YOUTH & CRIME

YOUTH & CRIME

Second Edition

John Muncie

SAGE Publications

London ● Thousand Oaks ● New Delhi

First published 1999

Reprinted 1999, 2001, 2002

SAGE Publications Ltd
1 Olivers Yard
London EC1Y 1SP

SAGE Publications Inc
2455 Teller Road
Thousand Oaks, California 91320

SAGE Publications India Pvt Ltd
B-42 Panchsheel Enclave
Post Box 4109
New Delhi 100 017

British Library Cataloguing in Publication data
A catalogue record for this book is available
from the British Library

ISBN 0 7619 4463 X
ISBN 0 7619 4464 8

Library of Congress control number available

Typeset by M Rules
Printed in Great Britain by The Cromwell Press Ltd,
Trowbridge, Wiltshire

Contents

List of Tables and Figures

Tables

Figures

Preface to the Second Edition

This is the second edition of *Youth & Crime*, which was first published in February 1999. Most of this new edition was written during the long hot summer of 2003. In the past five years an adult fear of, and obsession with, youth and crime has continued to dominate domestic political and media agendas. A bewildering array of new and old initiatives have been launched to tackle the 'problem'. Youth crime is excessively politicized. However, it is clear that this concern is not (and never has been) driven solely by fears of law breaking. Adult anxiety has consistently been expressed in terms of youthful vulnerability, nuisance and misbehaviour and has focused on the simply undesirable, worrying and disobedient as well as criminality. New Labour's 1998 legislation The Crime and Disorder Act arguably, for the first time, put law breaking and violation of social and moral codes on the same legal footing. This Act, together with further legislation which received Royal Assent at the end of 2003, focuses as much on the 'anti-social' as it does on the 'criminal'.

This book cannot be (and is not) simply about crime as committed by young people. Any serious analysis must confront the issue of how and why certain aspects of young people's behaviour have come to be perceived as particularly problematic at some times and why they are considered as deserving a criminal justice-based rather than a social welfare-based response. In this sense neither is the book simply about young people. It is just as much concerned to explore the nature of adult fear and the limits to which they are prepared to go in attempts to allay their anxieties. But how far are these fears warranted? Are young people a threat? Do they need to be listened to rather than ignored and punished? Are the courts the best way to deal with their conflicts and troubles?

As before, an underlying intention has been to provide an accessible introduction to these questions to facilitate undergraduate study and teaching. The aim remains not one of resolving issues but, as stated back in 1998, of providing the reader with enough knowledge to render them 'less unsure of the complexities involved'. As a result, I have forsaken the opportunity to radically restructure the text, but have kept faith with the ability of the original chapters to progressively explore the key issues involved.

Chapter 1 examines current parameters of the 'youth crime problem' as expressed through media representations, political discourses and statistical data.

It now includes new material on youth victimization, drugs and street crime as well as updating those assessments of the extent of disorder as can be gleaned from police records, self report studies and victim surveys. Vitally, it reveals the constantly shifting parameters and meaning attached to the two key concepts: those of 'youth' and 'crime'.

Chapter 2 draws upon social history research to reveal how much of our current obsession is far from unprecedented and novel. Moreover it shows how the identification of 'troublesome youths' is inseparable from the various policies that have been formulated for their control. The chapter provides an important reminder that whilst adult concern may be persistent, the precise means through which it is articulated is subject to continual dispute and change. One of the key insights from recent work in this area has been to underline the gender-specific nature of problem identification and policy response.

Chapter 3 looks at a diverse range of criminological theory – from anthropology, biology, psychology to sociology – which has attempted to discover the causes of youth crime. These theories – largely rooted in positivism – continue to make a significant impact not only on academic understandings but also on public perceptions and policy formulation. Of note has been a growing faith in theories that claim to be able to predict future delinquency by identifying the 'risk factors' embedded in our early lives.

Chapter 4 explores a different range of theories which are more concerned with the relationship between crime and how and why certain behaviours become criminalized whilst others do not. As some have put it, 'if you steal £10 you are condemned as a menace to society, if you steal £10 million you are lauded as an entrepreneurial financier'. Radical criminology is primarily concerned with revealing how crime is 'created' through relations of power and the capacity of state institutions to confer criminality on others. Further, postmodernism warns of any unreflective juxtaposition of the referents of 'youth' and 'crime' such that young people are constantly denied their place as legitimate citizens.

Chapter 5 underlines the point that the 'problem of youth' is not simply one of crime by examining how youth lifestyles, in the form of gangs, subcultures, consumer groups and countercultures, have been, and continue to be, constituted as a 'threat'. The chapter now draws extensively on the insights offered by a cultural criminology designed to reveal the linkages between youth marginality, the transgressive, media representations and processes of both commodification and criminalization.

Chapter 6 examines how youth is also a prime site of regulation; how social policies in employment, housing and welfare have become progressively submerged within criminal justice agendas. Traditional policy boundaries are now blurred in an interlinked series of interventions designed to reconstitute youth welfare through the zero tolerance policing of public space, the targeting of incivilities and the 'anti-social', the identification of dysfunctional families and the prevention of social exclusion through new moralities of inclusion. Issues of child protection and welfare have become merged with those of the 'anti-social' and the criminal.

Chapter 7 analyses the diverse and contested strategies that make up the complex of contemporary forms of youth justice. Since 1997 New Labour has placed youth justice reform at the top of its 'modernizing' agenda. Much of this, in the form of restorative justice, evidence-led practice, partnerships and adherence to principles of 'what works', seems to herald some new beginnings. However, the 'new' is also submerged within a persistent authoritarianism and populist punitiveness. Comparative research now confirms that England and Wales lock up more young people than any other country in Europe. But why are we so markedly different? What is it that seems continually to feed our punitive obsession so that we are more concerned to punish rather than to understand?

Those familiar with the first edition will here find a wide range of new material on such issues as anti-social behaviour, street crime, victimization, social exclusion, drugs, gangs, surveillance, crime prevention and policing as well as a sustained critical analysis of youth, social and criminal justice policies as they have been reconstituted over the past five years. To make sense of these developments, theories of risk assessment, governance, globalization and cultural criminology are introduced and assessed. I have retained as much of the original text as seemed appropriate for a critical reading of the present. Chapters 2, 3 and 4 on history and theory have largely undergone reworking and updating. Chapters 1, 5, 6 and 7 on contemporary representations, political interventions and policy initiatives have, as might be expected, been substantially revised and rewritten. Throughout though, the primary aim has been to provide *a critical introduction*, to encourage critical reflection on the array of political talk, media stories and academic research about young people with which we are daily bombarded.

In essence the book is intended to challenge prevailing conceptions not only of 'crime' and 'disorder' but of the very meaning of 'youth' itself. To do so, it deliberately moves beyond traditional criminological concerns and draws insights from other academic disciplines such as cultural studies, gender studies, media studies, social policy, social work, political science and human geography. The chapters may appear discrete but are in fact overlapping. It has become increasingly difficult to hold on to youth issues as separate entities as if, for example, criminology has no relevance for cultural studies or social policy to criminal justice agendas.

In some respects this might be said to amount to the construction of a comprehensive *youth criminology*. Certainly, youth studies has traditionally been viewed as a minor field in both sociology and criminology, somewhat surprisingly for the latter, given that most of its research and theoretical output has been driven by studying the young as the 'most criminogenic age'. Conversely, youth leisure pursuits and questions of style have tended to remain in sociology and cultural studies. It has taken the emergence of a cultural criminology in the 1990s to begin to break down these disciplinary boundaries. Conversely again, social policy and criminology have traditionally been viewed as separate disciplines with barely any mutual exchange. The seeping criminalization of social policy and particularly the impact of theories of governance in conceptualizing how young people are constituted in time and space are, however, beginning to break down these barriers. So maybe the time is right to talk of a specific multi-disciplinary *youth criminology*?

The case for such is compelling but we should be continually mindful that the adjunct of 'criminology' will always be a stumbling block, unless criminology itself can break out of its continuing obsession with the referent of a legal definition of 'crime'. Nevertheless, there is clearly a potential for studies of youth (and crime and disorder) to carve out a distinctive space as a meeting ground for key debates in the social and human sciences in which issues of citizenship, entitlement, identity and social justice can be re-formulated and re-expressed. Within this the voices of young people themselves will hopefully be given a (up to now denied) central space.

That said, this book also remains wedded to its past. It continues with some traditional means of presentation by supplying *key terms*, *a glossary*, *summaries* and *study questions* to aid its digestion. Each chapter also concludes with a list of *further resources* of relevant websites and suggestions for further in-depth reading. Hopefully these will provide the inspiration and encouragement to advance the project that has been started here.

As ever, I am indebted to many people in producing this book. The most important remain: the thousands of Open University students with whom I have been fortunate to work; my numerous colleagues in criminology and social policy at the OU and elsewhere; and above all Pauline Hetherington, who has done more than most to make this second edition fit for consumption. It goes without saying that none of it would have happened at all without the continual encouragement and support of Mirander Nunhofer at Sage.

Once more this book is dedicated to Lynn and Ella. Their unremitting reminder that, whilst some things stay the same, everything changes, is an important lesson for us all.

John Muncie
December 2003

1 **Youth Crime: Representations, Discourses and Data**

Overview

Chapter 1 examines:
- how young people have come to be regarded as a threat;
- how the 'problem of youth' is frequently collapsed into the problem of crime and disorder;
- how young people are represented in media and political discourses;
- the nature and extent of young offending;
- young people as offenders and as victims of crime;
- the usefulness of the concepts of 'youth' and 'crime'.

Key Terms

corporate crime	persistent offending
crime	protracted adolescence
criminalization	recording of crime
delinquency	reporting of crime
deviance	representation
discourse	self reports
folk devil	social constructionism
hidden crime	status offence
moral panic	victim surveys
official statistics	youth

This introductory chapter is designed to promote a critical understanding of the youth–crime nexus. The equation of these two categories is widely employed and for many is accepted as common sense. Stories about youth and crime appear regularly in the media and the official crime statistics seem to show that this preoccupation is entirely justified. But how far do the media reflect social reality and how much are they able to define it? How valid and reliable are the criminal statistics? By asking these questions, the chapter draws attention to how the state of youth and the problem of crime come to be defined in particular circumscribed ways. Its critical starting-point is to view 'crime' and 'youth' as social constructions. That is, it explores how certain images and notions of youth crime have come to be institutionalized, sedimented or 'taken for granted' as facts and objective knowledges. It also pays attention to the ways in which these 'constructions' have been challenged, or can be contested, by empirical and theoretical research. In short, it provides an overview of the presences and absences routinely employed in discourses of the 'problem of youth'.

The Threat of Youth

1.1

There is no neutral English noun which can identify a period of 'youth' with the same certainty and impersonality as 'child' or 'adult' (Springhall, 1983–4, p. 20). While 'child' and 'adult' are largely neutral terms connoting what is generally viewed as a normative period in life, 'youth' and 'adolescence' usually conjure up a number of emotive and troubling images. These range from notions of uncontrolled freedom, irresponsibility, vulgarity, rebellion and dangerousness to those of deficiency, vulnerability, neglect, deprivation or immaturity. As such, 'youth' is largely defined in terms of what it is lacking; by what it is *not* rather than by what it is (Furlong and Cartmel, 1997, p. 41). This section explores how these troubling, and often contradictory, notions are 'resolved' in media and political discourses.

Innocents and Demons

On 12 February 1993, 16 video cameras in a shopping centre in Liverpool filmed two 10 year old boys abducting 2 year old James Bulger. He was found two days later battered to death near a railway line. This particular murder was to form a watershed in media and political responses to youth crime, and not simply because of its apparent brutality. The Bulger case had at least three related consequences. First, it initiated a reconsideration of the social construction of 10 year olds as 'demons' rather than as 'innocents'. Second, it coalesced with, and helped to mobilize, adult fear and moral panic about youth in general. Third, it legitimized a series of tough law and order responses to young offenders which came to characterize the following decade.

The death of James Bulger triggered widespread moral outrage. It was also given widespread and sensational press coverage, both nationally and internationally. The story conformed perfectly to what Chibnall (1977) refers to as the five informal 'rules of relevancy' that govern how popular crime journalism decides what is *newsworthy*: that is how news is *selected* and how it is *presented*. These 'rules' are visible and spectacular acts, physical or sexual violence, graphic presentation, notions of individual pathology, and demands for a firm deterrent and retributive response.

In June 2001 the two boys convicted of the murder were released on parole. The tabloids had long condemned the fact that they had been held in secure units (rather than prison), where according to the *Sun* (9 January 2001) they had enjoyed a 'luxury life' of 'treats, trips and gifts'. When they were granted life-long anonymity to protect them from vigilantes, the *Daily Mail* (9 January 2001) declared this to be 'NO JUSTICE'. On the tenth anniversary of the murder, the *Sunday Mirror* (9 February 2003) asked where the two boys might be now: 'ON HOLIDAY (ALL EXPENSES PAID, OF COURSE)', with round-the-clock protection by armed police, was the reply.

Ten years on, the Bulger murder was still being talked about as 'iconic', galvanizing a mistrust of youth in general and fears of a failing justice system, of child abduction and of 'stranger-danger' in particular (Brown, 2003, p. 52).

However, the murder of children by strangers is rare; children are at far more risk from parents and carers. The murder of a child by other children is also rare. There have been only 27 such murders in the previous 250 years – most notably the case of 11 year old Mary Bell, who killed two small children in 1968. So the story of James Bulger was exceptional: indeed 'unthinkable' (James and Jenks, 1996, p. 315). But being unusual and unexpected, it was automatically considered newsworthy. In Hall's (1978, p. 22) words, 'it's as if newspapers set out each day with the unspoken assumption that things in the world will be exactly as they left them yesterday. The bigger, the more unexpected, the more violent the change, the bigger the story.' This is what is new; this is what makes the news.

Franklin and Petley (1996) and Davis and Bourhill (1997) provide detailed assessments of the newspaper reportage of the trial of the two boys who were eventually convicted for the murder of James Bulger in November 1993. For all but the *Financial Times* and the *Morning Star* it was the front-page headline story. The *Daily Mail* carried 24 separate articles; the *Daily Express* an eight-page supplement. One of the *Daily Mail*'s headlines 'THE EVIL AND THE INNOCENT' (25 November 1993) set the tone for some intensive media agonizing over 'HOW COULD IT HAPPEN?' However, it was the video footage from a security camera of James Bulger being led hand in hand by one of the 10 year olds out of the shopping centre that made the case famous. The blurred and shaky image was replayed endlessly on television. As Alison Young (1996, p. 112) argues, it invites feelings of helplessness and horror as we watch the boys slowly disappear from view with the voyeuristic knowledge that death is to follow. As such, the event 'always existed as much as an image of itself as it did in itself' (Young, 1996, p. 137).

A recurring theme in media representations of the case was the juxtaposition of innocent childhood and children as inherently evil. Innocence was easily imputed to James Bulger; he was the symbolic epitome of an ideal child. Normally, 10 year old children would also be media-idealized as innocent victims. But, as Hay (1995) argues, herein lies the crux of the event. We are forced to confront the uncomfortable notion that 10 year olds may not be innocent at all. As the *Sunday Times* (28 November 1993) put it: 'we will never be able to look at our children in the same way again . . . Parents everywhere are asking themselves and their friends if the Mark of the Beast might not also be imprinted on their offspring.' And so it was that one of the preferred media explanations of 'why it happened' dwelt on the theme of 'evil'. The *Daily Mirror* (25 November 1993) described the 10 year olds as 'Freaks of Nature' with 'hearts of evil'. Elsewhere, terms such as 'boy brutes', 'monsters', 'animals' and the 'spawn of Satan' abounded. For many, the case demanded that *all* children be regarded as a threat and that childhood be redefined as a time of innate evil. As James and Jenks (1996) suggest, it was not just two children who eventually were put on trial, but the very nature of childhood itself.

Other dominant explanations dwelt on an assumed decline in moral responsibility as a result of '1960s permissiveness'. The disintegration of the nuclear family, single parenting and the influence of media violence (particularly the film *Child's Play 3*, 1991) were all cited as key precipitating factors. William Golding's novel *The Lord of the Flies* (1954) was repeatedly referenced as 'evidence' of the horror and evil that is unleashed when children are free from the discipline of adults (*Guardian*, 16 February 1993; *Daily Mail*, 25 November 1993). As a result, any number of alternative 'readings' based on welfare, health, psychology, victimology, psychiatry, behavioural science or economics were subsumed by, or were ruled out in favour of, the law. Once the killing was coded as 'crime', it was the legal process and the assumption of individual responsibility which 'laid down the agenda for what could be reported and commented upon as "news"' (King, 1995, p. 173). To do otherwise would necessitate the questioning of some fundamental inequalities in society. And such questions do not conform to the imperatives of newsworthiness (Muncie, 1984, p. 20).

The Prime Minister's initial reaction was simply that we should 'condemn a little more and understand a little less' and the Home Secretary opined that no excuses could be made for 'a section of the population who are essentially nasty pieces of work' (*The Times*, 22 February 1993). The two 10 year olds – Jon Venables and Robert Thompson – were eventually sentenced to be detained for a minimum of eight years. This was raised to 10 years by the Lord Chief Justice and to 15 years by the Home Secretary (a decision subsequently declared to be illegal in July 1996). Much of this punitiveness was inspired by the *Sun* urging its readers to plead with the Home Secretary that the boys should be locked up for life. In 1999 The European Commission of Human Rights ruled that both their trial and their sentencing violated articles of the European Convention on Human Rights and the 'right to a fair trial'. It also ruled that sentencing decisions must be reserved for those independent of government. As a result the Criminal Justice and Court Services Act 2000 removed such power from the Home Secretary and handed it to the courts.

The Bulger case also came to symbolize something much broader; it became a signifier for a generalized 'crisis' in childhood and a breakdown of moral and social order (James and Jenks, 1996; Davis and Bourhill, 1997). In a climate of general anxiety about crime, the exceptional murder of an infant by two boys, barely at the age of criminal responsibility themselves, was viewed as symptomatic of a prevailing youth crime wave, even though they bore no obvious relation to each other. As Hay (1995, p. 204) argues,

> One mediated event . . . does not in and of itself constitute a moral panic. Through the process of discursive amplification, the 'event' is translated from a particular conjuncture that must be understood in its own terms, to an event which is seen as emblematic and symptomatic of broader processes – moral decay, social malaise and the destruction of the social fabric of the family and thus society itself. The shadow of such a threat only becomes identifiable by virtue of the event itself. Yet once the event is seen in this context, the nature of the submerged threat becomes immediately obvious and this in turn makes sense of a multitude of formerly unrelated, yet nonetheless individually troubling phenomena.

In the early 1990s, a raft of youth troubles – most notably truancy, drug taking, disturbances on housing estates in Oxford, Cardiff and Tyneside following police clampdowns on joyriding, and images of 'youth out of control' and 'one-boy crime waves' – had already raised levels of public concern. The Bulger case provided 'the strongest possible evidence to an already worried public that there was something new and terrifying about juvenile crime' (Newburn, 1996, p. 70). Individual TV images, such as that of an 11 year old in a balaclava mask being arrested after crashing a stolen car, galvanized politicians of all parties, the police, judges and magistrates to demand more effective measures to deal with young offenders. Indeed, just 10 days after the Bulger murder, the Home Secretary announced plans to establish a new network of secure training units for 12–15 year old offenders.

The Prime Minister also promised a crackdown on 'bail bandits', whereby those committing further offences whilst on bail (or if there was the slightest reason to believe they *might* reoffend), would be automatically remanded in custody ('I'LL LOCK UP YOUNG VILLAINS' – headline, *Daily Mail*, 22 February 1993). 'Truancy Watch' was launched in autumn 1993. Above all, a sense that the courts and law and order agencies had become impotent to deal effectively with offending was widely propagated and this mood persisted for much of the decade. In the run-up to the 1997 general election, a bewildering array of *additions* to the youth justice system in England and Wales were proposed, including curfews for children, the naming of young offenders in court, the shaming and public humiliation of offenders, parental control orders, fast-track punishment for 'persistent' offenders, the adoption of 'zero tolerance' campaigns to prosecute even the most petty and minor of offences, secure training centres for 12–15 year olds and the removal of the legal presumption of *doli incapax* for 10–13 year olds. Indeed, all of these measures were acted upon in the following six years. For good measure the Anti Social Behaviour Act 2003 introduced new powers for the police to disperse 'intimidating' groups of two or more people, criminalised noise nuisance and graffiti and restricted the sale of aerosol paint to children (see Chapters 6 and 7).

The role of the media, and particularly the symbolic purchase of the Bulger case, no doubt played a part in this escalation of fears and change in political mood. By comparing the Bulger case with a similar murder in Norway in 1994, Franklin and Petley (1996) were able to argue that the contemporary British press and judicial system were particularly 'punitive, harsh and unforgiving'. The initial sentence of Venables and Thompson was widely condemned as being too soft. Not only was the recommendation of eight years seen as too lenient but the conditions of their custodial confinement were viewed as akin to a 'holiday camp' (*Today*, 25 November 1993). In contrast, the language used by the Norwegian press and judiciary was more conciliatory. There the murder of a 5 year old by three 6 year olds was phrased in terms of a 'tragic accident', in which it served no purpose to simply apportion blame to those involved. Moreover in most European countries, Venables and Thompson would have been considered much too young to be prosecuted at all. In England the age of criminal responsibility is 10, across Europe it is usually 14 or above. The only European country to have an age of criminal responsibility below the age of 10 is Scotland (see Table 7.1). Comparison of the media and legal treatment of Venables and Thompson with that of the two 8 year olds – Barrett and Bradley – in a similar murder case in Stockport in 1861 is also informative. Though also initially demonized, the jury in 1861 delivered a judgement of manslaughter and was widely supported for having done so. Barratt and Bradley were sent to a reformatory for five years with public support, rather than resentment, for the prospect of their rehabilitation (Rowbotham et al., 2003). Most pernicious, perhaps, was the way in which reaction to the death of James Bulger firmly located violence solely with youth. As Scraton (1997a, p. 164) concludes: 'what a terrible irony this represents given the apparently insatiable appetite that much of the adult, patriarchal world has for violence, brutality, war and destruction.'

In these ways the Bulger case came to signify something more than an isolated tragic event. It set in motion fears about juvenile crime in particular and young people in general which continued to be reflected in youth imprisonment rates some 10 years later (see Figure 1.1).

Demons have invaded the innocents. Children and young people are the 'dangerous other'.

Figure 1.1 *The Punitive Decade: penal reforms and young people in prison 1992–2003[1] and future projections[3] (England and Wales)*

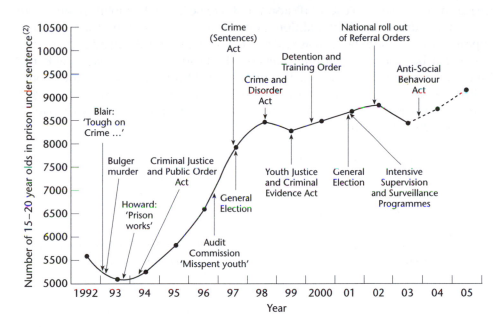

Source: derived from Home Office (2003a) *Prison Statistics for England and Wales 2002* Cm5996, p.6 and p.66 and Home Office (2003b) *Prison Population Brief* May 2003, p.12 and p.20.

Notes: (1) Does not include remands, non-criminal prisoners or those held in the privately run Secure Training Centres. (2) At 30 June 1992-2002; at 31 May 2003. (3) Home Office Prison Population projections based on June 2003.

Youth in the News: Dangerous, Deficient and Vulnerable

Images of dangerousness are arguably the most familiar public appearance of youth encapsulated in the threat and danger of the mob or gang. It is a recurrent theme vividly illustrated by the headline 'LORD OF THE FLIES GANGS RULE ESTATES' (*Sunday Times*, 17 August 2003) as evidence of what can happen in areas of high child population density whether in Britain or it is claimed in Baghdad and Beirut. A sequence of moral panics about 'depraved youth' has been a dominant and recurring feature of media representations of young people. In 1950s Britain, for example, these fears were premised on the image of a teenager who had no respect for authority and lived in a world that was generally dismissive of anything adult. Teddy boys were Britain's first post-war teenage 'folk devils', popularized as violent, depraved and sex-crazed (see Chapter 5.2). In the 1960s, such themes as student revolt, drug usage, sexual permissiveness, football hooliganism, vandalism and truancy combined to amplify the level of public concern. In the 1970s black youth, mugging, punks, violence in schools and groups of 'vicious young criminals' were the most potent symbols of a now 'rapidly deteriorating youth condition'. In the 1980s the sight of thousands of young people rioting on the streets added a new dimension to this social preoccupation with youth disorder. In the 1990s panics about joyriding, alcopops, Ecstasy, girl gangs and persistent offenders were the latest in a long history of despairing but 'respectable fears' (Pearson, 1983) to be joined by mobile phone thefts and bail bandits in 2002. In addition, popular music, styles of dress and personal appearance continue to be cited as evidence of young people's disregard for authority, whether it be teddy boy 'brothel creepers', skinhead 'shaved heads', long-haired hippies, the anarchy of punk rock, the 'unrestrained hedonism' of rave, the hooded jackets and baseball caps of rap or the carrying of replica guns as a 'fashion accessory'.

In 1961 the British Medical Association (BMA) offered the following despairing analysis of British youth:

> Looked at in his worst light the adolescent can take on an alarming aspect: he has learned no definite moral standards from his parents, is contemptuous of the law, easily bored. He is vulnerable to the influence of TV programmes of a deplorably low standard . . . [and] reading matter [which is] full of sex and violence. (cited by Pearson, 1983, p. 17)

Thirty-five years later, it seemed little had changed. The Chief Executive of the School Curriculum and Assessment Authority expressed his opinion that:

> a family breakdown, a 'synthetic pop culture' and a lack of identity among bewildered youngsters all contributed to a failure of a growing number of pupils . . . some young people have little sense of their own worth. Some have little sense of basic values. Some have no sense of identity as members of a community. Some are unaware that they have responsibilities as well as rights. (*Daily Mail*, 20 September 1996, p. 25)

And in 2002 a newspaper editorial claimed:

> Young people, but particularly young men, want to defy the law and do bad things because it is 'cool' to do so . . . Young people have lost it [respect], for one another as well as for the older generation' (*Daily Mirror*, 12 July 2002).

The very idea of 'youth', seems increasingly certain to attract adult fear, concern and censure. But as Clarke (1984) has argued, the potency of such images owes little to realism but instead reflects the way the 'state of youth' acts as a social metaphor for the state of society. Dangerous youth is the cornerstone of a number of key concerns about a disordered present. Are the streets safe? Are schools too permissive? Are parents failing to exercise proper control? Is television a corrupting influence? Are the courts too soft on young offenders? And so on.

In contrast some young people are also portrayed not so much as depraved but as deprived, not necessarily of material wealth and power (though this is usually the case), but of moral standards, proper guidance, training and self responsibility. Such 'deficiency' is characteristically viewed as part and parcel of the peculiarities of adolescence. Bizarre dress, 'blatant' sexuality, irresponsibility and moodiness are somewhat disparagingly passed off as 'just a phase they are going through' which will be 'grown out of'. As a result young people are typically viewed as being at a 'vulnerable' stage: capable of being corrupted by all manner of 'evil' influences, unless their behaviour is tightly regulated and controlled. Such control is often justified in terms of giving young people 'protection' (from others and themselves). The notion that youth are a problem both to society *and* to themselves is a recurring theme in media and youth research (Wyn and White, 1997, p. 21).

Although the sources of 'youth' imagery are wide and varied, including personal experience, television news, radio, film, TV sitcoms, and so on, it is apparent that one of the key agencies that informs the public about youth is the national and local press.

One of a very few quantitative content analyses of British newspapers to focus specifically on young people was carried out in the late 1970s (Porteous and Colston, 1980). Throughout June 1979 Bradford University's Social Work Research Unit scanned eight national daily newspapers and two local (Yorkshire) papers to discover what *particular* images of youth were propagated by this medium. Any article that involved young people between 11 and 19 years was categorized according to size, location and content, and each was assigned an evaluation category (positive, negative, neutral) based on the researchers' assessment of the general feeling about adolescents which each article might arouse in the 'average' reader. A total of 913 articles were analysed. The local *Bradford Telegraph and Argus* contained most stories (15 per cent of total), followed by the tabloids (between 10 per cent and 12 per cent of total), the broadsheets (between 7 per cent and 9 per cent of total), and the *Morning Star* (2 per cent of total). Stories relating to sporting events accounted for 11.4 per cent of this coverage and education 6.7 per cent, but most notably 34.9 per cent of all reports of youth were related to crime in one form or another. Of these the most frequent categories were crimes such as burglary, theft, vandalism and breach of the peace (9.2 per cent), murder (5.1 per cent) and sex crimes (2.3 per cent). Reporting was also frequent where adolescents were the victims of crime. The authors concluded that 'according to our daily press, a typical adolescent is a sporting youngster, criminally inclined, likely to be murdered or injured in an accident' (Porteous and Colston, 1980, p. 202).

However, the researchers' own evaluation of these articles produced a symmetrical distribution of moral connotations. They considered that 24 per cent offered positive images of youth, 24 per cent negative images and 52 per cent neutral images: suggesting that the press does not simply depend on wholly negative representations. Nevertheless, as they argued, the press does not simply reflect reality, but defines it in a specific way. In particular, the high propensity of crime stories was considered to be a gross caricature of young people's lives: 'Such a menu is generally unedifying, factually incorrect and socially divisive' (Porteous and Colston, 1980, p. 206). Similarly, there were many aspects of young people's lives which the press barely mentioned. The Bradford study found little discussion of education or employment issues. Only 2 per cent of articles discussed youth (un)employment, despite the fact that the number of school-leavers without a job was growing rapidly. In 1979 over 20 per cent of under 18s were unemployed. Stories concerned with education amounted to a mere 6.7 per cent of the total (almost half of these appearing in the *Guardian*'s weekly feature 'Education Guardian').

Moreover the 'positive' aspects of 'youthfulness' that were given coverage, were largely accounted for by the atypical careers of a small number of media and sporting personalities. As the Bradford study reported, entertainers, sports stars and the children of the aristocracy and the famous 'tend to commandeer the limelight in a stereotyped presentation of the good life' (Porteous and Colston, 1980, p. 206). In contrast other young people only appear to be newsworthy when they are singled out as dangerously criminal or naively vulnerable to physical attack. A tripartite image of youth emerges: they are either gifted, dangerous or innocent.

Twenty years later the charity Children's Express monitored over 400 stories in local and national newspapers and found a similar degree of stereotyping. Young people were routinely parodied as victims, demons, cute, brilliant, brave or as adult accessories (Neustatter, 1998). Clarke (1984) concludes that the link between these separate and diverse images lies in their assumption of the *different* or *deviant* nature of *all* young people. So although the images of dangerousness, deprivation, vulnerability and so on find their pinnacle in those singled out for media attention, the implications of such imagery carry over to inform adult reaction to the invisible mass. All young people are variously coloured by a dominant imagery of 'being adolescent', of 'lacking adulthood', of 'posing a threat' ('WHO'S AFRAID OF TEEN TERROR?': *Observer*, 1 August 1999).

The youth question then, is 'the site of a singular nexus of contradictions' (Cohen, P., 1986, p. 54). At one time feared, young people are at another time pitied for their vulnerability. They are simultaneously constituted as in need of control, but also protection. They are the constant object of fascination. The adult gaze is fixed on youth as something both desirable and threatening. Desirable, because youthful energy remains a part of adult longing; desirable too because it is here that new styles and fashions are generated that are ripe for commercial exploitation. In this sense 'youth' is also a commodity. But a fear of youth is never far beneath the surface. Too much freedom is dangerous when unsupervised and unregulated. Above all, youth is treated as a key indicator of the state of the nation itself. Young people are the nation's future. To secure that future and to solve the problems of the present, 'youth' is a consistent referent.

As a result, Phil Cohen (1997) has argued that young people have to carry 'a peculiar burden of representation'. Their condition is increasingly seen as being 'symptomatic of the health of the nation, or the future of the race, the welfare of the family, or the state of civilization as we know it'. If we want to control crime, it seems, we must first tackle 'the youth problem'.

Crime in the News: Enemies Within and the Criminal 'Other'

Various critical studies of the relation between media representations of youth and crime have identified a number of key and recurring processes:

- A distortion of the nature and incidence of crimes against the person. Whilst personal violence crimes account for only 6 per cent of all recorded crime, on average British newspapers devote 64.5 per cent of their crime reporting to such cases (Williams and Dickinson, 1993, p. 40). Similarly, studies of the provincial press by Ditton and Duffy (1983) in Strathclyde and by Smith (1984) in Birmingham found that media reportage consistently and dramatically distorted the 'true' picture of crime. Surette (1998) refers to this as 'the law of opposites'.
- Definitions of youth crime are structured within particular explanations proffered by the 'primary definers' of politicians and law enforcement agencies (Hall et al., 1975). The credibility of their definitions is enhanced by their official and institutional standing such that a 'deviance-defining elite' is able authoritatively to set its own moral and legal agendas (Ericson, 1991, p. 223). Such agendas may be contested and, in certain circumstances, negotiated, but the organization of journalistic practice generally seeks out and promotes the views of those in authority (Schlesinger and Tumber, 1994, p. 20).
- Stereotypical images of offenders and their behaviour encourage understandings of events in terms of the simple dichotomies of good (the victim) and evil (the offender). Such stereotyping and dismissive labelling may be used to deny legitimacy to the actions of whole groups – they become defined as the nation's 'folk devils', as the 'criminal other' (Cohen, S., 1973a; Hall, 1978).
- In particular, *atypical* crime events (such as youth violence) are selected as newsworthy. But these are presented as *stereotypical* (symptomatic of a general youthful moral decadence) and contrasted with visions of the 'normal world' which are *overtypical* (adults as law-abiding) (Young, 1974).
- The media do not simply reflect reality, they define it in a particular way. To prolong an event's newsworthiness, other apparently similar (but unrelated) incidents are sought out (Hall, 1978). In this way public concern and fear are directed from a single incident and towards the possibility of 'crime waves' through which the whole of society appears threatened (Cohen, S., 1973a). The reaction to particular crime incidents at particular times, it is argued, has more to do with fears of social transformation than with any significant shifts in the actual behaviour of youth (Taylor, 1981a).
- This process is now commonly referred to as a 'moral panic' in which clear boundaries are drawn between 'right' and 'wrong' and which need to be secured through retributive and deterrent responses towards offending (Goode and Ben-Yehuda, 1994). The term 'moral panic' was first used by Jock Young (1971, p. 182) to illustrate the process whereby an initial concern over drug taking in Notting Hill, London prompted the police to set up specialist drug squads, thereby ensuring that the 'problem' was *amplified* by increasing the number of drug-related arrests. A 'fantasy crime wave' was created (see Chapter 4.1).

- Crime news is a commodity. Its intrinsic 'market value' tends to override other news-making criteria, such as accuracy or relevance (McQuail, 1993, p. 253). As a result it has been contended that public images of youth crime are 'popular' only in so far as they are the consequences of information provided by law enforcement sources with a vested interest in 'crime control' and by media sources with a vested interest in 'newsworthiness' (Muncie, 1984, p. 23). News values also militate against any balanced public knowledge of sentencing practices. The popular misconceptions that crime is always rising, that most crime is violent and that the courts routinely hand out unduly lenient sentences are all fuelled by a steady 'repetitive' stream of atypical and unrepresentative stories emanating from the media (Sanders and Lyon, 1995; Hough and Roberts, 1998). Nevertheless numerous researchers have concluded that there is no simple deterministic relationship between media reportage and the formation of public opinion. Whilst media representations do have an effect, they are unlikely to be received passively, but rather interpreted by an 'active audience' (Roshier, 1973; Livingstone, 1996; Reiner, 2002).

- At the end of the twentieth and beginning of the twenty-first century it appears that there has been something of a shift from discrete panics to a perpetual period of moral crises in which a fact/fiction dichotomy has been dissolved. Crime-as-news has blended into crime-as-entertainment. 'Reality' TV, crime reconstructions, live newscasts and CCTV footage have fused 'facts' with institutional values and popular myths. Mass media and law enforcement agencies have become inextricably related in constituting the 'realities' of crime, justice and order (Osborne, 1995; Brown, 2003). It may be disturbing to acknowledge, but it has become increasingly difficult to disentangle the 'fact' from the 'fiction'.

Collectively, these processes may not determine public reaction, but they remain a key source of political sensitization. In political discourse young people tend to be a perennial source of anxiety. Law and order enthusiasts, for example, have warned us of a delinquent syndrome in which youth seems to delight in crudity, cruelty and violence. The characteristic expression of this is that young people have suffered unduly from single parenting or from the permissiveness of parents and have developed into a dangerous and undisciplined mob. In the 1970s, Patricia Morgan, for example, readily equated violence and destruction with youth, and talked of this 'new barbarism' as the major cause of urban breakdown and moral decline in Britain (Morgan, P., 1978, pp. 12–13). In the 1990s, Digby Anderson echoed such sentiments by claiming that the 'yobs and criminals' had been 'allowed to take over' (*Sunday Times*, 2 June 1996). Government ministers foresaw the imminent destruction of society epitomized by Margaret Thatcher's denunciation of the football hooligan in 1985 as the 'new enemy within'. The threat of youth violence was equated with trade union militancy and international terrorism. MPs called for flogging and the use of stocks to punish offenders (*The Times*, 14 March 1981), with one Conservative MP contemplating flogging criminals live on television before or after the weekly National Lottery draw in order to humiliate and deter (*Independent*, 20 March 1995). Chief constables have readily associated youth with a lack of discipline, and with violence and crime serious enough to threaten the very stability of society (Pearson, 1983, p. 5). In popular and political discourse the 'problem of crime' is almost synonymous with 'youth crime'. Increasingly, it seems, the young have come to be defined only as a social problem, rather than representing any positive or creative possibilities for the future (Muncie, 1997a; Waiton, 2001).

In turn such 'excessive' fears feed into political debate and policy formulation. For example, in 2002 the *Sun* launched its 'crusade against crime' with the headline 'ANARCHY IN THE UK' and seven subsequent pages detailing the failures of the justice system 'to smash crime with an iron fist' (*Sun*, 8 March 2002). It followed this with the assertion that 'our streets are ruled by muggers and yobs' (*Sun*, 18 March 2002). The newspaper was responding to the Metropolitan Police Commissioner's claim of undue delays in court procedures, excessive use of bail, and processes that favour defendants over victims. The campaign also reflected the Lord Chief Justice's call for a 'robust sentencing policy' for mobile phone thieves first made in January. It was also a response to the assertion that muggings had risen in London, particularly after September 11, 2001, when police were 'diverted from crime fighting to anti-terrorism' (*Sunday Times*, 30 December 2001). By early 2002 the *Mirror* (21 February 2002) was already announcing that we are 'drowning in a tidal wave of violent crime'.

The Home Secretary first responded by announcing an extension of electronic tagging of young offenders on bail (*Independent*, 27 February 2002). At the end of March, the Prime Minister made the unprecedented move of convening a taskforce with seven cabinet ministers to combat street crime. Meanwhile the *Mirror* (20 March 2002) ran with the headline 'VILE LAWLESS TEENAGERS TERRORISING THE STREETS' and the *Daily Express* (25 March 2002) declared that 'KIDS OF FOUR TURN TO CRIME'. By April a robbery reduction initiative based on the principles of zero tolerance and fast-track courts was in place in ten police areas. On 22 March 2002 the *Daily Express* argued 'AT LAST WE GET TOUGH ON YOBS' as on-the-spot fines for low-level offenders were introduced. One local authority began drawing up plans to impose curfews for under 15 year olds (*Guardian*, 26 March 2002). Docking child benefit from the parents of young offenders was proposed. Extra resources were released to finance over 2,000 new places in secure units and prisons (*Guardian*, 18 April 2002) and to pay for a more intensive policing of truants (*Guardian*, 26 April 2002). Further the Home Secretary insisted that children as young as three should be monitored for signs of nascent criminality. In May a mother was jailed for 60 days for failing to ensure that her children attended school.

As a result of these initiatives, the Prime Minister claimed street crime would be soon brought 'under control'. By September reductions of some 16 per cent were announced, but only amidst allegations of a selective use and intepretation of the statistics (*Guardian*, 13 September 2002).

Debate continues over whether the year 2002 did in fact witness a 'tidal wave' of street crime associated with violence. The British Crime Survey reports that there was a 25 per cent fall in all crime and a 24 per cent fall in violence between 1997 and 2002/3. The risk of being a victim of crime was reduced to an all-time low. Police recording of violent crimes, however, increased by 2 per cent (Simmons and Dodd, 2003). This might suggest that the police recorded more crime when fewer offences were being committed. It is a process that fuels political expediency and media sensationalism as well as heightening public fear. In 2002 almost three-quarters of the public still believed the crime rate to be increasing (Simmons and Dodd, 2003). Repeated claims were being made that the justice system was too soft, particularly when the tabloids questioned the proposition 'TOUGH ON CRIME?' by devoting eleven pages to gruesome pictures and harrowing accounts of violence *(Daily Mirror*, 12 July 2002). In contrast research on sentencing practices revealed magistrates and judges bowing to media and political pressure by bypassing fines in favour of community penalties; by jailing offenders who would have previously received community penalties; and by imposing longer sentences. As a result the adult prison population rose from 36,000 in 1991 to 62,000 in 2003 (Hough et al., 2003). The number of under 18 year olds sentenced to detention increased from 4,000 in 1992 to 7,600 in 2001 (NACRO, 2003b). Over the decade custodial rates increased by 71 per cent for adults, but by 90 per cent for young people (see Chapter 7).

Such punitiveness appears unrelenting. In 2003 the *Sun* (15 October) launched its 'Shop a Yob' campaign promising to name and shame the 'guilty', condemning the 'politically correct claptrap' of 'soft courts' and advocating the setting up of 'tough work camps' for the 'animals who make your lives a misery'. In promoting such views the media regularly claim they are simply responding to public opinion. The nature of populist punitiveness is, however, far from straightforward. 'Public opinion' is often presented as some undifferentiated and homogeneous entity and its divergences and complexities rarely fully acknowledged and understood. Public attitudes to crime and punishment often exhibit a degree of tolerance that is frequently lost when asking bald generalised statements about sentencing preferences. When presented with concrete descriptions of actual cases, the public tend to be less punitive. When given adequate information about the range of legal punishments available, the public are less likely to endorse the use of imprisonment (Hough and Roberts, 1998). The more detail that people are given about the circumstances of any given crime, and the more time they are given to reflect on appropriate penalties, the less likely they are of perceiving the courts as being 'too soft' (Gillespie and McLaughlin, 2003).

The Extent of Offending and Victimization

1.2 The 'true facts' of offending by young people (or any other group) have been, and will remain, unknowable. There are three main means by which crime rates have been estimated – recorded statistics, victim surveys and self report studies – but none can claim to provide an objective and incontrovertible picture. The problem arises because all quantitative data depend not only on which behaviours are perceived and *defined* as crime, but also on the *validity* of the various statistical measures and on the range of *interpretations* that can legitimately be made of any figures, no matter how they are produced. Most obviously, changes in policing priorities, or changes in what the law counts as crime, or shifts in public tolerance will all affect statistical representations of the youth crime problem. It might be tempting, then, to discard all such measures as 'worthless'. Yet they cannot be so readily dismissed. They provide valuable insights into self, police and court definitions of crime and tell us much of the organizational constraints and priorities of the criminal justice system. They cannot, however, be expected to aid our understanding of an 'independent entity of crime' for, as Lea and Young (1984, p. 15) acknowledge, 'by its nature no such fact exists'.

The Social Construction of Official Statistics

The main sources of data on the extent of offending in England and Wales are the annually produced *Criminal Statistics* (based on crimes recorded by the police) and the *British Crime Survey* (BCS) (based on victim interviews). In Scotland similar statistics appear in *Recorded Crime Scotland* and the Scottish Executive Justice Department conducted its own victim surveys in 1993 and 1996.

The first National Crime Survey was carried out in 1972 in America. It surveyed a representative sample of the population and questioned them on their experience of being a victim of crime. The aim was to shed light on hidden crime by uncovering those crimes committed (and for which a victim was recognized) which were not reported to the police. Predictably, these early victimization surveys revealed that the extent of crime may be up to five times greater than that detailed in official statistics. The first British Crime Survey (BCS) was carried out in 1982 (Hough and Mayhew, 1983) and by 2000 had been repeated eight times. Since then it moved to an annual cycle with 40,000 interviews with those aged 16 and over conducted each year. Collectively these are the most commonly referred to sources of information on offending rates and patterns and are regularly used by politicians, the media and criminological researchers. They offer us the following picture of young offenders, somewhat confusingly classified as *children* (between ages 10–13), *juveniles* (between ages of 10–17), *young persons* (between ages 14–17), *young adults* (between ages 18–20) and *adult* (21 and over). It is of interest to note that in contrast the UN Convention on the Rights of the Child insists that the term *children* be used to describe all those under the age of 18.

- The peak age of known offending is 18 for males and 15 for females, but adults account for more than 75 per cent of all detected crime.
- Between 1992 and 2001 the number of juveniles convicted or cautioned (or reprimanded and warned following the 1998 Crime and Disorder Act) fell by 21 per cent.
- Theft and handling stolen goods account for just under a half of all youth crime. Violence against the person accounts for less than 14 per cent of indictable offences. In 2001, 50 per cent of these were dealt with by reprimand and warnings, suggesting their less serious nature.
- Approximately 80 per cent of youth offenders are male.
- 33 per cent of males and 9 per cent of females born in 1953 had been convicted of an offence before the age of 46. (Source: Home Office, 2002; Simmons and Dodd, 2003; NACRO, 2003a.)

These statistics have been more or less constant over the past decade but they also paint a controversial and contradictory picture. First, they imply that youth crime is becoming less of a problem as crime rates have generally, sometimes dramatically, fallen, but they still maintain that 'youth' is the most criminogenic age. The Audit Commission (1996) estimated that the under-18s committed about 7 million offences a year. Second, they suggest that the 'crime problem' is a problem caused predominantly by males. Third, it seems that youth crime is made up largely of less serious property offences. Violent crime, sexual offences and robbery are rare, whilst the number of drug offences seems only to escalate for young adults. Finally, there is a widespread belief that whatever these figures do tell us, they represent the tip of an iceberg. Many other offences are not detected, others are not recorded by the police or a conviction is not secured. Indeed, the Audit Commission (1996, p. 14) argued that only 3 per cent of offences lead to arrest and action by the criminal justice system. If this is the case, then the official statistics provide a particularly skewed vision of the nature and extent of young offending.

The first and most paramount 'fact' about the *Criminal Statistics* is that they are both partial and socially constructed (Muncie, 1996, p. 22). This is so for a number of reasons, outlined below.

Public Reporting

The *Criminal Statistics* depend initially to a large degree on those crimes *reported* to the police by the public. Although the police do detect some crime, in the main they rely on the general public or victims to bring crime to their notice (Bottomley and Pease, 1986, p. 34). Yet not all crimes are reported, for a variety of reasons: there may be ignorance that a crime has occurred (for example, computer fraud and many instances of corporate crime and state crime); there may be no obvious victim (for example, certain drug offences); the victim may be powerless (for example child abuse); there may be distrust of the police (for example, by certain youth cultures); the offence may seem too trivial (for example, shoplifting); the offence may be considered to be youthful 'high spirits' (for example, brawls); or the victim may have no faith that the police will take the offence seriously (for example, racial harassment) (Jupp et al., 1999).

The 1996 British Crime Survey (which bases its data on reports from victims) found that the main reasons for not informing the police were that the incident was not considered serious or that the police would not be able to do much about it or would not be interested. Some felt that the incident was better dealt with privately without recourse to formal agencies. Vehicle vandalism, assault and minor theft had particularly low reporting rates. Burglary with loss and motor vehicle theft had almost 100 per cent reportage rates, presumably in order to meet insurance company requirements (Mirrlees-Black et al., 1996, pp. 24–6). This latter observation has caused many to query the validity of the assumption that crime is always on the increase. As Jenkins (1987, p. 25) perceptively argued: 'the total has about it an eerie, suspicious regularity. It advances relentlessly in step with the proliferation of telephones, of police computers and of household insurance . . . we could be victims of nothing more offensive than a wave of being middle class'.

Police Recording

Even when an incident is reported to the police, it will not count as crime unless the police *record* it as such. As Walker (1983, p. 286) noted, although the police have a statutory obligation to record crimes, considerable discretion remains about whether it is considered sufficiently serious to warrant their attention. The 1994 British Crime Survey estimated that 40 per cent of offences reported to the police were not recorded (Mayhew et al., 1994), whilst eight years later, the 2002/3 survey found it had increased markedly to 70 per cent (Simmons and Dodd, 2003).

Coleman and Moynihan (1996, p. 35) argue that the police recording of offences depends on three broader contexts: the political context at the time of the offence, the organizational context of policing priorities and the situational context of how the offence is reported and by whom. For example, in the 1950s when crime was not a political issue, there was little or no incentive for the police to record large numbers of offences. It had no financial (increased resource) implications and if there seemed little chance of a 'result', then such recording would only reflect poorly on subsequent clear-up rates. For many years Nottinghamshire, somewhat surprisingly, has had one of the highest crime rates in England and Wales, but this has been accounted for by the tendency of the Nottingham police to record minor thefts and to record multiple and continuous offences as separate crimes (Farrington and Dowds, 1985). This particular recording policy was subsequently considered worthy of national implementation and a National Crime Recording Standard was introduced in 2002.

Similarly, how a reported offence is recorded by the police – as 'theft from a person' or 'robbery' or as 'attempted break in' or 'criminal damage', for example – will affect the rate at which certain crimes are believed to being committed. Indeed, Farrington (1996), commenting on the statistical decline in juvenile crime since the 1980s, is able to argue that this has been illusory and simply reflects an increasing police practice at the time to deal with many juvenile offenders informally. Perhaps the clearest example of crime rates being affected by police targeting and recording occurred in 1932. Then, London's Commissioner of the Police ruled that all cases classified as 'suspected stolen' should be redesignated as either 'lost' or 'stolen'. The result was that recorded thefts increased by over 300 per cent in one year (Williams, 1994, p. 49)!

Creating Crime Waves

Changes in law enforcement and in what the law counts as crime preclude much meaningful discussion over whether youth crime is forever rising (or indeed falling) (Muncie, 1996, p. 24). Pearson (1983, p. 216), for example, notes how successive pieces of welfare-inspired legislation governing the treatment of young people in the early twentieth century encouraged law enforcement agencies to proceed with cases they might previously have dealt with informally. The end result was more young people being dealt with in court, creating the impression of a 'crime wave' when all that had changed was the readiness of official agencies to intervene (see Chapter 2.4).

Pearson (1983, p. 217) elaborates on this process by noting how after 1977, the distinction between minor and major criminal damage was abandoned in favour of a classification of all as 'known crimes'. This resulted in an apparent doubling of vandalism in one year: 'adding at a single stroke a sixth of a million indictable offences to the criminal records'. Similarly, Singer (1996) details how changes to juvenile offender law in New York in the late 1970s effectively *recriminalized* youth by redefining previous acts of delinquency as 'crimes' and delinquents as 'juvenile offenders'. In the wake of a media and political 'moral panic' about a 'crisis' in youth crime, the age of criminal responsibility was lowered, ensuring that juveniles were placed in New York's adult criminal justice system. Taylor (1998) also notes how changes in police priorities and politics will effect what is recorded. He argues that increases in crime between 1914 and 1960 can be accounted for by senior police officers 'playing the crime card' in order to increase police numbers and powers. In the 1990s with the advent of performance indicators, 'cuffing' of cases was revealed as common practice as the police tried to improve clear-up and detection rates to politically acceptable levels (*Guardian*, 18 March 1999).

Whilst victimization surveys are undoubtedly a more reliable means of measuring crime than police statistics, they too suffer from a range of methodological problems (Coleman and Moynihan, 1996, pp. 74–82). Inevitably they only measure criminal incidents where a victim can be identified or where a victim accepts such a status. 'Victimless' crimes such as some drug offences or consensual sexual acts will not be recognized and for crimes such as domestic violence there may be an unwillingness to accept a 'victim' status. For corporate crime, individual victimization is not only likely to be unknown, but its extent may be enormous. Other shortcomings include the lack of representativeness of the chosen samples, the problem of victims' memory recall and indeed whether respondents can always be relied upon to tell the truth. Moreover questions relating to *youth* victimization remain conspicuously absent from the BCS (it only included specific information on under-16s in 1992).

Self evidently, changes in legislation and in the number of arrests and sentences represent not actual changes in the level of crime, but changes in the capacity of the criminal justice system to process individual cases. More police and more prisons, coupled with the political will and resources to support law enforcement, have an infinite ability to increase the amount of recorded crime. As Christie (2000) argues, there is always an unlimited well of unrecorded crime to be tapped and as techniques of mass surveillance increase, so too will more 'crime' be discovered. This again is likely to impact most strongly on young people: their 'crimes' usually occur in the most visible of public places – the street, the shopping mall, the football ground. In contrast many 'adult' crimes will remain hidden at work (pilfering), in the home (domestic violence), the corporate boardroom (fraud, embezzlement) or in the corridors of power (state atrocities, illegal arms dealing). As such, increases in police resources will almost inevitably lead to a statistical rise in *certain kinds* of crime, just as prison building programmes will create more prisoners of the same kind. New legislation meanwhile remains capable of criminalizing ever wider sections of the population. For example, Nick Cohen (2003) notes that since 1997, New Labour has created 661 new criminal offences and has launched hundreds of anti-crime initiatives. Many of these have been directed at non-conformist and anti-social behaviour or that previously considered 'irritating' (see Chapter 6).

Table 1.1 outlines the various processes whereby an incident may, or may not be, eventually registered as an official crime statistic. In Box's (1981, p. 208) words, it illustrates how 'official data are social products'.

Table 1.1 *The social construction of youth crime*	
Event	**Mitigating factors**
Incident occurs	Visible or hidden? Recognized as crime?
Reported	Serious or trivial? Police able to act? Trust in police?
Recorded by police	Serious or trivial? Organizational priorities? Law and order directives? Status of complainant?
Arrest	Nature of evidence? Sufficient police resources and time? Possibility of a 'result'?
Charge/court/sentence	Legislation reform? Legal representation? Social status of offender? Previous convictions? Political climate of 'law and order'?

Self Reports and Hidden Crime

Given the doubts about the validity of official statistics, criminologists have increasingly turned to other measures. Self report studies, which ask people to list the crimes they have committed (whether they have been detected or not), were pioneered in the USA in the 1940s. Since then they have been widely used as a means not only to gain a more accurate picture of 'hidden crime' but also to shed light on why offending occurs and the degree to which it correlates with other social factors, such as gender, 'race' and socio-economic position. They have, in the main, been directed at young people.

Most self report studies conclude that young offending is far more widespread than the official statistics would have us believe. In a study of 1,400 London schoolboys, Belson (1975) reported that 98 per cent admitted having at some time kept something they found (legally, theft); 70 per cent had stolen from a shop and

88 per cent had stolen from school. Yet only 13 per cent had been caught by the police and only half of these were subsequently sent to court. Similarly, Rutter and Giller's (1983, p. 27) summary of youth self report research found that *inter alia* 82 per cent admitted breaking windows of empty houses, 70 per cent had stolen from a shop and that almost no one admitted no offences at all. Risk of prosecution ranged from 8 per cent (shoplifting) to 60 per cent (breaking and entering).

In 1992/3 Graham and Bowling (1995) interviewed a national sample of 1,721 young people aged 14–25 about their family life, school experiences, lifestyles and offending behaviour. Twenty-three offences were covered, ranging from shoplifting to serious assault. Similar to previous studies, they found offending to be widespread with over a half of males and a third of females admitting that they had committed an offence at some time. For a majority, however, these were restricted to no more than one or two minor property offences. A follow-up study in 1998/9 (Flood-Page et al., 2000) found little overall change, but with an increase in the population of 14–17 year olds admitting an offence.

The prevalence of crime as an everyday part of young people's lives was also substantiated by research in Edinburgh (Anderson et al., 1994). On the basis of questionnaires completed by 1,150 11–15 year olds and 120 face-to-face interviews in 1990, this study found that two-thirds admitted to committing a crime in the previous nine months: the majority being rowdiness, fighting in the street or shoplifting. The largest survey to date involved a nationwide sample of 14,500 11–17 year olds in 2000/1. Almost half reported having knowingly broken the law at some stage. A third of 14–15 year olds admitted shoplifting. Twenty per cent of 15–16 year old boys admitted attacking someone intending serious harm. The survey, on the other hand, also found that offending was infrequent and that most young people were law-abiding most of the time (Beinart et al., 2002).

From studies such as these it is clear that a majority of people have broken laws and rules at some time in their lives. To this degree transgression may be considered a typical, rather than abnormal, form of behaviour. It is, as Durkheim (1895/1964) argued, a normal and enduring feature of the social order. However, the major contribution of self report studies has been to seriously question widely held beliefs about the correlations of class position, 'race' and gender to criminality. Both Anderson et al. (1994) and Graham and Bowling (1995) found that middle-class children were just as likely to be involved in crime as working-class children. Indeed, a survey by the British Household Panel in 2001 based on interviews with 1,000 13–15 year olds found that those from higher-income families were *more* likely to commit vandalism, play truant and take illegal drugs (*Guardian*, 25 February 2001). The relationship between social class and offending that is reflected in the *criminal statistics* (and accepted by many criminological theories) is at best tenuous and probably non-existent. As Box (1981, p. 91) concludes: 'self report studies have on the whole failed to reveal the significant inter-class differences implied in official statistics . . . Only if this single fact is kept in the forefront of the reader's consciousness can there be sustained a critical stance towards many sociological theories on delinquency.' This suggests strongly that official statistics reflect not patterns of offending but patterns of policing. As a result the relative criminality of certain groups of young people has been exaggerated. For example, inner-city working-class youths face a greater risk of arrest than middle-class youths engaged in similar activities but in areas where the police presence is lower. Ethnic minority youths are statistically more likely to be stopped and searched by the police (Burke, 1996), but self report studies show that those of Indian, Pakistani and Bangladeshi origin have significantly *lower* rates of offending and that for Afro-Caribbeans the rate is no higher than for whites. Self report data also cast some doubt on the relative lack of offending by young women. Up to the age of 17, offending rates are not dissimilar to those of young men, but female offending then drops sharply, while male property offending increases. Graham and Bowling explain this differential by noting that those young women who have completed full-time education, left home, formed stable partnerships and had children are more likely to stop offending abruptly than those who have not. For males, however, passing these landmarks has no such effect: 'they tend to lag behind young women in virtually every area of social development' (Graham and Bowling, 1995, p. 56). As has been widely reported, for young men the transition to adulthood and maturity seems to have been significantly extended (Leffert and Petersen, 1995). And so too it seems has the length of time before young men 'grow out of crime'.

Despite these seemingly 'incontrovertible' findings, it would be misleading to take self report studies at face value. They too have a number of limitations. Most obviously they depend on the willingness of interviewees to admit their 'criminality' to researchers. Second, they are often administered by questionnaires which have notoriously high non-completion rates, particularly from ethnic minority groups. This in itself may result in highly skewed samples (Coleman and Moynihan, 1996, p. 59). Third, they tend to check offending against a relatively small list of 'standard' and sometimes trivial offences. Other areas of hidden crime such as domestic violence, child abuse and corporate crime are rarely (if ever) analysed. As a result the parameters of the 'crime problem' and assumptions about 'typical offenders' are not seriously challenged and tend only to be confirmed by self reports (Box, 1981, p. 81). Because they have focused almost exclusively on young people, valuable comparisons to adult offending cannot be made.

Youth Victimization

The vast majority of research on youth and crime in the UK has focused exclusively on young people as offenders rather than as victims of crime. The first attempt to reverse this priority was Mawby's (1979) study of 11–15 year olds in two Sheffield schools. He found that 40 per cent had had something stolen from their person and that 25 per cent had suffered a physical assault. Overall 67 per cent said that they had been a crime victim. Nevertheless it was not until the 1990s that the issue was given much sustained attention. Anderson et al.'s (1994) pioneering work in Edinburgh established that criminal acts are committed against young people with 'alarming frequency'. They found that over a period of nine months half of their sample had been victims of assault, threatening behaviour or theft (Anderson et al.,

1994, p. 39). Moreover some 52 per cent of young women and 36 per cent of young men recalled that they had suffered from adult harassment, ranging from being 'stared at', to importuning and indecent exposure. Whilst for males such offences decreased as they grew older, for females they increased to the extent that 30 per cent of 14–15 year olds had experienced 'touching' or 'flashing' (Anderson et al., 1994, p. 59).

In a follow-up study in Glasgow (Hartless et al., 1995), high levels of victimization were again found to be common, with 82 per cent of a sample of 208 12–14 year olds recalling they had been victimized in the previous year. Sixty-eight per cent of young women had been sexually harassed, whilst two-thirds of young men had suffered from assault *and* theft. On average a quarter of the sample admitted that they themselves had committed an offence, leading the authors to conclude that young people are 'more sinned against than sinning'. Similarly, Brown's (1998, p. 92) research in Teesside, which compared rates of youth and adult victimization, found that 'young people endured levels of victimization which would not be tolerated by adults'. Moreover, all three studies concluded that whatever the known rates of victimization, young people were often reluctant to report offences committed against them.

Specific questions about youth victimization have only once been included in the British Crime Survey: that of 1992. From a sample of 1,350, in just six months a third of 12–15 year olds claimed that they had been assaulted at least once, a fifth had had property stolen, a fifth had been harassed by people their own age and a fifth harassed by an adult. Again it was notable that the risks of theft and assault were substantially higher than for the adult population, but that few incidents were reported to the police (Aye Maung, 1995). The MORI Youth Survey (2002) of 5,000 school children revealed that 35 per cent had been physically attacked, 45 per cent threatened, 34 per cent racially abused and 34 per cent suffered from theft in school alone. A survey for the Howard League (press release, 11 April 2002) of 11–15 year olds found that only 4 per cent believed they had never been a victim of crime. The 2003 report on Crime in England and Wales which collates BCS and police statistics (Simmons and Dodd, 2003) also confirmed that young men aged 16–24 were most at risk of violent crime.

Openly racist harassment and bullying is endured by many black and ethnic minority children on a daily basis. Racially motivated violence (as reported to the police) increased by 250 per cent between 1989 and 1996, marking the UK as having one of the highest levels of such incidents in Western Europe (Human Rights Watch, 1997). All ethnic minority groups are more likely than whites to be victims of both household and person offences. Pakistanis are most at risk, being particularly vulnerable to vandalism of their houses and cars and to serious threats. Afro-Caribbeans are most at risk of assaults and acquisitive crime (Fitzgerald and Hale, 1996; Percy, 1998).

The murder of the black teenager, Stephen Lawrence in 1993 and the unrelenting campaign by his family to expose police and judicial racism catapulted racial violence and hate crime to the forefront of issues to be addressed by law enforcement and community safety agencies in the late 1990s. Six years after the murder, the Macpherson report confirmed what black and Asian communities already knew or suspected about police ambivalence, institutional racism and lack of accountability. But the report lacked an acknowledgement of the long history of violent racism in Britain. It dwelt on the failures of policing rather than on the daily experience of racist violence, threat and intimidation. Although survey research has burgeoned since the early 1980s, statistical snapshots of particular events are incapable of grasping the incessant and enduring process of such victimization (Bowling, 1999).

What is remarkable about these emergent discourses is that even they fail to note one of the more alarming facets of youth victimization. Significantly the British Crime Survey, for example, has not asked about experience of youth victimization and violence in the home. Children under 1 year old are more at risk of being murdered than any other age group, with 46 deaths per million of population compared with a national average of 16 per million. Parents are the principal suspects in 78 per cent of all child homicides (NSPCC, 2003). The extent of domestic child abuse remains largely unknown although research by the NSPCC (2002) estimated that 1 in 10 young adults have suffered serious abuse or neglect during childhood and it noted that over 600 children are added to child protection registers every week. While the issue was recognized as long ago as the late nineteenth century, it has generally been clouded in a discourse of cruelty and neglect or subsumed within a more general concern about juvenile delinquency. Criminological research has concentrated either on the degree to which parental abuse and neglect 'causes' future delinquency or on the relationship between delinquent activity and the risk of victimization (Lauritsen et al., 1991; Esbensen and Huizinga, 1991). Within criminology little has been done to expose the routine of violence – from slapping to serious assault – endured by young people in their own homes. The corporal punishment of children is widespread and often justified in the name of discipline and delinquency prevention. Ironically, studies in the USA, such as Straus (1994) have revealed that greater use of corporal punishment correlates not with a decrease but with *increased* rates of street violence, depression and alcohol abuse. Attempts to outlaw corporal punishment in Britain have always floundered because of accusations of 'nanny state' interference. New Labour has banned child-minders from using corporal punishment but not parents, on the grounds that it constitutes 'reasonable chastisement'. Since Sweden banned smacking a decade ago, child deaths at the hands of parents have fallen to zero. In Britain it is running at one a week (*Observer*, 4 May 2003).

In the child sexual abuse investigations of the 1980s in Cleveland, Orkney and Rochdale, blame was passed from parents to social workers for unnecessarily removing children from their families. Notions of family sanctity and privacy have always precluded widespread use of criminal prosecutions. A psychological, medical or welfare focus obscures the fact that criminal offences have been committed. Child victims continue to be marginalized by use of the term 'abuse' rather than 'assault' (Morgan and Zedner, 1992, p.20). Further ambivalence is created by a prevailing political concern that the publicizing of child abuse and children's rights is likely not only to undermine respect for authority and self-discipline but also to threaten family life itself. Despite moments of apparent visibility the issue of child victimization remains peripheral to mainstream law and order debates and absent from most criminological agendas (Saraga, 2001). Attempts to legislate against child abuse have never approached the 'constant stream of law and order legislation for youth crime' (Brown, 1998, p.86).

In addition, Morgan and Zedner (1992) draw attention to the fact that young people not only suffer from physical and sexual abuse and bullying but are witness to numerous and prolonged instances of parental violence in the home. Children are often 'indirect victims'. Over a third of households burgled each year include children who may be traumatized as a result, but are rarely considered to be victims themselves. Interviews with the relevant professional and voluntary agencies reveal not only a very low awareness about the effects of crime on children, but because of an overwhelming concern solely with sexual abuse, none of the welfare agencies consider it their responsibility to provide child victims with support and advice (Zedner, 1994). The NSPCC survey of the strategies developed by Crime and Disorder partnerships found that over half did not refer to child protection or the safety of young people at all. Even those that did tended to equate safety solely with reducing young offending: 'it is disappointing that the vast majority of partnerships prioritise dealing with young people only as perpetrators of crime and anti-social behaviour' (Mason, 2001, p.17).

Just as alarming is the growing number of revelations about the extensive abuse of children who have been in the *care* of local authorities. In the language of social work, young people who are in the care of local authorities are known as 'looked after children'. Over the past decade there have been between 7,000 and 11,000 young people in residential care at any one time in England, Scotland and Wales. Their treatment has long been a cause for concern, with allegations of systematic violence by residential staff surfacing throughout the 1980s and 1990s. Significantly such victimization, even when proved, has tended again to be clouded in terms of 'abuse' and 'mistreatment' rather than criminal violence (Muncie, 2003b). Any resultant inquiries have either been hidden from public view or at best restricted to identifying a small number of individuals who have taken advantage of the powerless. The main policy response has been to tighten checks on applicants for residential posts, rather than to overhaul residential care policies (Corby, 1997).

The issue came to a head in 2000 with the publication of *Lost in Care* – the Waterhouse report into abuse at children's homes in North Wales. Following allegations of sexual abuse in similar homes in Leicestershire, Islington, Dumfries, Buckinghamshire, Northumbria and Cheshire, the Waterhouse tribunal of inquiry was established in 1996. It uncovered widespread and organized abuse of boys and girls in North Wales between 1974 and 1990. Although by 1996 12 people had already been convicted, Clwyd County Council had refused to publish 14 prior reports partly for fear of compensation claims. Waterhouse eventually heard 259 complaints, named 200 workers in more than 40 homes and found evidence not only of daily physical assault but also of gross sexual exploitation and emotional abuse. It attributed at least 12 deaths, by suicide or in suspicious circumstances, to the experience of being 'in care'. Such criminal violence, it was concluded, was the result of a catalogue of failure by those – at all levels – who were supposedly responsible for delivering children's services (*ChildRight* 2000, no. 164, pp. 3–5).

A further inquiry into allegations of institutional violence in council-run care homes in Lancashire was launched in 2000. It joined at least 22 other similar inquiries being conducted elsewhere in England and Wales, including investigations into church abuse. Between 1995 and 1999, 21 priests were convicted of child abuse. It has been estimated that six out of ten women and a quarter of men have experienced 'some kind of sexual abuse or interference' before the age of 18 (Bauman, 1997, p. 274).

On reviewing much of the available research, Furlong and Cartmel (1997, p. 93) argue: 'In many respects, the concentration on young people as the perpetrators of crimes has left us blind to the extent to which young people are victims . . . while adults express concerns about "lawless" youth, many crimes are also committed against young people by adults.' Similarly, Brown (1998, p.96) concludes that 'young people have to *earn* their status as victims, whereas they are eagerly *ascribed* their status as offenders'. The relative powerlessness of young people has always placed them at potential risk of adult victimization. Such a risk is exacerbated at times when the *potential* of youth is subjugated to that of 'threat'. Ironically, seeking their protection and regulation often ensures that they are placed in those same family and institutional settings that are a key source of their victimization.

Patterns of Offending and Non-offending

1.3 Despite the shortcomings of official statistics, self reports and victim surveys, it remains widely assumed that age is a major indicator of involvement in crime. Because proportionately more ethnic minority and working-class youth and fewer female youth are dealt with by the youth justice system, it is also believed that the crime problem is predominantly a problem of young males from lower social class and ethnic minority communities. This focus on youth has also encouraged research into how criminal careers are formed and developed. In popular idiom, the 'truant of today' will eventually be the 'criminal of tomorrow'. And for a small number, offending will not be transient, but will be both frequent and persistent. This section provides a critical assessment of these 'taken-for-granted' notions.

Criminal Careers

The 'criminal career' approach suggests that offending is part of an extended continuum of anti-social behaviour that first arises in childhood, persists into adulthood and is then reproduced in successive generations (Farrington, 1994; 2003). Whilst offending by the vast majority of young people is believed to be widespread, much of this is transient and minor, arising from 'having fun' and rowdyism rather than from any calculated decision to engage in criminality. Nevertheless the chance of acquiring at least one criminal conviction during a lifetime affects four out of ten males and one in ten females. But according to Farrington (1996), a relatively small number – about 5 per cent of males – become 'chronic offenders' who then go on to account for about a half of all known offending.

One of the most ambitious projects to investigate why delinquency begins and to assess how far criminality can be predicted was the Cambridge Study in Delinquent Development. In 1961 a sample of 411 working-class boys aged 8 was selected from six primary schools in Camberwell, London. Girls were not included. Only 12 boys were from ethnic minorities. They were contacted again when aged 10, 14, 16, 18, 21, 25, 32 and 46 to examine which of them had developed a 'delinquent way of life' and why some had continued a 'life of crime' into adulthood. Analysis of the latest data began in 2003. About a fifth of the sample had been convicted of criminal offences as juveniles and over a third by the time they were 32. But half of the total convictions were amassed by only 23 young men – less than 6 per cent of the sample. Most of these 'chronic offenders' shared common childhood characteristics. They were more likely to have been rated as troublesome, impulsive and dishonest at primary school. They tended to come from poorer, larger families and were more likely to have criminal parents. They had also experienced harsh or erratic parental discipline. Six 'risk factors' were eventually suggested by the researchers as the most likely predictors of future criminality (Farrington, 1989):

- socio-economic deprivation (e.g. low family income/poor housing);
- poor parenting and family conflict;
- criminal and anti-social families;
- low intelligence and school failure;
- hyperactivity/impulsivity/attention deficiency;
- anti-social behaviour (e.g. heavy drinking, drug taking, promiscuous sex).

In addition those convicted at an early age (10–13) tended to become the most persistent offenders. On this basis Farrington (1994, p. 566) contends that future 'chronic offenders' could have been identified with reasonable accuracy at the age of 10. He argues that

> children from poorer families are likely to offend because they are less able to achieve their goals legally and because they value some goals (e.g. excitement) especially highly. Children with low intelligence are more likely to offend because they tend to fail in school. Impulsive children . . . are more likely to offend because they do not give sufficient consideration and weight to the possible consequences. Children who are exposed to poor child rearing behaviour, disharmony or separation on the part of their parents are likely to offend because they do not build up internal controls over socially disapproved behaviour, while children from criminal families and those with delinquent friends tend to build up anti-authority attitudes and the belief that offending is justifiable. The whole process is self-perpetuating. (Farrington, 1994, pp. 558–9)

Using the same sample Farrington et al. (1996) subsequently maintained that if children had a convicted parent by the time they were 10, then that was the 'best predictor' of their becoming criminal and anti-social themselves. Criminal behaviour, it was argued, was transmitted from parents to children: simply put, crime runs in the family.

Such risk analysis has become more and more common since the 1990s as interest in crime prevention research has burgeoned. Something of a consensus around the precipitative factors of family conflict, truancy, drug use, irresponsible or lack of parenting, low intelligence, delinquent friends and community disorganization has emerged (Goldblatt and Lewis, 1998; Rutter et al., 1998; Flood-Page et al., 2000; Youth Justice Board, 2001; Farrington, 2002; Beinart et al., 2002). The problem, however, remains of deciphering which of these numerous variables has more pertinence with some people at some times. The degree to which they interrelate and react remains uncertain. And whilst they may correlate with *recorded* offending, their applicability to all rule breaking – as self reports indicate – is at best tenuous; their connection to the causes of crime is dubious and their potential to inform effective programmes of risk management and crime prevention remains questionable (see Chapters 3.1, 6.4 and 7.4).

Using an ethnographic, rather than statistical and personality measurement approach, Foster's (1990) study, which spanned the generations in one area of south-east London in the early 1980s, also found that parental attitudes to education, street life and crime were replicated (through subtle processes of parental reinforcement) by their children. Youth crime served as an apprenticeship to adult offending when, for example, techniques could be learnt to minimize the risks of detection and arrest. But all this occurred in a context whereby many of their illegal activities were not considered as crime: 'these were not criminal "careers", just ordinary people whose everyday world took for granted certain kinds of crime' (Foster, 1990, p. 165). As a result, whilst the Cambridge study is a good example of the degree to which various social and personality factors correlate statistically with 'known' offending, it fails to capture the broader context in which such offending takes place. It assumes that legal definitions of crime are shared by all communities. Foster's analysis shows clearly that this is not the case. The issue becomes not simply one of law breaking, but of conflicting cultural and moral values embedded in different material realities. Moreover, the Cambridge study substantiates public concern about lower-class criminality, but only because the range of other types of criminal activity typically associated with white-collar and corporate crime are not identified as problematic. It may be able to shed some light on the characteristics of those offenders who are recorded in the official statistics, but it tells us little about the extent, causes and meaning of offending *per se*.

From a different theoretical perspective, Craine and Coles (1995) used the concept of 'career' to explore how young people in inner-city Manchester coped with unemployment and social deprivation in the 1980s and the realization that the prospect of a traditional 'career' in the formal labour market had largely disappeared. The alternative 'careers' that were developed included market trading and social security fraud (working and claiming), 'fencing' stolen goods, unlicensed street trading, acting as 'lookouts', 'touting' and 'hustling'. As with Foster's (1990) informants, these 'edge of crime' activities were regarded as quite legitimate. For some this ethos may have heralded a progression to organized shoplifting, robbery and drug dealing whereby crime came to be a major means of earning a living. But, above all, the 'drift into crime did not involve a major moral dilemma for the young people concerned. Rather it was the result of a series of incremental choices to access the alternative opportunity structures around them' (Craine and Coles, 1995, p. 20). The picture of 'crime careers' painted by the Cambridge study is one of inadequate and morally damaged individuals. For Craine and Coles it is a matter of young people reacting rationally to the (lack of) opportunities available to them.

Persistent Offending

From mid 1991 onwards, stories have appeared regularly in the press about some young people who, it is argued, are so involved in crime that they seem to account for much of the crime in the areas where they live (Newburn, 1996, p. 69), as evidenced by the following lead stories:

> ONE-BOY CRIME WAVE (*Daily Mail*, 10 September 1992)

> Hardcore child super crooks are bringing fear to Britain's streets . . . they are our number one crime problem . . . they account for 90 per cent of offences. (*Daily Star*, 30 November 1992)

> RATBOY: A 14 YEAR OLD BECOMES A BYWORD FOR TROUBLE. (*Independent*, 9 October 1993)

> 73 CONVICTIONS OF THE SMIRKING TEARAWAY: THUG AGED 14 IS UNMASKED (*Daily Mail*, 14 March 2000)

The epitome of this was 'Ratboy'. Alleged to have committed 55 offences by the time he was 14, one boy in north-east England first came to the notice of the police when he was 10, for burglary. After two cautions his parents volunteered him for local authority care, from which he absconded 37 times. In February 1993 he was found hiding in a ventilation duct. A local newspaper could not print his name, so invented the nickname Ratboy. Next day he was front-page national news. With the construction of images of sewers, of a hidden underworld and of secret tunnels running beneath the urban landscape, the boy became a symbol of all juvenile crime against which the police and courts were 'impotent' to act (despite the existence of local authority secure units). But in many other respects the boy did not live up to the prevailing stereotypes of dangerous and outcast youth. He did not come from a broken home; he was not violent; he did not grow up in some 'urban wasteland'; he became a 'symbol surrounded by clichés' (*Independent*, 9 October 1993). Again in 1993 an 11 year old crashed a car through a fence. When he appeared on television in a black ski mask, he became Balaclava Boy. Spider Boy, Homing Pigeon Boy,

Boomerang Boy and The Terror Triplets have all followed until New Labour decided that in certain circumstances young offenders could be publicly named.

Again it is worth noting that such fears are not new. In the mid 1970s the Magistrates' Association had warned of 'a minority of tough, sophisticated young criminals . . . who deride the powerlessness of the courts to do anything effective' (cited by Rutherford, 1986, p. 61). But such clichés once more fed into a growing public and political concern about *persistent* young offenders in the 1990s. In July 1992 a Home Affairs Committee was established to inquire into all aspects of juvenile crime and the youth justice system, looking in particular at the 'problems of persistent offenders' (HAC, 1993, p. vii). Noting conflicting evidence from the Association of Chief Police Officers (ACPO) which claimed that the rate of juvenile offending had *increased* by 54 per cent during the 1980s and Home Office statistics which had recorded a 37 per cent *decrease*, the Committee tentatively concluded that

> one possible explanation . . . is a growth in the numbers of persistent offenders . . . If there is a small but growing number of juvenile offenders responsible for many offences, it is possible to reconcile the indisputable fact that the number (and rate, to a lesser extent) of known juvenile offenders has fallen over time with the more speculative assertion that the number of offences committed by juveniles has risen. (HAC, 1993, p. xii)

Asked to provide specific numbers, ACPO suggested it was 'a very, very small handful'. A survey of all police forces eventually came up with the number of 106 (HAC, 1993, p. xiii). More reliable research based on self reports estimated that 8 per cent of all 12–30 year olds could be classified as serious persistent offenders (Flood-Page et al., 2000).

In March 1993 the Home Secretary announced his intention to introduce a new sentence, the secure training order, and a new institution, the secure training centre, to deal with those children aged 12, 13 or 14 identified as seriously persistent juvenile offenders. It was notable that this commitment was made some time before Home Office-sponsored researchers into the issue had had time to report. Hagell and Newburn (1994) assessed the extent of 'persistence' by sampling all those 10–16 year olds arrested three times or more in 1992 in one Midlands county and two London boroughs. Of a total of 531, 74 were also eventually interviewed. Fourteen per cent were girls. The most common offences were traffic, non-residential burglary, theft from shops and car theft. Violent offences were exceedingly rare, as was offence *specialization* (such as burglary and car theft). The mean number of offences per reoffender was 5.6, with the majority committing three 'known' offences. Only two had committed more than 40. On the basis of such data, Hagell and Newburn (1994) further query the possibility of arriving at some objective definition of 'persistence'. They compared three definitions:

1   those top 10 per cent of 10–16 year olds who were arrested and known to have committed offences or alleged to have committed offences in one year;
2   those 10–16 year olds who were known or alleged to have committed ten or more offences in three months;

3 those 12–14 year olds who had committed three or more offences punishable by imprisonment, one of which having been committed whilst subject to a supervision order (the secure training order criteria).

Inevitably, no two definitions of 'persistence' produced similar figures and in particular they often did not identify the same individuals. The first two definitions led to the identification of 30 'persistent offenders', but 15 identified by definition 1 did not appear in definition 2. Twenty-five offenders met the third definition. Only eight were identified by all three. Similarly, Crowley's (1998) study of three local authorities found only ten young offenders who would meet the secure training order criteria. The study also found that whilst the vast majority had experienced disrupted educational histories and were already 'known' by the social services, it was impossible to define these offenders as being of a particular 'type'. Most young reoffenders are not 'hard core' in the sense of being continually engaged in serious crime, but are more likely to be repeat minor offenders. Hagell and Newburn (1994, p. 122) concluded that 'a discrete group of persistent offenders cannot be identified' and that 'any definition of persistence will inevitably be arbitrary'. Undeterred, New Labour defines a persistent young offender as those 'aged 10–17 years, sentenced on three or more occasions for one or more recordable offences in the past three years' (Home Office, 1997a). Three per cent are now thought responsible for 25 per cent of all offences. In 2001 a new Intensive Supervision and Surveillance Programme was launched to target those who had committed four or more offences in the previous year.

However, interviews with the most persistent offenders reveal stories of chaotic and disruptive lives, neglect and abuse, time spent in children's homes, school exclusions and psychological intervention or counselling: 'what they hoped for in the future was to settle down, have families and find work. What they saw in the future was usually less rosy' (Hagell and Newburn, 1994, p. 130; Crowley, 1998; Liddle and Solanki, 2002). Nevertheless the image of a 'persistent hard core' of 'superpredators' (*Sunday Times*, 16 February 1997) continues to feed popular and political debate. Despite widespread criticism from agencies and organizations working with young offenders (Children's Society, 1993), the secure training centres proposed by the Conservatives were first condemned and then supported by New Labour. By 2003 three had been opened, all privately managed, and were holding some 170 10–17 year olds. The question of persistence has also been tackled from another angle: namely that intervention at an early age – particularly in the form of secure institutions – is unlikely to prevent reoffending and may only succeed in cementing 'criminal careers'. In Crowley's (1998) sample more than a half had spent time in institutional care. Bailey et al. (1994) found that of all those sent to a secure unit, 80 per cent had previously been in local authority care. Only 7 per cent had had no previous psychological or psychiatric contact. Similarly, Boswell (1995) found that 91 per cent of all 10–17 year olds who had committed the most serious offences had experienced abuse or loss in their earlier life. Criminal convictions can have substantial long-term consequences, not only in terms of gaining access to housing or employment, but also in informing the courts' attitude to dealing with further offences. Reoffending rates on leaving secure units are also high – estimated by NAJC (1993) to be between 70 and 80 per cent. This suggests that some types of intervention are not only inappropriate, but may also encourage the kinds of behaviour that they are designed to treat or deter (see Chapter 7).

Young Women as Non-offenders?

Farrington (1996) contends that those factors that are known to protect young people against offending include having a resilient temperament, an affectionate relationship with at least one parent, parents who provide effective and consistent discipline and maintain a strong interest in their children's education. However, one of the strongest predictors of non-offending seems to be that of gender. Only one in six of all known young offenders is a young woman. In general their crimes are also less serious, with theft and handling stolen goods by far the most common. Such data have led Newburn and Stanko (1994, p. 1) to observe that 'the most significant fact about crime is that it is almost always committed by men'.

Nevertheless some reservations about the validity of such a bald statement should be noted. Self-report studies, for example, suggest that although fewer girls than boys do break the law, the difference is not marked. Anne Campbell (1981, p. 22) notes that whilst official statistics in 1976 produced a ratio of male to female offending of 8.95:1, results from self reports of 16 year old schoolgirls showed a ratio of 1.33:1. She argues that when young women commit crime they follow the same pattern as young men in terms of which acts they commit. In contrast, Walklate's (1995, p. 6) review of the statistical data concludes that while 'men and women commit similar crimes albeit at different rates, women appear to commit the more serious crimes at a much lesser rate than men'. This is even more the case when the largely hidden crimes of domestic violence are taken into consideration. Moreover as self report studies (Graham and Bowling, 1995; Flood-Page et al., 2000) found, the rate of offending for young women peaks earlier and recedes at an earlier age than that of young men. So although at ages 12–14 a similar proportion of boys and girls admit offending, by the age of 17 males outnumber girls 3:1 and by the ages of 22–25 it is 11:1.

It is clear then that even though it would be misleading to view young women as non-offenders, significant gender-based differences in rates and frequency of offending still need to be explored. Until the 1970s the most common form of explanation of female crime was firmly tied to biology. For example, Cowie et al. (1968) linked female delinquency to abnormal 'hormonal balance' and argued that 'sex chromosome constitution is one of the basic factors determining liability to delinquency'. West (1967) accounted for girls' deviance in psychodynamic rather than social terms: wayward girls are likely to show neurotic symptoms and 'psychopathic traits', he argued. The dominance of such biologically based analyses is reflected again in the widespread assumption that the delinquency of young women is related to 'deviant' sexuality, promiscuity and/or prostitution.

Thus delinquent girls are viewed as doubly deviant: delinquent for breaking the law and abnormal for contradicting dominant feminine roles. Traditionally, they have been more likely to be declared in need of 'care, protection and control' than boys (Worrall, 1999 and see Chapter 7.2). Much of this is a hangover from a psychological approach to youth developed at the turn of the century. Traditionally, adolescent boys have been seen primarily as ambitious, and in need of mental growth and challenge, while adolescent girls were viewed as emotional, prone to weepiness, flirtatious and in need of social protection (Frith, 1984, p. 50).

Since the 1970s many of these assumptions have been challenged by a feminist critique of both traditional and contemporary youth studies. Such a critique has pointed out not only that issues of female deviance have generally been neglected (most studies are of boys) but also that the prevalence of psychological interpretations has led to some gross distortions of patterns of young women's conformity and deviance (McRobbie, 1978, 1980; Heidensohn, 1985). The new feminist studies have argued in particular that gender roles are socially constructed rather than biologically determined, and have revealed the key role played by dominant ideologies of femininity in shaping the differential experiences and responses of young women to their position of structured subordination.

In accounting for lower rates of offending, recent enquiries have focused on questions of culture, ideology and social control. For example, Sue Lees (1986) has detailed how masculine and feminine behaviours are subject to different social rules and operate according to different norms. Characteristically these act to constrain girls' behaviour to a much larger degree than boys'. For instance, girls' potential income and spending power is lower than that of boys. Parents guard girls' leisure time much more closely. Through a variety of informal means of control emanating largely from a sexual division of labour, girls' behaviour outside the home is carefully constrained. In turn, such controls are linked to dominant ideologies about women's natural place being in the home, revolving around a culture of domesticity rather than street-based leisure or employment. A key element in the construction of these gender-related opportunities is the different ways in which male and female sexuality are defined. While it is expected that boys will 'sow their wild oats', the implications for girls of becoming known as receivers of the 'wild oats' is often drastic and irreversible. A long list of derogatory labels – slag, slut, scrubber, whore, easy lay – awaits the independent or promiscuous girl, terms for which there are no male alternatives. To remain 'respectable', young women must suppress their sexual desire. This double standard of sexual morality is central to explaining women's subordination within a 'natural career' of marriage, home and children, and continually acts to restrict young women's freedom of movement (Lees, 1986, p. 82).

There is indeed a continuity of control in women's offending and non-offending lives (Heidensohn, 1985). As Worrall (1999, p.46) put it: 'The criminalisation of a small group of girls the welfarisation of a larger group and the socialisation of all girls are processes which form a "pyramid" of gendered social control.' By 2000 it seemed as if the shape of this pyramid was shifting towards criminalization. Fuelled by media-driven panics about a 'new breed' of girl gangs, the numbers of girls convicted of indictable offences rose, the use of diversionary measures (cautions, reprimands and warnings) decreased, and the numbers in prison rose from 86 in

1999 to 120 in 2002. Repeated promises over some 20 years from the government and the Youth Justice Board to remove all under 18 year old girls from prison service custody remain to be met (NACRO, 2001; Howard League, 2003).

Violent Crime: 'Yobs' and Aggressive Masculinity?

Overall men account for nearly nine out of every ten people found guilty of indictable offences and are responsible for 92 per cent of convicted cases of violence against the person. Statistics such as these have long been available, but it is only in the past decade that it has seriously been suggested that the problem of crime may indeed be a 'problem of men'; or perhaps more precisely termed a problem of 'maverick masculinities'. This academic interest coincided with increasing public and political concern about the apparently growing anti-social behaviour of the young urban male which the Prime Minister referred to in 1994 as a 'yob culture'. As Ros Coward (1994, p. 32) recalls:

> yob is a species of young white working class male which if the British media is to be believed, is more common than ever before. The yob is foul mouthed irresponsible, probably unemployed and violent. The yob hangs around council estates where he terrorises the local inhabitants, possibly in the company of his pit-bull terrier. He fathers children rather than cares for them. He is often drunk, probably uses drugs and is likely to be involved in crime, including domestic violence. He is the ultimate expression of macho values: mad, bad and dangerous to know.

Such images pervaded the crime discourse of the early 1990s and were returned to in 2000 when Tony Blair declared that 'we need to tighten the law significantly in respect of what I call the yob culture'. The term captures many of the real and imaginary fears of crime and disorder, although it is unclear at what point shouting, swearing and drinking and so on turn from the irritating to the 'yobbish'. More significantly, Coward (1994, p. 33) argues, the yob has come to carry the 'weight of a masculinity' now deemed to be unacceptable. Not that such images are at all new. The 'yob' (back slang for 'boy') has been regularly demonized since Victorian times and has most recently been found in the black-leathered bike rider of the 1960s 'rocker', in the 'mindless mentality' of the 1970s football hooligan and in the 'boorish' lager lout of the 1990s.

But in the 1990s, images of the 'yob', as Coward (1994) contends, became to a degree legitimized by right-wing notions of a dangerous underclass (Murray, 1990) and by feminist critiques of masculinity (Campbell, 1993). For Murray, unmarried and unemployed men are akin to primitive beasts lacking any civilizing influence. For Beatrix Campbell, the 'threat' of masculinity is more complex. Her analysis of the various riots of 1991 in Britain's working-class housing estates draws attention to what was 'self-evident' but publicly rarely acknowledged: they were perpetuated in the main by young men. While public debate circulated between unmarried mothers failing to exercise control over their male offspring, and unemployment and urban deprivation creating legions of the dispossessed, Campbell (1993) stresses how the abandonment of certain communities by the state has not caused a crisis of masculinity, but unleashed it in extreme forms. Young men on council estates became engaged in a militaristic culture of crime: celebrating war and force as ways of sorting things out (Campbell, 1993, p. 323). Unemployment had denied men access to legitimate masculine status. Joyriding, drugs, ram raiding, burglary or rioting on the streets became the key means by which *young men* in economically deprived areas could assert themselves as men. In contrast, Campbell argues, *young women* responded to the same circumstances of deprivation by forging self help and constructive solidarities and provided the only means through which their communities could be sustained. Moreover, she contends that on the streets, and particularly in the context of car crime, joyriding and police chases, it is a similar display of masculinity that is being expressed by the perpetrators and the law enforcement agencies alike.

Indeed, crime, rather than being abnormal, can provide an avenue to express some socially revered values. Stan Cohen was one of the first to note that 'we must realise that some of our most cherished social values – individualism, *masculinity*, competitiveness – are the same ones that generate crime' (Cohen, 1973b, p. 622, italics added). Or as Connell (1995, Chapter 4) contends, violence and crime are key contexts in which a particular collective conception of masculinity is 'made'.

Such notions have also been applied to youth crime through the study of football hooliganism. Dunning et al. (1988) argue that 'aggressive masculinity' is not only tolerated in some lower-working-class communities, but is positively sanctioned as an 'important source of meaning, status and pleasurable emotional arousal' (Dunning et al., 1988, p. 210). This is not to deny that male violence does not exist elsewhere, indeed it is a common characteristic of all social classes, but it takes on a particularly visible form in those groups who are excluded from the status to be found in educational and occupational success. However, openly violent behaviour is rarely uncontrolled or random. It takes place in specific places and in culturally approved contexts, to the degree that perpetrators of indiscriminate violence are liable to be labelled 'nutters' by their peers (Dunning et al., 1988, p. 212).

Trying to find 'violent crime' predominantly in 'masculinity' remains a vexed issue. Coward (1994, p. 35), for example, notes how the equation has simply 'become a way of attacking the least powerful men in our society'. Indeed, demonizing the 'yob' can serve to hide the continuities between their behaviour and that of other men (Walklate, 1995, p. 179). Similarly, Stanko (1994) argues that the discourse of male violence is fixated on the predatory crimes of the street. Not only does this tend to overlook the fact that working-class male youth are likely to be both the perpetrators *and* victims of such crime, but it detracts from the hidden violence used by men against women in the home. A focus on *masculinity* denies that there may be many and varied masculinities (Connell, 1995). It also ignores female violence. Campbell's (1981) study of 251 16 year old schoolgirls, for example, found that 89 per cent of them had been involved in at least one physical fight. The key variable may indeed not be gender alone, but, as Segal (1990, p. 27) contends, how gender and class combine to reflect back the 'increased barbarism' created by the social divisions and inequalities of contemporary capitalism. The limitations of a 'doing gender' approach have also been commented upon by Walklate (2001, p.73) when she argues: 'debate which proceeds under its umbrella strains to fit all kinds of criminal behaviour occurring in all kinds of contexts within its terms'. It is both simplistically universal and tautological.

Drugs: Crime and Criminalization

The scourge of drugs is one of the greatest evils facing society today. They destroy lives, ruin families and undermine communities. (Jack Straw, Home Secretary, cited in the *Guardian*, 3 January 1998)

Drugs can tear communities apart and make thieves and villains out of those who would under normal circumstances be law-abiding citizens. (David Blunkett, Home Secretary, cited in www.drugs.gov.uk, press release, 21 January 2003)

Tackling drug use has become a centrepiece of New Labour's strategy to control criminal and anti-social behaviour. Yet the use of drugs for experimental, recreational and social reasons appears to be widespread. Miller and Plant's (1996) survey of 7,722 15 and 16 year olds found that 94 per cent had drunk alcohol, a third had smoked cigarettes in the past 30 days and that 42 per cent had at some time used illicit drugs, mainly cannabis. In Graham and Bowling's (1995) self report study of 14–25 year olds, 45 per cent of young men and 26 per cent of young women admitted to illegal drug use at some time. The rate was significantly *higher* for white than ethnic minority populations. Similarly, data derived from successive British Crime Surveys estimated that around one in two young people has tried a prohibited drug at some point in their lives and 25 per cent in the last year (Ramsay and Percy, 1996; Ramsay and Spiller, 1997; Ramsey et al., 2001; Aust et al., 2002).

Statistics such as these appear to suggest that half of the population have engaged in criminal activity, simply through their use of illegal substances. Moreover, in the 1990s, a number of media, probation and police sources came to argue that drug use was a significant factor in driving young people towards other forms of crime – most commonly expressed as a 'need' to thieve or rob in order to finance an 'expensive' drug habit. The National Association of Probation Officers claimed that nearly a half of all property crime and theft that had been cleared up had been committed to fund drug and alcohol dependence (cited by Matthews and Trickey, 1996, p. 3). A Home Office study – the NEW-ADAM survey – initiated in response to requests from the Association of Chief Police Officers, found that 65 per cent of all people arrested in Britain tested positive for some illicit drug (Bennett et al., 2001). In these ways a drugs–crime connection has become widely assumed.

However, the BCS studies also reported that whilst illicit drug use amongst young people is widespread, it is an episodic rather than ongoing activity. Only 18 per cent of 16–24 year olds admitted to having taken illegal drugs in the previous month.

The picture is also confused when measured against the use of particular *types* of illicit drug. By far the most common monthly use was cannabis (17 per cent), followed by Ecstacy (3 per cent), amphetamines (2 per cent), cocaine (2.1 per cent), amyl nitrate (1.5 per cent), LSD (0.3 per cent), solvents (0.2 per cent), with use of heroin and crack cocaine extremely rare (0.1 per cent) (Aust et al., 2002). Moreover whilst some research studies have shown a relation between use of heroin or crack cocaine and acquisitive crime, in general there appears to be no direct causal relationship to support the popular perception that drug use invariably results in anti-social, criminal or violent behaviour. Researchers have come to recognize that any reliable investigation of a drugs–crime connection must take into account the relevance of historical shifts in law enforcement, specific forms of drug use, local variations and subcultural factors. All of these tend to be missing from national surveys such as the BCS.

The idea of a 'drugs problem' is probably no more than a hundred years old. In the eighteenth century opiates (opium, morphine and heroin) were freely available and widely used for pain relief. Opium was used – as laudanum – to calm distressed children, and explored for creative reasons by a succession of Romantic poets, notably Coleridge, Wordsworth and Thomas De Quincy. In the mid nineteenth century Britain fought two major wars to compel the Chinese government to continue importing British opium grown in India (Porter, 1996). In the early 1900s cocaine use was marginal in Britain but it was widely used in the USA, where it was a primary ingredient of Coca-Cola. The origins of an overtly penal response to such drug use lie amidst a complex of imperialist, racist and political concerns in the 1910s. In the USA, the Harrison Narcotics Act of 1914, aimed at regulating and controlling opiates and cocaine, made it illegal for doctors to prescribe such narcotics to patients. It was largely designed to placate white fears of Chinese opium use and black cocaine use. As a result whole new *criminal* classes of addicts were constructed. The addict became, not a medical problem, but a criminal one (Beirne and Messerschmidt, 1991, pp. 139–40). In turn, criminalization created a black market and a narcotics underworld. In Britain, the Dangerous Drugs Acts of 1920 and 1923 similarly initiated a 'criminal' model of addiction, even though the regulation of supply was left in the hands of doctors as well as the Home Office (Pearson, 1991).

The next wave of drug control legislation surfaced in the 1930s. This time, in the USA, it was directed at Mexicans with the 1937 Marijuana Tax Act being introduced not because of any medical evidence of marijuana's effects but because of racist attitudes towards those minorities who used it. In Britain cannabis has been prohibited since 1928 and until 1971 was considered, legally, to be on a par with heroin. Current concern about its use originates from the mid 1950s, associated in the main with jazz and black music cultures. However, it was not until the 1960s that young people, in particular, were believed to be the major source of the nation's 'drug problem', epitomized by the use of cannabis, amphetamines and LSD in various bohemian and youth subcultures (see Chapter 5). As Porter (1996, p. 4) concludes:

perception of a 'drugs problem' is quite modern; it has little to do with the substances involved and much to do with social crisis and the strategies of politicians, police and experts . . . the formulation of theories of addiction and the pursuit of criminalization have together created a problem that will not easily go away.

Of all the illegal drugs currently in circulation, it is heroin that has received the lion's share of criminological research, although it should be remembered that cannabis remains the most widely used and accounts for over 90 per cent of all drug seizures. Various researchers (Parker and Newcombe, 1987; Pearson, 1987; Parker et al., 1988) noted a sharp increase in heroin use in particular cities in the north of England and Scotland during the 1980s. Research based in Merseyside suggested that there was a very close relationship between increases in theft and burglary between 1981 and 1986 and the presence of a large number of young, unemployed heroin users. Yet as Parker and Newcombe (1987) point out, most acquisitive crime continued to be committed by non-heroin users and most opiate-using offenders had committed crimes *before* beginning their heroin use. A causal relationship between heroin use and crime is thus far from established. Equally, Pearson (1987, p. 5) notes that the problem was highly scattered and localized, often concentrated in areas with high levels of unemployment and thus arguably reflective more of poverty and deprivation rather than of wilful criminality.

By the 1990s fears of a heroin 'epidemic' were largely superseded by a new set of concerns about Ecstasy, amphetamines, and poly-drug use where a mix of drugs used in combination (alcohol, cannabis, Ecstasy, amphetamines) was believed to have become a 'normalized' practice (Measham et al., 1994). In such 'pick and mix' usage, clear distinctions between the legal and illegal have become eroded. All of this throws the drugs–crime debate into further disarray. Certainly both Parker, Measham and Aldridge's (1995) research in the north-west of England and Matthews and Trickey's (1996) research in Leicester suggest that amongst 13–16 year olds there is no direct link between drug use and crime. In the Leicester sample only six (of 758) respondents admitted that their drug use was financed by crime. Only a small minority had problems of drug dependency. As a result, most reviews of the literature in Britain and internationally are able to conclude that only a small proportion of crime is drug-driven (Hough, 1996 and see Table 1.2).

This is not to deny, however, that illicit use of drugs – particularly cannabis – has not become an increasingly normal aspect of young people's recreation. The normative nature of drug usage is such that it can no longer be simply attached to particular youth cultures, but has transcended class and gender boundaries. As Parker (1996, p. 296) put it, 'perceptions of how to create and take "time out" are in transition in the UK'. As such, it is all the more anachronistic to pathologize drug usage as evidence of some delinquent or damaged personality (Perri, 6. et al., 1997).

Table 1.2   Drugs and crime
• Around four million people use illicit drugs each year.
• Most illicit drug use is relatively controlled, 'recreational' use of cannabis and Ecstasy (though the latter is declining).
• Drug use is more prevalent in affluent urban areas than in areas of low income housing.
• There is no persuasive evidence of any causal link between drug use and property crime. Criminals may use drugs but drugs do not cause crime.
• A very small proportion of users – less than 5 per cent of the total – have chaotic lifestyles involving dependent use of heroin, crack/cocaine and other drugs.
• An even smaller proportion of users – perhaps around 100,000 people – finance their use through crime.
• The majority of those who steal to buy drugs were involved in crime before their drug use became a problem.
• If appropriate drug treatment is given to this group, they reduce their offending levels.
• Police crackdowns have no impact on drug availability or on levels of crime.
Source: Derived from www.drugscope.org.uk/druginfo/evidence-select/drugscrime.htm

The case for normalization has been most forcefully put by the north west England longitudinal study of recreational drug users (Parker et al., 1998; Parker et al., 2002). This traced the changing attitudes to drug use of 465 young people between 1991 to 1995 and again in 2000. Various measures of normalization appear to have been met, particularly in acceptance, availability and use of cannabis. Not only did informal friendship networks make the drug readily available, but usage rates increased with age and had by the age of 22 become further accommodated into everyday lifestyles. As Parker et al. (2002, p. 959) explain:

> That so many otherwise law-abiding citizens have collectively socially reconstructed an illegal act, the supplying of controlled drugs, which carries severe penalties is a good example of the interplay of the dimensions of normalisation; availability and access of drugs continues to grow but is only made possible by socio-cultural accommodation of 'sorting' by youth populations.

Further evidence of the normalization of cannabis might also be seen in New Labour's decision in 2002 to downgrade it to a C classification, with possession to be treated on a 'seize and warn' basis. Decriminalization and legalization however, were ruled out (*Guardian*, 11 July 2002). A potential two-year prison sentence remains for possession, if it involves 'flagrant disregard for the law'. Penalties for supply have been increased from 5 to 14 years. Drug monitoring, testing and treatment may continue apace but often coercively practised and with punitive outcomes.

As a result the political urgency to fight a 'war on drugs' still holds the potential to criminalize large numbers of the relatively law-abiding, particularly considering the apparently widespread use of Ecstasy and cocaine. What criminal and social policy still fails to reflect is that for most young users drugs are *not* a problem; they do not interfere with other aspects of their lives; they are quite simply a rational lifestyle choice (Coffield and Gofton, 1994; Hammersley et al., 2002).

The 'Youth'–'Crime' Connection

1.4 To develop a critical understanding of youth crime it is necessary to move beyond the world of representation and data and the limited discourses of crime that they implicitly encourage. The supposed truism of criminology – that crime is predominantly an activity of the young – can be challenged in various ways. First we need to be clear what we mean by 'crime'. Second, we need to look more attentively at the meaning of 'youth'. The meaning of both concepts appears self evident. In themselves they are rarely subject to critical attention, but closer examination reveals them to be inherently unstable, flexible and shifting categories.

The Problem of 'Crime'

Crime is commonly understood to be behaviour that is prohibited by criminal law. In other words, no act can be considered a crime, irrespective of how immoral or damaging it may be, unless it has been made such by state legislation (Michael and Adler, 1933). This legal definition appears clear-cut and uncontroversial, but in the case of young people especially, it is unable to capture the full extent of those behaviours widely considered to be troublesome. Criminologists have also used the terms 'delinquency' and 'anti-social behaviour' to refer to youth misconduct in order to include behaviour that may be deemed a 'nuisance' as well as that which is liable to criminal sanction.

For young people, the terms 'crime' and 'delinquency' collide to attract critical attention to a much wider set of 'problem' behaviours than is usually afforded to adults. For example, 'being incorrigible', running away from home, truancy and drinking alcohol in public are considered to be problematic only when committed by young people. Indeed, in the USA they are commonly termed 'status offences'. Legal definitions of crime can only consider an act to be criminal once it has been identified by law – thus criminals cannot be identified until processed and convicted by the courts. But, as we have seen (Section 1.2), not all of those who break the law are detected and convicted. The study of youth crime is severely hampered and is particularly one-dimensional when restricted only to those who are 'known' offenders. In addition, legal definitions imply there is some underlying consensus about what constitutes criminality and what does not, but conceptions of crime clearly vary from place to place and change over time. For example until relatively recently slavery, non-consensual intercourse within marriage, and all forms of execution were exempt from criminal sanction. Wilkins (1964, p. 46) goes so far as to claim that 'there are no absolute standards. At some time or another, some form of society or another has defined almost all forms of behaviour that we now call "criminal" as desirable for the functioning of that form of society.' The picture is further confused because many of the 'crimes' that we attribute to young people – vandalism, joyriding, mugging, hooliganism – are media-inspired terms and not specific offences recognized by the law.

As a result, some sociologists have suggested that 'crime' is not simply a violation of the criminal law, but occurs whenever social and moral codes are infracted (Sellin,

1938). Here the terms 'deviance', 'non-conformity' and 'anti-social conduct', as well as that of 'delinquency', are employed to capture acts of 'wrongdoing' that are missed by the law. Such a definition may indeed be useful, not so much in unearthing youth crime but in drawing attention to a vast array of behaviours from corporate fraud, swindling, domestic violence, abuse and harassment to violations of human rights and crimes committed by the state, which are usually omitted from the public discourse of 'crime'. Because the term 'crime' is not the object but the product of criminal law and because it is of such emotive and political value, some have argued for its abandonment in preference of the more sensitizing notions of 'social injury' and 'social harm' (Hulsman, 1986). As the criminal law is in the main directed against forms of behaviour associated with the young, the working class and the poor, we should not be surprised to find that, officially, it is these groups that are 'found' to be the most criminal. To break out of this impasse, Presdee (1994) argues that notions of youth crime should be replaced by the ideas of transgression, of 'doing wrong', of desire and seeking excitement (see Chapter 5.5). Only then will we be able to capture a sense of 'wrongdoing's' ubiquitous nature, its presence throughout all sections of society and its essential motivations. Focusing on the law and official statistics simply reproduces a partial and pernicious view of where, when and why 'offending' occurs in society.

By the 1960s a critical school of criminology had started to address the issue not of why young offending occurred, but of how particular images of crime were *constructed* and maintained. Becker (1963), for example, argued that there was no intrinsic reason why any reference to behaviour should be included in a definition of crime at all. Crime, he argued, is a consequence of social interaction, a result of a negotiated process that involves the rule violator, the police, the courts and lawmakers who have *labelled* that person's behaviour as criminal. It is not behaviour in itself that constitutes crime. Crime only occurs once it is *criminalized* through public perception and social reaction. So there is nothing intrinsic to any behaviour that makes it criminal and there cannot be specific kinds of motivation to engage in crime if there are no categories of activities or people that are inherently criminal (see Chapter 4.1). In this way it has been argued that our main sources of information about (youth) crime – namely the media and official statistics – are social constructions. They identify *certain* people as criminal and reproduce *recognizable* criminal populations, but tell us little about the extent and meaning of crime *per se*.

From a Marxist perspective, Chambliss (1975) argues that acts are defined as criminal only when it is in the interest of the ruling class to define them as such. In capitalist societies, 'crime' performs the vital function of diverting the lower classes' attention away from the condition and source of their exploitation and allows the ruling classes to expand penal law in order to ensure that the lives of the working classes (and particularly the young working classes) are subject to tighter regulation. Behaviours are criminalized to maintain political control and to counter any perceived threat to ruling-class rule (most notably in the form of 'dangerous' youth). For Sumner (1990), 'crime' again is neither a behavioural nor a legal category, but a means of applying *social censure* to complex practical conflicts and moral debates. 'Crime' and 'deviance' are matters of moral and political judgement:

in short they are ideological concepts that maintain existing power relations and justify inequality (De Haan, 1991). This is most clearly seen when we find that a wide range of behaviours that cause the most injury, suffering and loss – poverty, political atrocities, fraud, embezzlement, illegal arms dealing, domestic violence, child abuse, denial of human rights, environmental pollution, genocide, workplace death and injury and so on – are rarely, if ever, considered within discourses of 'crime'. Even when they are, they are unlikely to attract the same degree of moral condemnation (Box, 1983; Cohen, 1993; Muncie and McLaughlin, 2001). Significantly, these 'crimes' are not usually the work of young people. If our concern with youth crime is driven by fears for social stability, personal safety and social justice, then we need to look elsewhere to discover where the most dangerous threats and risks to our person and property lie (Muncie, 2000a, p. 220).

By focusing on how the 'problem of youth crime' is constructed through statistical measures and by media, political and public discourses (and by revealing the significant absences in those discourses), it also becomes possible to recognize that we are not simply dealing with a problem of aberrant behaviours, but with problems of definition, representation and political reaction. 'Youth crime' is a problem, not simply in its damaging consequences, but also in the way it is commonly understood and conceptualized. As Sheila Brown (1998, p. 119) concludes, 'youth criminology perhaps remains the field most trapped by its past and most confounded by uncritical supposition'.

The Problem of 'Youth'

The concepts of 'youth' and 'adolescence' can be deconstructed in much the same way. There are no precise moments that mark when childhood ends and adulthood begins. Does youth begin at the age of 10 when we can be held responsible for criminal behaviour (8 in Scotland)? Does it start at 16 when we can leave school? And does it only end at the age of 26 when we can claim the full rate of housing benefit? (see Table 1.3 and Mizen, 2004 pp. 5–9). Though the teenage years of 13–19 are usually taken as synonymous with adolescence, for young men especially this period appears to have expanded significantly since the 1970s. Adulthood is usually defined in terms of gaining independence from the family home and full employment. For many, these possibilities have been foreclosed by extended periods of training and education and rising levels of debt. A growing trend is for young adults to stay living with their parents: 57 per cent of 18–24 year olds did so in 2001 compared to 55 per cent in 1997 (*Guardian*, 13 March 2003). Autonomy is denied. However, this general trend also masks a growing polarization between, on the one hand, those leaving school at 16, risking low pay and unemployment and, on the other, a middle-class majority deferring entry into the labour and housing markets. Social inequalities of class, gender and 'race' are being exacerbated. Scraton (1997a, p. 182) explores these anomalies by noting that on the one hand, then, there is the denial of children as rational, responsible persons able to receive information, participate in frank and open discussions and come to well reasoned and appropriately informed decisions about their interpersonal relationships (family, friends, sexual), about school and about developing sexuality. On the other there is the imposition, using the full force of law, of the highest level of rationality and responsibility on children and young people who seriously offend. The paradox is that the same sources appear to propose that childhood represents a period of diminished adult responsibility governing certain actions while being a period of equal responsibility governing others.

Indeed, as Table 1.3 shows, criminal responsibility is one of the first 'rights' that are afforded to children. The image of young people as a 'threat' endows them with more power than they actually possess. Or as Phil Cohen (2000, p. 228) so succinctly puts it: 'it is precisely because they pose no real threat to the body politic that unemployed young people are made to carry the enormous burden of symbolising the moral crisis of civil society'.

Phil Cohen (1986, p. 6) identifies four major assumptions that lie behind most political, policy and professional reactions to the 'youth question':

1 Youth is a unitary category with certain psychological characteristics and social needs common to the age group.
2 Youth is an especially formative stage of development where attitudes and values become anchored to ideologies and remain fixed in this mould in later life.
3 The transition from childhood dependence to adult autonomy normally involves a rebellious phase which is itself part of a cultural tradition transmitted from one generation to the next.
4 Young people in industrial societies experience difficulty in making successful transitions and require professional help, advice and support to do so.

These 'common senses' continually resurface in political and media discourses as explanations of why young people can never be freed from moral, legal and social regulation.

However, whilst 'youth' may share some characteristics simply because of their age or class position, their lifestyles and opportunities are differentiated by 'race', gender and a diverse array of social, economic and cultural realities. 'Youth' is not a stable undifferentiated category, but one of diversity, flexibility, adaptability and individualized meanings (Miles, 2000, p. 160). For Wyn and White (1997, p. 11) 'youth' is a *relational* concept whose meaning can only be captured through attention to how age is 'socially constructed, institutionalized and controlled in historically and culturally specific ways'. For example, as we have noted, the connotations attached to 'youth' and 'adolescence' continually create a conflicting set of expectations for girls. Barbara Hudson (1984) argues that adolescence is a 'masculine' construct. Typical aspects of adolescence – soul searching, rebellion, peer group conformity, offending – are masculine images. Attempts by girls to comply with such notions not only imply a lack of maturity, but also a lack of femininity on their part (Hudson, 1984, p. 35). Such contradictions are most striking in the control of girls' sexuality:

In matters of sexuality the discourse of adolescence is clearly at variance with the discourse of femininity. According to the terms of the adolescence discourse, adolescence is a time for shifting allegiances, rapidly changing friendships, whereas femininity involves the skill to make lasting relationships with the ability to care very deeply for people. (Hudson, 1984, p. 47)

Table 1.3 *Becoming an adult: Rights and responsibilities*	
Age	**Rights and responsibilities**
5	Drink alcohol in private
8	Be held responsible for a crime in Scotland
10	Be held responsible for a crime in England, Wales and Northern Ireland
	Be taken into the 'protective custody' of 'intensive fostering'; be sent to a secure unit for 'grave' offences
12	Be held in a secure training centre
	Own a pet
13	Seek part-time employment
14	Open a bank account
	Pay adult fare on public transport
15	Be sent to a young offenders institution
16	Enter or live in a brothel
	Pay taxes
	Consent to sexual intercourse
	Have a homosexual relationship (lowered from 18 in 2000)
	Leave home/marry with parents' consent
	Leave school
	Seek full-time employment
	Buy a knife (introduced in 1996)
	Buy tobacco (to be raised to 18?)
	Drive a moped
	Buy a lottery ticket
	Buy aerosol paint (introduced in 2003)
17	Drive a car
	Join the army
	Own an airgun (raised from 14 in 2003)
18	Vote in elections (to be reduced to 16?)
	Serve on a jury
	Buy alcohol
	Claim partial income support
	Marry without parents' consent
	Be tried in a magistrates' court
	Buy fireworks (raised from 16 in 1997)
	Bet in a betting shop
	Entitled to lower rate of national minimum wage
	Get a tattoo
21	Adopt a child
	Become an MP
22	Entitled to adult rate of national minimum wage
25	Claim adult rate of income support
26	Claim full rate of housing benefit

In general, sexuality and sickness are firmly interwoven into images of deviant girls to a degree that is absent in images of deviant boys. The study of relations between crime, gender and generation not only reveals how the experience of 'being young' differs fundamentally for boys and girls, but how common-sense and everyday notions of 'youth' are largely predicated on gender-specific assumptions. In general, the troubling aspects of being an 'adolescent' remain contained within and derived from analysis of male criminal deviance: both the 'youth' and 'crime' discourses are to a large extent gender specific.

The experience of being young in Britain is further mediated by racial background. The majority of black youths in this country form a specifically racialized section of the working class (Sivanandan, 1976); they are subject to specific pressures of deprivation and oppression because of their 'race'. In education, black youths have encountered various racially specific forms of disadvantage: schools have generally failed to develop curricula that are non-ethnocentric and, for many, cultural differences are likely to be recast as 'educational problems', resulting in higher rates of school exclusion (*Independent*, 19 June 1996). Also, for black youth, racism and harassment are daily facts of life (*Guardian*, 23 July 1996). Yet their demonization as the criminal 'other' has been a recurring feature of post-war Britain, whether it be 'the pimp' of the 1950s, the 'black activist' of the 1960s, the 'mugger' of the 1970s, the 'rioter' of the 1980s or the 'yardie drug dealer' of the 1990s (Keith, 1993, p. 42). It should not be surprising then to find that one of the repeated grievances of Afro-Caribbean youth is the degree of interference and harassment they receive from the police on the streets.

By way of some contrast, a recurring grievance of 'Asian' youth has been the lack of protection afforded to them by the police. This has led to the establishment of organizations for their own protection, such as the Southhall Youth movement founded in 1976. For years idealized images of 'Asian' family life had promoted a view – supported by self report studies – that 'Asian' youth were more likely to encounter crime as victims than as offenders. However, following disturbances in Bradford in June 1995, contrary images of gangs, drugs and family disintegration came to the fore. As Webster (1997) argues, the activities of a core offending group spilt over to inform media discourse and police reactions to whole ethnic populations with the end result that 'Asian' young people were both 'racialized' and 'criminalized'. For example, despite a growing presence of young black and 'Asian' young women in higher education in the 1990s their reservoir of talent remains largely ignored (Mirza, 1992; Malek, 1997).

These cases illustrate that 'youth' is not a unitary category and that social reaction is coloured by popular perceptions of 'race' and 'gender'. But such differentiation can also be glossed over in political and professional discourse. Images of *all* young people as potentially troubled or troublesome remain; they all need strict control or guidance. Any behaviour that may undermine the 'natural' authority of adults is subject to regulation. Rarely are young people allowed the right to speak for themselves (Qvortrup et al., 1994, p. 2). The equation is simple enough. Young people experience biological and physiological changes during puberty. This causes psychological disturbance and deviant ways of behaving which can only be resolved either through adult professional support or overt control.

When young people are constituted as *deprived* and *deficient* of standards of morality and discipline, then all manner of intensive supervision, guidance, training, fostering and mentoring programmes are initiated. In November 2002 Tony Blair outlined his vision of civic responsibility and rights; at the root of which lay the 'new opportunities' of New Deal employment programmes, the minimum wage, Sure Start nursery provision, poverty reduction and the expansion of education and training. However, in return Blair expected 'a tougher approach to anti-social behaviour'. The 'something for something' society. Failing to accept 'opportunity' is constituted as evidence of *depravity* and *dangerousness* such that more punitive interventions are entertained. A continuum of social policy and criminal justice programmes has been created (see Chapters 6 and 7). Targeting those below the age of 10 to identify 'future problem behaviour' becomes an issue of criminal justice rather than social welfare. The homeless are threatened with jail unless they get off the streets. A 'new unacceptable culture of worklessness' is identified. 'Littering and graffiti are criminalized . . . Young people are routinely at the sharp end of such demonisation: a process which readily creates "icons of evil", fosters fears about "us" and "them" and erects rigid moral boundaries between the deserving and the undeserving' (Goldson, 2002). The attributions of the 'feral', 'yob' and 'super-predator' further strip young people of humanity and access to rights. Intervening in young people's lives comes to be an expected essential process. Given the dangers and potentials of 'youth' – and the limited discourses of depravity, and deficiency in which they are caught – the 'doing nothing' option is unthinkable. Or as Mizen (2004 p. 15) puts it, the construction of youth is an important 'politically constituted method of division' which allows the state to 'go about its everyday business of managing social relations by organising them into real distinctions and categories that work to obscure the exploitative content of social life.'

Summary

- The first issue to be addressed in the study of youth and crime is to be aware of the problems involved in reaching an adequate definition of 'youth'. At what age do people suddenly become adult? Traditionally 'youth' has been associated with adolescence and the 'teenager', meaning everybody between the ages of 12 and 20, but by no means all of this age group share the same interests or concerns. Most notably, growing up male, growing up female and growing up in different communities involve different activities, different constraints and different opportunities. Youth is a social relation.

- In much media and political debate the terms 'teenage', 'adolescence', 'youth' and 'generation' have been trapped in a negative discourse to describe a condition which is considered both troubled and troublesome. These images in the main derive from a predominantly bio-psychological literature dating back to the first decade of the twentieth century but persist as a successful newsline for the press, television and radio and as a potential vote winner for politicians.

- Similar problems arise when trying to reach an adequate definition of 'crime'. Legal definitions reflect only what is sanctioned by the criminal law and fail to recognize other more serious 'social harms'. Conversely, in the case of youth, the concepts of 'delinquency' and 'anti-social behaviour' extend the parameters of crime to include a host of trivial 'nuisances' and 'misconducts'.

- Young people are widely perceived not to be rational and responsible enough to be fully empowered, but are deemed fully rational and responsible if they offend.

- The extent of youth crime is unknowable. There are no reliable statistical indices. To this extent what is known about young offending is a social construction – a product of particular social reactions and policing practices which become embedded as 'facts', not only in official statistics, but also in popular and political discourses.

Study Questions

1 What can be learned about youth crime by studying crime statistics?
2 Why do media, politicians and law enforcement agencies attach so much significance to the transgressions of young people?
3 In what ways can 'youth crime' be considered a social construction?
4 The 'youth crime problem' is an illusion, a trick to deflect our attention from more serious crimes and social harms. How far do you agree?
5 'The issue of youth crime is less to do with breaking the law and more to do with fears for the nation's future.' Discuss.

Further Resources

An overview of many of the issues raised in this chapter is provided by Newburn (2002). Statistical measures of youth offending can be found at the Home Office's Research

Development Statistics website at homeoffice.gov.uk/rds Another useful source is the annually produced *Youth Crime Factsheet* produced by the voluntary organization NACRO (National Association for the Care and Resettlement of Offenders) and accessible on nacro.org.uk/data/briefings All such sources should however, be read alongside some critical commentary such as Coleman and Moynihan's *Understanding Crime Data* (1996).

There is still no single text which explores media representations of youth and crime, but Hall's (1978) analysis of football hooliganism in the press provides important insights, while Davis and Bourhill (1997) catalogue how the media were implicated in creating a 'crisis' about childhood in the 1990s. The most thorough self report studies are those associated with the Youth Lifestyles Survey first conducted in 1992 (Graham and Bowling, 1995) and repeated with a larger sample in 1998 (Flood-Page, 2000). Anderson et al.'s (1994) Edinburgh study was also pathbreaking. Its discovery of widespread victimization called into question the usual ways of understanding the 'youth problem'.

Anyone seriously interested in youth drug use and the possibilities for reform can do no better than start with Parker, Aldridge and Measham's *Illegal Leisure* (1998). The landmark text on black youth and crime is Hall et al.'s *Policing the Crisis* (1978). For a good introduction to gender and crime see Walklate's (2001) *Gender, Crime and Criminal Justice*, though this does not focus exclusively on young women. Phil Cohen's (1997) *Rethinking the Youth Question* and Wyn and White's (1997) *Rethinking Youth* both provide important insights into shifts in the meaning of being young.

The role of the state in (re)constructing childhood is the subject of Goldson et al.'s edited collection (2002). Sheila Brown's (1998) *Understanding Youth and Crime* does more than most to force us to acknowledge that 'youth crime' is a product not of absent fathers, single mothers, lack of discipline and so on but of the production and consumption of partial knowledges.

2 Histories of Youth Crime: The Deprived and the Depraved

Overview

Chapter 2 examines:
- the 'invention' of childhood;
- why juvenile delinquency emerged as a major social problem in the early nineteenth century;
- the relevance of the concepts of 'deprived' and 'depraved' for the treatment of young people in trouble;
- the significance of 'adolescence' in understanding youth crime in the early twentieth century;
- the origins of 'hooliganism';
- the role of medico-psychological discourses in consolidating the 'youth problem' in the inter-war years.

Key Terms	
adolescence	idealist history
child savers	reformation
dangerous classes	rescue
depravation	revisionist history
deprivation	social crime

Is youth crime a relatively new phenomenon? Is the situation far worse now than in the past? Can historical research shed any light on how best to treat young offenders? This chapter traces the origins and development of discourses of juvenile delinquency (in the context of changing policies and practices of youth justice primarily in England and Wales) from the early nineteenth century to the 1930s. This focus on history is informed not simply by a curiosity with the past, but because it guards against the impression that the problem of youth crime is either timeless or relatively recent. Similarly, it is only by placing crime (and the reaction to it) in precise socio-historical contexts that we are able truly to grasp the meaning and significance of our subject matter. However, any brief excursus into social history must bear two vital matters in mind. First, historical research is not a simple matter of telling facts in an unproblematic fashion. It is a profoundly political subject in its own right. Second, it is not possible simply to recall a single, uncontested history. This chapter deals with *competing* interpretations of youth crime and youth justice. Whilst legislative and organizational landmarks might be placed quite accurately, the extent of crime and delinquency and the purpose of youth justice remain the subject of dispute and controversy.

Broadly speaking, a basic distinction between idealist and revisionist histories can be made. Until the 1970s most histories of youth crime and punishment told a story of reformers who struggled against the 'cruel and barbaric' practices of the past and initiated the movement towards the more humane methods of dealing with young offenders of the present. History was constructed 'from above', concentrating almost exclusively on the reforming zeal of powerful and notable individuals. The history of youth crime was told as one of progress from cruelty to enlightenment in how the young criminal was treated. Contemporary assessments of the nature and extent of offending were largely taken for granted.

During the 1970s this version of events came to be questioned by revisionist accounts of historical change. In short, revisionism was more intent on retelling the story of crime and reform in the context of changing socio-historical circumstances, economic interests, power relations and a strengthening of state power. Reform was analysed not so much in terms of benevolent progress, but as an insidious extension of centralized power and control. Above all, it was argued that it was impossible to view reform as a simple reaction to a growing problem of youth crime. Rather, it was only through the developing legal powers and institutions of juvenile justice that the 'problem' of childhood and youth could be constituted and defined. Notions of youth as either innocent or dangerous were only fully realized in those developments of criminal law and in the expansion of institutional interventions that characterized the early to mid nineteenth century. Revisionism also questioned the motives of the humanitarian reformers themselves, arguing that they were driven as much by self and class interest as they were by conscience. Above all, it is argued that it was only through the particular motives and moralities of the reformers that attention was drawn to new categories of youthful behaviour and the very concept of juvenile delinquency invented. The revisionist concern then is not so much with unearthing the causes and extent of youth crime, but with identifying the ways in which certain behaviours and groups of the population were subject to processes of criminalization – how some children and youth came to be considered as criminal.

This chapter tries to capture something of the spirit of these debates while remaining alive to the possibilities of a 'new revisionism' which neither condemns reform as overt repression nor celebrates it as a successful humanitarian crusade. In particular it focuses on the historical controversies of two particular moments: (i) the emergence of 'juvenile delinquency' as a discrete social problem in the early nineteenth century and (ii) the significance of the concept of 'adolescence' in understanding youth crime in the early twentieth century. Throughout it is informed by Pearson's (1983, 1993–4) and Humphries' (1994) insistence that the identifying of young offending as particularly troublesome is nothing new. British social history – at least from the eighteenth century – is replete with 'respectable fears' in which the present is compared unfavourably with the past. A common and recurring complaint is that the behaviour of young people is worse than '20 or 30 years ago' or 'in my day' or 'before the war'. However, such assumptions fail to stand up to sustained historical scrutiny.

Whether it be the 2000s (truancy and street crime), the 1970s (football hooligans), the 1950s (teddy boys), the 1930s (immoral youth), the 1890s (street gangs), the 1860s (garrotters) or the 1830s (street arabs), young people's behaviour has consistently been singled out as symbolic of national moral decline and as indicative of some new and unprecedented problem in which things have 'gone too far' (see Table 2.1). In addressing the pressing problems of the day, it seems that the Victorians suffered from the amnesia that inflicts many contemporary readings of the present.

Table 2.1   *A catalogue of complaints*

- 'I think it's something from the early to mid-1990s, and beyond, getting worse because of more single parent families, lack of authority.' (Police Commander, 2002)
- 'In the last 30 years the balance in the criminal justice system has been tilted too far in favour of the criminal and against the protection of the public.' (Home Secretary, 1993)
- 'We will never get reasonable behaviour among the young until we bring back National Service. Without decent standards to guide them, the young have become lawless. Before the war there was little lawlessness. We need to return to those days.' (Newspaper editorial, 1985)
- 'Over the past 20 years or so, there has been a revulsion from authority and discipline.' (Newspaper editorial, 1981)
- 'The adolescent has learned no definite moral standards from his parents, is contemptuous of the law, easily bored.' (British Medical Association, 1961)
- 'The passing of parental authority, defiance of pre-war conventions, the absence of restraint, the wildness of extremes, the wholesale drift away from churches are but a few characteristics of after-war conditions.' (Boys' club leader, 1932)
- 'Their vulgarity and silliness and the distorted, unreal, Americanized view of life must have a deteriorating effect and lead to the formation of false ideals.' (Social commentator and advocate of boys' clubs, 1917)
- 'Our young people have no idea of discipline or subordination.' (Chief Constable, 1904)
- 'The manners of children are deteriorating . . . the child of today is coarser, more vulgar, less refined than his parents were.' (Howard Association, 1898)
- 'Insubordination to parental authority, leading to insubordination to all authority is very general.' (Clergyman, 1849)
- 'Morals are getting much worse. When I was young my mother would have knocked me down for speaking improperly to her.' (Newspaper editorial, 1843)
- 'They are links which have fallen off the chain of society which are going to decay and obstruct the whole machine.' (Politician, 1788)
- 'I would there were no age between 10 and three-and-twenty, or that youth would sleep out the rest; for there is nothing in the between but getting wenches with child, wronging the ancientry, stealing, fighting.' (*The Winter's Tale*, Act III, scene iii, *c.* 1610)

Source: Derived from Pearson (1983, 1985, 1993–4)

We are just as likely to find complaints about social change, permissive decline, the break-up of the family, 'disturbing' tendencies of modern life, the deterioration of manners and the growing numbers of irresponsible youth surfacing in the nineteenth century as we do in the present. Moreover each new complaint seems to gather strength from a prevailing assumption that 'nothing like this has had to be endured before'. As Pearson (1983, pp. 242–3) eloquently concludes:

If this long, connected history of respectable fears tells us anything at all, then it is surely that street violence and disorder are a solidly entrenched feature of the social landscape. Hence they are going to be much more difficult to dislodge than if we imagined that they had suddenly appeared from nowhere . . . it will help first to repossess the past if we are to understand the present and build the future.

The Social Construction of Childhood and Youth

2.1 A catalogue of complaints about youth behaviour may be traced back at least through two centuries, but childhood has not always been a time in the life cycle to which much importance was attached. Often the reverse was true. Infanticide or abandonment of the newborn was not uncommon in Europe as late as the eighteenth century, and the practice of disposing of illegitimate children continued into the nineteenth. Cultural beliefs partly determined who should or should not survive. Boys were considered of much greater value than girls and any child who was imperfect was likely to be subject to a premature death. Even when allowed to live at birth, a child's survival was tenuous owing to high mortality rates among babies and young children.

This may in part explain why childhood received so little attention, to the extent, as the social historian Philippe Ariès (1962, p. 28) maintains, that the various languages of the Middle Ages and later did not possess words to distinguish infants from juveniles or juveniles from adults. Ariès' radical notion was that prior to the seventeenth century there was no conception of childhood, adolescence or youth. Unsurprisingly, his work has not gone unchallenged. For example Pollock's (1983) study of diaries and autobiographies led her to conclude that there has been no time in which parental indifference predominated. Parents have always held an emotional attachment for their children. Some conception of childhood has always existed. Nevertheless in pre-industrial societies children mingled with adults in everyday life, in work, in leisure and in sport to a far greater degree than they might do today. They did not live in a separate world or behave differently and were not subject to different codes of morality and propriety. So children were quite 'naturally' and 'happily' involved in any number of activities – drinking alcohol, manual work, gambling – that we might now define as inappropriate in order to safeguard their 'innocence' and morality (Empey, 1982, p. 33). As a result there could be no conception of childhood as a social problem in itself. Some children might be 'selected as problematic by particular value judgements' – but not to the extent that it demanded a legal response (Dingwall et al., 1984, p. 208).

The process of strictly distinguishing a period of childhood and a morality of childhood began in the late Middle Ages, largely from within the aristocracy and nobility. The most obvious influences came from Renaissance humanism and moralists of the Protestant Reformation (Cunningham, 1995). There were two important emphases. First, children gradually became seen as innocents and as objects of affection, especially within the family, but second, they were seen by moralists as rather odd creatures – fragile maybe, but also capable of bringing into the world a corrupt nature and evil disposition. These two images, described by Hendrick (1997, pp. 37–40) as the 'Romantic child' and the 'Evangelical child', collided in the view that children were in need of both protection *and* discipline/regulation. What was emerging was a modern concept of childhood in which a child was thought to require a moral and educational training before entering adult life. Moreover, given children's vulnerability, such training could not be undirected. Thus the moralists placed responsibility not only on the Church, but also on the family and the school to raise children in a proper fashion. By the eighteenth century a vision of the ideal child had been developed and widely projected – a child who was dependent, submissive to authority, obedient, modest, hard-working and chaste. If children did not meet such standards then the fault lay primarily with parents and, second, with schools which had failed to exercise an appropriate measure of discipline.

Historical analyses have suggested that both this ideal concept and its practical implementation were formative influences in the origins of the nuclear family. During the Middle Ages, children were common property and, except for a few early years, were not necessarily raised by their own parents. However, by the seventeenth century direct responsibility was placed on natural parents to provide a safe and disciplined upbringing. The irony in this development and the instigation of an ideology of parental responsibility was that, although not solely confined to aristocratic and bourgeois elites, such conceptions of childhood and family did not have much (if any) purchase upon the material conditions of life or the culture of the mass of the population. For them the necessity to make children economically active as soon as possible precluded any consideration of instigating prolonged periods of childhood training and dependency. There was then a clear class differentiation in conceptions of childhood (Thane, 1981, p. 9). Only the privileged classes could afford the 'luxury of childhood with its demands on material provision, time and emotion' (Jenks, 1996, p. 64). As a result, as late as the mid nineteenth century the majority of children participated in acts which, if committed today, could not only result in their being defined as delinquent but could require their parents to be charged with negligence or contributing to their children's delinquency.

Much of this was the outcome of child labour being an economic necessity for many families. Children were viewed as a vital source of family income and were placed in work as soon as they could be economically active. Child labour from the ages of 4 or 5 was a long-established practice in the rural farms and fields, where children performed tasks including straw plaiting and preparing raw materials for such domestic industries as lace making. With the onslaught of the industrial revolution, the children of the poor formed the bulk of factory labour. In the late eighteenth century it has been estimated that, because of the high birth and death rates, 40 per cent of the population were under the age of 15 (Morris and McIsaac, 1978, p. 1). In particular they worked in the mines, traversing the narrower roadways and in the mills, where they crawled under machines to clear waste.

Such a situation remained unquestioned, not only by families who needed to maintain a level of income, but also by factory owners who were acutely aware of the benefit of maintaining such a cheap source of labour. In the first decades of the nineteenth century, 80 per cent of the workers in English cotton mills were children (Gillis, 1974, p. 56). Children were legally the property of their parents and were used by them as family assets. Among the poor, the labour of children was exploited; among the rich, their marriages were contrived, all to the economic advantage of their parents. This degree of complacency was bolstered by the law. Not until 1889 did cruelty to children by parents become a specific criminal offence. Children were also held to be adult if above the age of 7 and were held responsible for any misdemeanour. There was no special provision for young offenders. For example on one day in 1814 five children between the ages of 8 and 12 were hanged for petty larceny (Pinchbeck and Hewitt, 1973, p. 352).

All of this lends credence to the notion that childhood and youth are not universal biological states, but social constructions in particular historical contexts. It is clear that for a majority of young people in the early nineteenth century, the modern concepts of 'childhood' or 'youth' had little or no bearing on their lives. However, whilst eighteenth-century conceptions of the child were at best ambiguous and class specific, by the twentieth century 'childhood' had become recognized as a universal condition. This was made possible not only through changes in economic and social conditions, but by the establishment of identifiable age groups in law and in medical, psychological, educational and welfare discourses and policies. As a result notions of 'childhood as constructed' continue to be highly influential in many criminological texts because they reveal connections between socio-economic transformations, adult perceptions and the ability to recognize 'delinquency'. They reveal how, as the concept of childhood expanded, it became possible to define certain behaviours as new and unique social problems.

Discovering Juvenile Delinquency

2.2 Most historians agree that youthful behaviour was first identified as a major social problem in the early nineteenth century through a mixture of contemporary accounts, social surveys and empirical investigations. These permitted a problem to be identified but they presupposed existing conceptions of how youth should behave, what relation should exist between different age groups and what should be the appropriate role of the family. In the early nineteenth century, with the rapid growth of industrial capitalism, factory production and high-density urban populations, the condition of the labouring classes became the object of considerable middle-class concern – whether this was fear of their revolutionary potential, disgust at their morality or alarm at their impoverishment and criminal tendencies. The need to ensure a reliable, healthy and willing workforce to maintain factory production produced a wide range of reformist initiatives which have variously been interpreted as humanitarian in motive or repressive in intent. Many of these centred on the delineation of juvenile delinquency as a distinctive social problem, demanding special and immediate action.

Depravity, Destitution and Urbanization

In early nineteenth-century Britain it was commonplace for children to work in many industries including textiles, mining, agriculture, domestic service, docks and machinery and metals. The first attempts to restrain child labour came from landowners hostile to manufacturing, adult trade unionists seeking limitations of adult hours of work, or from middle-class intellectuals and humanitarians who were appalled at the exploitation and brutalization of young workers and the violence thereby done to the 'nature' of childhood itself (Thompson, 1963, p. 367; Hendrick, 1997, p. 40; Cunningham, 1995, pp. 138–45). As a result of such pressure, the 1819 and 1833 Factory Acts stipulated that no child under the age of 9 was to be employed in the mills and factories, and hours were limited to eight per day for those under 13, and 12 hours for those under 18. This legislation marked the first step in acknowledging a 'universal' childhood. Whilst the Acts were consistently contravened, where the law was upheld it indirectly compelled families with children to seek further employment in order to compensate for lost wages. And while parents were at work, children were left to their own devices or neglected. Similarly, the urban youth population often grew more rapidly than the now restricted work opportunities. A growing number of children were thus effectively unemployed and unsupervised. In Hendrick's (1997, pp. 40–5) terms, the 'Factory Child' was replaced by the 'Delinquent Child'.

Vagrancy and the sight of children eking out a living on the street (gambling, selling necklaces, matches, braces or boxes of dominoes) increasingly came to be viewed as a serious social problem. Mayhew's (1861) vivid descriptions of the rookeries in the East End of London catalogued the activities of such young 'precocious' traders, 'daring' thieves and 'loutish' vagabonds. Children attracted to the streets as a result of the 'brute' tyranny of parents, association with costermongers, orphanhood or destitution, necessarily lived on the edge of crime. There was no clear demarcation between honest work and illegal trading for those existing on a subsistence level on the streets of Britain's newly industrialized cities. It was in such conditions that bands of young pickpockets and other 'artful dodgers' thrived, whose independence and street-wise lifestyle were anathema to the growing number of middle-class journalists and social commentators. Such observers tended to carry with them their own bourgeois conceptions of childhood and youth as a period of dependency and vulnerability. They expressed concern not simply about the need to control criminality, but about the need to tackle a 'premature precocity', symbolized by promiscuity, irreligion, pauperism and knowledge of 'the adult world and its pleasures'. In short the problem was viewed as having as much a moral as a criminal character.

As Mayhew (1861, p. 479) described it:

Each year sees an increase of the numbers of street-children to a very considerable extent, and the exact nature of their position may be thus briefly depicted: what little *information* they receive is obtained from the worst class – from cheats, vagabonds, and rogues; what little *amusement* they indulge in, springs from sources the most poisonous – the most fatal to happiness and welfare; what little they know of a *home* is necessarily associated with much that is vile and base; their very means of existence, uncertain and precarious as it is, is to a great extent identified with petty chicanery, which is quickly communicated by one to the other; while their physical sufferings from cold, hunger, exposure to the weather, and other causes of a similar nature, are constant, and at times extremely severe. Thus every means by which a proper intelligence may be conveyed to their minds is either closed or at the least tainted, while every duct by which a bad description of knowledge may be infused is sedulously cultivated and enlarged.

It was from such concerns that the first public body to investigate youth crime – the Society for Investigating the Causes of the Alarming Increase of Juvenile Delinquency in the Metropolis – was established in 1815 (Shore, 1999, p. 20). Whether or not the rate of crime was in fact increasing at the time is statistically unanswerable, as the Society's report contained no figures, but it is clear that it was contemporary conviction that this was the case. The Society's evidence was taken from interviewing children already incarcerated in prison, and it concluded that the main causes of delinquency were the 'improper conduct of parents', the 'want of education', the 'want of suitable employment' and 'violation of the Sabbath'. In addition the report made much of the failures and criminalizing tendencies of existing legal procedure, police practices and penal regimes:

Dreadful is the situation of the young offender: he becomes the victim of circumstances over which he has no control. The laws of his country operate not to restrain, but to punish, him. The tendency of the police is to accelerate his career in crime. If when apprehended, he has not attained the full measure of guilt, the nature of his confinement is almost sure to complete it; and discharged as he frequently is, pennyless, without friends, character or employment, he is driven, for a subsistence, to the renewal of depredations. (Report of Committee into Juvenile Delinquency, 1816, p. 25)

The Society proposed a separate system of dealing with the young offender: one that depended on the 'mildness of persuasion' and the 'gentleness of reproof' rather than the infliction of bodily punishment. It was such beliefs that helped to encourage voluntary effort to provide institutions whose aim would be to reform, and not merely punish, delinquent youth.

These concerns about youth were also indelibly tied to the growing fear of crime and disorder in general that captured the imagination of the early Victorians. The criminal statistics that began to be published annually from 1810 painted a disturbing picture of incremental rises year on year. Whether this measured 'real' crime or was merely a reflection of improved record keeping and expanding law enforcement is a problem that afflicts 'readings' of criminal statistics then as now (Weiner, 1990; Muncie, 2001 and see Chapter 1.2). Nevertheless, although they did not distinguish between adults and juveniles, select committees in London in 1816 and in Surrey and Warwickshire in 1828 were in no doubt that crime was being committed at a much earlier age than formerly and that the prime cause was parental neglect. When such statistics were refined to include a wide range of factors, including age, it became possible to gain a more detailed account of the population that was being processed through the criminal courts. From 1834, when information on the age and education of offenders was first included, it became possible to claim that crime was increasing out of all proportion to population rises and that such increase was greatest among the young. As a result a number of unofficial enquiries produced by magistrates, teachers and church officers (or indeed any professional whose occupation brought them into contact with the world of the working-class street) began to give specific consideration to delinquency as something separate from crime *per se*.

It is clear that in the early nineteenth century with the expansion of the criminal law, previous concerns over sin were being replaced with concerns over delinquency and crime – in particular property crimes and the defence of property. 'Crime' was gradually assuming its modern meaning: a 'vehicle for articulating mounting anxieties about issues which really had nothing to do with crime at all: social change and the stability of social hierarchy. These issues invested crime with new meanings, justified vastly accelerated action against it, and have determined attitudes to it ever since' (Gatrell, 1990, p. 249). The rapid growth of towns seemed to promote moral dissolution: the crowding, fast pace and young population acting to 'dangerously stimulate the passions' (Weiner, 1990, p. 19). The working population, and especially the young, were believed to be in desperate need of 'moral guidance' and 'civilized order'.

Legislation, Prosecution and Criminalization

These fears were galvanized by dramatic images of gangs of 'naked, filthy, roaming, lawless and deserted children', believed to number more than 30,000 in London alone in 1848 (Lord Ashley cited by Magarey, 1978, p. 16). But accurate estimations of the extent of 'delinquency' were impossible, not least because of its ill-defined nature. Nevertheless Susan Magarey (1978) contends that there was some justification for these growing fears, particularly in the newly recorded prison statistics of the 1830s. The number of under-17s imprisoned increased from some 9,500 in 1838 to around 14,000 in 1848. However, she finds that this rise is explicable less with reference to 'increased lawlessness' and more by changes in the position of children in relation to the criminal law and the subsequent criminalization of behaviour in relation to which previously there may have been no official action. First the presumption that the under-14s were *doli incapax* (incapable of evil) fell into disuse. Second, the Vagrancy Act 1824 and the Malicious Trespass Act 1827 considerably broadened legal conceptions of 'criminality' to include, for example, suspicion of being a thief, gambling on the street and scrumping apples from orchards and gardens. Previous nuisances were transformed into criminal offences. Third, the remit given to the Metropolitan Police in 1829 included apprehension of 'all loose, idle and disorderly persons not giving good account of themselves'. This alone made many more street children liable to arrest.

Magarey estimates that between 1838 and 1856 summary convictions for vagrancy accounted for more than 20 per cent of all juvenile convictions, while those for malicious trespass, larceny and being a known or reputed thief accounted for 30 per cent. She argues that 'at least half of the increasing numbers of juvenile prisoners were in prison as a result of the creation of new criminal offences, an extension of the powers of justices of the peace and a widespread readiness to treat children as young as 9 or 10 as fully responsible adults' (Magarey, 1978, p. 23). In these ways juvenile delinquency was 'legislated into existence'. Similarly, Shore (1999, p. 150) concludes that 'a lack of willingness to overlook the crimes of children combined with the decreasing use of acquittal verdicts implies a conscious inclination to draw children into the criminal justice system'. If not created, then policing and legislative action in the early to mid nineteenth century certainly accentuated the 'problem of delinquency'.

Rescue and Reformation

Legal recognition of the juvenile offender as being in some way different from the adult also emerged in the field of penal reform. Although the introduction of the penitentiary and the reform of the local prisons in the early nineteenth century did not entail any special differentiation on the basis of age, the emphases placed upon separation, classification and categorization highlighted age differentials and led to various conclusions being drawn about the position of the young. The Society for the Improvement of Prison Discipline and the Reformation of Juvenile Offenders (1817), for example, was convinced of the need to separate the juvenile from the hardened adult criminal in order to avoid the former's moral contamination. Similarly, the Society advocated the establishment of separate, highly controlled institutions in which young offenders could be reformed and reclaimed. May (1973, p. 12) argues that 'cellular isolation clearly revealed the mental and physical differences between children and adults' and she notes how this led prison inspectors to conclude that 'so marked is the distinction in the feeling and habit of manhood and youth that it is quite impractical to engraft any beneficial plan for the lengthened confinement of boys upon a system adapted to adults'. So the early period of modern imprisonment permitted the apparently unique needs of the young to be recognized. Refinements in prisoner classification brought the particular case of the *young* offender to the fore.

In 1823 a separate convict hulk (prison ship) for juveniles was introduced. In 1838 the first penal institution solely for juveniles was opened at Parkhurst. Yet as Weiner (1990, p. 132) notes, its regime was hardly less repressive than that afforded to adults. It was 'decidedly of a penal character' and its founder assured the Home Office that there was 'no reason to doubt that a strict system of penal discipline is quite compatible with the means requisite for the moral and religious improvement of the offender'. Prisoners were manacled and confined to their cells except for brief periods of exercise and religious instruction. Yet this severity was viewed as philanthropic, Parkhurst's governor claiming that 'every punishment is a weapon drawn from the armoury of truth and love . . . and directed for their real happiness' (cited by Weiner 1990, p. 133). Parkhurst, however, did little to undermine the prevailing view that *all* offenders should be held fully responsible for their actions, and long before its conversion to a women's prison in 1864, its administration had ceased to speak of its role as one of reformation and rescue.

Pressure to develop separate institutions (other than prison) for young offenders was also mounting from voluntary organizations such as the Philanthropic Society and the Society for the Suppression of Juvenile Vagrancy. As early as 1756 the Marine Society had established a system whereby delinquent children of criminal parents or those who had been deserted could avoid institutional confinement by being sent to sea. It was, as Radzinowicz and Hood (1990, p. 134) concluded, 'more a policy of sweeping the gutters, of flushing out, than of reintegrating the poor, the unemployed and the depraved into society'. By contrast the Philanthropic Society (for the Prevention of Crimes and the Reform of the Criminal Poor; by the Encouragement of Industry and the Culture of Good Morals, among those Children who are now trained up to Vicious Courses, Public Plunder, Infamy and Ruin), which had been founded in 1788 on the initiative of Robert Young, aimed to reform the depraved *and* the deprived. Accordingly, an asylum with no surrounding wall was established for 60 children to provide as far as possible a 'normal' home, with each child assigned to a local manufacturer for industrial instruction. This was complemented by daily prayers and compulsory attendance at church each Sunday. In 1792 further property was acquired in Southwark complete with its own dormitories and workshops, and this was the first full-scale institution for delinquent and potentially delinquent children of both sexes. The early 'family system' was replaced by a 'house' master supervising groups of 45 children, and admissions were eventually to be restricted to those who had already been convicted of a criminal offence. By 1806 the asylum had three sections: the reform as a prison school for young delinquents; the manufactory for the employment of partially reclaimed delinquent boys; and the training school for girls (Pinchbeck and Hewitt, 1973, pp. 419–30).

The distinguishing feature of such schools was the principle of self-instruction under surveillance, whereby discipline and order were viewed as the vehicles for self improvement and beneficial activity. This has led such revisionist theorists as Michel Foucault (1977) to argue that discipline served as an education for similar degrees of order which were being demanded in the factories, workhouses, poorhouses and prisons across Europe. The schools were essentially a disciplinary machine for the arrangement and classification of bodies and the promotion and regulation of preferred activities. Classification of pupils and inmates provided a principle of order in itself, by setting standards to be followed and instituting schedules of reward and punishment (Rush, 1992). The separation of male and female delinquents was similarly designed to prepare children for future roles. At Southwark, girls were employed in making, mending and cleaning their own and the boys' clothes and keeping the house clean, while the boys were employed in shoemaking and ropemaking. Girls were sent out as menial servants for domestic labour, while boys were apprenticed to local employers.

Whilst these early initiatives were to flounder by the end of the eighteenth century, they were revived and augmented by the reformatory movement of the 1840s. Inspired by the establishment of the Mettray reformatory near Tours in France, which instituted a regime of strict self denial, religious zeal and continual exercise for delinquents and vagrants, the Philanthropic Society established its own agricultural farm at Redhill in Surrey in 1849. Lauded as a great success, the cause was subsequently taken up by such philanthropists as Mary Carpenter, the daughter of a Unitarian minister. A forceful critic of penal regimes such as at Parkhurst, she was convinced that reformation depended on meeting the perceived needs of children for care and support as well as overt discipline. The causes of crime were seen to lie firmly in deficiencies in working-class family life, in the low moral condition of parents and in parental neglect. Preventing the contamination of youth and restoring their moral guardianship in the family were to serve as the principles for 'humanitarian' reform:

> The child must be placed where the prevailing principle will be, as far as practicable, carried out – where he will be gradually restored to the true position of childhood . . . He must perceive by manifestations which he cannot mistake that this power, whilst controlling him, is guided by interest and love; he must have his own affections called forth by the obvious personal interest felt in his own individual well being by those around him, he must, in short, be placed in a family. (Carpenter, 1853, p. 298)

Carpenter's language was notably gender specific, but concern was directed as much at girls as boys. Whilst boys were considered at risk of criminal offending, girls were viewed as especially vulnerable to moral, and in particular sexual, transgressions. Carpenter herself argued that criminal women and girls were blatantly depraved – 'they are, as a class, even more morally degraded than men' (cited by Gelsthorpe, 1984, p. 2). And as Zedner (1991, p. 43) argues, in Victorian discourses about crime, female criminality was viewed as particularly abhorrent: not only transgressing legality and femininity but also being a source of moral contagion in itself. Criminal women were widely represented as 'utterly depraved and corrupted beyond repair'. One of the key aims of the reformatory movement was the control of female sexuality (Shore, 2002, p. 168).

Given a set of 'commonsense' presuppositions about the true nature of childhood, femininity and masculinity and the increasing accumulation of empirical data organized directly around these presuppositions, it is not surprising that a specific set of conclusions surrounding the nature and causes of delinquency was to emerge in Victorian society. A view of childhood as an essentially innocent and dependent state requiring nurture and discipline on the part of parents led to a certain definition of delinquency in particular, but also of youthful behaviour in general. It was not just criminal behaviour that was of concern to the nineteenth-century reformers. Whilst there was a recognition that economic and social conditions connected with the criminal propensities of the young, this was subordinated to a consideration of the *moral* dimension of the problem. In the reformatories the 'rescue' of children was dependent on their understanding 'the value of labour' rather than learning specific industrial skills: 'The salutary fatigue of the body removes from the mind evil thoughts and renders it necessary to devote to repose the hours which in the towns are given to vicious pleasures' (Carpenter, 1853, p. 306). The terms that emerged to describe the problem were 'unnatural independence', 'deterioration', 'contamination' and 'parental neglect and irresponsibility'. Delinquency and youth behaviour in general became firmly associated with the conditions of working-class family life. Victorian concern also encompassed orphans, the illegitimate, the deserted, the independent young and anyone who failed to live up to middle-class assumptions of normal family life. As May (1973, p. 16) argues, the Victorian social investigators and reformers produced such damning reports of the conditions of existence for working-class children because the realities of slum childhood violated their sense and image of their own protected childhood. Concern was directed not only towards these children, but also towards the failings of parents – the apparent absence of supervision and control; the failure to imbue their children with proper moral habits. Such parental shortcomings were viewed as the root cause of what was seen as the 'progressive career of the delinquent child'. The roots of social disorder were tied directly to the family and the moral life of the poorer classes.

Above all, such reformist conceptions of childhood and interpretations of delinquency marked a major shift in how the troublesome young should be dealt with. They tended to relieve the young from full responsibility for their actions and emphasized the central role that family and family life should play in the creation of obedient and respectable citizens. When the family failed, the state had a duty to intervene – not simply to punish offending but to compel responsible behaviour on the part of parents. For the first time it became quite appropriate for the state to act *in loco parentis* – to intervene in working-class life in order to ensure that children were 'properly' educated, moralized and disciplined. In doing so it was believed that the chain that links the deprived child of today to the criminal of tomorrow would be broken (McLaughlin and Muncie, 1993, p. 160). It was not necessary for a child to have committed an offence for intervention and removal from home to be justified.

In the abiding concern for categorization, Carpenter labelled the deprived as the 'perishing' and the depraved as the 'dangerous' classes. Advocating industrial schools for the former and reformatories for the latter, her initiative was to gain legal status in the 1854 Youthful Offenders and 1857 Industrial Schools Acts. Under the 1854 Act, courts were allowed to sentence any child convicted of an indictable or summary offence to a reformatory for between two and five years; under the 1857 Act, children found begging or who had no visible means of subsistence and were deemed to be beyond parental control could be sent indefinitely to an industrial school. By 1860 there were 48 certified reformatories in England and Wales holding about 4,000 young offenders. The development of industrial schools was slower, but by the end of the century reformatories and industrial schools held more than 30,000 inmates. The state had come to assume the responsibility of parents for one in every 230 of the juvenile population (Radzinowicz and Hood, 1990, p. 181).

The reforming zeal was not without its critics. Traditional advocates of the principles of classical justice argued that age could not be taken as a sufficient index of responsibility and that *no* circumstances should preclude the necessity of punishment in dealing with offenders, whether juvenile or not. In contrast to the reformist discourse of welfare and treatment, May (1973, p. 25) notes a continuing and influential body of opinion that punishment should fit the crime and not be mitigated by personal circumstances; that juveniles should be treated as all other offenders; that 'the idea of pain might be instantly associated with crime in the minds of all evildoers'. Carpenter's proposals were thus subject to legislative compromise. Before entering a reformatory, a 14-day prison sentence had to be served. The maintenance of the reformatories was to be paid for partly by the state, but also through parental contribution. Moreover, the 1854 Act was only advisory and magistrates could continue to send juveniles to prison if they so decided. Stack (1992, p. 117) estimates that between 1856 and 1875 sentences to reformatory detention formed only 12.6 per cent of all child commitments to prison. The reformatory system was thus grafted on to the existing institutions of punishment and justice and did not replace them.

With the establishment of industrial schools, the issue of parental responsibility was more acute. Here parents were again required to contribute to the maintenance of their children and denied the right to bring their children up as they wished, even when no criminal offence had been committed. Such institutional intervention was legitimized in the name of care and protection, centring not so much on material as on moral care. There was a double incentive for parents to try and conform to the dominant morality and middle-class child-rearing practices: both the fear of losing their child and the burden of maintenance that attended such separation. Parents who failed to provide such care in effect signed away their rights to their children.

Such tensions between reclamation and punishment for the deprived and depraved alike have continued to impact on the rationale and practices of a separate system of justice for juveniles (see Chapter 7). But, significantly, it was only through the initiation of such disputes that the concept of the 'juvenile delinquent' achieved not only public and political recognition, but also its own legal status. Before the reformatory and industrial school movements of the 1840s, May (1973, p. 29) argues, it was impossible to talk with any precision of the existence of the *juvenile* offender:

> The establishment of separate institutions gave the juvenile delinquent a new legal status. The operation of the English penal and educational systems and the perceptions of social investigators had resulted in new distinctions between the child and the adult. The acceptance of Mary Carpenter's belief that 'children should not be dealt with as men but as children' was a seminal point in the evolution of the modern child.

Similarly, Stack (1992), working on data derived from judicial and prison statistics between 1856 and 1875, finds that almost all custodial sentences for juveniles were given for relatively minor crimes against property, usually larceny and petty theft.

The juveniles, however, were not drawn equally from all sections of society. Most were working class and male and significantly many more were Irish than English. Irish children were roughly four times more likely to end up in prison and reformatories than their counterparts in the general population. As Green and Parton (1990, p. 24) argue, 'The Irish in particular were stigmatized as wild and uncivilized, little different in habits and appetites, according to the more xenophobic observers, from the pigs with which they sometimes shared a residence.' But in general the young urban poor were viewed almost as a 'separate race' in need of ever watchful surveillance and regulation. Similar to Magarey's (1978) analysis, Stack (1992, p. 129) argues that the three factors which 'encouraged' the increased prosecution of children were: the growing availability of formal methods of prosecution, the decline in informal means of chastisement and the expanded activity of the police. It was the very existence of the sentencing alternatives of reformatories and industrial schools that enabled 'juvenile delinquency' gradually to take on its modern meaning as a clearly identifiable and distinctive social problem (see Table 2.2). The first half of the nineteenth century constitutes a distinct watershed in ways in which the debate about youth and crime came to be packaged and stereotyped.

Table 2.2 *The origins of juvenile delinquency*

Many authors have argued that the young offender was a Victorian creation. The reasons lie not simply in any growing visibility of juvenile waywardness, but in a complex of factors including:

- humanitarianism and control of child labour;
- religious zeal and need for moral guidance;
- bourgeois philanthropy and attempts to combat neglect;
- expansion of the scope and severity of the criminal law;
- fear of social disorder;
- fear of crime;
- fear of moral destitution;
- changes in the legal status of the young.

Pre-industrial Traces: Disorderly Youths

Something of a new orthodoxy emerged in the 1970s which challenged previous historiographies and the assumption that juvenile justice developed as a humanitarian response to a real and dramatic increase in youth crime. Though the term itself was coined in 1776, revisionist histories have largely accounted for the origins of juvenile delinquency as a creation of early nineteenth-century processes of industrialization, urbanization and criminalization. As a regulatory discourse, the concept was only fully realized in law as a result of the heated debates about reformatories in the 1840s (Rush, 1992). The precise origins of juvenile delinquency, however, remain a matter of some debate. The prevailing view that delinquency was a Victorian creation has subsequently been revised by more detailed empirical research on the rate of juvenile prosecutions in the period 1790–1820. Revisionist histories have also been subject to their own 'revision'. King and Noel (1993) acknowledge that between the mid seventeenth and the late eighteenth centuries, juvenile delinquency was rarely regarded as a distinct and serious problem. However, their analysis of records at the Old Bailey suggests that a sea change in offending and prosecution was in place well before the 'moments of discovery' believed by Magarey to be the 1820s and by May to be the 1840s. In particular there was a marked shift in the peak age of offending, from between the ages of 20 and 21 in 1791–3 to between 17 and 19 by 1820–2. In addition the numbers of offenders under 17 coming before the Old Bailey rose nearly fourfold (King and Noel, 1993, p. 22).

Was this then the period in which modern conceptions of juvenile delinquency first emerged? If so, in London at least, the 'problem' arrived long after urbanization and well before 'the city's economy was affected, by anything that could be termed an industrial revolution' (King and Noel, 1993, p. 28). King's (1998) subsequent study of court records across England also notes a rapid increase in crime rates between 1782 and 1793, but yet no significant panic about delinquency. To address these anomalies, King suggests that a complex of changing attitudes of magistrates and prison reformers, growing fears about the social consequences of economic change and financial incentives offered to detective and policing agencies need to be taken into account when considering the root causes of the juvenile 'crime wave' in the 1810s and 1820s. In congruence with previous researchers, he concludes that alarm about 'the problem of juvenile delinquency' had little to do with substantial changes in levels of criminal activity and more to do with changing attitudes to childhood and the poor and the reactions of those who wrote about, investigated and prosecuted crime. The authors of the report of the Society for Investigating the Causes of the Alarming Increase of Juvenile Delinquency in the Metropolis in 1815 were only the latest in a long tradition of social commentators who had berated youthful disorder, mischief, merriment and idleness as indicative of a decline in national morality.

In the seventeenth century a major focus of concern was the apprenticeship system. Established in 1563, the system placed young men and women at the age of puberty with masters who were responsible for teaching trade skills and industrious habits. Initially systems of 'indoor' apprenticeship provided strict controls over virtually every aspect of the young person's life: from the ownership of personal possessions to clothing and hair style. Described by Smith (1973) as an identifiable subculture with its own standards, heroes and sense of fraternity, 'indoor' apprenticeship gradually declined through the century as the demand for more flexible working patterns evolved. Freed from the omnipresent strict regulation of their masters, apprentices were routinely condemned as idle, violent and profligate. Carnivals, initiation rituals and traditional customs provided seasonal occasions for apprentices to engage in revelry and rowdy behaviour. For example, as Pearson (1983, p. 192) records, London apprentices devoted Shrove Tuesday to the wrecking of brothels, ostensibly to prevent their own temptation during Lent. As a result a succession of new regulations and legal statutes were created to ban apprentices from visiting public houses and brothels, from attending tennis courts, bowling alleys and cock fights and from playing cards, dice and billiards (Smith, 1973, p. 151). Feast days, carnivals and traditional customs – May Day, maypoles, morris dancing, hobby horses, fertility rites – were condemned as relics of paganism, particularly their propensity to incite violence, disorder and debauchery. They were routinely censured as the source of 'all kinds of moral ruin' (Pearson, 1983, p. 196).

Davis (1971) records how festive life – masking, costuming, parades, farces, dancing, lighting fires, gaming and charivaris (a demonstration to humiliate some wrongdoer in the community) – persisted throughout Europe in the sixteenth century. Organized informally by friends, craft guilds or by 'fools' societies', Abbeys of Misrule regularly mocked the behaviour of local dignitaries and representatives of officialdom. They parodied their rulers in carnivals of mock justice. As one defender of the Feast of Fools proclaimed in 1444, 'Foolishness is our second nature and must freely spend itself at least once a year. Wine barrels burst if from time to time we do not open them and let in some air' (cited by Davis, 1971, p. 48). Above all, these events were led and orchestrated by groups of young, unmarried men. (Most men did not marry until their mid-20s, particularly in rural areas.) Such rituals of rebellion were not simply 'safety valves' but acted to define and maintain certain community values (especially with regard to marital fidelity) and provided avenues for criticizing the political order. In the violent revelry and rowdy charivaris of the sixteenth century it is thus possible to witness some of the characteristics of 'adolescence' or of youth subcultures that were to emerge some four centuries later (see Chapter 5). Whilst the Abbeys of Misrule gradually died out as a result of official censure and the decline of traditional rural customs, vestiges of the carnival can still be glimpsed in the confrontations, chants, slogans and rituals of street cultures of the twentieth century (Presdee, 2000). And it raises the intriguing proposition that juvenile delinquency was only capable of being recognized as a distinct social problem when the 'foolish' ribaldry and revelry of young people could no longer be tolerated.

Further, Griffith (2002) maintains that historians' obsession with the origins of delinquency at the turn of the nineteenth century has made them blind to traces of the problem stretching back to at least the sixteenth century. Cunningham (1995) too emphasizes that street children are a centuries old problem. Griffith (2002) notes how age-specific offences, penalties and policing measures were prevalent in the houses of correction, in transportation and in discourses of youth reformation which preceded the semantic twist of 'juvenile delinquency' by some 200 years. Nevertheless it was not until the 1810s that a willingness to prosecute rather than ignore juvenile offenders became apparent. Juvenile delinquency may not have been created as such at this time, but it underwent a dramatic reconfiguration in terms that are now familiar to us today.

Troublesome Adolescence

2.3 The concept of adolescence gained pre-eminence in the late nineteenth and early twentieth centuries to describe a period of life between childhood and adulthood which had its own particular problems of emotional adjustment and physical development. The rapidly developing psycho-medical disciplines of social psychology and child psychology gave traditional concerns about young people 'both a more profound substance and a new legitimacy' (Hendrick, 1990, p. 11). Delinquency was viewed as a 'natural' attribute of adolescence and consequently Victorian assumptions of a causal relationship between working-class culture and delinquency came to be challenged (though rarely superseded) by theorizing that focused on the age of *all* young people.

The discovery of adolescence by psychologists also coincided with specific renewed anxieties about working-class youth. In the 1880s amid the emergence of the 'boy labour market', dramatic increases in juvenile crime, the rise of socialism and threats to the British Empire and Britain's economic position, concern was expressed once more about undisciplined and independent working-class youth.

The twin concerns running through the complaints were that the urban working-class family was not fulfilling its regulatory functions and that the wage-earning capability of working-class youth enabled them to buy freedom from parental control (Springhall, 1986). Manifestations of this lack of discipline and independence were to be found in the street-based leisure pursuits of working-class adolescents. For the reformers of the late nineteenth century, independence and unwholesome leisure pursuits (e.g. street gambling and football) would inevitably result in delinquency and criminality. It was in this period that the term 'hooliganism' first emerged. The reformers saw their task as being to re-establish control over working-class adolescents in order to enforce their dependency. Consequently working-class youth and their families were subject to renewed interventions.

First, the moral crusades of youth organizations sought to impose the 'new norms of adolescence' and as a result the working class was subject to heavier policing. Youth clubs were set up to provide the discipline, regulation, guidance and improvement that working-class parents would/could not. Working-class girls also found themselves on the receiving end of specialist youth work because it was believed that too much independence from the family and home was socially undesirable (Dyhouse, 1981, p. 113). Second, the growing public concern about adolescence and its presumed direct connection with juvenile delinquency resulted in a number of important changes in the legal position of young people. A plethora of early twentieth-century legislation clarified the position of the child and the adolescent in criminal law. Probation was introduced in 1907, and the 1908 Prevention of Crime Act inaugurated specialist detention centres – borstals – for young people. In the same year the Children Act introduced juvenile courts. The primary assumptions underpinning this legislation were that juveniles were less responsible than adults for their actions and should not be subject to the full majesty of the law. But, such legislation (as in the early nineteenth century) can be read as not simply humanitarian in intent. Whilst separating juvenile from adult justice, it further cemented the notion that the troublesome young (once again) constituted an entirely *new* and *unprecedented* problem for the nation's future.

Inventing Adolescence

The invention of the *concept* of adolescence is usually attributed to Rousseau, writing in the 1760s. He likened adolescence to a second birth, and viewed it principally as a period of emotional turmoil, which led to various forms of moral degeneration, and most particularly sexual precocity. Rousseau's chief concern was that the young were becoming worldly-wise and sexually aware at too early an age. He proposed that the young should be 'protected' and segregated from adult life for as long as possible (Simmons and Wade, 1984, p. 17). Musgrove (1964, p. 43) thus argues that adolescence was *invented* at the same time as the steam engine. It was directly related to the prolonged education afforded to *upper-class* students and apprentices in the late eighteenth century. The debates among the parents of the gentry and the professional middle classes at this time were concerned with the relative merits of keeping predominantly male youth education in the home or moving it out into the hands of public schools. Despite strong pressures to the contrary, by the 1830s the public school system achieved ascendancy, giving to the young 'a status and importance which they had not hitherto enjoyed' (Musgrove, 1964, p. 64). However, this development was by no means uncontested: public schools had a reputation for generating insubordination and rebellion. In 1818, for example, riots at Winchester public school were finally dealt with by the military; and the last of the revolts by public school boys was not until 1851 at Marlborough. But by the mid nineteenth century, the reform of the public schools was established to the extent that the numbers of middle-class pupils rose significantly. In the process, the state of adolescence was born. Nevertheless the development extended only as far down the social hierarchy as the new bourgeoisie of industrialists, bankers and merchants. Adolescence at this time was still irrelevant to the mass of the labouring poor. It was not until the late nineteenth century and the advent of compulsory state education to the age of 13 that the concept of adolescence began to affect the children of the working classes.

It was a concept that gradually became endowed with pathological connotations. Adolescents were viewed as relatively unrestrained by the discipline of family or labour. Adolescence was replete with 'negative' and 'troubling' connotations. As Gillis (1974, p. 114) notes, 'what were the historically evolved social norms of a particular class became enshrined in medical and psychological literature as the "natural" attributes of adolescence'. Consequently, by the turn of this century, youngsters of all classes were viewed as sharing certain characteristics *solely because of their age*. Although originally related to the adult desire to regulate the increased leisure and period of dependency of middle-class youth, the equation of pathology with a particular period of life enabled all youthful behaviour to be subject to adult supervision and control. This was all the more anachronistic because, as Thane (1981, p. 16) notes, the children of the labouring poor still shared very fully the life of adults until well into the twentieth century, since they had to work for survival. Rather than being dependent, working-class youth remained very independent. Their material position contradicted much of what was scientifically considered to be the 'natural' attributes of 'adolescence'. Youthful independence thus became defined as a problem. Working-class youths in particular were viewed as morally degenerate and in need of stricter control. The label of 'adolescence', therefore, not only secured the view that *all* young people were potentially troublesome, but also that those (working-class) youths who did not or could not conform to this new view of being young were further stigmatized as 'delinquent'.

By the first decades of the twentieth century the concept gained scientific credibility and subsequently informed and underpinned a diverse and expansive range of initiatives designed to control and redirect youthful behaviour. Many historical accounts (Davis, J., 1990, p. 60; Hendrick, 1990, p. 101) see the role of the American psychologist Granville Stanley Hall as pivotal. In his *Adolescence, Its Psychology and Its Relations to Physiology, Anthropology, Sociology, Sex, Crime, Religion and Education* (1905), Hall argued that each individual relives the development of the human race from early animal-like primitivism (childhood) through savagery (adolescence) to civilization (adulthood). Such argument was clearly influenced by the ideas of Darwin concerning the origin and evolution of the human species. In this individual recapitulation of evolutionary development, adolescence was viewed as particularly troublesome because it was a stage in which young people were being pulled in two opposite directions – back to the primitivism of childhood and forward to the rational and civilized state of adulthood. Adolescents were characterized as half animal, half human, and the struggle between these impulses directly caused a period of emotional 'storm and stress': adolescence. Hall also went on to equate the 'barbarity' of adolescence with increased criminality. Thus for Hall, 'adolescence is pre-eminently the criminal age', and 'criminals are like overgrown children' (Hall, 1905, pp. 325, 338).

Although Hall's notions of evolution and adolescent development may appear as strange anachronisms of his time, his central premise that adolescence is marked by *pathological* storm and stress has continued to inform numerous psychological and psychoanalytical studies. His characterization of adolescence as a period of disturbance akin to sickness has been successfully popularized, such that it is widely accepted as 'commonsense'.

The discovery of adolescence by psychologists and educational reformers coincided with public concerns about working-class youth gangs and the 'boy labour problem'. Generally, delinquency appeared all the more threatening because it could now be viewed as an attribute of 'natural' social and psychological growth and could only indirectly be related to social and economic conditions: 'A stage of life, adolescence, had replaced the poverty of the working class, as the perceived cause of delinquent behaviour by the 1900s' (Springhall, 1986, p. 27). Or as Gillis argued, the concept of 'adolescence' had served to redefine the independence and legitimate traditions of youth as delinquent:

In reality the troubles of the children of the poor were deeply imbedded in the economic and demographic structure of society. The growing tendency to treat these as psychological and therefore as subject to clinical, rather than political or economic solution was at least as disturbing as the phenomenon itself. (Gillis, 1974, p. 131)

Nevertheless, Hendrick (1990, p. 120) argues that whilst the psychology of adolescence was to gain influence, it never superseded that of social class as the predominant object of the reformers' attention and concern. The debate between adolescence as 'natural' or 'socially constructed' is summarized in Table 2.3.

Table 2.3 *The nature of adolescence*	
Biological approach	**Social construction approach**
Adolescence caused by biological maturation	Adolescence created by changes in methods of schooling and shifts in the economy
Adolescence as universal	Adolescence as specific to particular cultures and economic structures. Originally a concept of the upper classes
Adolescence as pathological and problematic	Adolescence as normal, given social constraints/conditions
Adolescence as primarily a unitary category. Gender differences derive from biological differences. No class differentiation	Adolescence as variable according to class, 'race' and gender
The legitimization of medical and psychiatric interventions to solve the problem of adolescence	Changes in social conditions and social tolerance to alleviate the socially constructed problem of adolescence
Adolescence: the key concept in understanding youth	Adolescence: a term which obscures more than it reveals of young people's behaviour

'Hooliganism'

The word 'yob' derives from the late nineteenth century as backslang for 'boy'. It was widely used as a description for members of street gangs in the city slums. Most cities had well-known gangs – in Manchester the Ikey Boys and Scuttlers; in Birmingham the Peaky Blinders; in Glasgow the Redskins and the Beehive; and in London the Hooligans. The word 'hooligan' first entered common English usage during the summer of 1898. It was a word, like the 'teddy boy', 'mod' or 'skinhead' terms of the 1950s and 1960s, which emerged from working-class popular culture in London. Sometimes associated with the name of a notorious Irish family of the time, the Houlehans, its precise origins remain unknown. But the word was to become notorious after a rowdy August bank holiday celebration in 1898, when hundreds of people were brought to court on charges of assault, drunkenness and attacks on policemen (Pearson, 1983, p. 73). The Hooligans wore bell-bottomed trousers, colourful neck scarves, leather belts and steel-capped boots; the Redskins had cropped hair and wore red headbands. They were akin to what we would now call 'youth cultures'. The gangs battled with each other for territorial supremacy: some were violently racist and anti-Semitic, but the main 'enemy' was the police. The issue was largely one of who 'owned' and controlled the streets (Cohen, P., 1979). In August 1898 the term 'hooligan' was picked up by the newspapers and used as a generic term to describe all troublesome youths who might previously have been described as 'ruffians' or 'roughs' (Pearson, 1983, p. 75). It was a word that convinced 'respectable England' that it was suddenly engulfed by a new variety of crime.

In a report compiled by the Howard Association on Juvenile Offenders in 1898, the general impression given was that young people were becoming increasingly unruly, more vulgar and undisciplined. Magistrates and police believed themselves to be impotent in the face of what they considered to be a rising level of criminality and violence. In Parliament, MPs advocated the punishments of whipping and birching, and 'from the late 1890s to the First World War there was a flood of accusations against youth' (Pearson, 1983, p. 55). Urban youth was condemned as growing up in a 'state of unrestrained liberty' and 'irresponsible freedom' (Bray, 1911, pp. 102–3) in which parental authority, discipline and subordination were absent. Youth was believed to be not only lacking in discipline but excessively affluent, accusations that were directed mainly at those young people employed in various kinds of street work – paper-sellers, van boys, flower-sellers, barrel organ boys, messengers, and so on (Pearson, 1983, pp. 57–8).

Anxiety about the visible presence of youth on the streets was not about youth in general, however, but about working-class *male* youth. Concern was only directed towards girls when it was considered that they lacked domestic and moral surveillance. This might arise when they were away from home, working as domestic servants, or when their own homes were thought to offer inadequate protection from the temptations and 'moral danger' of the street. It was still considered inappropriate for girls to spend their work or leisure time outside the confines of the domestic sphere. As a result, whenever girls 'showed signs of cherishing anything resembling autonomy' (Dyhouse, 1981, p. 138), they were likely to find themselves subject to official intervention.

Between 1890 and 1910 the publication of 'scientifically' collected national statistics of juvenile crime appeared to confirm that the problem was indeed growing. Using figures based on police court records in Oxford, Gillis (1975, p. 99) notes that the juvenile crime rate rose from a decennial average of 29.6 offences per year in the 1880s to 99.2 in the first decade of the twentieth century. However, Gillis discovered that much of this rise was accounted for by such non-indictable crimes as drunkenness, gambling, malicious mischief, loitering, begging and dangerous play. This evidence suggests that the 'increase in crime' was due largely to efforts on the part of the police and the courts to control traditional working-class male youth leisure pursuits and working practices. Forms of street activity that had formerly been considered acceptable came to be perceived as indicative of a new social problem. As a Westminster police court probation officer giving evidence to the National Council of Public Morals in 1917 argued:

Our streets are now more rigidly supervised . . . there is a large and increasing army of officials whose duty it is to watch over child life. In many cases it has seemed to me that the zeal of these officers was not always adequately tempered by humanity and expediency. The practical result has been a systematic increase in the number of charges brought against children. (Cited by Springhall, 1986, p. 179)

As Pearson (1983, pp. 53–73) notes, a whole range of material and cultural innovations were transforming urban life in the late nineteenth century, such as football stadiums, 'penny dreadful' comics, bank holidays, the new unionism, the music hall, the fish and chip shop and the bicycle. Although we might now consider these as part and parcel of urban life, in the 1890s they were greeted as 'signs of an alarming development which threatened to destroy the "British way of life"' (Pearson, 1983, p. 62). All of these elements were considered to be inducements to depravity and crime. Music halls lowered moral standards, penny dreadfuls glorified criminality, football encouraged rowdyism and violence, on bank holidays seaside resorts were 'invaded' by the urban masses, and the increasing use of the bicycle caused a panic about 'hit and run' cyclists.

Stedman-Jones (1971) placed such 'respectable fears' in the context of a structural decline in established industries, trade depression, shortage of working-class housing and a bourgeois fear of socialism at the turn of the century. The preoccupation with youth disorder was invariably associated with wider social tensions. The moral panic about youth at this time (and also in other historical periods) was the surface manifestation of a deeper concern revolving around the place and passivity of the British working class.

The 'Boy Labour Problem'

The state of the juvenile labour market was a special object of concern for social reformers and policy-makers at the turn of the century. The transition from school to work was viewed as 'haphazard', occupational mobility was 'excessive' and working-class boys in particular were condemned to 'blind-alley' employment. Collectively these issues came to be known as creating the 'boy labour problem'. Industrial training was considered so woefully inadequate that after boys left school – usually between the ages of 10 and 14 – there was nothing but dead-end jobs for them, thus perpetuating a cycle of working-class poverty. The situation was exacerbated by the tendency of employers to take on low-paid juvenile labour in preference to adults. When young workers reached an age at which they would by law attract adult wages, they were commonly fired in order to make way for a new generation of juveniles. This practice not only deprived skilled adults of employment but also ensured that much of youth received no formal work training and thus regularly faced unemployment when they were discharged.

This came to be a matter of concern in the Edwardian era when lack of regular work, 'blind alley' jobs and occupational mobility were considered to be the root causes of the two 'vices' of indiscipline and precocious independence which manifested themselves in 'unruly' youth leisure on the streets. In part, this reconceptualization of working-class youth as a 'problem' was only made possible by the instigation of compulsory state schooling in the 1870s. This helped to set a norm for childhood and youth as a time for dependency, supervision, guidance and training from which wage-earning schoolchildren, school-leavers and child street traders obviously deviated. As Springhall (1986, p. 96) and Hendrick (1990, p. 9) argue, the concern of educationalists and reformers to 'safeguard' young people's welfare and employment prospects helped to construct new definitions of what could be considered troublesome and wayward behaviour. According to the Fabian socialist Sidney Webb, giving evidence to the Poor Law Commission in 1910, the young worker was 'indisciplined, precocious in evil, earning at 17 or 18 more wages than suffice to keep him, independent of home control and yet unsteadied by a man's responsibilities' (cited by Hendrick, 1990, p. 121). The social commentator and reformer Reginald Bray was convinced that the working-class family was devoid of discipline and supervision because parents were fearful of exercising their authority lest their sons leave and take their earnings with them. As a result, he argued, 'city bred youth is growing up in a state of unrestrained liberty' (Bray, 1911, p. 101). The debates of the time dwelt on these two themes: the failure of the working-class home and the freedom that came with wage earning. Both were presumed to give young workers a premature adult status, exposing them to undesirable influences and encouraging defiance of authority.

> The result is a species of man-child, in whom the natural instincts of boyhood are almost overwhelmed by the feverish anxiety to become a man. It is at this age that he begins, with disagreeable precocity, to imitate the habits of his elders – smoking daily an unwholesome number of cheap and nasty 'fags' . . . adding to his vocabulary the wealth of coarse and profane expletives . . . for his amusement a cheap theatre or music hall on Saturday night . . . followed by a starch and buttonhole promenade in the Sunday evening, probably with a girl . . . and a lively interest in any others he may happen to meet . . . It is an odd material, hard to mould and baffling . . . but the contradictions in it are after all only the inevitable result of premature face to face acquaintance with the hard facts of life. (Urwick, 1904, p. xii–xiii)

The reformers' concern was multi-faceted. It included worries about employment and unemployment, youth promenading on the streets, leisure, education and general health. By comparing the 'worldly-wise' activities of working-class youth with the extended period of education offered to public school boys, images of working-class depravity and deprivation abounded. Moreover these coalesced with general fears about the nation's physical and moral health. By the 1900s national efficiency became a key issue when the Boer War revealed an alarming proportion of volunteers as medically unfit. As John Davis (1990) has argued, the focus on youth at this time was not simply generated by fears of disorder, but by fears for racial preservation. Sidney Webb's description of undisciplined but also of 'weedy, narrow chested, stunted weaklings' (cited in Hendrick, 1990, p. 127) brought attention to the notion that young people were the nation's future. The 'boy labour problem' was just one element in a series of entangled debates about imperial security, social stability and the nation's assets that exercised the minds of early twentieth-century reformers and politicians. The newly identified 'adolescent' could be a source of national degeneration if left untutored, but was also capable of ennobling the race if educated, directed and organized in 'appropriate' ways.

Youth Organizations

It was in the context of the debates about 'adolescence', 'hooliganism' and 'boy labour' that numerous youth movements, clubs and organizations were formed. The urge to 'improve' working-class socialization and secure national unity underlay the Boys' Brigade, founded in Glasgow in 1883, and the Boy Scouts, founded in 1908. These were supplemented by many university, church and school missions designed to provide healthy activities that would extend public school virtues of *esprit de corps* and 'muscular' Christianity to working-class youths in order to improve their 'character' (Springhall, 1986, p. 149). The intention was to organize youth leisure and, as a result, protect young people from the 'vices of the street'.

Such organizations were designed to preserve the idealism of youths and redirect their wayward tendencies, while simultaneously improving physical health and promoting an ideology of nationalism. Accordingly by the turn of the century, 'the model adolescent became the organized youth, dependent but secure from temptation, while the independent and precocious young were stigmatized as delinquent' (Gillis, 1975, p. 97). However, as Blanch (1979) notes, although the principles of organized youth were to apply to all, they were most popular with the middle classes and with children of skilled workers. The majority of youths were excluded from youth clubs and organizations because membership fees could not be met or, more pertinently, because the principles of such organizations were alien to the customs of the adult-centred, working-class family. The end result of this move to 'organize' youth was to highlight divisions within youth and make its delinquent element more visible and detectable.

The more independent the youths, the more responsible they were for their own conduct and thus the more likely to be stigmatized as real or potential delinquents. It was a self fulfilling prophecy. As the historian Gillis (1975, p. 122) notes:

> The spread of secondary schools and youth organizations helped establish in the public mind what seemed to be a moral distinction between rough and respectable youth, for the school and athletic uniforms of the model adolescent produced their antithesis in the wide leather belts and bell-bottomed fustian trousers which were becoming the costume of many working youths at the turn of the century . . . The contrasts between the military style of the Brigades and Scouts on the one hand and the costuming of corner boys and girls on the other served only to create in the public mind an awareness of differences within the youth population which because they no longer followed class boundaries in an obvious manner could be interpreted as moral in nature.

Whilst the youth organizations were originally intended solely for boys, comparable movements were also established for girls to help them resist the temptations of sex, alcohol and undisciplined conduct. The Girls' Guildry was formed in Glasgow at the turn of the century as a combination of a senior Sunday school class, friendly club and female equivalent of the Boys' Brigade. Despite its aim to develop 'capacities of womanly helpfulness', the marching and military drill characteristic of their male counterparts were also adopted. Many condemned the Guildry for its encouragement of 'unladylike behaviour', and the Girl Guides (sister organization to the Boy Scouts) received a similar reception in the 1910s because of male prejudice against anything that could be seen as part of a general movement towards women's rights. It was not until it was acknowledged that women had played a vital role in the war effort of 1914–18 that organizations for girls gained in membership and credibility (Springhall, 1977, pp. 130–3). But the First World War also saw the first employment of women police officers to patrol military camps and munitions factories with the express purpose of 'protecting' young women from prostitution and 'controlling' large numbers of young female workers (Emsley, 1996, p. 35).

The ultimate aim of all such organizations was the elimination of working-class street cultures and the provision of a morally healthy alternative to such 'corrupt' influences as the music hall and the cinema. In the process the street and street corner leisure grew to be perceived as dangerous and were more rigorously policed. As Gillis (1975) and Weinberger (1993) concluded on examining prosecution data from Oxford and Manchester respectively, a combination of compulsory education, the regulation of street trading, increases in male and female youth independence and extended periods of leisure (coupled with the new notions of adolescence) resulted in a vast expansion of the means to monitor and regulate the presence of young people on the streets. In order to explore the statistical 'crime wave' of the 1900s, we thus need to move far beyond an examination of offending behaviour itself.

Child Saving

The concept of adolescence also had some immediate implications for juvenile justice policy. As delinquency was tied to a particular life stage that was both 'natural' and 'inevitable', adolescents were seen as less responsible for their behaviour. It then made little sense to subject young people to the full rigours of the law; rather their delinquencies could be treated and cured by special forms of intervention. But as Weiner (1990, p. 360) records, such a 'naturalization of delinquency' created two opposing tendencies: greater tolerance and heightened interventionism.

In many historical accounts of juvenile justice, the first decade of the twentieth century is lauded as a progressive milestone. In 1907 the Probation Act established community supervision as an alternative to prison and as a means to prevent reoffending through befriending, advising and assisting. In 1908 the Children Act established separate juvenile courts to hear criminal and care and protection cases, the imprisonment of children under 14 was abolished and special places of detention (remand homes) were set up to avoid any child being kept in prison, before trial. Imprisonment of 14–16 year olds was sanctioned only for those deemed 'so unruly' that reformatory detention would be unsuitable. Pinchbeck and Hewitt (1973, p. 144) refer to these developments as a 'Children's Charter' which provided 'a more comprehensive and child oriented legal system and more generous and liberal provisions for children in all walks of life'. Above all, the 1908 Act was viewed as the forerunner of a series of twentieth-century reforms in which humanitarianism and the welfare of the child are assumed to have become prominent in juvenile justice policy (see Chapter 7).

The juvenile courts were empowered to act upon both the criminal offender and the child who may have been found begging, vagrant, in association with reputed thieves or whose parents were considered 'unworthy'. The categories of criminal (the troublesome) and destitute (the troubled) were conflated. Morris and Giller's (1987) analysis, however, argues that the juvenile courts remained essentially criminal courts. The idea that the child was a wrongdoer prevailed and despite a range of available sentences – from fine, discharge and probation to committal to industrial school, whipping and imprisonment (if over 14) – the procedures for dealing with adults were usually thought to be the most appropriate for dealing with children. Although imprisonment for children under 14 ended, later in the same year the Crime Prevention Act set up specialized detention centres where rigid discipline and work training could be provided in a secure environment. The first of these was at Borstal in Kent, which gave its name to numerous similar establishments.

A more hard-hitting critique, Platt's (1969) account of the origins of the juvenile court in America, argues that we need to look beyond the rhetoric of benevolence and the 'child-saver's' concern for 'salvation', 'innocence' and 'protection'. Rather, he notes how ideologies of welfare enabled constant and pervasive supervision and allowed the state to intervene directly into any element of working-class life that was deemed immoral or unruly. Troublesome adolescents could now be depicted by the new bodies of professional psychiatrists, social workers and philanthropists as 'sick' or 'pathological'. As a result young people were imprisoned 'for their own good', were exempted from full legal rights and were subjected to correctional programmes which required longer periods of incarceration. Platt (1969, p. 176) is thus able to argue that the child-saving movement was far from libertarian. It used such rhetoric to justify a vastly increased level of intervention which denied working-class youth any initiative, responsibility and autonomy. At root, the state's intention was to implement more and more extensive networks to enforce industrious habits and discipline.

Morris and Giller (1987, p. 32) are more circumspect, arguing that 'the social construction of childhood did prevent the economic exploitation of juveniles . . . but most reforms were also implicitly or explicitly coercive . . . humanitarianism and coercion are essentially two sides of the same coin'. Garland (1985, p. 262) probably best captures the nuances of Victorian and Edwardian reform when he argues that it was 'constructed around an eclectic series of disparate and contradictory forms and logics which may sometimes be strategically related, but are never singular or uniform'. It is in such terms that he accounts for a new 'penal-welfare complex' emerging in the period 1895–1914, in which classical conceptions of punishment and generalized deterrence were contested and disrupted by positivist conceptions of reclamation and individualized treatment. The end result was new means of 'normalizing', 'correcting' and 'segregating' young people, which in their complexity and interrelation could no longer be simply viewed as either humanitarian or repressive.

The Consolidation of the 'Youth Problem'

2.4 During the First World War the number of juvenile offenders is assumed to have risen once more. The press reported that gangs of hooligans were terrorizing communities and the Home Office warned of a juvenile crime epidemic. It is estimated that at least 12,500 more children and young people were appearing before magistrates in 1916 than in 1914. Now it was the absence of fathers sent to war, the independence of married women employed in munitions and lack of parental and school discipline that were the most widely cited causes (Springhall, 1986, pp. 179–80; Smith, D., 1990, p. 122–5). The influence of the cinema was also believed to be encouraging new and dangerous trends of lawlessness either through imitating the new celluloid heroes and villains or by succumbing to the 'moral dangers of darkness' in the cinema itself. Charles Russell (1917, p. 6), a leading advocate of boys' clubs, warned that the cinema's 'vulgarity and silliness and the distorted, unreal, Americanized (in the worst sense) view of life presented must have a deteriorating effect and lead, at the best, to the formation of false ideals'. Juvenile crime was in large part viewed as resulting from the lack of opportunities for healthy recreation (Bailey, V., 1987, p. 12).

Oral histories of the period have however come to challenge these dominant images of adolescent depravity through which the problem of 'youth crime' could be defined predominantly in moralistic terms. By recording the 'voices from below', Humphries' (1981) study of property theft from 1890 to 1940, for example, illustrates that minor thieving was viewed by some working-class parents and children as a customary right and essential for family survival. Taking coal from slag heaps, wood from timber yards, vegetables from fields and poaching rabbits were an integral and historical part of working-class culture and committed because of economic necessity. Successive legislation prohibiting juvenile street trading only exacerbated the extent of the 'problem'.

By the 1920s the growing problem of juvenile delinquency became an established topic for British academics. Earlier emphases on economic factors were slowly replaced by a focus on the psychological conditions produced in the home and family. The crime rate, though reduced after the war, started to rise again in the late 1920s, coinciding with the years of the Great Depression. Unemployment and the continuing practice of 'boy labour' was once again promoted as a key causative factor. The preferred solution now was to 'improve' home conditions and family life. The rising problem of crime may have coincided with high levels of unemployment, but the problem was laid firmly at the door of working-class families. Young people may have been without jobs, but according to a growing medico-psychological discourse, what they really required was a stable and protective home life. For example Cyril Burt's *The Young Delinquent* (1925) arose from his work as an applied psychologist advising on the psychological difficulties of London children referred to him by magistrates. Using a definition of delinquency which spread from assault and theft to truancy, 'excessive bad temper' and 'excessive masturbation', he concluded that delinquency is 'nothing but an outstanding sample – dangerous perhaps and extreme, but none the less typical – of common childish naughtiness' (Burt, 1925, p. viii). The key factors, of some 170 considered, which propelled juveniles from 'naughtiness' to 'delinquency' were believed to be defective discipline, defective family relationships and particular types of temperament. Burt proposed that delinquency was multi-causal and complex, but that deficient personality coupled with broken homes were central. To tackle delinquency he advocated intervention by parents in the pre-school period, by teachers' reports at school and by supervision of school-leavers by after-care workers.

Such medico-psychological notions were not only to gain prominence in the emerging field of British positivist criminology (see Chapter 3.1), but remained influential at least up to the 1980s. Neglect and delinquency became conflated, such that the problem of juvenile crime was viewed as 'but one inseparable portion of the larger enterprise for child welfare' (Burt, 1925, p. 610).

In 1932 industrial schools and reformatories were amalgamated and reconstituted as approved schools. In deliberations before the 1933 Children and Young Persons Act, the Home Office Departmental Committee on the Treatment of the Young Offender had argued

> there is little or no difference in character and needs between the neglected and the delinquent child. It is often a mere accident whether he is brought before the court because he was wandering or beyond control or because he has committed some offence. Neglect leads to delinquency. (Home Office, 1927, p. 6)

The Act itself (section 44) stressed that

> every court in dealing with a child or young person who is brought before it either as an offender or otherwise, shall have regard to the welfare of the child or young person and shall in proper cases take steps for removing him from undesirable surroundings and for securing that proper provision is made for his education and training.

An earlier limited practice of having a specially selected *panel* of magistrates to hear juvenile cases was adopted as uniform for the whole country; restrictions were placed on the reporting of cases in newspapers; the age of criminal responsibility was raised from 7 to 10 (8 in Scotland); and above all the Act directed magistrates to take primary account of the 'welfare of the child'. In this, considerable responsibility was given to probation officers and social workers, recruited in the main from the Charity Organization Society: 'Regulation *within*, rather than removal *from*, the community was constructed as the dominant strategy for the delinquent' (Clarke, 1985a, p. 251).

However, whilst we might presume that such welfarism would lead to less formal means of intervention, in fact the reverse was true. As Springhall (1986, p. 186) comments, there is 'abundant evidence' to show that the effect of the 1933 Act was not to divert youth from court, but to actively encourage formal intervention. Because of the Act's 'welfare' focus there was an increased willingness to prosecute. As one contemporary declared:

> Experience shows . . . that each time a new statute relating to the young has been put into effect, the immediate result is an apparent rise in the number of offences. This 'rise' is not due to any 'wave' of crime among juveniles but to a desire on the part of those concerned with putting the law into motion, to make use of the new method of treatment. (Assistant Secretary at the Home Office cited by Smithies, 1982, p. 172)

Such a view was, however, not shared by all. Retributionists drew different conclusions. For them the 1930s had witnessed a real rise in juvenile crime attributable (once again) to adolescent 'mischief', the want of organized leisure, lack of employment, the proliferation of consumer goods, the influence of American gangster movies and lack of parental control. As Smithies (1982, p. 177) also notes: 'The popular press had built up a picture of juvenile offenders as "wasp-waisted loungers, who ape the methods of their film heroes", breaking the law in gangs and with impunity. They need an "intensive police clean up" to deal with them.' In opposition to welfarism, stricter punishments, including use of the birch, were strongly advocated and implemented. In 1939, 50 birchings were inflicted on boys under the age of 14. In 1941 there were over 500 (Smithies, 1982, p. 175). Indeed, the 1933 Act had retained a clause – section 53 – whereby those aged under 18 can, if convicted in a Crown Court for 'grave crimes', be detained for lengthy periods and in effect treated as if they were adults. Such powers remain today in the form of sections 90–92 of the Powers of Criminal Courts (Sentencing) Act 2000 (see Chapter 7). Corporal punishment was not abolished until 1948.

Such discourses and policy debates are, of course, now familiar to us, and serve as a telling reminder that whatever romantic images we may now hold about the inter-war years (or of earlier periods), these were certainly not voiced at the time. Images of youth as 'led astray' or as 'vicious hooligans' and ideas about welfare and punishment, treatment and control, 'moral danger' and wilful criminality continue to circulate around, and inform, the various contradictory policies and practices of contemporary youth justice. But what is clear is that having 'invented' the 'juvenile delinquent' in the early nineteenth century and the 'troublesome adolescent' in the early twentieth, increasing numbers of 'expert knowledges' (from social work, probation, child care, education and so on) have come to do battle over their respective place in the control and supervision of the young.

Summary

- This chapter has traced the origins and development of delinquency and juvenile justice policy from the early nineteenth century to the 1930s. It has explored changing conceptions of the young offender and revealed that definitions and explanations of crime are inseparable from the various policies and practices that have been constructed for the ostensible reason of its control. In other words, as revisionist historians have argued, the precise definition of troublesome behaviour is frequently only realized through the very means by which it is believed such behaviour might best be regulated and constrained.

- 'Juvenile delinquency' is as much an index of adult perceptions as a description of youth behaviour. As a result it is difficult to catch sight of the meaning and extent of young offending in any objective fashion. Instead we are forced to rely on the definitions and discourses created in the processes of political, social and legal intervention. What actually constitutes 'young offending' is in a constant process of (re)invention and (re)definition. In the early nineteenth century, the *juvenile delinquent* was created in the midst of wider concerns about unemployment, lack of discipline and moral degeneration. In the early twentieth century, the *troublesome adolescent* was invented in the midst of concerns for 'boy labour', street leisure and imperialism. In the mid twentieth century, notions of the *troubled offender* were constructed, reflecting the increased presence of welfare agencies and professionals at the time. Social concern may be persistent and recurring but the practices, issues and concepts through which it is articulated are subject to change.

- Hendrick (1997) notes how the eighteenth-century contradictory conceptions of childhood as inherently innocent (the Romantic child) or evil (the Evangelical child) have inspired a whole series of competing constructions of childhood, youth and delinquency. Young people have been relocated from mill, mine and factory into reformatories, schools, youth organizations, welfare agencies and the family. At each stage the nature of childhood has been defined differently (see Table 2.4).

- The chapter also illustrates some of the difficulties involved in working with the nebulous concept of delinquency. Changes in police practices, legislation and shifts in public perception of crime make it difficult to produce a consistent definition of what actually constitutes delinquency and what its causes might be. We are left with a series of contradictory and competing discourses of which one of the most familiar is that of national decline and moral degeneration. Above all, it is clear that delinquency is not simply a crime problem.

- The repeated fear has been that youth are getting out of control. Often the solution is believed to lie in the past, harking back to some mythical 'golden age' of peace and tranquillity when young people 'knew their place'. But these notions do not allow us to see the issue with any clarity. The recurring fears directed at young people probably tell us more about adult concerns for morality, national security, unemployment, leisure, independence, imperialism and so on than they do about the nature and extent of young offending.

Table 2.4 *Competing constructions of childhood 1800–1930*

The Romantic Child (from the eighteenth century) – the elitist portrayal of childhood as fundamentally different to adulthood; a time of 'natural' and 'original' innocence

The Evangelical Child (from the early nineteenth century) – the contrary image of childhood as inherently corrupt and in need of overt control and moral guidance

The Factory Child (from the early nineteenth century) – child labour as an economic necessity for the working classes, but also the object of philanthropic reform

The Delinquent Child (from the mid nineteenth century) – the separation of child from adult offenders and legal recognition of the difference of childhood

The Schooled Child (from the late nineteenth century) – childhood as a universal condition and defined as a state of dependence and ignorance in need of compulsory education

The Psycho-medical Child (from the early twentieth century) – childhood and adolescence as a time of emotional upheaval in need of constant psychological and medical monitoring in order to improve national efficiency. Delinquency redefined as 'subnormality'

The Welfare Child (from the early twentieth century) – children as vulnerable, in need of care and protection. Delinquency redefined as 'neglect' or 'lack of moral education'

The Psychological Child (from the mid twentieth century) – childhood as imbued with its own psychological and psychiatric problems. Delinquency redefined as 'disturbance' or 'maladjustment' or 'pathological'

Source: Derived from Hendrick (1997)

Study Questions

1   How can it be argued that the 'juvenile delinquent' was a Victorian creation?
2   Why was 'hooliganism' a cause for concern at the end of the nineteenth century?
3   Which is the greatest cause of youthful delinquency: unemployment, poverty or adolescence?
4   Is adolescence a biological fact or a socio-historical construction?
5   How different is a child considered 'deprived' from one considered 'depraved'? Should they be dealt with separately?

Further Resources

A useful overview of some of the most important social constructions of childhood since the end of the eighteenth century which illustrates the theme of historical variability is provided by Hendrick (1997). In contrast Pearson's *Hooligan: A History of Respectable Fears* (1983) traces a remarkable historical continuity in the identification of young people as particularly troublesome and threatening to the nation's future. Collectively May (1973), Magarey (1978), King and Noel (1993) and King (1998) provide the debate about the origins of juvenile delinquency with a much needed historical substance. Shore's *Artful Dodgers* (1999) does more than most to humanize the experiences of working-class children and offenders in the early nineteenth century by drawing on their own personal accounts. The edited collection by Muncie, Hughes and McLaughlin (2002) draws together many of these formative texts. Springhall's *Coming of Age* (1986) is a thoughtful overview of the period 1860–1960 which focuses on the impact of the concept of adolescence. Hendrick's (1990) focus is narrower, restricted to 1880–1920, but is important in placing the debates in the context of class, as well as age, relations. Bailey (1987) is one of a few to give sustained attention to the period 1914–48. Dyhouse (1981), Zedner (1991) and Shore (2002) also reveal the extent to which gender divided Victorian society and they remind us that until relatively recently, most social histories have been written by men and solely about men.

3 Explaining Youth Crime I: Positivist Criminologies

Overview

Chapter 3 examines:
- a diverse range of theoretical and empirical studies that have addressed the issue of why young people commit crime;
- theories that locate the causes of crime in the individual;
- theories that locate the causes of crime in social organization and social structures;
- the limitations and problems of attempts to isolate specific causes of crime.

Key Terms

aetiology	extroversion
anomie	genetic determinism
causal analysis	maternal deprivation
correlation	positivism
determinism	social disorganization
differential association	somatotyping
essentialism	status frustration
eugenics	strain

Explanations of youth crime are various, diverse and contradictory. In popular and political idiom, poverty, inequality and unemployment have been cited as precipitating factors, but so too have affluence and a concomitant fear of 'premature independence'. Single parenting, inadequate parental control, child abuse and broken homes provide another recurring set of causal images, but so do notions of inherent wickedness, lack of self control, greed and wilful irresponsibility. In addition, low IQ, media violence, illegitimacy, 'bad blood', drugs, homelessness, 1960s permissiveness, moral decline, masculinity, truancy, deprivation, alienation and run-down housing estates have all been evoked at one time or another as the key to understanding youth crime. The list could be expanded indefinitely. But significantly, all of these motivational conditions do not just exist in popular discourse, but are grounded, albeit sometimes implicitly, in some biological, psychological or sociological theory of crime causation.

This chapter and Chapter 4 introduce some of the major criminological paradigms that have attempted to explain youth crime. In particular this chapter focuses on the insights and modes of explanation offered by *positivist* and scientific criminologies. The origins of a scientific criminology are usually located in the late nineteenth century, when biological research (based on physiological and anthropological studies) attempted to explain crime with reference to hereditable disorders. In the early twentieth century this was complemented by psychological studies that purported that many criminals were of low intelligence and feeble-minded. At this time academic criminology in Britain was largely the domain of doctors, psychologists and psychiatrists. It was not until the 1960s that British sociologists began to make a sustained impact, although influential work on the relationship between the inner city, subcultures and crime had already been carried out in the 1930s in Chicago, USA. Much of this work – whether grounded in psychology, biology or sociology – is positivist in nature because it attempts to isolate key causal variables, located in particular individuals or in particular social situations or social structures. Chapter 4, in contrast, examines how positivism came under attack in the 1960s by a variety of *radical* criminologies and was subsequently reworked by a variety of *realist* criminologies in the 1980s and 1990s.

It would, however, be misleading to assume that criminologists have moved *en masse* from one explanation to another as the limitations of preceding theories were exposed. Each has a contemporary presence and relevance. Moreover positivist accounts tend to remain paramount in media and popular discourses, whether they are expressed in terms of crime being caused by pathological individuals, inadequate parents or social deprivation. Even within positivism, the academic search for the causes of youth crime is a highly contested terrain and one that is frequently reflected in competing political discourses.

Individual Positivism

3.1 The key characteristic of positivism is the application of the methods of the natural sciences to the study of social behaviour. It has generally involved the search for 'cause and effect' relations that can be measured in a similar way to which natural scientists observe and analyse relations between objects in the physical world. Positivism does not concern itself with the abstract and unprovable, but with the tangible and quantifiable. It is dominated by the search for 'facts'. Through gaining 'objective' knowledge about how behaviour is *determined* by physiological, psychological and environmental conditions, it is assumed that most social problems can be understood and treated through the 'positive application of science'.

This approach first emerged in the late nineteenth century and was a radical departure from the dominant understandings of crime, law and justice at the time. It is widely assumed that modern *scientific* criminology began with the advent of a criminal anthropology associated with the work of the Italian physician, Cesare Lombroso (1876). By studying the body shapes of executed criminals, Lombroso attempted to prove scientifically that those who broke the law were physically different from those who did not. His observations led him to conclude that:

- serious offenders were born to be criminal; such people had inherited certain physical characteristics – such as large jaws and strong canine teeth – which marked them out as criminogenic;
- criminality was biologically determined – individuals had no control over whether they were to become criminal;
- crime was generated by biological pathology and atavism. Physically, criminals were throwbacks to more primitive times when people were deemed to be 'savages'.

Such notions were in direct contrast to the prevailing judicial doctrine, which was grounded in principles of neo-classicism and which maintained that, with few exceptions, behaviour was a matter of free will and individual choice. People broke laws because they anticipated that the benefits would outweigh any loss. They acted largely out of hedonism, choosing behaviour that was pleasurable and avoiding that which would give pain. For much of the eighteenth and nineteenth centuries this meant that no defences of criminal acts could be entertained. And although strict adherence to such principles was gradually tempered by the recognition of mitigating factors such as age (see Chapter 2.2), the arrival of Lombroso's theory remained a significant challenge to the judicial orthodoxy. For, if criminality was determined by factors other than rational choice, then surely it made little sense to punish offenders. Rather their condition should be treated.

By the early twentieth century the development of a criminological science – positivism – was to become influential, not only in physiology, but also in medicine, psychiatry, psychology and sociology. Offending came to be thought of as being determined by biological and cultural antecedents. It was no longer viewed as simply self determining. A leading protagonist of the positive school, Enrico Ferri (1901, p. 161) argued:

> The illusion of a free human will (the only miraculous factor in the eternal ocean of cause and effect) leads to the assumption that one can choose freely between virtue and vice. How can you still believe in the existence of free will when modern psychology, armed with all the instruments of positive modern research . . . demonstrates that every act of a human being is the result of an interaction between the personality and the environment of man?

By searching for the specific causes (or aetiology) of *criminal* behaviour as opposed to other behaviours, positive criminology assumes that criminality has a peculiar set of characteristics. Accordingly, most research of this type has tried to isolate key differences between criminals and non-criminals. Some theorists have focused on biological and psychological factors, thus locating the sources of crime primarily *within* the individual and bringing to the fore questions of individual pathology and abnormality. This approach is central to *individual positivism*. In contrast *sociological positivism* (considered in Section 3.2 below) argues that the key causative factors lie in the social contexts *external* to the individual. Here crime is more a matter of social pathology. However, whether individual or sociological, a number of common threads run through all positivist modes of analysis (see Table 3.1).

Table 3.1 *Characteristics of positivist criminologies*
• Use of *scientific methodologies* in which quantifiable data (such as the criminal statistics) are produced and can be tested by further empirical investigation and scrutiny.   • Emphasis on the study of *criminal behaviour*, rather than the creation of laws, the functions of legal systems or the operation of criminal justice systems.   • The assumption that criminality is different from normality and indicative of various *pathological states*, such as degeneracy, feeble-mindedness and frailty. Abandonment of rationality in the aetiology of crime.   • The attempt to establish 'cause and effect' relations scientifically and thus to increase the ability to *predict* criminality (when particular criminogenic factors can be identified).   • The assumption that, as criminals are abnormal, their behaviour is in violation of some widely held *consensus* in the rest of society.   • *Treatment* or neutralization of causes, when these become known, with the ultimate goal of eliminating anti-social behaviour. As behaviour is involuntary and not a matter of choice for the offender, punitive responses are misplaced.

Physiology

In the early twentieth century several attempts were made to isolate the key physiological characteristics of known criminals. Goring (1913) studied over 3,000 male prisoners in and around London and compared them with various control groups of non-prisoners. Using correlational analysis – a then new statistical procedure for quantifying the degree of association between variables – he found that the criminal tended to be shorter in height and weigh less. He explained such difference with reference to notions of 'inbreeding within a criminal class' which generated a lineage of mental deficiencies within certain families. Similarly, Hooton (1939) found that criminals were marked by smaller heads, shorter and broader noses, and sloping foreheads. Criminals were (akin to Lombroso's theory of atavism) viewed as biologically inferior and made up an incorrigible, inferior class.

Such correlations of body build and behavioural tendencies reached their most sophisticated expression in the work of Sheldon (1949). His analysis of *somatotyping* suggested that the shape of the body correlated with individual temperament and mental well-being. A person's somatotype is made up of three components: endomorphy, ectomorphy and mesomorphy.

- *Mesomorphs* have well-developed muscles and athletic appearance. Body shape is hard and round. Personality is strong, active, aggressive and sometimes violent.
- *Ectomorphs* have small skeletons and weak muscles. Body shape is fragile and thin. Personality is introverted, hypersensitive and intellectual.
- *Endomorphs* have heavy builds and are slow moving. Body shape is soft and round. Personality is extrovert, friendly and sociable.

Analysing and comparing 200 boys in a reformatory with 4,000 students in Boston, Sheldon concluded that most delinquents tended towards mesomorphy. Ectomorphs had the lowest criminal tendencies. Glueck and Glueck (1950), using large samples of delinquent and non-delinquent boys, found similarly that there were twice as many mesomorphs among delinquents than could have occurred by chance. Sixty per cent of delinquents were mesomorphic, while only 14 per cent were ectomorphic, compared with 40 per cent of non-delinquents. The Gluecks contended that strength and agility may enable boys to fill a delinquent role. Endomorphs were too clumsy, and ectomorphs too fragile, to be successful delinquents. On reviewing a number of such studies, Wilson and Herrnstein (1985, p. 89) felt confident in concluding that criminals do differ in physique from the population at large. Physique, however, does not cause crime, but it does correlate with temperaments which are impulsive and given to uninhibited self gratification.

Such research into physiology is clearly controversial, particularly in Lombroso's case, where certain physical traits are considered to be reflective of a biological inferiority. With hindsight it is clear that his work was more informed by notions of racial and gender superiority at a time of Italian unification than it was by any scientific objective method (Valier, 2002, p. 17). By the early twentieth century anthropology had totally ruled out the possibility of an evolutionary throwback to earlier, more primitive species. Psychology and psychiatry were demonstrating that the relationship between crime, epilepsy and mental disorder, for example, was far more 'complex and involved than Lombroso supposed' (Vold and Bernard, 1986, p. 38). Clearly the leap from skull type to criminality to atavism does not necessarily mean that one causes the other. As is common with such studies, it is not *causes* that are revealed but *correlations*. Being athletic in stature may be correlated with delinquency, but this does not mean that either is the cause of the other. Both are probably influenced by other factors, including the adequacy of nutrition, extent of manual labour and social class position. Similarly, what Hooton and Sheldon were measuring was the characteristics not of the criminal *per se* but of the identified and processed criminal, who is most likely to be of working-class origin. Above all, any association between body type and crime remains in need of explanation. Are mesomorphs biologically predisposed to crime or is their criminality simply more socially visible? Such questions continue to plague physiological research, but its assumptions have had a major impact on popular conceptions of crime. Bull and Green (1980) showed members of the public and the police ten photographs of men and asked to match them with any of eleven particular crimes. For crimes of robbery, gross indecency, fraud, soliciting, car theft and drug possession, respondents readily and consistently put a face to a crime. However, none of the photographed men had ever been convicted of any crime! Similarly, Ainsworth (2000) notes how visual stereotyping is constantly reinforced by employing the same actors to play criminal roles in film and drama. We remain deeply wedded to the idea that criminals not only act, but also look different to the 'normal population'.

Genetics and the 'Pathological Family'

The earliest attempts to isolate a genetic cause of criminality involved analyses of the family trees of known criminals. Of note were Dugdale's (1910) study of the

Jukes and Goddard's (1927) study of the Kallikaks. Dugdale traced over 1,000 descendants of the Jukes – a New York family infamous for criminality and prostitution – and found 280 paupers, 60 thieves, 7 murderers, 140 criminals and 50 prostitutes. Goddard studied the descendants of Martin Kallikak, who had an illegitimate son by a woman of 'low birth' and subsequently married into a 'good' family. The relations of the illegitimate offspring contained substantially more criminal members than the latter. Both studies concluded that 'undesirable' hereditary characteristics were passed down through families. Criminal families tended to produce criminal children. Criminals were born, not made.

Goring (1913), though dismissive of physiological determinism, likewise argued that criminality was largely inherited and was linked to mental inferiority. His study of convicts discovered high correlations between the criminality of spouses, between parents and their children, and between brothers. He found that poverty, education and broken homes were poor correlates of crime, and so he was led to conclude that social conditions were insignificant explanations of criminality. He believed that criminality was passed down through inherited genes. Accordingly, in order to reduce crime, he recommended that people with such inherited characteristics should not be allowed to reproduce. This logic was fertile ground for the growth of *eugenics*, a doctrine concerned with 'improving' the genetic selection of the human race.

Most critical commentaries on this work – notwithstanding the question of its ethical position – have argued that it fails to recognize the potential effect of a wide range of environmental factors. Although Goring remained alive to such effects, the few social conditions he examined were subject to inadequate measures. The high correlation in the criminality of family members could just as easily be explained by reference to poor schooling, inadequate diet, unemployment, common residence or cultural transmission of criminal values. In other words, it was argued that criminality was not necessarily an inherited trait, but could also be learnt or generated by a plethora of environmental factors (Vold and Bernard, 1986, p. 86).

Nevertheless evidence from the Cambridge Study in Delinquent Development (see Chapter 1.3) continues to suggest that crime does indeed run in families. Farrington et al. (1996), for example, note that of 397 families, half of all convictions were concentrated in just 23. Convictions of one family member were strongly related to convictions of other family members. Three-quarters of convicted mothers and convicted fathers had a convicted child. Whilst these correlations suggest that criminality may be transmitted in certain families, they do not, as the researchers acknowledge, allow us to distinguish the relative importance of genetic and environmental factors. Nevertheless Farrington et al. (1996, p. 61) conclude that 'while offending (specifically) cannot be genetically transmitted because it is a legally and socially defined construct, more fundamental characteristics that are linked to offending (e.g. intelligence, impulsivity, aggressiveness) could be genetically transmitted'.

More rigorous research directed at isolating 'a genetic factor' has been carried out with twins and adoptees. These have attempted to test two key propositions:

- that identical (monozygotic or MZ) twins have more similar behaviour patterns than fraternal (dizygotic or DZ) twins;
- that children's behaviour is more similar to that of their biological parents than to that of their adoptive parents.

If either proposition could be supported, then the case for biological determinism would be stronger. In a review of research carried out between 1929 and 1961, Mednick and Volavka (1980) noted that, overall, 60 per cent of MZ twins shared criminal behaviour patterns compared to 30 per cent of DZ twins. More recent work has found a lower, but still significant, level of association. Christiansen's (1977) study of 3,586 twin pairs in Denmark found a 52 per cent concordance for MZ groups and a 22 per cent concordance for the DZ groups. The evidence for the genetic transmission of some behaviour patterns thus appears quite strong. However, telling criticisms have also been made of this line of research. For example a tendency to treat identical twins more alike than fraternal twins may account for the greater concordance. Thus the connection between criminality and genetics may be made through environmental conditions, derived from the behaviour of parents or from twins' influence on each other's behaviour (Einstadter and Henry, 1995, pp. 94–5).

As a result, Mednick et al. (1987) proposed that the study of adoptions would be a better test of a relative genetic effect, particularly if it could be shown that the criminality of biological parent and child was similar even when the child had grown up in a completely different environment. Using data from over 14,000 cases of adoption in Denmark from 1924 to 1947, Mednick et al. concluded that some factor *is* transmitted by convicted parents to increase the likelihood that their children – even after adoption – will be convicted for criminal offences. However, the question of exactly *what* is inherited remains unanswered. Rutter and Giller (1983, p. 179) argue that the mysterious factor is unlikely to be criminality as such, but rather 'some aspect of personality functioning which predisposes to criminality'. Or as Beirne and Messerschmidt (1991, p. 484) conclude, if prospective parents are routinely informed about the criminal convictions of biological parents, this may trigger a labelling process and a self fulfilling prophecy.

Nevertheless the evidence from twin and adoption studies has not ruled out the possibility that there is some genetic basis to some criminality and this type of research continues to attract research funding and publicity. In 1994 a new Centre for Social, Genetic and Development Psychiatry was opened at the Maudsley Hospital in south London to examine what role genetic structures play in determining patterns of behaviour (including crime). In 1995 a major conference discussed the possibility of isolating a criminal gene – the basis of which rested on the study of twins and adoptees (Ciba Foundation, 1996). One of the best-selling social science books of the 1990s, Herrnstein and Murray's *The Bell Curve* (1994), claimed that American blacks and Latinos are disproportionately poor, not because of discrimination, but because they are less intelligent. Further they suggested that IQ is mainly determined by inherited genes and that people with a low IQ are more likely to commit crime because they lack foresight and are unable to distinguish right from wrong. Such theory indeed remains attractive (to some) because it seems to provide *scientific* evidence which clearly differentiates 'us' from 'them' (see Chapter 4.2). Similarly, if certain people are inherently 'bad', then society is absolved of all responsibility. But as Einstadter and Henry (1995, p. 98) warn, such reasoning is also characteristic of totalitarian regimes 'whether in Nazi Germany or the former USSR and extending more recently to forced therapy in the United States'.

Further research has examined a wide range of biochemical factors in attempts to isolate an individual causal factor in the generation of deviant, anti-social, criminal or violent behaviour. These have included: hormone imbalances; testosterone, vitamin, adrenalin and blood sugar levels; allergies; slow brain-wave activity; lead pollution; epilepsy; and the operation of the autonomic nervous system. None of the research has, as yet, been able to establish any direct causal relationships. While some interesting associations have been discovered – for example, between male testosterone levels and verbal aggression, between vitamin B deficiency and hyperactivity, and between stimulation of the central portion of the brain (the limbic) and impulsive violence – it remains disputed that such biological conditions will automatically generate anti-social activities, which in turn will be translated into criminality. Indeed, most current research in this tradition would not claim that biological make-up *alone* can be used as a sufficient explanation of crime. Rather, some biological factors may generate criminality, but only when they interact with certain other psychological or social factors.

The tendency has grown for biology to be considered as but one element within *multiple factor* explanations (Wilson and Herrnstein, 1985). In terms that are consonant with those of classical (pre-positivist) criminology, they argue that individuals have the free will to choose criminal actions when they believe that the rewards will outweigh any negative consequences. Such a decision (freely made) is, however, influenced by inherited constitutional factors. Wilson and Herrnstein argue that low IQ, abnormal body type and an impulsive personality will predispose a person to make criminal decisions. Criminality for them is not a matter of nature versus nurture, but of nature *and* nurture. This approach is also a defining characteristic of *socio-biology*, developed in the 1970s and heralded by its advocates as a way forward in unifying the social and natural sciences. Generally, it is argued that some people carry with them the potential to be violent or anti-social and that environmental conditions can sometimes trigger anti-social responses. Socio-biologists view biology, environment and learning as mutually dependent factors. Jeffery argues, for example, that:

> We do not inherit behaviour any more than we inherit height or intelligence. We do inherit a capacity for interaction with the environment. Sociopathy and alcoholism are not inherited, but a biochemical preparedness for such behaviours is present in the brain which if given a certain type of environment will produce sociopathy or alcoholism. (Jeffery, 1978, p. 161)

Nevertheless it is acknowledged that the usual comparative controls of criminal and non-criminal are doubly misleading. Offenders in custody are not representative of criminals in general, but constitute a highly selected subset of those apprehended, charged and convicted. Control groups of the non-criminal are almost certain to include some individuals who have committed crimes but whose actions have remained undetected. Above all, the search for biological, physiological or genetic correlates of criminality is continually hampered because it is practically impossible to control for environmental and social influences and thus to be able to measure precisely the exact influence of a genetic effect. Nevertheless bio-chemical research has been given a significant boost through the Human Genome Project which reported in 2003 that it had 'cracked the code of life'. It is claimed that by sequencing and mapping human genes, doors will open not only to advancements in health care but also in law enforcement and criminal identification. Caspi et al. (2002), for example, claim to have identified a specific gene that triggers violence in some previously abused children. Once more the possibilities of a 'criminal gene' and 'gene therapy' (and fears of eugenics) are being publicly debated. Surprisingly these have, as yet, little or no presence in criminological conferences or texts.

The Adolescent Personality

Another form of individual positivism – often termed 'the psychogenic school' – has shifted the focus of causal analysis away from biologically given 'constitutional' factors and towards more 'dynamic' mental processes and characteristics.

The earliest versions of this work were applications of the principles of Freudian psychoanalysis. Briefly, Freud, while not directly addressing the issue of crime causation, argued that all behaviour is the result of tensions existing between unconscious drives (the id) and conscious understandings of self, morality and the social order (the ego and superego). Crime is the symbolic expression of such psychic conflict, when the individual has failed to learn and develop adequate measures of self control through which unconscious drives can be channelled into socially acceptable acts. The repression or inadequate control of the unconscious is usually related to a lack of intimate and trusting relationships in early childhood. Aichhorn (1925) concluded that delinquent children continue to 'act infantile' because they have failed to develop an ego and superego that would allow them to conform to prevailing social mores. In Freudian terms, the 'pleasure principle' has not been sufficiently controlled and adapted to the 'reality principle'.

Writers in the psychoanalytical tradition have been particularly influential in linking crime with the 'pathological' conditions of adolescence. Criminal behaviour is the result of a failure of psychological development in which the underlying latent delinquency of adolescence is allowed to govern behaviour. The earliest version of this argument was that of G. Stanley Hall (see Chapter 2.3) and his premise of an adolescent storm and stress (*Sturm und Drang*) has remained remarkably influential. In the 1950s Anna Freud, for example, argued:

Adolescence is by its nature an *interruption* of peaceful growth, and . . . the upholding of a steady equilibrium during the adolescent process is in itself *abnormal* . . . adolescence resembles in appearance a variety of other emotional upsets and structural *upheavals*. The adolescent manifestations come close to symptom formation of the *neurotic, psychotic*, or *dissocial* order and merge almost imperceptibly into . . . almost all the *mental illnesses*. (Freud, 1952, pp. 255–78, italics added)

In this way adolescence is viewed as a time of crisis in which the struggle between the forces of natural instinct and those of cultural constraints are acted out in behaviour patterns comparable to madness. The problem of adolescence derives from the conflict caused as instinctual drives are constrained by social learning and the demands of a *social* existence. Similarly, Eissler, writing in 1958, viewed adolescence as stormy and unpredictable behaviour marked by dramatic mood changes which manifest themselves as 'neurotic at one time and almost psychotic at another' (quoted by Rutter et al., 1976, p. 35).

Erikson (1968) went on to argue that adolescence is characterized by an 'identity crisis' in which the key task is to resolve a conflict between 'ego identity' and 'identity confusion'. Failure to achieve a positive resolution to such contradictions, he argued, will adversely affect development later in life. Although Erikson was at pains to show that such a crisis was predictable rather than unusual, he nevertheless uses the same medical terminology of 'symptoms', 'neuroses' and 'psychoses' to describe the adolescent condition. In this way the concept of adolescence is firmly associated with emotional disorder, impairment and pathology. It is an abnormal condition, reducible ultimately to universal biological determinants.

Applying such concepts to crime, Healy and Bronner (1936) compared two groups of children from a child guidance clinic and argued that the delinquent group showed greater signs of emotional disturbance. This was explained with reference to instability in family relationships and lack of affectional ties. Delinquency was viewed as a form of sublimation in which the delinquent attempted to meet basic needs that had not been met by the family. Similarly, Bowlby's (1946) study of *Forty-four Juvenile Thieves*, who were referred to a London child guidance clinic between 1936 and 1939, concluded that 'the prolonged separation of the child from his mother or foster-mother in the early years commonly leads to his becoming a persistent thief and an Affectionless Character'. Lack of affectional ties or *maternal deprivation* was viewed as the root cause of criminality.

Other psychoanalytic explanations for crime have focused on the inability to control pleasure-seeking drives, on parental permissiveness and on the acting out of feelings of oppression and helplessness. While such hypotheses continue to be highly influential both popularly and politically, they largely remain immune to objective scientific testing – a cornerstone of assessing the adequacy of any positivist criminological theory. This is because the reliance on unconscious factors, symbolic behaviours and the analyst's own interpretations of that behaviour place psychoanalysis beyond the boundaries of scientific demonstration.

Other psychologists and psychiatrists have attempted systematically to associate particular personality traits with criminal behaviour. Much of this has depended on the construction of performance tests, personality scales and measurements of intelligence. From these a wide range of traits have been singled out as indicative of delinquent and criminal propensities. They include extroversion, vivacity, defiance, resentfulness, suspicion, assertiveness, low IQ, excitability, impulsiveness and narcissism (for example, Glueck and Glueck, 1950). West and Farrington's longitudinal research (1973, 1977; Farrington and West, 1990) of 411 working-class London boys followed their development from the age of 8 onwards. By the age of 21, about 30 per cent of the sample had some sort of official record of delinquency. A scale was devised to measure 'anti-social' tendencies, based on attitudinal measures and such activities as smoking, loitering, tattooing, heavy drinking, gambling and promiscuous sex. West and Farrington found that those who scored high on anti-social attitudes and behaviours were more likely in the future to have criminal records than those who scored low. The authors concluded that a 'delinquent' way of life – particular attributes of personality and lifestyle – was clearly connected to officially recorded criminality.

In a review of research concerned with the backgrounds, circumstances and attitudes of future offenders, Farrington (1996) details numerous risk factors including: being the child of a teenage mother, impulsive personality, low intelligence and poor performance in school, harsh or erratic parental discipline and parental conflict, as well as peer group influences and socio-economic status. More narrowly focused, a review of 94 personality studies conducted between 1950 and 1965 by Waldo and Dinitz (1967) found that over 80 per cent of these studies reported statistically significant personality differences between criminals and non-criminals. The studies generally concluded that criminals were more 'psychopathic' than non-criminals. Similarly, Wilson and Herrnstein (1985, pp. 187–8) conclude that such personality traits as conflict with authority and low personal attachments (on a psychopathic deviate scale), bizarre thought and withdrawal (on a schizophrenia scale) and unproductive hyperactivity (on a hypomania scale) all correlate with criminal tendencies.

Another form of personality measurement was devised by Eysenck (1964). He focused on two basic dimensions: *extroversion*, a continuum from extroversion to introversion along an E scale, and *neuroticism*, a continuum from unstable to stable along an N scale. He found that those having high NE personalities were the most likely also to have deviant characteristics. Eysenck attempted to explain such results by adopting a multi-factor approach which incorporated biological, individual and social levels of analysis. The basis of his theory was that through genetic endowment, some people are born with a particular structure of the cortex of the brain which affects their ability to learn from, or adapt to, environmental stimuli. The extrovert was considered to be cortically underaroused and sought to gain stimulation through impulsive behaviour. The introvert was considered to be cortically overaroused and avoided stimulation through adopting a quiet, reserved demeanour. Eysenck argued further that extroverts condition less efficiently than introverts, thus affecting their ability to develop an effective conscience and behave in a socially acceptable manner. The basic principles of Eysenck's theory are as follows:

- Children learn to control anti-social behaviour through the development of a conscience.
- A conscience is developed through conditioning whereby children are deterred from 'wrong' acts by disapproval and punishment, in which certain acts become associated with fear and anxiety.
- The effectiveness of conditioning depends mainly upon the child's personality in terms of E (extroversion) and N (neuroticism).
- The extrovert requires a higher level of stimulation than others, lacks inhibition, and engages in more 'risky' behaviour.
- High E and high N personalities have poor conditionability and are the least likely to learn self control.
- Dramatic and impulsive behaviour, unhindered by conscience, means more potential crime.
- High N and high E personalities will be over-represented in offender populations.

Eysenck's theory combines elements of biological determinism with social conditioning, and he argues that it is universally applicable, given that all personalities are made up of N and E factors. It also retains an environmental component. As Eysenck explains:

> The very notion of criminality or crime would be meaningless without a context of learning or social experience and, quite generally, of human interaction. What the figures have demonstrated is that heredity is a very strong predisposing factor as far as committing crimes is concerned. But the actual way in which the crime is carried out and whether or not the culprit is found and punished – these are obviously subject to the changing vicissitudes of everyday life. (Eysenck, 1970, p. 75)

During the 1970s Eysenck's theory generated a great deal of empirical research. The findings have been somewhat inconsistent, but the general pattern to emerge was that offender populations did appear to be high on the N scale, but within the normal E range. The key element of Eysenck's theory – extroversion – thus appears to be subordinate to that of neuroticism – a factor regarded simply as intensifying behaviour of any kind. A direct correlation between extroversion and criminality remains unproven (Crookes, 1979). In response to such limitations, Eysenck added a third dimension of psychoticism (characterized by such personality traits as insensitivity, aggression, foolhardiness and lack of concern for others) but this has also shown mixed results, in particular missing a critical 'hedonism' factor (Burgess, 1972).

The logic that youth crime and deviance are symptomatic of some personality disorder continues to be popular. In Rutter and Smith's (1995) review of the scientific evidence on whether psychosocial disorders among 12–26 year olds have increased in the second half of the twentieth century, it is simply assumed that crime (as well as suicide, depression, eating disorders and use of alcohol and psychoactive drugs) is a 'disorder' which is amenable to causal explanation. Of the tentative causes which are promoted, family break-up, parental confrontation and increased individualism are given prominence. In particular, a weakening of internalized moral values is attributed to a rise in freedom in the post-war era and thus a growing number of young confused people living in a moral vacuum divorced from the positive influence of adults.

Assessment

If we assume for the moment that all young people do go through a period of inner turmoil, is this caused by an unalterable biological law or by adjustments necessitated by particular environments, cultures and moments in history?

Margaret Mead's famous work *Coming of Age in Samoa* (1928) set out to contradict biological positivism in particular. If a culture could be discovered in which adolescents did not appear to suffer 'storm and stress', it was argued, then biological determinism could be declared invalid. Over a period of several months Mead studied the behaviour of 25 adolescent girls in three villages on the Manu'an island of Tau in Eastern Samoa. She reported that while social ranking by age existed, their adolescence was not characterized by any form of role confusion, conflict or rebellion. She concluded that the state of adolescence was not universal, but culturally variable. The stresses of adolescence were socially, rather than biologically, determined. For Mead, the adolescent anxieties so troubling middle-class America in the inter-war years were produced through young people being confronted with a wide range of occupational choice, extreme competitiveness, and conflicting standards of sexual morality, rather than being biologically inevitable.

This cultural determinist approach was criticized some 50 years later. Derek Freeman's visit to Samoa in the 1940s convinced him that Mead's analysis was full of inaccuracies. For, whereas Mead claimed that the behaviour of Samoan adolescents was untroubled and that adolescence was 'the age of maximum ease', Freeman (1983, p. 262) notes relatively high rates of delinquency in the 14–19 age group, characterized by rape and male aggression. Mead's book rapidly attracted popular attention largely due to her portrayal of Samoa as a paradise of adolescent free love and pre-marital sexuality. However, Freeman's observations again contradict such assertions. He discovered a cult of chastity in which high value was placed on female virginity prior to marriage and noted how the Samoan girl was strictly watched and guarded from the time of her first menstruation. What for Mead was unrestrained sexual promiscuity was for Freeman a custom of *moetotolo* (sleep crawling), whereby young men would compete to deflower any sexually mature virgin, and if a young man was successful he would claim her as his own. Such a practice usually involved a man sexually assaulting a sleeping woman through force or deceit in a manner which in the West we would describe as 'surreptitious rape' (Freeman, 1983, p. 244). Above all, Freeman claimed that any attempt to explain behaviour in purely cultural terms must be 'irremediably deficient'. Instead he argues for a synthesis of biological and cultural variables.

In addition, the pathological connotations of a universal and biologically based 'adolescent personality' have also been widely critiqued. For example, Fass's (1977) study of college youth in the 1920s reported that the young were essentially conformist, rather than hostile to parental attitudes, and she was struck by the absence of 'storm and stress' in young people's lives. Springhall (1983–4) suggests that one reason why some adolescents have problems of adjustment is simply because parents and teachers expect them to have such problems. In a 1970s survey, 80 per cent of teachers stated that adolescence was a time of great stress, while 60 per cent of adolescent pupils denied that they had ever felt miserable or depressed. Springhall concludes:

> The misleading images of the disturbed adolescent can be blamed, according to taste, on: unrepresentative sampling techniques, the threat presented to the adult by certain deviant forms of adolescent behaviour or on the role of the professional hand-wringers of the mass media in publicizing the sensational behaviour among the young . . . The ordinary public can thus be forgiven for holding a stereotyped version of adolescence as a social problem which requires to be dealt with either through separate institutions or by handing out heavier forms of punishment. (Springhall, 1983–4, p. 34)

In general, individual positivism assumes that all human behaviour is determined by biological, psychological or environmental factors, or a combination of these. What is noteworthy is that such theory focuses on individual motivations and provides us with very specific representations of the young criminal as either 'born bad', for example, through genetic inheritance, or 'made bad', for example, through inability to develop a conscience. The issue of crime causation is often alluded to, but in the spirit of developing vigorous scientific methods of analysis what emerges is a series of correlations rather than 'proven' cause–effect relations.

Individual positivism formed the bedrock of criminological studies for the first half of the twentieth century and has regained importance since the 1990s. For some, because of advances in our understanding of genetic structures, it offers a way forward in understanding criminality which is 'free' from a multitude of complicating social variables. For others it is little more than a dangerous political gambit to segregate those deemed to be physically or emotionally unfit. Indeed, from within psychology, positivism has been attacked for its lack of attention to processes of human cognition and social learning in which individuals are viewed as capable of self reflection and self development, rather than as beings who simply act upon pre-given determinants. In addition some sociologists have argued that there is 'meaning' in all social activity. Thus whilst theorists, such as Eysenck, characterize deviant behaviour as pathological, it has also been argued that deviancy is a meaningful behaviour pattern which becomes undesirable only when judged and labelled by others.

Hollin (1989, pp. 60–1) points to two major limitations of theories that attempt to replicate principles of scientific determinism. First, the more that criminological research has developed, the more the number of variables thought to be important in crime has increased. Even if such variables were capable of adequate measurement, controlling for their relative effect is probably impossible. This leads to sampling variations between studies so that results are always difficult to replicate. We are thus left with a long list of correlations, which though interesting in themselves, shed no light on the question of causation. Second, psychological research continues to unearth more and more variables, but then attempts to explain crime with reference to existing psychological theory that is designed to account for some psychological abnormality. Thus criminal behaviour becomes a genetic defect, an extreme of personality development, a failure of family socialization and so on. Finally, it is always worth questioning that if crime and delinquency are as widespread as self report studies indicate (see Chapter 1.2), what sense does it make to impute some biological or psychological disturbance (learnt or otherwise) to these forms of behaviour?

Nevertheless, theories based on individual positivism continue to have widespread popular and political appeal. Notions of adolescent disorder, parental neglect, 'bad blood' and psychopathology all have their root here. The search for the aetiology of crime by identifying a criminal type, a criminal gene or a criminal personality will continue because of a general reluctance to believe that youthful criminality is in any way 'normal'.

Sociological Positivism

3.2 Most of the explanations of crime that were examined in Section 3.1 focused on the characteristics of individual criminals and attempted to identify certain behavioural or physiological anomalies or abnormalities which distinguish the criminal from the non-criminal. The sources of crime were, in the main, found to lie *within* the individual. In contrast, sociological approaches stress the importance of social factors as causes of crime. Their broad aim is to account for the *distribution* of varying amounts of crime within given populations. This mode of analysis in fact predates the work of Lombroso, and can be traced back to the work of the French statistician, Guerry and the Belgian mathematician, Quetelet, in the 1830s. They analysed official statistics on variables such as suicide, educational level, crime rate and age and sex of offenders, within given geographic areas for specific time periods. Two general patterns emerged: types and the amount of crime varied from region to region, but within specific areas there was little variation from year to year. Because of this regularity it was proposed that criminal behaviour must be generated by something other than individual motivation. Quetelet (1842) found that the factors most strongly tied to criminal propensity were gender, occupation and religion, as well as age. Fluctuations in crime rates were explained with reference to changes in the social, political and economic structures of particular societies, while crime itself was viewed as a constant and inevitable feature of social organization. He argued:

> Society includes within itself the germs of all the crimes committed, and at the same time the necessary facilities for their development. It is the social state, in some measure, which prepares these crimes, and the criminal is merely the instrument to execute them. Every social state supposes, then, a certain number and a certain order of crimes, these being merely the necessary consequences of its organization. (Quetelet, 1842, p. 108)

Such an analysis was clearly associated with the emergence of a sociological form of positivism first developed by philosophers such as Comte and Saint-Simon in the mid nineteenth century. Comte's insistence that society both predates and shapes the individual psychologically provided the foundation for *sociological positivism*. At the turn of the century its most influential advocate was Émile Durkheim (1895/1964). He argued, in a similar way to Quetelet, that in any given social context, the predictability of crime rates must mean they are social facts, and thus a normal phenomenon. Crime is rarely abnormal – it occurs in all societies, it is tied to the facts of collective life and its volume tends to increase as societies evolve from mechanical to more complex organic forms of organization. Above all, crime and punishment perform a useful function for society because they maintain social solidarity, through establishing moral boundaries and strengthening the shared consensus of a community's beliefs and values. Crime, then, is positive – an integrative element in any healthy society. In other words, Durkheim reasoned that societies without crime must be extremely repressive and incapable of adapting to social change.

Many of these early sociologies of crime were at direct odds with the premises of individual positivism. However, although the level of analysis is different, the mode of analysis remains very much the same. Sociological positivism continues to view the individual as a body that is acted upon, and whose behaviour is determined, by external forces. Little or no role is given to the processes of choice, voluntarism or self-volition. While Durkheim argued that crime is a normal social fact, he also acknowledged that in given contexts its rate might be abnormal. Thus crime is also

Table 3.2 *Individual and sociological positivism compared*	
Individual positivism	**Sociological positivism**
• Crime caused by individual abnormality or pathology	• Crime caused by social pathology
• Crime viewed as a biological psychiatric, personality or learning deficiency	• Crime viewed as a product of dysfunctions in social and economic conditions
• Behaviour determined by constitutional, genetic or personality factors	• Behaviour determined by social conditions and structures
• Crime as a violation of the moral consensus	• Crime as a violation of a collective conscience surrounding legal codes
• Crime varies with temperament, personality and degree of 'adequate' socialization	• Crime varies from region to region depending on economic and political milieux
• Crime as an abnormal individual condition	• Crime as normal: a social fact, but certain rates of crime are dysfunctional
• Criminals can be treated via medicine, therapy and resocialization	• Crime can be treated via programmes of social reform

regarded as some form of pathology: if not the abnormality of individuals, then dysfunctions in social systems. The study of crime remains in the tradition of scientism, essentialism and positivistic method: that is, it can be measured and evaluated by means of statistical methods and empirical data. It also assumes that there must be something about crime that differentiates it from normal behaviour. A consensus, or in Durkheim's terms a 'collective conscience', exists which marks out the criminal from the non-criminal. The role of social conflict between individuals and among competing groups is downplayed. Finally, as both individual and sociological positivism maintain that it is theoretically possible to specify causes, they also hold that it is theoretically possible to 'treat' or 'correct' the aberrant condition (see Table 3.2).

Social Ecology and Criminal Areas

Social ecology explanations of crime have traditionally been influenced by human geography and biology. As Quetelet had observed, crime is always subject to uneven geographical distribution. Urban areas appear to have higher recorded crime rates than rural areas, and within cities there are presumed to be 'criminal areas' or 'hot spots' of crime. To explain these patterns of crime distribution, analogies were made between the ecology of plant life and human organization. Cities were viewed as akin to living and growing organisms. The analogy, as Downes and Rock (1995, p. 70), suggest, was attractive to 'sociologists who were searching for metaphors and principles to advance their own new and rather incoherent discipline . . . just as plants, insects and animals translate a physical terrain into a mosaic of distinct communities, so people become separated into a network of unlike communities which form an intelligible whole'. Such an approach allowed the prevalent paradigm of individual positivism to be challenged. Above all it was claimed that because particular areas maintained a regular crime rate even when their populations completely changed, there must be something about particular places that sustains crime.

In the 1920s and 1930s sociologists at the University of Chicago embarked on a systematic study of all aspects of their local urban environment. Park, a newspaper reporter turned sociologist, and Burgess, his collaborator, were especially influential. They noted that, like any ecological system, the development and organization of the city of Chicago were not random but patterned, and could be understood in terms of such social processes as invasion, conflict, accommodation and assimilation. They likened the city to a living and growing organism and viewed the functions of various areas of the city as fundamental to the survival of the whole. The city's characteristics, social change and distribution of people were studied by use of Burgess's concentric zone theory. The city was divided into five areas: zone 1, the central business district; zone 2, a transition from business to residences; zone 3, working-class homes; zone 4, middle-class homes; and zone 5, commuter suburbs. Zone 2 – the zone in transition – was a particular focus of study. Here the expansion of the business sector continually meant that residents were displaced. It became the least desirable living area. It was characterized by deteriorating housing stock, poverty, pawn shops, cheap theatres, restaurants, casual workers, new immigrants and a breakdown in the usual methods of social control.

Park and Burgess (1925) hypothesized that it was in zone 2 that crime and vice would flourish. Shaw (1929) set out to test this hypothesis by using juvenile and adult court and prison statistics to map the spatial distribution of the residences of delinquent youths and criminals throughout the city. Among his conclusions were the following:

- Rates of truancy, delinquency and adult crime varied inversely in proportion to the distance from the city centre. The closer to the centre of the city, the higher the rate of crime.
- Areas showing the highest rates of juvenile delinquency also had the highest rates of adult crime.
- The rates reflected differences in the make-up of different communities. High crime rates occurred in areas characterized by physical deterioration and declining populations.
- Relatively high rates of crime persisted in zone 2 despite the fact that the composition of the population in that area had changed significantly over 30 years.

These observations suggested that it was the nature of neighbourhoods, and *not* the nature of the individuals who lived there, that determined levels of criminality. As a result, this line of reasoning has been termed 'environmental determinism'.

The concentration of crime and delinquency in a zone of transition was viewed as indicative of processes of *social disorganization*. As industry and commerce invaded and transient populations entered such areas, community ties were destroyed and resistance to deviance lowered:

> In this state of social disorganization community resistance is low. Delinquency and criminal patterns arise and are transmitted socially just as any other cultural and social pattern is transmitted. In time these delinquent patterns become dominant and shape the attitudes and behaviour of persons living in the area. Thus the section becomes an area of delinquency. (Shaw, 1929, pp. 205–6)

This early work was thus clearly positivist in orientation. Subsequently Shaw and McKay (1942) developed the notion of a delinquency area into a *cultural transmission* theory of delinquency. This held that within transitional (zone 2) areas, particular forms of crime became a cultural norm: they were learnt and passed on through the generations. Shaw and McKay (1942, p. 436) proposed that:

> This tradition becomes meaningful to the child through the conduct, speech, gestures and attitudes of persons with whom he has contact. Of particular importance is the child's intimate association with predatory gangs or other forms of delinquent and criminal organisation. Through his contacts with these groups and by virtue of his participation in their activities, he learns the techniques of stealing, becomes involved in binding relationships with his companions in delinquency and acquires the attitudes appropriate to his position as a member of such groups.

Originally such factors as overcrowding, slum housing and poverty were viewed as causal factors in themselves; now structural factors were relegated to the minor role of predisposing symptoms of the more significant processes of social and cultural transmission. A shift away from structural determinism (and thus away from positivist modes of analysis and understanding) was a key element of the Chicago School's later studies. Using detailed case studies of the 'career' of individual offenders, *appreciative studies* of the criminal's own perspective and attitudes were promoted in which the principles of positivism were rejected in the detailed study of interactional, learning and associational processes.

A key influence was Sutherland's theory of *differential association*. His central hypothesis was that crime is not caused by personality or environment, but is the product of learning. It is learnt just as any other behaviour is learnt. From association with others, the potential delinquent or criminal learns definitions favourable to deviant behaviour. When these definitions exceed the frequency and intensity of definitions favourable to conformity, the chances of criminality are higher. The basic principles of differential association, first formulated in the 1930s, were subsequently detailed by Sutherland and Cressey (1970, pp. 77–9) as follows:

- Criminal behaviour is learned.
- Criminal behaviour is learned in interaction with other persons in a process of communication.
- The principal part of the learning of criminal behaviour occurs within intimate personal groups.
- When criminal behaviour is learned, the learning includes techniques of committing the crime and the specific direction of motives, rationalizations and attitudes conducive to crime.
- The specific direction of motives and drives is learned from definitions of the legal codes as favourable or unfavourable.
- A person becomes delinquent because of an excess of definitions favourable to violation of law over definitions unfavourable to violation of law.
- Differential associations may vary in frequency, duration, priority and intensity for each individual.
- The process of learning criminal behaviour by association with criminal and anti-criminal patterns involves all the mechanisms that are involved in any other learning.
- While criminal behaviour is an expression of general needs and values, it is not explained by those general needs and values since non-criminal behaviour is an expression of the same needs and values (for example, it is not the need for money that inspires crime, rather the learnt method that is used to acquire it).

A key to understanding Sutherland's theory lies in his argument that learning does not necessarily have to occur through association with criminals, but rather with people who may not consistently support, or adhere to, strict legal codes. However, the theory does not explain why some people associate with those who approve of law violation while others in similar circumstances do not. A problem remains too of defining exactly *what kinds* of association favour such violations. Nevertheless, there have been numerous subsequent observations that appear to confirm the centrality of learning crime via association. Rutter and Giller's (1983, p. 249) review of the relevant positivist research finds that most delinquent acts are committed in the company of other children; an individual's delinquency is strongly associated with parental and familial criminality; children living in high delinquency areas, or attending a high-delinquency school, are also likely to become delinquent themselves; and the probability of committing a specific delinquent act is statistically related to the prevalence of delinquency in one's peer group.

The Chicago School simultaneously developed two contradictory notions of crime causation. Individual behaviour was viewed as determined by social disorganization, but also as imbued with an element of freedom of action, particularly in the learning of patterns that were favourable to law violation. The two notions are theoretically incompatible (Taylor et al., 1973, p. 114). Above all, the normative learning of behaviours implies a level of social organization which the concept of *disorganization* tends to deny. Thus subsequent researchers, such as Matza (1964), abandoned the concept in favour of that of cultural *diversity* or *differential* social organization.

Nevertheless, the notion of a delinquent or criminal area remained influential in a number of British studies in the 1950s and 1960s. In particular, London, Birmingham and Liverpool (cities that seemed to replicate the turbulent and expanding Chicago of the 1920s) were subject to a similar environmental analysis in attempts to explain the relatively high incidence of recorded crime in inner-city working-class areas. For example, Terence Morris (1957) found that the areas of peak crime rates in Croydon were two of the inter-war council housing estates and two older residential areas noted for slum housing and physical deterioration. From this he argued two points:

1   The type of housing and the housing policies of local authorities were central in creating criminal areas.
2   The chances of becoming delinquent were related to the strength of delinquent influences in the local environment.

Further British area studies widened the focus to include the study of differential access to housing space, of policies concerning the allocation of publicly owned housing, and of the effects on people compelled to live in low-grade housing in 'rough' areas. The concepts of social *class* and differential access to *power* became central to understanding the continuing 'competitive struggle for space' (Rex and Moore, 1967; Damer, 1977; Gill, 1977).

The collaboration of some geographers and sociologists in the 1980s once more suggested that understandings of *space* and *place* should be included in any adequate theory of criminality. The problem faced by such an endeavour reflects the contradictions encountered by the Chicago studies. While it is clear that official crime rates are concentrated in particular areas, can it be unequivocally claimed that it is such places that create crime? Similarly, while the ethnographic study of criminal careers in specific localities has shed light on the importance of individual motivations and social interactions, this micro level of analysis often appeared blind to the effects of structural constraints. Nevertheless, new versions of spatial analysis (Brantingham and Brantingham, 1984; Bottoms and Wiles, 1992) have succeeded not only in substantiating that crime is spatially as well as socially defined, but that it is a natural and normal expression of social interaction given the organization of particular localized communities. It is how individuals recognize the role of space in their own biographies and how space mediates the relationship between individual and environment that creates different *opportunities* for crime. Interest in this area has also burgeoned in the UK as a result of New Labour's attempts to regenerate certain 'deprived' and 'high crime' neighbourhoods through a combination of 'empowerment funds' and 'strategic partnerships'. The aim is to reduce crime and stimulate local economic enterprise by not only improving the physical environment but also providing better access to health, education and housing resource. Such a policy tends to assume a direct link between crime and urban decline. Hancock's (2001) Merseyside study, found that, contrary to governmental claims of equitable partnerships, local regeneration initiatives rarely addressed local needs. Rather 'regeneration' was more designed to attract 'outsiders' (as consumers and as labour) than to expand local employment opportunities. When 'renewal' takes the form of developing a night time economy, for example, it may act to increase local fears and anxieties rather than secure their abatement. The relationship between urban regeneration and crime reduction is clearly complex. To fully understand the role of social and spatial divisions in generating crime, fear and perceptions of safety further detailed and intimate knowledge of specific community dynamics is required.

Anomie, Strain and Subcultures

The proposition that crime is a consequence of societies based on values of competitive individualism and structured by a high division of labour was first formulated by Durkheim at the turn of this century. He argued that a society without deviance is impossible because it is inconceivable that humans are so inflexible that none will diverge from a norm or ideal. Moreover some form of behaviour will always be liable to be defined as dissensual in order to reaffirm the conformity of a majority:

> Imagine a society of saints, a perfect cloister of exemplary individuals. Crimes, properly so called will there be unknown; but faults which appear venial to the layman will create there the same scandal that the ordinary offence does in ordinary consciousness. (Durkheim, 1895/1964, pp. 68–9)

Crime has a positive function in affirming the moral consciousness of society. It is also positive in challenging and effecting change in that consciousness:

> There is no occasion for self congratulation when the crime rate drops noticeably below the average level, for we may be certain that this apparent progress is associated with some social disorder. (Durkheim, 1895/1964, p. 72)

Thus crime is both an expression of individual freedom and a necessary and desirable precursor of social change. The rate at which individuals deviate from the norm is related to the degree of integration and cohesiveness by which society is governed at particular times. For example, the higher rate of suicides in times of economic crisis is explained by the lack of regulation in society at such times. Because society encourages individualism and unlimited aspirations, situations arise when such aspirations cannot be realistically achieved. Unless society imposes new regulations on aspirations, then a social state of anomie or normlessness will occur, resulting in personal crises and a higher tendency towards suicide:

> No living being can be happy or even exist unless his needs are sufficiently proportioned to his means. In other words if his needs require more than can be granted or even merely something of a different sort, they will be under continual friction and can only function painfully. (Durkheim, 1897/1952, p. 246)

In the 1930s Merton elaborated on this theme of unobtainable or unrealistic aspirations to apply the concept of anomie beyond suicide to all forms of deviance. Following Durkheim, Merton (1938) argued that socially produced aspirations could exceed what is obtainable through available opportunities. But whilst Durkheim claimed that anomie resulted from a failure to regulate behaviour, Merton proposed that such a condition was generated from *strains* in the social structure that actively encouraged individuals to develop unrealistic aspirations. Anomie was viewed as dependent on the degree of divergence between cultural goals – through which success and status in society are defined – and institutionalized means – the acceptable methods of achieving such goals. For Merton, the cultural goal of American society – the American Dream of open and infinite opportunity for all – had come to overemphasize the ambition of monetary and material gain. The ideal that anyone, regardless of class origin, ethnicity or religion, could achieve material wealth stood uneasily against the essentially closed opportunity structure by which American society was in reality constrained. Such a situation produces a structurally induced strain in which the cardinal American virtue of ambition ultimately promotes the cardinal American vice of deviant behaviour (Merton, 1957, p. 200). Because aspirations are encouraged to be endless, but in reality are blocked by what the social structure makes possible, large sections of the American population find that they cannot achieve their goals through conventional means. In this way intense pressure for deviation is produced.

Merton continued by analysing how such 'breakdowns in the cultural structure' are responded to by a series of *individual* adaptations. These are depicted not as individually perverse or destructive, but as reflections of the range of options available to people, given their position within the social structure. He identified five possible modes of adaptation – conformity, innovation, ritualism, retreatism and rebellion. About each he asks whether cultural goals and institutionalized means for their realization are accepted or rejected.

- *Conformity* describes the acceptance of goals and means, and is the most frequently used adaptation.
- *Innovation* occurs when the value of attaining goals is accepted and acted out irrespective of the impropriety, immorality or illegality of the chosen means. For example, for those groups situated in lower echelons of the social hierarchy, the problems of poverty and restricted opportunity may be 'solved' by innovative and deviant adaptations. This situation may explain the higher rate of property crime in poor areas. Merton points out that poverty does not cause crime, but when combined with acceptance of cultural goals, the possibility of criminal behaviour is increased.
- *Ritualism* is explained as typically lower middle class, as opposed to innovation which is seen as typically working class. In ritualism, aspirations are abandoned in favour of strict adherence to institutionalized means – 'the perspective of the frightened employee, the zealously conformist bureaucrat' (Merton, 1957, p. 150). Such modes of 'playing it safe' however remain deviant because of non-compliance with dominant cultural goals.
- *Retreatism* similarly involves a rejection of cultural goals, but here institutionalized means are also abandoned. Rather than coping with structural strains, the retreatist opts out altogether. Drug addicts, vagrants, alcoholics and psychotics are viewed as such highly individual deviants seeking their own rewards outside of the dominant value system.
- *Rebellion* involves not only a rejection of goals and means, but also the intention of altering the social structure from which such norms emanate. The non-conforming rebel challenges the status quo and attempts to institutionalize *new* goals and means for the rest of society.

In sum, Merton suggested that the very nature of American society generates crime and deviance. The more the cultural goal of material success is advocated, the more the power of institutionalized norms to regulate behaviour is diminished. Criminality becomes prevalent once certain modes of adaptation – particularly innovation – are practised successfully and observed by others. But for Merton such criminality is not simply deviant, because it is also generated by conformity to the widely accepted goal of pecuniary success.

The theory of anomie, as proposed by Durkheim and Merton, subsequently provided a platform for the development of *subcultural* theories of delinquent and criminal behaviour. Albert Cohen's (1955) research on delinquent boys and the subculture of the gang in Chicago, for example, accounted for their actions as lower-class adaptations to a dominant middle-class society which discriminated against them. However, Cohen noted that the Mertonian modes of adaptation to strain failed to account for the non-utilitarian, malicious and negative forms of their behaviour. Delinquents, he argued, usually steal items of minor value or are involved in acts of petty vandalism. How could this be explained within Merton's utilitarian framework in which all actions were viewed as a rational means to an end? Accordingly Cohen developed the notion of *status frustration* in preference to that of anomie. He viewed the gang as operating *collectively* within a different value system from that which, according to Merton, characterized the whole of American society. The development of specialized vocabulary, internal beliefs and innovative ways of dressing and acting, he argued, represented a total inversion of dominant values. Status frustration becomes visible in negative forms of behaviour whereby the dominant goals of ambition and achievement, deferred gratification and respect for property are rejected and reversed. By a process of *reaction formation*, dominant values are inverted to offer a collective solution to restricted opportunity in which 'the delinquent conduct is right by the standards of his subculture precisely because it is wrong by the norms of the larger culture' (Cohen, 1955, p. 28).

Similarly, Cloward and Ohlin (1961) explain working-class deviance as a collective, rather than an individual solution. In this version of strain theory, however, the problem for the delinquent is to achieve a high status position in terms of lower-class, rather than middle-class, criteria. By combining anomie and differential association theory, these authors were able to explain why one form of adaptation was preferred to another. The answer lay in the differential availability throughout the social structure of legitimate and illegitimate means to gain material and status success. Thus they argued that a *criminal subculture* develops mainly in lower-class neighbourhoods where the successful criminal is not only visible to young people, but is willing to associate with them. Although denied access to the conventional role models of people who have achieved success via legitimate means, these youths do have access to criminal success models. In more disorganized neighbourhoods access even to a criminal subculture is denied. In such situations a *conflict subculture* is more likely to arise in which the lack of legitimate and illegitimate opportunities for material success is solved by achieving status through fighting and violence.

Strain and subcultural theories have, in the main, been largely concerned to explain high rates of delinquency within the lower classes. They take the criminal law and statistical representations of offending rates as given. They propose that both the origins and development of juvenile delinquency are structurally determined, and as such also offer a *general* framework for understanding all crime by contending that the denial of legitimate opportunity acts as the major precipitative factor. In this regard they can be clearly located in a tradition of positivist and determinist modes of analysis. However, subsequent studies, based in particular on self reports, have found that most people from all social classes commit acts for which they could be adjudicated criminal or delinquent. Strain theory is thus said to be both class and gender biased. In ignoring both the ubiquity of crime, and its white collar variants, it conveys the impression that lawlessness is exclusively a lower-class and male phenomenon (Lilly et al., 1989, p. 76).

The degree to which behaviour is determined by structure and class position has also been questioned. Matza's (1964) research found that individual members of a gang were only partially committed to subcultural norms. Rather than forming a subculture which stands in antithesis to the dominant order, he argues, the delinquent 'drifts' in and out of deviant activity. This is made possible because there is no consensus in society – no set of basic and core values – but a plurality in which the conventional and the delinquent continually overlap and interrelate. Instead of viewing delinquent acts as a direct expression of delinquent norms and thus system determined, Matza was more concerned to illustrate how their diversity was dependent on particular individuals and situations. This line of enquiry was ultimately to provide a critique of all positivist modes of thought, not just its strain theory variant, in its insistence that *pluralism* rather than consensus and *interaction* rather than determinism provided more adequate means of studying social behaviour (see Chapter 4.1).

Nevertheless, traces of strain and anomie theory can be found in numerous subsequent American and British analyses. Adopting a Marxist perspective, Greenberg (1977), for example, argues that the high rate of property crime among youth in America is a response to the disjuncture of the desire to participate in the consumer society and being prevented from securing legitimate funds to enable such participation. From a labelling perspective, Cohen (1973a) writing of the mods and rockers in 1960s Britain, claims that in part they were driven by 'desperation' because of their exclusion from the leisure goals of mass teenage culture. In Lea and Young's (1984) left realist perspective, youth crime is viewed as a response to the 'relative deprivation', and 'perceptions of injustice' engendered when expectations are not met by real opportunities. In Agnew's (1992) 'revised' and social psychological strain theory it is stressed that when the theory is expanded to focus on all *negative relationships* which may generate anger, despair or resentment – that is, relationships in which individuals are not treated equitably or as they might wish to be – then it has the potential to explain a broad and diverse range of delinquencies from theft and aggression to drug use. Researching the experiences of youth homelessness and street crime in Canada, Hagan and McCarthy (1998) propose an integration of strain with a social capital theory of crime in order to explore how unemployed and disrupted families provide a limited 'social capital' for their children and how this subsequently impacts on their success or failure to reach cultural goals. So whilst the functionalist and essentialist nature of Mertonian strain theory has been widely criticized, the notion that crime may be generated by unequal and restricted opportunities continues to inform some radical and realist 'readings' of youth crime (see Chapter 4).

Assessment

Compared to individual positivism, sociological theories appear less interested in crime as a specific pattern of behaviour and more in *probabilistic* accounts of variations in crime rates given particular social, geographical and economic circumstances. They focus on general patterns of criminality rather than on individual motivations. Nevertheless, early versions of sociological criminology continued to harbour major positivist principles. The concern remained to isolate key causal variables, such as anomie, social disorganization and criminal area, and to infer that such conditions *determined* rates of criminality. Crime remained a violation of a social order that was considered to be based on a consensus of legal and moral codes. As Laurie Taylor (1971, p. 148) has remarked, 'it is as though individuals in society are playing a gigantic fruit machine, but the machine is rigged and only some players are consistently rewarded . . . nobody appears to ask who put the machine there in the first place and who takes the profits'. Little room was given to the contrary positions that crime may be a freely chosen course of action and that it may be due to *different* forms of socialization, rather than lack of socialization.

Many of the basic principles of positivism came to be questioned during the 1940s, particularly from within the 'appreciative' strand of the Chicago School. Positivism was criticized for:

- denying the role of human consciousness and meaning in social activity;
- presenting an overdetermined view of human action;
- assuming that there is an underlying consensus in society, of which crime is a key violation;
- ignoring the presence and relevance of competing value systems, cultural diversity or structural conflict;
- equating crime with *under*socialization or social *dis*organization rather than accepting the validity of different forms of social organization.

Such critiques suggested that non-positivist forms of analysis may offer more fruitful lines of enquiry. The relevance of space, place and economic constraints may remain acknowledged, but their relation to crime is not asserted as determining. Moreover, in such seminal works as Matza's *Delinquency and Drift* (1964), young people are not only (re)bestowed with a degree of free will, but positivism's search for motivational and socio-economic causes of crime is placed in doubt. The main questions of positivism – 'Who is deviant?' 'Why do they do it?' – ignore that crime is not only *action*, but also *infraction*. Actions only become 'crime' when they are defined as such by legal and other institutions.

Whilst positivism retains popular and political appeal in both its individual and sociological variants, it is by no means universally accepted. Some would argue that the use of the scientific method remains superior to conjecture or polemic, but such methodology carries no automatic guarantee of uncovering the 'truth'. Inaccurate assumptions, misinterpretations, misapplication of findings and inadequate measures for testing can all conspire to produce not only misleading but also dangerous conclusions. Assumptions are likely to be made about exactly which factors, from a myriad of the potentially relevant, are worthy of study. In this, the selection of particular variables will depend on *a priori* assumptions the scientist holds about the nature of human behaviour. There is also the potential misuse to which some theories can be put. As McCaghy points out:

> Since there are several possible theories concerning the fundamental nature of man, it should not be surprising that since the advent of positivism every human appendage has been measured, every emotion plumbed, every social influence probed and every bodily fluid scrutinized. As a further result of such theories, social environments have been engineered, parts of the brain removed, families counselled, organs lopped off and many sorts of chemicals injected into the human system. All this has been done in the apparently limitless search for answers to the question of why some ignore or disobey others' concepts of righteous behaviour. (McCaghy, 1976, p. 9)

Summary

- This chapter has reviewed a wide variety of criminological theory which has attempted to find the causes of youth crime in a range of biological, personality and environmental conditions. Despite their obvious differences, in the main they all share the basic assumption that criminality is a behavioural problem and that people are propelled into crime by circumstances over which they have no control. This is one of the defining characteristics of positivist criminology: that crime is *caused* either by individual 'pathologies' and/or by precipitative social and economic conditions.

- The chapter has not been designed to provide answers to the many issues and debates about what causes young people to commit crime, but to compare different theories and suggest ways in which they can be subject to critical enquiry. The simple desire to discover the 'facts' of youth crime causation is far from a straightforward exercise. This is partly because, even within positivism, there is no *one* criminology but a variety of competing positions. Table 3.3 provides a summary of some of the major theories and theorists which occupy this field. It is also partly because although positivism is capable of revealing *correlations* between offending and such factors as age, personality, peer groups, urban space and so on, it can never unequivocally state that any *one* factor is the chief causative agency.

Table 3.3   *Positivist theories of youth crime*

Theory	Explanation of crime	Key theorists
Somatotyping	Mesomorphic body type	Sheldon (1949)
Genetics	Heredity	Mednick, Gabriella and Hutchings (1987)
Bio-social	Multi-factor, including genetics, rational action, lack of discipline, personality, low IQ	Wilson and Herrnstein (1985) Farrington (1996)
Personality	Extroversion/psychopathology, affectionless character/psychosocial disorder	Bowlby (1946) Eysenck (1964/1970) Rutter and Smith (1995)
Anomie and strain	Disjunction between high aspirations and restricted opportunities/status frustration	Merton (1938, 1957) Cohen (1955) Cloward and Ohlin (1961)
Social ecology	Breakdown of urban communities	Shaw and McKay (1942)
Differential	Beyond positivism?: learnt through association, exposure to an excess of influences, favourable to violations of the law	Sutherland (1939)

- No one theory can, or should, be expected to be capable of accounting for all forms of youthful criminal conduct. The category of 'youth crime' covers a wide variety of behaviours and activities – from petty theft to violence – and in itself is subject to changing legal, moral and social definition. Indeed, most of the theories we have considered focus not on all forms of youth misbehaviour and legal transgression but on those that have come to the notice of official agencies and are recorded in the criminal statistics. Again this may have inadvertently led to some peculiar biases and narrow essentialist visions. Because such statistics consistently reveal strong correlations between offending and young, male and low-income sections of the population, it is to these groups that most academic research (and public outrage) is directed. In particular, positivism's largely uncritical use of official crime statistics has helped to cement the following propositions as universal criminological 'truths':

– Crime is committed disproportionately by males.
– Crime is committed disproportionately by 15–25 year olds.
– Crime is committed disproportionately by unmarried people.
– Crime is committed disproportionately by people living in large cities.
– Crime is committed disproportionately by people who have experienced high residential mobility and who live in areas characterized by high residential mobility.
– Young people who are strongly attached to their school are less likely to engage in crime.
– Young people who have high educational and occupational aspirations are less likely to engage in crime.
– Young people who perform poorly at school are more likely to engage in crime.
– Young people who are strongly attached to their parents are less likely to engage in crime.
– Young people who have friendships with criminals are more likely to engage in crime themselves.
– People who believe strongly in the importance of complying with the law are less likely to violate the law.
– Being at the bottom of the class structure increases rates of offending for all types of crime (apart from white-collar crime).
– Crime rates have been increasing in most countries since the Second World War. (From Braithwaite, 1989, pp. 44–50.)

• Whilst these associations undoubtedly have some validity (and many criminological theories have substantiated them or taken them for granted), they do allow statistical indices to set the research and policy agendas. In contrast, self report studies have revealed that not only is young offending more widespread, but that it is not simply the province of working-class urban males who have 'failed families' or who have 'failed' at school or who live in 'failing' neighbourhoods. Moreover, as will be discussed in Chapter 4, crime is not simply a behavioural problem. It is also a means of stigmatizing what is considered to be 'undesirable' and of legitimating the control of particular sections of the population while ignoring the legal, social and moral transgressions of those considered to be 'worthy citizens'. Nevertheless, as Sumner (1994, p. 137) eloquently concluded: 'a sizeable chunk of criminology today [still] remains locked in the emotional-conceptual-political prison within which Lombroso did a long sentence'.

Study Questions

1   How far is youth crime determined by constitutional factors such as physiology and genetics?
2   How far is youth crime determined by the 'pathological' conditions of adolescence?
3   How far is youth crime determined by social factors, such as 'strains' in the urban environment and economic deprivation?
4   Is youth crime normal or pathological?
5   How can it be maintained that 'young people are propelled into crime through circumstances beyond their control'?

Further Resources

For a thorough understanding of the divergences and disputes in positivist theories of youth crime (and in criminology in general), all of the authors cited in Table 3.3 deserve attention. In addition there are numerous overviews to be found in general criminology textbooks (such as Beirne and Messerschmidt, 1991) and in theoretical reviews (one of the most comprehensive and accessible being Einstadter and Henry, 1995). Both of these latter references are American. In Britain, numerous explorations of criminological theories have been published since the mid 1990s. For example, Tierney's *Criminology: Theory and Context* (1996) is an introductory text focusing on historical shifts and resonances; White and Haines' (2000) *Crime and Criminology* and Hopkins Burke's (2001) *Introduction to Criminological Theory* clearly illustrate theoretical diversity. Valier's *Theories of Crime and Punishment* (2002) is a critical and appreciative text which does more than most to explore the social and cultural contexts from which principal theories of crime – from the eighteenth century to the present – have emerged. All include specific chapters devoted to a critical examination of positivist knowledges. On youth and crime specifically, Rutter et al.'s (1998) *Anti Social Behaviour by Young People* (largely an update of Rutter and Giller, 1983) reviews numerous theories and indeed restricts itself to those that are largely positivist in nature. Rutter and Smith (1995) and Farrington (1996; 2002) are two contemporary exponents of positivist and predictive 'knowledges', whilst one of the best critiques remains that in Chapter 2 of Taylor et al.'s *The New Criminology* (1973).

4 Explaining Youth Crime II: Radical and Realist Criminologies

Overview

Chapter 4 examines:

- the emergence of radical criminologies in the 1960s and 1970s;
- theories that argue that crime is a social construction and is 'caused' by social control;
- the distinction between 'crime' and 'criminalization';
- the relevance of gender in constructions of youth crime;
- the appropriation of the crime debate by 'realist' criminologies in the 1980s and 1990s;
- problems inherent in any attempt to discover the 'cause' of youth crime.

Key Terms

classical Marxism	left realism
critical criminology	modernity
deviancy amplification	postmodernism
drift	racialization
ethnographic research	rational choice
hegemonic masculinity	relative deprivation
interactionism	right realism
labelling	underclass

This chapter explores how the 'positivist orthodoxy' discussed in Chapter 3 was subsequently challenged by a range of radical criminologies first emerging in the 1960s and reworked by realist criminologies which surfaced in the 1980s and 1990s.

The *radical* criminologies were marked by a deep scepticism of any theory that proposed that crime was 'caused' in a simple cause–effect fashion. Although adopting diverse research agendas from analyses of labelling and moral panics to structural conflict and gender issues, they were more concerned to explore processes of criminalization – how crime was 'created' through the power to define behaviour as illegal rather than by biological, personality or social defects.

The *realist* criminologies can be considered as products of the 1980s and 1990s and are epitomized by the attempts of some sections of the right to reintroduce notions of individual moral culpability into the 'crime debate' and by some sections of the left to reintroduce notions of social causation.

The chapter concludes by examining a number of key problems in any attempt to unearth the causes of youth crime. Most significantly, it asks why it is, after over one hundred years of academic endeavour, no one 'cause' is deemed irrefutable.

Why is it that we seem to be left with a never ending series of disputes and debates? Why does the 'youth crime problem' seem to lie beyond resolution?

Radical Criminologies

4.1 The term 'radical criminology' is used here as a convenient umbrella term under which a number of diverse theories (whose chief characteristic is one of anti-positivism) can be drawn together. This section examines how the perspectives of interactionism, labelling, Marxism, critical criminology and gender studies have shifted the object of enquiry away from explanations of why a pathological few transgress legal codes, towards an analysis that focuses more on the activities of competing interest groups and how processes of law creation and enforcement are implicated in the causation of the (young) criminal (see Table 4.1).

Table 4.1   *Characteristics of radical criminologies*

- Human action is voluntaristic (to different degrees), rather than determined (or in some formulations, voluntary in determining contexts).
- Social order is pluralistic or conflictual, rather than consensual.
- Economic policies lead to immizeration and force people to consider turning to crime as a viable survival strategy.
- Criminalization strategies are class, race and gender control strategies that are consciously used to depoliticize political resistance and to control economically and politically marginalized neighbourhoods and groups.
- Moral panics about crime being out of control are used to deflect attention away from inherent structural conflicts.
- Orthodox crime control strategies are incapable of tackling the crimes of the powerful and state crimes.
- Legal categories that claim to be gender neutral are riven with male assumptions of what constitutes normal or reasonable behaviour.

The first traces of such approaches were found in the 1930s within the *interactionist* school of sociology. In contrast to positivism, interactionism presents a view of the world which emphasizes the flexibility of individual responses to social situations. Rather than viewing behaviour as determined by 'external' forces, interactionism is more concerned with questions of human choice, voluntarism and the variability of meaning in everyday life. It owes much to a philosophy of 'subjective realism' and echoes the appreciative strand of the 1930s Chicago School of sociology (see Chapter 3.2). For example, George Herbert Mead (1934) argued that 'the self' is a social construct and that the way in which individuals act and regard themselves is in part a consequence of the way others see and react to them. The focus is thus shifted away from macro social structures and their determining effect, to the meso and micro personal interactions that make up social life. As human action is deemed voluntarist, it is forever changing and adapting to social conditions. In this conception of human nature it makes no sense to depict the social order as consensual. Rather, that order comprises a set of fluid relationships embracing conflict, domination, exploitation and disagreement, as well as co-operation and consensus.

Neither does it make much sense to argue that criminality is *caused*. If criminals were as different from the law-abiding as positivists assumed, then individual criminality would be a more permanent and all-pervasive phenomenon. In *Delinquency and Drift*, Matza (1964) argues forcefully that delinquency is transient and intermittent. Juvenile delinquents are not that different from other juveniles. This is because, rather than being at polar extremes, conformist values and non-conformist values often intersect and propagate similar desires, such as for hedonism, fun and excitement. The delinquent is committed neither to the mainstream nor to a delinquent culture, but *chooses to drift* between one or the another 'in a limbo between convention and crime responding in turn to the demands of each, flirting now with one, now with the other, but postponing commitment, evading decision' (Matza, 1964, p. 28). Moreover delinquents are able to move freely between delinquency and conformity, by adopting various rationalizations to justify their behaviour. According to Sykes and Matza (1957), these techniques of *neutralization* include:

- denial of responsibility (I didn't mean it);
- denial of injury (I didn't really cause any harm);
- denial of victim (he deserved it);
- condemnation of condemners (they always pick on us);
- appeal to higher loyalties (you've got to help your mates).

In these ways positivism's rigid separation of the criminal and non-criminal and its insistence that criminality is not chosen but determined by external pressures, is called into question. Matza argues that most delinquents 'grow out of' crime precisely because they are never seriously committed to it in the first place.

Interactionism was also a crucial reference point for a *pluralist* conception of crime and deviance. Deviance could no longer be viewed simply as a pathological act that violated consensual norms, but was something created in the *process* of social interaction, in which some people who commit deviant acts come to be known as deviants whereas others do not. Tannenbaum (1938, p. 19), for example, argued that 'the process of making the criminal is a process of tagging, defining, identifying, segregating, describing, emphasizing, making conscious and self conscious; it becomes a way of stimulating, suggesting and evoking the very traits that are complained of. The person becomes the thing he is described as being.'

In short, interactionism opened up a new line of critical enquiry by posing definitional rather than behavioural questions – 'Who defines another as deviant?'; 'How does that person react to such designation?' In addressing such questions, it was necessary not only to begin to study how rules/laws were created, but also to ask in whose interests they were enforced. Thus the subject matter of criminology was considerably expanded to incorporate theories of power, social order and the state and processes of social control and resistance. The meaning of 'crime' itself became politicized.

Labelling and Moral Panics

The labelling perspective is distinctive because it begins from the assumption that no act is intrinsically criminal. What counts as crime and deviance is forever problematic because deviance only arises from the imposition of social judgements on others' behaviour. Such judgements are established by the powerful through the formulation of laws and their interpretation and enforcement by police, courts and other controlling institutions. But these formulations and interpretations are by no means constant: they change according to historical contingencies and individual discretion. Thus exactly what constitutes 'crime' and 'deviance' is subject to historical and social variability. Neither can be 'objectively' defined because their existence always depends on a series of negotiated transactions between rule makers/enforcers and rule violators.

As Becker (1963) argued, behaviour may be labelled criminal, but it is not this behaviour in itself that constitutes crime. Behaviour is *criminalized* by processes of social perception and reaction as applied and interpreted by agents of the law. Crime exists only when the label and the law are successfully applied. Labelling logically contends that without the enforcement and enactment of criminal law there would be no crime. Ditton (1979, p. 20) is thus able to argue that 'the reaction is constitutive of the criminal (or deviant) act. In fact the reaction *is* the "commission of the act".' It is implied that we will never discover youth crime simply by looking at youthful behaviour for there is nothing intrinsic to any behaviour which automatically makes it 'criminal'.

The twin concepts of 'label' and 'career' are central to labelling in explaining how deviance is first constructed and subsequently cemented in future behaviour. Lemert (1967) distinguished between primary deviance – isolated, relatively insignificant rule breaking (e.g. petty theft, classroom misbehaviour) – and secondary deviance – the construction of a deviant identity as a result of social reaction to the initial act. In making this distinction, Lemert emphasizes first that deviance is a process, and second that social control is not simply a response to deviant activity, but plays an active and propelling role in the creation and promotion of deviance. This proposition that *social control causes deviance* effectively stood the premises of positivist criminologies on their head. Labelling also raised a number of questions about how the labelled react to their newfound status and change their lifestyle to accord with their new identity. A number of studies were published in the 1960s and 1970s which attempted to reveal the process of *becoming* a marijuana smoker, a juvenile delinquent, a prostitute, a homosexual and so on. In each, it is the application of a stigmatizing label that is considered pivotal in informing future behaviour patterns. Lemert (1951), for example, argued that whilst most youths commit some delinquent acts, only a few are eventually labelled as delinquent. Official reactions (condemnation, treatment, punishment) to this few do not deter or reform but initiate processes that push the labelled delinquent towards further delinquent conduct. If there is no official reaction, delinquent behaviour may dissipate or at least will not accelerate, because the notion of a delinquent 'career' will not be established.

The implications of attaching a particular label to certain behaviours are evident in Cohen's (1968, 1973c) analyses of 'vandalism'. Vandalism is not a legal category but a label attached to certain incidents of property damage, defacement or destruction. Conjuring up images of 'barbarity', 'ignorance' and 'ruthlessness', it is differentially applied; denying 'meaning' to certain actions whilst turning a blind eye to others. As Cohen (1968, p. 17) remarked:

> painting 'Fink College is the Best' on a wall is not vandalism, painting 'Stop Making Bombs' is. Destroying property during rags is 'youthful exuberance' and after all 'for a good cause', but destroying property during a political demonstration is 'thoughtless hooliganism'.

By categorizing 'vandalism' into five main types – acquisitive, tactical, vindictive, play and malicious – Cohen (1973c) provides meaning and sense for behaviours that are commonly condemned as 'meaningless' or 'senseless':

- *Acquisitive vandalism*, Cohen argues, is in some respects akin to petty theft. Damage is done in the course of acquiring money or property such as stripping lead, removing street signs and looting coin boxes.
- *Tactical vandalism* is a conscious tactic used to advance some end other than acquiring money or property through the use of slogans and graffiti of a political nature.
- *Vindictive vandalism* is a form of revenge against persons or institutions believed to be the source of personal grievance. Cohen argues that much school vandalism is of this type.
- *Play vandalism* is motivated by curiosity and the spirit of competition and skill. The fact that property may be destroyed is often minor or incidental.
- *Malicious vandalism* is the category that most closely corresponds to dominant media and public images of apparently mindless and wanton destruction. But Cohen contends that such actions can also be explained by reference to a variety of subjective feelings – boredom, despair, failure and frustration – and that they can be rendered intelligible through understanding the context in which they occur.

Pearson (1975) also usefully directs our attention to another form of 'vandalism' – that indirectly performed by planners and architects. Following observations in a Cardiff park, he noted how juvenile vandalism became more frequent when the park was closed and rescheduled for office development. As he rightly questioned: 'Just who are the vandals in the park?'

Such critical readings of media labels in the 1960s and 1970s not only granted 'meaning' to criminality and thus 'humanized' the deviant (Muncie and Fitzgerald, 1981), but enabled alternative definitions of crime to be promoted. For example, as environmental protection groups have increasingly asked: which is the more serious, dumping toxic waste in the sea or breaking windows in derelict factories? And why is one routinely labelled as 'vandalism', whilst the other is not?

Above all, the labelling perspective denies that criminality is driven by any peculiar motivation or that criminals are a species apart. Rather crime is ordinary, natural and widespread and requires no more special an explanation for any everyday activity. What needs explanation is the complex process by which moral entrepreneurs and agencies of social control are able to realize the public identification of certain people as criminal; how social reaction and labelling can produce and reproduce a recognizable criminal population. One of the characteristic ways in which the non-conformity of some sections of society is 'demonized' is through the generation of 'moral panics' and perceptions of 'crime waves'.

The first systematic empirical study of a moral panic in Britain was Stan Cohen's research on the social reaction to the 'mods and rockers' disturbance of 1964 (Cohen, 1973a and see Chapter 5.2). Groups of working-class youths arrived in the seaside resort of Clacton over the Easter bank holiday, Clacton being the traditional meeting place for holidaying youths from the East End of London. Easter 1964 was cold and wet and the facilities and amusements for young people were strictly limited. Shopkeepers were irritated by the lack of business, and the young people's boredom was fanned by rumours of café owners refusing to serve some of them. Eventually scuffles between groups of youths broke out, windows were broken, beach huts vandalized, and those on scooters and bikes rode up and down the promenade. Such 'rowdyism' was by no means new (Pearson, 1983; and see Chapter 2) but it was to receive front-page outrage in the national press. The media spoke of a 'day of terror'; of youngsters who 'beat up an entire town'; of a town being invaded by a mob 'hell-bent on destruction'. Youths were presented as being engaged in a confrontation between easily recognizable rival gangs – 'mods' or 'rockers'. They were described as affluent young people from all social classes who deliberately caused trouble by acting aggressively towards local residents and in the process destroying a great deal of public property.

Cohen's research, on the other hand, found no evidence of any structured gangs. He argued that the groups were not even at the time polarized within a mod–rocker distinction. Rivalries were more likely to have been built around regional identities. Most young people did not identify with either group. Motorbike or scooter owners were in a minority. The young were not particularly affluent – in the main being unskilled or semi-skilled manual workers. Above all, Cohen argues, the total amount of serious violence and vandalism was not great. The typical offence throughout was not assault or malicious damage, but threatening behaviour. A few days after the event a journalist was forced to admit that the affair had been 'a little over-reported'.

By then, though, the media outrage had set in train a series of interrelated responses. First, it initiated a wider public concern which obliged the police to step up their surveillance of the two groups. The result was more frequent arrests, which appeared to confirm the validity of the initial media reaction. Second, an emphasis on the antagonism between the groups, and their stylistic differences, encouraged the youths to place themselves in one or other of the opposing camps. This polarization cemented the original image and produced more clashes on subsequent bank holidays. Third, the continuing disturbances attracted more news coverage, increased police activity and further public concern. As such a *deviancy amplification spiral* was set in motion (Wilkins, 1964). The media's distortion of the initial events in 1964 resulted in an amplification of youthful deviance both in perceived and in real terms. Youths began to identify with the label attached to themselves and thus believed themselves to be more deviant and separate from the rest of society. They had been singled out as society's 'folk devils' and acted out that role accordingly in subsequent years.

The moral panic thesis not only identifies instances of media exaggeration and distortion, but maintains that such selective reporting can actually *create* crime waves and social problems. The media can stir up public indignation and engineer concern about certain types of behaviour even when there is nothing new about that behaviour or when its real threat is minimal. Young (1974) goes further and argues that there is an institutionalized need in the media to create moral panics in order to make 'good copy' (see Chapter 1.1).

Having established the processes through which the agencies of social reaction – in the form of the media, police and the judiciary – are implicated in the creation of a social problem, Cohen addressed himself to the question of why this process should have occurred at all in the 1960s. He argued that we need to examine such responses in the context of wider developments in society at the time. The mid 1960s was the time of a supposedly new permissiveness, the beginnings of 'Swinging London', a rise in working-class youth spending power, the onslaught of a new consumerism, and the decline of traditional working-class communities. It was, above all, a time of rapid social change. For Cohen the ensuing public anxiety, uncertainty and anomie were resolved by identifying certain social groups as scapegoats or folk devils. They became the visual symbols of what was wrong with society. But in the meantime the more intractable and structural problems to do with relative deprivation and a continuing restricted opportunity structure were overlooked and passed by.

During the 1970s youth was to play a central part in this diversionary process. In *Policing the Crisis*, Hall et al. (1978) reused the concept of moral panic in identifying a series of such panics to do with permissiveness, vandals, student radicals, football hooligans and so on, culminating in 1972–3 with the moral panic of 'mugging'. Hall et al. show how the news media, working with images from the New York ghetto, defined the incidence of street robberies by youth in Britain's inner cities as an outbreak of a new and dangerous kind of violent crime. What was previously known as 'snatching' or 'getting rolled' – or in the nineteenth century as 'garrotting' – was now defined as 'mugging'. Hall et al. trace the way this definition was employed to justify not only a new category of crime, but also punitive sentencing and an image of a generalized breakdown of law and order in society. Also, as the panic developed, mugging became defined almost exclusively as a problem with black youth – they became the primary folk devils.

As Cohen had previously concluded, Hall et al. also noted how such problems were publicly defined as lawlessness, rather than the results of social deprivation or class and racial inequality. The notion of moral panic was central to both studies in explaining how particular sections of youth (working-class/black) become identified as worthy of police and judicial attention. The implication of such identification was, however, extended by Hall et al. For them a moral panic is the first link in a spiral of events leading to the maintenance of law in society by legitimized rule through coercion and the general exercise of authority. The sudden defining of the historically recurring event of street crime as a mugging creates the impression of a crime wave and provides government with the legitimacy to institute repressive legislation which ultimately affects the quality of life of all members of society. For example, as was evident by the late 1970s, the enunciation of authoritarian policies, if repeated often enough, is able to form the terrain of any debate concerned with issues of law and order. As Hall succinctly commented with regard to football hooliganism: 'the tendency is increased to deal with any problem, first by simplifying its causes, second by stigmatizing those involved, third by whipping up public feeling and fourth by stamping hard on it from above' (Hall, 1978, p. 34) (see Figure 4.1).

Figure 4.1   *Moral panics and authoritarianism (Muncie, 1987, p. 44)*

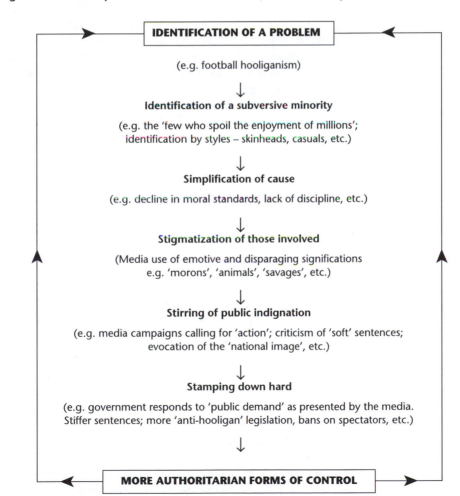

Subsequently the concept of 'moral panic' has been critiqued for a lack of any precise theoretical grounding (Plummer, 1979); for being a polemical rather than an analytical concept (Waddington, 1986); and for simplifying complex processes of media representation, public perception and pressure group contestation (McRobbie, 1994). By the mid 1980s its theoretical integrity was to be seriously questioned. By then the term had become widely used by the media as a means through which daily events could be sensationalized. It became part of a normalized rhetoric rather than an exceptional intervention. McRobbie and Thornton (1995) are persuasive in their argument that moral panic, rather than being an unwanted label designed to denigrate youth cultural pursuits, has become something to be actively pursued by youth themselves. The global domination of rave in the 1980s, for example, was in part dependent on its marketing as a 'dangerous' subcultural activity by the consumer industries. The growing prevalence of niche media, lobbies, pressure groups and commercial interests has made it virtually impossible to talk of discrete moral panics (or discrete youth cultures), but more an 'endless debate' about deviance, difference and personal identity (see Chapter 5). Moral panics do now appear as continually contested, rather than as accepted proof of moral malaise. Nevertheless the continual (re)surfacing of moral panics directed at certain behaviours or groups – hooligans, teenage mothers, drug users and so on – can still tell us something of significance about the nature of social order. As Goode and Ben-Yehuda (1994, p. 52) have argued:

> it is entirely likely that moral panics serve as a mechanism for simultaneously strengthening and redrawing society's moral boundaries – that line between morality and immorality, just where one leaves the territory of good and enters that of evil. When a society's moral boundaries are sharp, clear and secure and the central norms and values are strongly held by nearly everyone, moral panics rarely grip its members – nor do they need to. However, when the moral boundaries are fuzzy and shifting and often seem to be contested, moral panics are far more likely to seize the members of a society.

Classical Marxism, Critical Criminology and Processes of Criminalization

Although it can be said that labelling retains a logic – there can be no crime without legal sanction – a number of authors have argued that it remains limited if employed without any analysis of the social and political structures in which such labels are constructed and upheld. Being born out of the relatively vague pluralist notions of value diversity and cultural diversity, labelling fails to explain why some behaviour patterns have been defined in a historical and political context as deviant, while others have not. Is deviance merely born out of a relatively unstructured heterogeneity and diversity, or are certain classes and groups in society consistently afforded the power to assert their definitions as the only 'correct' ones? A key question – whose law and whose order is being protected? – was notably overlooked by the labelling perspective.

Labelling clearly opened up the area of analysis of how deviance was defined and processed by the defining agencies, and how conformity to social rules and norms was secured. However, these relations are not simply subjective encounters, but social processes set in objective historical conditions. Control agencies have an institutional location and function within a particular structure of power. To apply the insights of labelling to concrete situations, it was necessary to consider the issue of social control within a broader analysis of social structure or the state. It was necessary to explore how the abstract notion of social control connected to the maintenance of social order in particular types of social formation (see Chapter 6.1). Such analysis required a general model of society and the state to which crime and deviance could be related. In this context the insights of Marxist analyses of crime and the law in capitalist societies have been drawn upon (Marx, 1859, 1865; Marx and Engels, 1848).

One of the core elements of classical Marxism is that all social phenomena are explainable in terms of each society's means of production or economic relations. In a capitalist economy the private ownership of the means of production and control over the exchange of wealth creates both structural inequality and structural conflict. In this respect classical Marxism clearly challenges positivist conceptions of the social order as consensual. However, it also retains a view of human action as grounded in degrees of determinism. The exploitation of the proletariat by the bourgeoisie is viewed as endemic to such societies. From this perspective deviance can be seen as an expression of a struggle in which the economically powerless attempt to cope with the exploitation and poverty imposed upon them. While Marx wrote little on crime *per se*, a number of influential propositions have been derived from his general analysis. First, that crime is not caused by moral or biological defects, but by fundamental conflicts in the social order. Second, that crime is an inevitable feature of existing capitalist societies because it is an expression of basic social inequalities. Third, that working-class crime results from the demoralization caused by labour exploitation, material misery and the appalling conditions at home and in the factories. Fourth, that in certain respects such crimes as theft, arson and sabotage may be considered a form of primitive rebellion – a protest or rebellion against bourgeois forms of property ownership and control. Finally, Marx stressed that the extent and forms of crime could only be understood in the context of specific class relations and the nature of the state and law associated with particular modes of production.

The Dutch academic, Bonger (1916), was the first systematically to apply a theory of social order based on the notion of structural conflict to the topic of crime. His argument is encapsulated in the following propositions:

- Notions of immorality and criminality are socially and historically variable.
- The criminal law exists to protect the interests of the powerful.
- Capitalism is held together by coercive exploitation rather than co-operative consensus.
- Capitalism encourages egoism and greed. In the pursuit of such 'pleasures' both proletariat and bourgeoisie become prone to crime as their sense of responsibility towards each other is diminished.
- Poverty prompts crime to the extent that it creates a desperate need for food and other necessities.

- Crime also results when there is a perceived opportunity to gain an advantage through illegal means and/or when opportunities to achieve pleasure are closed off by a biased legal system.

For Bonger the competitive and individualist tendencies of capitalism actively encourage an unbridled egoism in which acts of criminality are likely to flourish. Significantly, he recognized that crime was not confined to the working classes. The bourgeoisie was also criminogenic because of the opportunities for crime that accompanied their power and because of a lack of morality within capitalist modes of production. The higher rate of recorded criminality in the working classes was viewed as a product of inequitable economic relationships in a context of general poverty.

It was not until some 60 years later that subsequent researchers (e.g. Quinney, 1970; Chambliss, 1975) developed the notion that the mode of economic production impacts on the types of social relations (including crime) experienced in society, by formulating such premises as the following:

- Acts are defined as criminal because it is in the interest of the ruling class to define them as such.
- The ruling class will violate laws with impunity while members of the subject classes will be punished.
- Criminal behaviour is a consequence of the repression and brutalization of capitalism.
- Crime diverts the working class's attention from the exploitation they experience; it contains their resistance.
- Crime will persist in capitalist societies because of the fundamental tendency of such societies to promote inequality and class conflict.

The proposition that patterns of crime are intimately connected to modes of economic production has been taken up in a number of ways. For example, Spitzer (1975) argued that deviants and criminals are 'constructed' when certain groups create problems for those who rule. In other words, those who call into question the social conditions under which capitalist production takes place (for instance, the bohemian or New Age traveller who refuses to perform routine wage labour) or those who fail to comply with processes of socialization for production roles (e.g. those who refuse to be schooled) or those who adopt deviant patterns of consumption (e.g. those who use drugs for escape) are likely to find themselves criminalized.

Greenberg (1977) 'appropriates Marxian theory for criminology' by identifying a number of *structural* sources of youth crime. The most significant of these are exclusion from work, extended schooling, dependence on peers for approval, and obstacles to the acquisition of legitimate sources of funds. In consumerist societies, young people face considerable pressure to turn to illegitimate means to finance their increasingly important leisure activities. Youth property crimes serve as an alternative to work. Similarly, interpersonal violence, committed largely by males, is viewed as symptomatic of masculine status anxiety. Exclusion from the labour market, inability to achieve traditional cultural expectations, and structural constraints on status attainment imposed by the economic and political order all combine to generate male criminality.

In these ways, classical Marxism has been developed to promote a more complex analysis of why certain behaviours are criminalized by the state while others are not, and how a capitalist economic system itself is capable of generating certain patterns of crime (Beirne and Messerschmidt, 1991, p. 498). For example, in Britain, Taylor et al., writing under the auspices of *The New Criminology* (1973), attempted to fuse such Marxist principles with the insights gained from interactionism and labelling. They sought to synthesize an interactional approach to deviance, focusing on its meaning for the individuals involved, with a structural approach grounded in the analysis of political economy, class relations and state practices. Taylor et al. (1973, pp. 270–8) argued that, above all, a 'fully social theory of deviance' must include the connections between:

- *the wider origins of the deviant act* (the economic and political contingencies of advanced industrial society);
- *the immediate origins of the deviant act* (the interpretation and meaning given to deviance by individuals);
- *the actual act* (the rationality of individual acts and the social dynamics surrounding them);
- *the immediate origins of social reaction* (the contingencies and conditions crucial to the decision to act against the deviant);
- *the wider origins of deviant reaction* (the political and ideological concerns of the state);
- *the outcome of social reaction on the deviant's further action* (the conscious decisions made by an individual to respond to sanctions);
- *the nature of the deviant process as a whole* (the necessity to integrate all elements of the deviant process while being alive to the conditions of social determination and self-determination).

However, *The New Criminology* was not only an attempt to develop the parameters of an adequate criminological theory; it was also designed to promote a form of radical politics. Its insistence that inequalities and divisions in material production and ownership are intrinsically related to the social factors producing crime, brought notions of the possibility of a crime-free society to the fore: a society based on principles of socialist diversity and tolerance. The intention, then, was also to construct the parameters of a radical praxis.

This politicization of criminology was indeed a logical extension of the critical questioning of social science and its role in research, teaching and policy making that had emerged in the 1960s. Becker (1967) brought such questioning directly into criminology and the sociology of deviance by asking social scientists: 'Whose side are you on?' Social science in general, and individual positivism in particular, were charged with lending the state a spurious legitimacy and functioning as little more than a justification for oppressive power. What such a critique managed to achieve was a radical reconstitution of criminology as part of a more comprehensive sociology of the state and political economy, in which questions of political and social control took precedence over behavioural and correctional issues. By the mid 1970s such reflections on the construction of crime became pivotal in the formulation of a *critical criminology* (Taylor et al., 1975; Hall and Scraton, 1981).

For example, Howard Parker's (1974) classic ethnographic research on juvenile theft in an inner-city area of Liverpool adopts a theoretical framework that attempts to capture a dialogue between micro and macro structural variables. In his *View from the Boys*, Parker records how he spent three years 'hanging out' with the lads of 'Roundhouse'. According to the official crime statistics, 'Roundhouse' was the most 'delinquent' area of Liverpool. However, Parker found that delinquency was neither a core part of the 'Boys' activities, nor the aspect of their behaviour which cemented the group together. Rather they were a loose-knit peer group who had experienced the problems associated with having few educational qualifications in a high unemployment area. Collectively they had turned to a highly instrumental form of delinquency – stealing 'catseyes' (car radios) as a solution to their lack of money. Such theft was important mainly because it provided the resources with which the boys could participate in and enjoy leisure. 'Roundhouse' was in general a 'condoning community' towards most kinds of delinquency. Thus theft was regarded as acceptable, if it was from people outside of the local area. The Boys only 'became delinquent' in the eyes of outsiders, social workers, the police and the courts – the 'Authority Conspiracy'. Accordingly the Boys' commitment to the dominant social order was ambiguous. Moral restraint tended to be community bound, extending beyond only in relation to their fear of authority. Parker concluded that the Boys' involvement in theft was not the 'real problem' at all. Rather these were accommodative and rational solutions arrived at by some working-class youth faced with the constraints of a particular social and economic context.

In a similar vein, Ian Taylor (1971) attempted to account for the rise of football hooliganism in the 1960s, not as the mindless activity of some pathological individuals, but as a rational reaction to changes in the game itself. Noting that hooliganism is often transient and incidental (cf. Matza's (1964) notion of 'drift'), he argued that it is explicable as a reaction to an increasing 'bourgeoisification' and 'internationalization' of football by which traditional elements of working-class support and control have been consistently undermined. Historically the game 'belongs' to that class in terms of social composition and organization of local teams and supporters. The rank and file supporters of the 1930s could see themselves as part of a collective and democratically structured organization united through the primary values of masculinity and collective participation which were derived from their experiences of the labour process. However, during the post-war years, soccer's identification with working-class culture was undermined by such transformations as the construction of grounds as commercial 'stadia', the elevation of certain players to media stars, the increasing hold of the petit bourgeoisie over directorships, and the incorporation of soccer into the range of respectable national sports. With the development of international competitions, still further separation was engendered between local culture and the club. This resulted in an uneasy coexistence between the club and the traditional working-class supporter. The latter's 'drift' into hooliganism, Taylor argued, is an elementary form of protest and resistance to clubs he once helped to create and which now ignore or reject his contribution.

However, the clearest example of how 'critical criminology' could be applied to youth crime in a specific historical period was Hall et al.'s (1978) analysis of mugging and the crisis of hegemony in the British state in the 1970s. As we have seen, their work began with an analysis of the mugging scare in Britain in 1972 and examined its US social history but eventually went behind the label to reveal how the state used concerns about law and order to divert public concern from economic and political crises. Above all, Hall et al. made clear how crime can be defined differently at particular historical moments. This has little to do with actual events, but reveals how the state uses 'crime' to prepare the ground for a general exercise of legal constraint and political control. Condemning crime as a product of 1960s permissiveness, the British state was able to construct public unease about historically recurring street crimes – now labelled as muggings – into popular mobilization of fear and anxiety which were drawn upon to legitimize the construction of an 'exceptional' form of 'authoritarian state'. In an increasingly divided society, the 'young black mugger' became one of the few symbolic sources of unity. The state, faced by a crisis of hegemony brought on by Britain's post-colonial economic decline and reflected in industrial disputes, attempted to regain its legitimacy by defining the crisis as one of lack of respect for the rule of law. The crisis was deflected on to youth, crime and particularly 'race'. The crime debate not only became politicized, but was also significantly racialized: a specific section of society was construed as a 'type' by referring to a limited number of their physical or cultural attributes (Solomos, 1988).

Critical criminology also made significant contributions to understanding aspects of youth crime through its impact on youth subcultural and social history research. In particular it reasserted the centrality of class analysis and modes of resistance in the study of youth subcultures (see Chapter 5). In its insistence that crime can only be analysed within its precise socio-historical setting, it also encouraged numerous revisionist histories of how the 'youth crime problem' is socially constructed in particular historical periods (see Chapter 2). Critical criminology, in myriad forms, continues to flourish. Its opposition to those cultures of control, scientism, patriarchy, positivism and correctionalism associated with orthodox criminology remains vital in understanding and challenging how power is determined, knowledge legitimated and social order maintained (Carrington and Hogg, 2002).

Feminist Perspectives and Gender Studies

The vast majority of criminological theories – positivist and radical – have traditionally focused on *male* offenders, *male* juvenile delinquents and *male* prison populations. The issues of gender and crime and women and crime remained absent from much criminological discourse until the 1970s. Female deviance was largely perceived as relatively insignificant, given women's under-representation in the official crime statistics. If explained at all, it was with reference to biological difference. Male deviance was accounted for with reference to a host of individual, social and economic factors but very rarely with reference to men's gendered position (see Chapter 1.3).

A critical feminist criminology (Klein, 1973; Smart, 1976; Leonard, 1982) first took the form of a critique of the *neglect* and *distortion* of women's experiences that characterized the criminological enterprise. It was noted how such concepts as anomie, strain and subculture had only been applied to male populations. But the exposure of criminology as the criminology of men also marked the starting point of feminist attempts to find alternative ways of conceptualizing the social world. As Leonard (1982, p. 11) asked: 'Why is crime so rampant among men . . .? What does this imply about the traditional role of men or about our society?'

First, *liberal feminists* (Oakley, 1972) noted how *role theory* may be used to explain differential rates of criminality. Here it is argued that women are socialized to different roles and are subject to more forms of social control than men. The protection and supervision of women and their training to be non-aggressive, dependent and restrained highlight the way in which females are purportedly less predisposed to delinquency. Such an approach challenged traditional notions of sex roles as 'natural' and revealed how gender differences are socially constructed. It also revealed how criminality and masculinity may be linked because the sorts of acts associated with each (aggression, status achievement) have much in common. As Oakley (1972, p. 72) concluded, 'the dividing line between what is masculine and what is criminal may at times be a thin one'.

Second, *radical feminists* (Millett, 1970) argued that crime is intimately related to structures of masculine power and privilege. Patriarchal societies are based on sets of social relationships through which men maintain power over children and women. The power attributed to men is realized in sexual violence and is often condoned by the state. Thus rape, domestic violence and sexual harassment are not so much a problem of male deviance as a problem of dominant notions of acceptable *masculinity*. In short, much criminality (and the subjugation of women) can be accounted for as a problem of patriarchal society which encourages aggression for men and passivity for women.

Third, *socialist feminism* (Rowbotham, 1973) combined insights from Marxist analyses of class and capitalism, and radical feminists' analysis of patriarchy to produce accounts that prioritized neither class nor gender. It is the *interaction* of these relations that structures crime in any given society at any given time. Criminality is the product of the unequal distribution of power in both the market and the home.

These three perspectives have decisively demonstrated that not only has criminology traditionally ignored female crime, but that the issue of gender and crime can be approached in a variety of ways. Whilst liberal feminism emphasizes gender role socialization, it has been criticized for lacking a structural explanation of the origin of those roles (Smart, 1976, p. 69). Neither does it explain why a considerable number of women do commit crime, if their socialization into conformity is as effective as assumed. Similarly, the assumption within radical feminism that all women are universally subjugated to male power within the monolith of patriarchy has been critiqued for its essentialism and reductionism. It imputes a single and unitary male personality (Messerschmidt, 1993). In contrast, socialist feminism has come under attack for simply grafting 'gender' on to an uncritical reading of Marxism, for failing to recognize the structuring context of 'race' and for propagating a determinist analysis from which notions of human action or intent remain absent (Carlen, 1992).

Such points of dispute within feminism and between feminism and criminology have led some writers to adopt an explicitly 'anti-criminological' position. Brown (1986), for example, argues that feminists working within criminology have by necessity uncritically adopted some of its key referents such as 'crime' and 'deviance' and that this has often led to 'unwanted consequences and obstacles to thinking and empirical analysis'. She maintains that awareness of feminist issues or the recording of discriminatory practices do not in themselves amount to a 'feminist analytical project'. Above all, 'in its wish to restore women to their place in criminology or to demonstrate their exclusion from it, feminist criminology has failed to be sufficiently critical of the discipline itself' (Brown, 1986, pp. 366–7). Acceptance of its empirical referents has meant that it has remained 'trapped in essentialist categories obstructing the production of new knowledge' (Carlen, 1992, p. 53). Smart (1990, p. 70) similarly states that 'the core enterprise of criminology is problematic, that feminists' attempts to alter criminology have only succeeded in revitalizing a problematic enterprise'. In this view the problem of criminology, in whatever form, is that by definition it always returns to notions of 'crime' and will be forever drawn to 'scientific' analyses and solutions:

> The thing that criminology cannot do is deconstruct crime. It cannot locate rape or child sexual abuse in the domain of sexuality, or theft in the domain of economic activity, or drug use in the domain of health. To do so would be to abandon criminology to sociology; but more importantly it would involve abandoning the idea of a unified problem which requires a unified response. (Smart, 1990, p. 77)

For Smart, the alliance of feminism and criminology is likely to be more damaging for the former, and beneficial only to the latter. Since the 1970s feminism has developed into a broadly based scholarship and political practice addressing questions of philosophy, representations and political engagement. It no longer needs to work through, or be attached to, more restrictive disciplines, such as criminology. Equally, Cain (1989, 1990) notes how feminist criminologists have been increasingly forced to 'transgress criminology, to break out of it'. In order to accomplish this, Cain (1990) advocates three strategies of *reflexivity*, *deconstruction* and *re-construction*. This involves a distancing from dominant and limiting discourses, recognizing their internal inconsistencies and illogicalities and facilitating moves for women outside or beyond them with impunity. This, by necessity, is a gender-specific exercise:

> Studying women as women and comparing different groups of women, rather than women and men, takes off the blinkers of the male-as-yardstick and male commonsense, so that *new* thoughts can come into the social and criminological worlds. (Cain, 1990, p. 9)

Yet Cain (1990, p. 12) suggests that a 'transgressive criminology' must also tackle the questions of 'what in the social construction of maleness is so profoundly criminogenic: why do males so disproportionately turn out to be criminals?'

As we have noted, some critical criminologists (Greenberg, 1977) had begun to frame their explanations of youth crime in terms of a 'masculine status anxiety' induced by exclusion from the labour market, but the question of exactly how masculinity was constituted remained unanswered. In the 1990s a small but growing literature emerged to 'take masculinity seriously'. The key figure here is the Australian academic Bob Connell (1987, 1995). His chief insight was to recognize 'multiple masculinities', in contrast to the one-dimensional vision of male dominance propagated by radical feminism. This involves recognizing that masculinities may be black as well as white, homosexual or heterosexual, and working class as well as middle class and that all are subject to change, contingency and open to challenge. Connell (1995, p. 77) accepts that a 'hegemonic masculinity' based on a dominant ideal of heterosexual power and authority currently stands at the head of a gender hierarchy among men, but that it is always contested by a series of alternative, subordinate forms, notably from gay men. Male power, then, is not absolute, but historically variable and a contested terrain of social practice.

In his work *Masculinities and Crime*, Messerschmidt (1993, Chapter 4) applies this analysis of diverse and contested masculinities to youth crime. Different forms of crime by young men are patterned through various interpretations of masculinity generated by 'structures of labor and power in class and race relations'. Crime provides a means of 'doing masculinity' when other resources are unavailable. Where class and 'race' position combine to reduce conventional opportunities for the accomplishment of hegemonic masculinity, then crime provides a ready replacement (Messerschmidt, 1993, p. 88). But crime takes different forms according to how different class and ethnic groups come to define their masculinities. So he argues that for white middle-class youth, 'crime' takes the form of vandalism, minor theft and drinking outside of the constraints of school. For white working-class youth, masculinity is constructed around physical aggression and, for some, hostility to all groups considered inferior in a racist and heterosexist society. Lower working-class racial minorities find their masculinity in the street gang. Whilst the white middle class may envisage a future in mental labour and the white working class in manual labour, both of these routes are perceived as closed to ethnic minority youth. Crime, such as robbery, provides the opportunity to accomplish a particular form of masculinity based on toughness and physical power. In these ways Messerschmidt (1993, p. 117) argues that 'unique forms of masculinity' are situationally accomplished through engaging in different forms of crime. But each represents an attempt to meet the 'cultural ideals of hegemonic masculinity' that are denied to young people elsewhere, whether it be in the home, at school or in work (see Chapter 1.3).

Whilst these analyses clearly provide some important insights into the variable relationships between gender (and class and 'race') and crime, they continue to prioritize structural determinants. As Jefferson (1997; 2002) remarks, they tell us little of why only a particular minority of men from a given 'race' or class background come to accomplish their masculinity in a crime option whilst a majority do not. He suggests that future enquiry should not restrict itself to the issue of structural constraints but should also encompass a theory of subjectivity – a psycho-social criminology – capable of reworking 'the fragile, contingent and contradictory character of masculinity (and femininity) without losing sight of the social' (Jefferson, 1997, p. 536). As both Katz (1988) and Presdee (1994; 2000) have noted, criminological knowledge has consistently failed to recognize the subjective gratifications involved in 'doing masculinity' and 'doing crime'. Unless we also understand the pleasures to be derived from the 'drama of crime' we will never have a complete picture of youthful criminality (see Chapter 5.5).

Assessment

Within the broad classification of 'radical criminology' there is a diverse range of theories which contest the behavioural questions posed by positivist criminologies. Crime is to be found less in individual characteristics and environmental conditions and more in relations of power and selective processes of criminalization. In labelling this is expressed in terms of a 'society' that creates rules. Within Marxism and critical criminology it is expressed in terms of 'a capitalist state' that has the power to criminalize those behaviours that are deemed 'threatening'. In some feminist perspectives it is expressed in the social construction of 'hegemonic masculinities' within patriarchal societies. All such notions have shifted the criminological agenda away from popular ideas about causation. As a result they have been critiqued for addressing 'political interpretations to the detriment of posing or answering empirical questions' (Rutter and Giller, 1983, p. 264). In tandem they have come under fire for an apparent lack of political pragmatism and a failure to be policy prescriptive. For example, it has been noted that critical criminology's pursuit of structural change and a tolerance of diversity smacks of utopianism and may be able to offer little practical help to those on the receiving end of repressive control systems or to those members of the working class who suffer most the effects of everyday criminal actions (Tierney, 1996, pp. 284–5). It tended to romanticize the deviant (via ethnographic and subcultural studies – see Chapter 5) and underplayed the damaging consequences of some youth crime. To this extent Young (1986), adopting a left realist position, argued that a focus on criminalization and moral panics fails to 'take crime seriously': not only by ignoring causal explanations, but also allowing the right to dictate the terms of the 'law and order' debate (see Section 4.2 below).

Radical feminist theory has also been critiqued for its view that social classes are subordinate to gender inequalities and for assuming a universal female subjugation. Explanations of male violence against women have also been treated in biological terms or as simply a reflection of masculine power and deviance. Above all, the unreflective use of such terms as 'patriarchy' and 'capitalism' has been critiqued as reductionist in its characterization of male/class power as universal. Historical changes in, and various forms of, patriarchy and capitalism tend not to be accounted for (Beirne and Messerschmidt, 1991, p. 526). Or as Walklate (2001, p. 75) puts it, the key questions of how and when masculinity and/or social class become the key variable in committing crime, remain unanswered. Neither has the impact of criminal justice on different subject populations been adequately theorized. As Ahluwalia (1991) points out, whilst gender analysis has a certain validity, it also needs to be sensitive to racial and ethnic differences. In all of this debate between class and gender, the experiences of black women have remained largely hidden and ignored. What is called for is a critical criminology that remains alive to the primary determining contexts of patriarchy, class and 'race' (Scraton and Chadwick, 1991), but which also avoids using such terms as 'women' or 'blacks' as universal and homogeneous categories (Rice, 1990).

Realist Criminologies

4.2 The developments we have noted within critical criminology occurred during the 1970s and 1980s at a time when, as De Haan (1990, p. 20) noted, 'a wave of law and order' was 'washing over the western world'. Against a backcloth of spiralling recorded crime rates, industrial unrest and urban disorders, Conservative politicians depicted crime as the outcome of a broader decline in moral values. In Britain and the United States 'law and order' was a key electoral issue in the 1980s, which fuelled and fed off a growing public concern for, and fear of, crime. Both Reaganism and Thatcherism's rise to power were built on an appeal to the logic of social authoritarianism, in which free market economics, reduced state welfare intervention and increased state punitive intervention were paramount. The most manifest outcome of such economic and political doctrines was long-term unemployment, economic marginalization of certain groups and attempts to reduce crime by strengthening the deterrent impact of the criminal justice system. Within this context, police powers were extended, tougher sentencing options were given to the courts and the use of imprisonment expanded, such that by the 1990s the United States could claim the highest incarceration rate in the world and Britain the highest in Europe.

On both sides of the Atlantic the rhetoric of the radical right presented a popularly received picture that criminality was voluntaristic – a course of action chosen by pathological individuals with no self control who, without coercive control, threatened the very moral fabric of society. Thus the dominant public/political debate about crime came to be focused almost exclusively on images of youth violence and lawlessness in which it made no sense to treat or rehabilitate offenders; rather, the emphasis was firmly on securing the means for their vindictive punishment. New right 'realist' criminologists such as Van den Haag and James Q. Wilson, writing in the mid 1970s, departed from the prevailing liberal consensus by simply claiming that crime emanates from wicked, evil people who are insufficiently deterred from their actions by a criminal justice system deemed to be chaotic and ineffective. In their view, the only remedy lay in capital punishment and the strengthening of penal sanctions.

The almost wholesale capture of the political terrain of law and order by the 'new right' forced sections of the left to rethink their position, and to move closer to the mainstream in an attempt to counter some of its more reactionary policies. In particular, the self styled school of *left realism* gradually dissociated itself from the 'new' and critical criminologies and attempted to formulate alternative law and order policies in which the problem of crime would be 'taken seriously' and accountable programmes of crime control would be implemented. Politically this necessitated the forging of alliances with centrist Labour or Democratic parties and the overcoming of any latent reluctance to become engaged in day to day issues of crime and criminal justice policy.

'Realist' criminologies, whether of the right or the left, are thus primarily concerned with developing responses to a perceived intensity in the public's fear of crime. They concentrate more on those crimes that are at the centre of public concern, namely youth crime, street crime, violence and burglary, than on crimes of the powerful or those crimes perpetuated by the state itself. Similarly, they are more concerned with developing defensible measures of crime control than with exploring issues concerned with the power to criminalize. The urge to 'become real' thus represents a significant move away from radical criminologies and a selective reworking of some aspects of positivist criminologies.

The 'New Right': Freedom and Discipline

The term 'new right' escapes easy definition. Broadly speaking it refers to the merging of a number of schools of thought whose primary analytic orientation was to the concepts of individual freedom, self responsibility and justice (Tame, 1991, p. 127). These concepts have, however, been activated in a variety of intellectual movements including Christian fundamentalism, economic liberalism, traditional conservatism, racism, fascism and indeed any expression of anti-socialism. Belsey (1986, p. 173) usefully picks out two, seemingly contradictory, ideologies around which the 'new right' can be defined, namely neo-liberalism and neo-conservatism. However, whilst neo-liberalism emphasizes *laissez-faire* market economics in which the individual is to be protected through freedom of choice and minimal state interference, neo-conservatism stresses the need for strong government and social authoritarianism in order to create a disciplined and hierarchical society in which individual needs are subordinate to those of the 'nation'.

Within criminology this paradox of freedom and discipline has been reflected in the politically influential work of Hayek (1983), van den Haag (1975), Wilson (1975) and Gottfredson and Hirschi (1990). Hayek's conception of the social order, for example, whilst clouded in the rhetoric of individual freedom, assumes that 'civilization' rests on the restraining and taming of primordial instincts. Such 'bad' instincts, however, are deemed to be not those of egoism or aggression, but of altruism and solidarity. It is the latter that need to be kept in check in order to maintain individual freedom and choice within a market-based economy. The problem for Hayek is that 'primitive' instincts such as demands for social justice, welfare or egalitarianism continually threaten to disrupt the efficient running of a capitalist society. Because of this inherent instability, the 'spontaneous' market order also requires a strong state to uphold it.

Similarly, van den Haag's work on the role of punishment is characterized by a defence of the efficacy of deterrence and a reaffirmation of the existence of individual free will and responsibility. He argues that the 'paramount duty of governments is to provide a legal order in which citizens can be secure in their liberties' (van den Haag, 1975, p. 3) and that such liberty fundamentally rests on the meting out of retributive punishment to those who threaten it. Lamenting a 'worldwide decline in punishment and therewith of respect for law' (1975, p. 155), van den Haag argues for an increase in penalties in which 'social authority' once more finds its nerve to support capital punishment: 'When murder no longer forfeits the murderer's life (though it will interfere with his freedom), respect for life itself is diminished, as the price for taking it is. Life becomes cheaper as we become kinder to those who wantonly take it' (van den Haag, 1975, p. 213). He advocates a series of sanctions ranging from fine through prison, exile and banishment to the death penalty, in which the task is 'not to dream up an order that can do without punishment, but rather to consider how punishment can be just and effective' (van den Haag, 1975, p. 265). Crucially, effectiveness rests on devising a series of threats that will reinforce resistance to temptation and deter most people from crime for most of the time. Temptation is not the sole property of criminals; rather:

> They are like us. Worse, we are like them. Potentially we could all be or become criminals. Which is why deterrence is necessary. The population cannot be neatly split into two disconnected groups – potential offenders and untempted citizens. Beginning with Adam, people have been temptable even though most people do not commit crimes. They do not, not because they are healthy, but because they are deterrable and deterred when credible threats are made. (Van den Haag, 1975, pp. 118–19)

In turn, 'credible threats' rest on the certainty and severity of punishment:

> What the prospective criminal is certain of – the size of the punishment – matters if being certain of it does: being certain of punishment deters from crime only if the punishment is sizable. (Van den Haag, 1975, p. 115)

Within this logic, questions of the causes of crime are sidestepped, in favour of an almost sole focus on techniques of crime control. Van den Haag (1975, p. 77), for example, argues that theories of crime causation may be fascinating, but none promises to 'tell much that can be applied to crime control now' or suggests 'modification of its instruments such as punishment'. Similarly, Wilson (1975, pp. 233, 235) dismisses the search for the causes of crime as utopian:

> Though intellectually rewarding, from a practical point of view it is a mistake to think about crime in terms of its causes and then to search for ways of alleviating those causes. We must think instead of what it is feasible for a government or a community to do . . . Wicked people exist. Nothing avails except to set them apart from innocent people.

Indeed, Wilson's work *Thinking about Crime* is in part devoted to establishing the failures of positivist criminologies by arguing that individual positivism tended to promote causal variables that were difficult to isolate and that sociological positivism was simply wrong. This opposition to the notion of the social causes of crime is encapsulated in his conclusion that poverty is not related to crime because the most dramatic increase in recorded crime occurred during the period of post-war economic growth and relative prosperity in the United States. Criminality is simply accounted for by the existence of 'lower class' people who 'attach little importance to the opinion of others'; are 'preoccupied with the daily struggle for survival'; and are 'inclined to uninhibited, expressive conduct' (Wilson, 1975, pp. 41–2).

In a later work, *Crime and Human Nature*, Wilson and Herrnstein (1985) conclude a lengthy survey of causal and correlational factors by arguing that a 'criminal personality' probably does not exist. Instead, 'personality traits' such as impulsiveness and lack of regard for others are cited as key factors in criminality, particularly when these traits are found in 'discordant families'. They stress that criminality rests on choice; a choice, however, that is mediated by the perceived consequences of the costs and benefits of such action. The criminal, as described by Wilson and Herrnstein (1985, p. 61), is a person without a conscience, but who is capable of reacting to a variety of influences in which 'the larger the ratio of the rewards (material and non material) of non crime to the rewards (material and non material) of crime, the weaker the tendency to commit crimes'.

This attempt to merge aspects of positivism with an essentially voluntaristic conception of human nature has been questioned by Gottfredson and Hirschi (1990). They contend that the key factor underlying criminal behaviour is lack of self control, rather than positivist notions of criminal propensity. The concept of self control suggests that 'people differ in the extent to which they are restrained from criminal acts', whereas the concept of criminality suggests that 'people differ in the extent to which they are compelled to crime'. They thus construct an image of the 'offender' as 'impulsive, insensitive, physical (as opposed to mental), risk-taking, short sighted and non-verbal' (Gottfredson and Hirschi, 1990, pp. 88, 90). Crime may not be an automatic consequence of low self control, but this is viewed as its primary distinguishing feature. In turn self control derives from factors affecting calculation of the consequences of one's acts and, most crucially, on effective socialization. Thus the major 'causes' of low self control, it is argued, are ineffective child rearing, poor parental supervision and discipline, working mothers and broken families: in short a lack of self control in the home (see Chapter 3.1).

These realist propositions have arguably come to dominate mainstream criminology in the twenty-first century. Attention has shifted towards the *circumstances* surrounding the commission of different criminal acts rather than attempting to understand or deal with the offender. Rational choice theory, for example, is based on the premise that most offenders are reasoning and normal rather than pathological. Crime is understood as rational action performed by ordinary people but also acting under particular pressures and exposed to specific opportunities and situational inducements. Crime rates have increased in advanced industrial societies because opportunities have increased. For a crime to occur, two events must coincide: the opportunity for the commission of the criminal act must present itself; and the individual must decide that the gains to be had from taking the opportunity outweigh both the chances of being caught and the penalty should s/he be apprehended (Clarke, R., 1992; Felson, 1998). However, contemporary neo-conservative theorizing on crime not only rests on the doctrines of free will and rational action but is also heavily informed by notions of moral culture, moral decline and parental permissiveness. Its formative ideas are listed in Table 4.2.

Table 4.2   *Characteristics of neo-conservatism*

- The search for the causes of crime in terms of predisposing social factors (deprivation, unemployment, poverty) is misguided because improvements in social conditions in the 1950s and 1960s did not herald a decrease in crime, but rather an increase.
- Crime, essentially, has biological roots that are not amenable to individual treatment or social engineering. Wicked people exist; nothing avails but to set them apart from the innocent. Thus it is impractical to try and 'cure' crime.
- Individuals commit crime through rational choice. Lack of self control and a lack of individual responsibility are at the root of all criminality.
- Crime is a symptom of declining moral standards epitomized by 1960s permissiveness, welfare dependence, liberal methods of child-rearing, family breakdown, illegitimacy, single parenting and the lack of effective means of discipline. Collectively these factors have been instrumental in the development of a dependent, demoralized and dangerous 'underclass'.

Whilst these 'new realists' obviously differ in theoretical sophistication and are not ideologically homogeneous, Platt and Takagi (1977) argue that they have a unity of interest and purpose in that they:

- focus almost exclusively on those crimes that are either specific to, or concentrated within, the working class (e.g. street crime);
- are basically uninterested in the causes of crime, except to divorce it from questions of political economy;
- concentrate on questions of control and deterrence to the detriment of questions of social justice.

An Underclass?

The new and reinvigorated themes of neo-conservative criminology, emphasizing individual responsibility, self control and deterrence, first found a ready market in the 1980s when Conservative politicians and ideologues were mounting a vigorous moral campaign against various forms of deviance. And these themes have continued to underpin part of the reforming agenda associated with successive Labour governments since 1997. In Britain, Thatcher made crime a primary election issue in 1979 by attaching it to a general concern to re-establish 'Victorian values' and overturn the supposedly permissive culture of the 1960s. Left-wing and liberal theory and policy were denounced not only for a failure to respond to public concerns, but because of their role in accelerating a process of 'demoralization' (Davies, 1987) rooted largely in their indifference to 'family disintegration' (Dennis, 1993).

A critique of critical criminology was mounted, denouncing its support for civil liberties, welfare rights and organized labour and condemning progressive trends in social policy as evidence of a monolithic political correctness (Morgan, P., 1978; Dennis and Erdos, 1992). Some sections of the right also re-emphasized the moral dimension of social theory. For example, Scruton (1980) and the journal he founded, the *Salisbury Review*, achieved notable success in promoting conservatism as the only defensible ideology in which the virtues of authority, order and discipline could be protected. In moral and political terms, such ideology has been translated into critiques of welfare dependency, illegitimacy and single parenting as central to the formation of a 'criminogenic' underclass. These themes indeed proved just as attractive to Labour, as they did to Conservative politicians (Muncie, 2000b).

The term 'underclass' was first used by Myrdal (1964) to describe the unemployed, but it was not until some 20 years later that it entered the public domain through the work of a New York journalist, Ken Auletta (1982). He argued that a sizeable number of North America's poor never assimilate into society, but remain trapped in an underclass characterized by dependency on state benefits, denial of the work ethic, failed morality and rejection of family norms. This group also contains those individuals who commit most traditional street crime and are the most likely to be involved in urban riots. Whilst the term remains poorly defined, it has been used by both left and right to describe those sections of society who are not engaged in gainful productive work. For some observers on the right, 'the underclass' is young and homeless. For others it almost invariably refers to those sections of the black population who are welfare dependent. Illegitimate births, crime, child abuse, drug dependency, single mothers, promiscuity and begging have all been cited as its key features. In contrast, for some of those on the left, the 'underclass' is a pejorative label to describe those who have been systematically excluded from the labour market. They point out that a succession of such labels has been consistently attached to the poorest members of society in order to mark them out as either politically dangerous or as marginal outsiders – from the 'undeserving poor', 'dangerous classes' and 'social outcasts' of the nineteenth century to the 'culture of poverty ', 'scroungers' and 'work-shy' of the twentieth (Mann, 1991). Broadly speaking the right focus on the pathology and culture of the underclass (promoting an ideology of 'idle, thieving bastards': Bagguley and Mann, 1992), whilst the left emphasize industrial decline, recession, political marginalization and deprivation.

The chief protagonist on the right is the American, Charles Murray. In his influential work *Losing Ground* (1984), he argued that much of the federal welfare system should be abolished because it encourages state dependency and fecklessness and undermines communal sources of social solidarity. In particular, welfare benefits have enabled young mothers to live independently of fathers, so increasing numbers of young people have grown up without viable male role models. This culture is then passed on to the next generation. Young men, who by nature are 'essentially barbarians' until they are civilized by marriage, turn to drugs and crime and a vicious circle is created. For Murray, it is not poverty or unemployment that creates an underclass, but the 'affluence' and independence afforded to young women through their welfare entitlement. In the USA the underclass debate has focused almost exclusively on crime, 'race' and youth.

In 1990 Murray applied his argument to the situation in Britain and claimed that increasing rates of illegitimacy, violent crime and drop-out from the labour force were clear signs that an underclass was in emergence. These three factors, he argued, were intimately related:

> when large numbers of young men don't work, the communities around them break down, just as they break down when large numbers of young unmarried women have babies . . . Supporting a family is a central means for a man to prove to himself that he is a *mensch*. Men who do not support families find other ways to prove that they are men, which tend to take various destructive forms. As many have commented through the centuries, young males are essentially barbarians for whom marriage – meaning not just the wedding vows but the act of taking responsibility for a wife and children – is an indispensable civilising force. Young men who don't work don't make good marriage material. Often they don't get married at all; when they do they haven't the ability to fill their traditional role. In either case, too many of them remain barbarians. (Murray, 1990, p. 37)

In subsequent analyses Murray (1994; 2000) focused more directly on illegitimacy. His tone was also more apocalyptic. The restoration of the two-parent family, through marriage, he argued, was the only way to ensure the survival of 'free institutions and a civil society'. His view of Britain in 2000 was even bleaker than that presented a decade earlier. Noting an increasing rate of illegitimacy throughout British society, especially in the working classes, he conjures up a future vision of increasing segregation between 'New Victorians' (characterized by a levelling off of illegitimacy among the upper middle classes) and the 'New Rabble' (characterized by increasing rates of illegitimacy among the working classes). Affluent, well-educated sections of the population will edge back towards traditional morality; poorer sections will continue to degenerate into an underclass characterized by more violence, more crime, more widespread drug addiction, fewer marriages and more unemployment. The breakdown of the family results in a breakdown of the socialization of the young which is then reflected in a higher propensity for violent behaviour.

As before, Murray's solution to this 'crisis' was resort to the prison and a reduction in welfare benefit levels for single, unmarried mothers in order to encourage the avoidance of pregnancy for women who have no husbands. In Britain this analysis was largely shared by such self styled 'ethical socialists' as Norman Dennis and George Erdos. They argued that children from 'fatherless families' would grow up without appropriate role models and supervision and would thus reduce their own chances of becoming competent parents. For Dennis and Erdos (1992) it is 'commonsense' that family breakdown and rising crime will go hand in hand. Such a vision percolated through to Conservative policy-makers in the UK. Single parenting has often been cited as a chief cause of moral decline and rising lawlessness. In 1995 it was suggested that single mothers should be ineligible for state support unless they had first tried and failed to have their children adopted (*Guardian*, 14 August 1995). The notion of a 'parenting deficit' has also informed Labour Party policy. In 1998 parenting orders were introduced to give courts powers to force parents to take responsibility for their children's care and control. In 2001 a new offence of 'aggravated truancy' was introduced carrying a three-month prison sentence for those parents who fail to ensure their children attend school regularly. Once again the root cause of youth crime is viewed in terms of a breakdown of morality associated with dysfunctional families and a feckless underclass (see Chapter 6.4).

In Britain the 'underclass and crime' debate has continued to circulate around the moral decline vs. unemployment axis. For some it is not welfare dependency, but cuts in welfare provision, the widening of class differentials and the exclusion of the poor that account for the existence of an underclass (Jordan, 1996). Thus structural factors, such as economic recession, are the root cause of increased rates of crime.

One of the most thorough attempts to test this proposition was made by Box (1987). He reviewed over 60 studies that have attempted to discover if there is an empirical relationship between unemployment and crime, and between income inequality and crime. He found that 33 studies reported a positive relationship between unemployment rates and crime rates, while 18 reported a negative or statistically insignificant relationship. Regarding income inequality and crime, 12 found a positive relationship; five did not. Such research is bedevilled by the question of how crime rates can be most adequately measured: by arrest, conviction, victimization or self report data (see Chapter 1.2)? Most research has relied on official data, and this has tended to find a relationship between job instability and crime. However, the self report data are less strong. The possibility arises, then, that unemployment may have only a slight effect on criminal behaviour, but is a very strong determinant of police recording and arrest rates. Box thus ends in agreement with Freeman's (1983) conclusions from his US research:

> Despite differences and weaknesses among the studies, a general finding emerges: namely that rises in unemployment and/or declines in labour participation rate are connected with rises in the crime rate, but the effect tends to be modest and insufficient to explain the general upward trend of crime in the period studied. The labour participation rate is, moreover, often found to have a closer link to crime than does unemployment, suggesting that those who actually leave the labour force are the most crime prone. (Quoted by Box, 1987, p. 78)

Similarly, a review of research in Britain for the Home Office in 1982 concluded that:

> Since crime goes up during periods of low unemployment and many crimes are committed by people in employment or of school age, it is clear that unemployment is not the sole determinant, or even the major determinant, of crime. Against this, some evidence of a

> relationship persists suggesting that unemployment is a factor in the causation of crime, although it may not be a major factor; furthermore it appears to be inter-related in some complex way with other aspects of economic disadvantage or social deprivation. (Tarling, 1982, p. 32)

However, as Dickinson (1995) observes, such reviews of long-term trends may miss some salient and specific correlations. He notes that in a period of relatively full employment, pre-1970, there is indeed no statistical relationship between crime and unemployment rates, but that since 1970, when unemployment began to rise, recorded crime has exhibited cyclical fluctuations in line with the numbers out of work. Moreover for certain crimes, such as domestic burglary committed by men under the age of 25, there appears to be a close and contemporaneous relationship with unemployment levels. Dickinson concludes that whilst this is no simple relationship, being out of work must be regarded as a major factor motivating crime.

Nevertheless, Box (1987) contends that it is not unemployment but the relationship between income inequality and crime that is the stronger. Of all the studies he reviewed, Box found that each concluded that the greater the contrast in economic privilege, the higher the rate of property crime and non-fatal violence. He concluded that 'any crime control policy which fails to recognise that the uneven distribution of income is strongly related to criminality activity fails to get to grips with a major underlying structural factor which generates a strong motive to commit crime' (Box, 1987, p. 96).

Similarly, Field's (1990) Home Office research argued that economic factors have a major influence on trends in property and personal crime. Using levels of personal consumption (i.e. the amount that people spend on average during a year), he found that when personal consumption falls, property crimes rise. Conversely when consumption levels rise, so do personal offences. What this research suggests is that it is not absolute poverty or deprivation that necessarily causes crime, but a sudden loss of income or increasing levels of social inequality between the 'haves' and 'have-nots'. This notion of 'relative deprivation' has been most forcefully promoted by advocates of left realism.

Left Realism: Relative Deprivation

The emergence of a left realist criminology in Britain in the 1980s can be viewed as both a product of, and a reaction to, the dominant 'law and order' political climate at the time. Initially, it promoted itself by advancing a virulent attack on critical criminology (in particular for what it viewed as its *left idealist* tendencies). Lea and Young in their pivotal work, *What Is To Be Done about Law and Order?* (1984, p. 266), for example, condemned the left's 'myopia about crime' and for simply 'turning their back on the problem'. Accusing the left of adopting crude reductionist arguments (crime caused by poverty; criminal law as the direct expression of a ruling class); and of underestimating and romanticizing the nature of working-class youth crime (as relatively minor, as primitive rebellion, as constructed through state engineered moral panics), Young (1975, 1979, 1986) argued that the political arena was left wide open to Conservative campaigns for law and order. In contrast he argued for the development of a left *realist* theory and praxis:

> The central tenet of left realism is to reflect the reality of crime, that is in its origins, its nature and its impact. This involves a rejection of tendencies to romanticize crime or to pathologize it, to analyse solely from the point of view of the administration of crime or the criminal actor, to underestimate crime or to exaggerate it . . . most importantly it is realism which informs our notion of practice: in answering what can be done about the problems of crime and social control. (Young, 1986, p. 21)

From the first murmurings of discontent with the original formulations of a critical criminology by two of its originators (Young, 1975; Taylor, 1981b), left realism developed the following propositions:

1 *Crime is a real problem.*   Left realism tries to avoid the over-dramatization of crime by the right and the minimization of its impact by the left. By contrast it argues that it 'takes crime seriously'. Thus working-class crime (street crime, burglary, personal violence) is viewed as a problem of the first order. 'Street crime is the most transparent of all injustices' (Lea and Young, 1984, p. 75). It notes that most crime is intra-class and intra-racial; committed by relatively disadvantaged perpetrators on similarly relatively disadvantaged victims. The task of the left is to accept this reality, try to understand it and do something about it, rather than deny it.

2 *Crime has specific causes.*   Left realism is critical of both the right and the left for their abandonment of the search for the causes of crime: a neglect that has facilitated the rise of utilitarian forms of crime control and punishment. It argues that crime can best be explained with reference to the processes of *relative deprivation* and *marginalization*. Access to the labour market is seen as vital to the working class in general and a black 'underclass' in particular. When such access is denied, young people are pushed to the margins of society, as peripheral to the economic process of production and consumption and to the political process of democratic representation. Left realism suggests that one adaptation to marginalization (and to the feeling of relative rather than absolute deprivation) is the emergence of a criminal subculture. Whilst rejecting any direct causal link between deprivation and crime, Lea and Young (1984, p. 81) stress that is the *perception* of injustice derived from deprivation that is central. Thus the notion of a *relative* deprivation (derived from anomie theory and Runciman, 1966) is utilized to explore the contradictions involved when expectations are not met by real opportunities. This situation explains the growth of street crime and disorder amongst the most relatively deprived section of the working class, namely young, inner-city, Afro-Caribbean males.

3 *Fear of crime reflects social reality.*   Again in contrast to critical criminology's insistence that most crime is by and large a minor problem and that the media and other state agencies exaggerate its seriousness for wider political gain, realism maintains that criminology should begin its analysis from problems as people experience them. For example, as the Islington Crime Survey (Jones et al., 1986) found that 36 per cent of local residents saw crime as a major problem; that 56 per cent worried about being burgled, that 46 per cent had been a victim of street robbery and that a third of women avoided going out at night for fear of sexual harassment, then these should be the proper and central concerns of criminologists.

4 *The need for an accurate victimology.* The major empirical base for realism is the local victim survey because, it is argued, this provides an accurate reflection of people's concerns and a realistic picture of the nature and extent of crime (in contrast to officially recorded statistics or national surveys, for example). Realism argues that criminology has traditionally ignored the victim, or, even worse, has preferred to view the offender as victim. The survey provides a means by which public attitudes to crime and policing can be measured and thus a basis for developing a social policy that is responsive to the voice of the 'consumer'.

5 *The need for effective means of crime control.* Lea and Young (1984, Chapter 5) are particularly critical of the police and their failure to 'clear up' much of the crime in the inner cities. This is viewed as a reflection of a loss of public confidence, a decline in consensus policing and subsequent discriminatory policing which further aggravates the crime problem. The political solution offered by left realism is greater democratic control and community accountability of the police. Such developments would restore public confidence, increase willingness to report crime and thus aid police efficiency and community protection. Coupled with the advocacy of alternatives to custody, victim restitution schemes and the minimal use of the penal sanction, the realists argue for reduced central state intervention and its replacement by localized inter-agency and community-based forms of crime prevention and control.

6 *The need to merge theory and political practice.* The key rationale for the development of a left realism was to 'combat the tendency of a divided and disillusioned public to move to the right' (Lea and Young, 1984, p. 272). Thus it initially aligned itself with the British Labour Party in an effort to overcome the right's monopoly on matters of law and order and to construct an alternative social democratic set of criminal justice policies which it hoped might be taken seriously by parliamentary bodies.

Latterly, Young (1992, p. 27) attempted to draw these elements together by referring to a 'square of crime' in which the interactions and relationships between police and other agencies of crime control, the public, the offender and the victim must be accounted for. This implies a fourfold aetiology of crime. It includes, but moves beyond, the traditional focuses on the causes of offending, to the factors that make victims vulnerable, the social conditions that affect public perceptions of control and tolerance, and the social forces that propel the formal agencies, such as the police. The four parts of the square, it is maintained, must be explained with reference to the micro level of interaction, the meso level of control agency administration and bureaucracy and the macro level of the economic and political domains. In this way it is argued that realism is not a denunciation of *The New Criminology* but is its more sophisticated version: a version that avoids partial explanation and reductionism and which is comprehensive and pragmatic enough to explore and respond to the 'complex reality of crime as it is experienced in everyday life' (Matthews, 1987a, p. 380).

This agenda touched a nerve in many of those on the left, and has been taken up, with various degrees of enthusiasm, by academics in other Western countries. In the United States the work of Currie (1985) mirrored that of left realism in so far as it was designed to provide a pragmatic counter to the criminologies of the 'new right'. This version differs to the extent that crime is considered endemic in a society built on principles of competition, conflict and individualism. To attack the roots of the crime problem, 'we must build a society that is less unequal, less depriving, less insecure, less disruptive of family and community ties and less corrosive of co-operative values' (Currie, 1985, p. 225). In short an effective crime control strategy lies outside of the criminal justice system and in the fields of education, training and employment, through which fundamental economic, cultural and political practices can be challenged. Brown and Hogg (1992) and McQueen (1990) have similarly attempted to assess the relevance of realism in an Australian context. They argue that it represents more of a politically strategic response to the dominance of the 'new right' in Britain and USA, than it does a fully worked out 'theory' in its own right. In Canada, MacLean's generally sympathetic account still acknowledges that left realism is the product of a 'specific political configuration' and that there are some 'important theoretical and ideological biases inherent in the discourse' which are 'deserving of sceptical scrutiny' (MacLean, 1991, p. 246). In particular, left realism appears to be driven by popular conceptions of 'crime' and fails to acknowledge that the issue of what actually constitutes a criminal occurrence is far from settled (see Chapter 1.4).

Indeed, it has been claimed that the import of 'realism' (whether left or right) necessarily narrows the crime debate to a focus on those visible intra-class (and youthful) crimes of the street. Accordingly, other (non-youth) crimes such as fraud, embezzlement and corporate crime tend to be overlooked. Although this may be the case, there are certain crucial differences between left and right realism. Whilst both are critical of utopianism and claim to be rational responses to increased levels of public fear of crime, left realism insists that neo-liberalism and neo-conservatism are part of the problem and not its solution (see Table 4.3). As Young (1990, p. 10) maintains, realism argues for the minimum use of coercive sanctions, the decriminalization of certain (e.g. drug) offences, and 'that only socialist intervention will fundamentally reduce the causes of crime rooted as they are in social inequality'.

Table 4.3   *Right and left realism compared*

Right realism	Left realism
• Rejection of utopianism in favour of neo-conservatism	• Rejection of utopianism in favour of democratic socialism
• Acceptance of legal definitions of 'crime'	• Acceptance of legal definitions of 'crime'
• Primary focus on 'crime' as represented by official statistics	• Primary focus on 'crime' as perceived by victims
• Fear of crime as rational	• Fear of crime as rational
• Reworking of genetic and individualistic theories	• Reworking of subcultural, anomie and structural conflict theories
• Crime caused by lack of self control	• Crime caused by relative deprivation, social injustice and marginalization
• Prioritizing order (rather than justice) via deterrent and retributive means of crime control	• Prioritizing social justice via programmes of crime prevention

Source: Derived from Young (1990)

Assessment

Realist criminologies encompass a plethora of notions of crime causation as evidenced in the divergent approaches taken by neo-conservatism and left realism. Whilst the former combines elements of free will, genetics and social control theory and marks something of a return to the principles of individual causation, the latter combines elements of anomie (relative deprivation) and subcultural theory and marks something of a return to the principles of social causation. Both accept that crime is becoming more of a problem and stress the urgent need to address that problem with feasible and effective measures of crime control.

The neo-conservative account of crime causation, however, does not address why individuals choose to commit particular types of crime rather than others. It is simply assumed that innate propensities have been unleashed by weakened social bonds. Also the claim that coercion is essential for the maintenance of social order is not demonstrated. Coercion may lead to greater injustice and the further separation of 'criminals' from 'non-criminals'. It does not aid reintegration. Reducing welfare benefits in order to break the 'dependency culture' of an underclass encourages a widening of income differentials and the raising of social tensions which may also eventually be expressed in rising levels of crime (Brake and Hale, 1992, p. 115).

Much of the left realist agenda has also come under critical scrutiny, in particular for its abandonment of critical criminology and its seeming return instead to the 'citadels of the old criminology' (Cohen, 1988, p. 9). Indeed, in its attempt to revive an aetiology of crime, it draws extensively on American subcultural theory of the 1950s (see Chapter 3.2). In particular the utilization of such theory to assert the existence of a specifically *black* youth criminal subculture came under virulent attack for its racist connotations (Ginsberg, 1985; Gilroy, 1987a). More generally, the primary focus on 'crime' as perceived by victims tends to ignore, or at best underplay, the more damaging consequences of corporate crime, white collar crime and crimes of the powerful. The realist agenda then does little to challenge political and media-driven definitions of what constitutes 'serious crime' and fails to capture the harm caused, for example, by workplace injury, occupation-related diseases and environmental pollution (Pearce and Tombs, 1992). Much of this stems from a theoretical orientation grounded in the notion of relative deprivation, rather than class/gender/'race' exploitation.

Left realism's reliance on the concept of an 'underclass' is also controversial. The concept of class implies some reproduction over time and a degree of common identity for its members, but it remains as yet unclear whether a distinct and permanent 'underclass' of a marginalized black youth culture empirically exists. Moreover as Taylor (1992, p. 107) has commented, in the context of the 1990s, it may be time for radicals to give up the obsession with class and examine other 'stressed social relations' associated with class fractions, gender and ethnicity.

Finally, realism's programme for social reform based on proposals for enhanced police accountability and community-based crime prevention has been condemned as 'simplistic' and 'naive'. As Sim et al. (1987, p. 54) argue, 'their policy prescriptions have become no more than "constructive criticism" welcomed by the police and incorporated as an integral part of social democratic politics'. Similarly, Jefferson et al. (1992) have questioned the 'realism' involved in the narrow focus on individual victims of crime in which working-class street and property crime remain the key components of the 'crime problem'. The key issue for the left, they argue, should remain the way in which crime is activated by the new right to justify coercive and authoritarian state practices, and latterly the way in which the 'victim of crime' has been reconstructed as a *consumer* of police, and other agency, service. Realism's commitment to a community-based crime prevention policy renders its position very similar to the early 1990s notion of the 'new right' that crime is 'caused' by a lack of vigilance on the part of the 'active citizen'.

Politically, then, there is some merging and co-option of the concerns of left realism by the right. This view – that left realism has failed to challenge right-wing ideology, but by accepting some of its key premises has become a part of it – has indeed been latterly accepted by some of its orginators who, in particular, have noted how much of its agenda has been usurped by an authoritarian New Labour since the late 1990s (Young, 2003). Whilst left realism continues to be a serious and politically committed project to tackle the issue of intra-class and intra-racial crime, the problem remains of how far the theoretical gains made by critical criminology have been jettisoned in the search for a social democratic law and order politics (Carrington and Hogg, 2002).

Beyond Criminology?

4.3 If criminology has been traditionally conceived as the scientific study of the causes of crime, then it is clear that the paradigm of critical criminology has moved far beyond the original remit. Critical criminologies are as much an examination of political economy and state formations as anything we might like to call crime. Feminist criminologies have shifted the study of crime into addressing questions of patriarchy and gender roles. These avenues of enquiry are able to move beyond the issue of crime causation because they do not take the concept of 'crime' for granted. 'Crime' is not something that can simply be described with reference to what is, or is not, circumscribed by the law. 'Crime' is not simply law-breaking behaviour, but is something constructed through the processes of interaction, social reaction and power. Thus the search for the cause of 'crime' in general, and 'youth crime' in particular, is abandoned. Not only has a hundred years of positivist criminology, with its persistent problem of distinguishing cause from correlate, been unable to isolate a specific cause, but the whole endeavour, it is argued, is doomed to failure, because 'crime' refers not to a unified phenomenon, but to a diverse multitude of behaviour patterns. If one accepts Hester and Eglin's (1992, p. 269) proposition 'that "crime" is a status accorded to some acts and not to others, at some times and in some places and not others, and that those acts are engaged in to some degree by most people at least some of the time', then it is highly questionable whether it warrants any special explanation at all. However, such a view is inimical to new right and left realist (as well as positivist) criminologies. For the latter 'crime', and particularly 'youth crime', remains a major social problem about which something needs to be done. This impasse in itself accounts for the current fragmented, diverse and contradictory nature of criminology. Criminology appears united only in its fascination with its key referent – 'crime' – but is racked by internal debate and controversy because what actually constitutes 'crime' is forever changing and open to dispute.

Modernity and Postmodernism

This chapter and Chapter 3 have introduced a number of theoretical approaches which, despite their obvious and clear divergences, are all grounded in rationalistic and meta theories about the relationship between individual behaviour, cultural values and social structure. Despite their points of difference, all the approaches we have considered assume that social reality is ultimately 'knowable' and 'understandable' when the 'correct' terms of reference, concepts and mode of research are employed.

These attempts to make sense of the social are characteristic of *modernist* modes of thought. Modernism attempts to use the rational knowledge of science, law and technology to construct the social into an essentially ordered totality and is underpinned by faith in the 'master narratives' of progress, self-advancement and emancipation (Morrison, 1995, p. 453). Such fundamental premises have, however, been called into question through the challenge of *postmodernism*. For example, a postmodern perspective views the modernist project of developing objective and scientific means to understand the social as misguided and redundant. The questions it asks are unanswerable; the answers it formulates are too dogmatic (Einstadter and Henry, 1995, p. 289). Postmodernism views the world as replete with an unlimited number of models of order, each generated by relatively autonomous and localized sets of practices which are incapable of being explained by any 'scientific' theory. Whereas modernism strives for universality and the overcoming of relativism in theory and practice, postmodernism accepts relativity as a lasting feature of the world. Postmodernism challenges us to accept that we live in a world of contradictions and inconsistencies which is not amenable to objective modes of thought. Assumptions about the 'real' and the 'virtual' (and how they might be distinguished) are less readily sustained. More knowledge produces less certainty and less ontological security (Valier, 2002, p. 175). Modernist theory (of which criminology is but one example) simply serves to impose a pre-defined meaning and structure on the disordered social; if anything, it moves us further from the truth, rather than helping us to understand it. Grand theorizing is rejected by postmodernism in favour of a pluralist and appreciative relativism. As Bauman (1993, p. 245) explains:

What the post-modern mind is aware of is that there are problems in human and social life with no good solutions, twisted trajectories that cannot be straightened up, ambivalences that are more than linguistic blunders yelling to be corrected, doubts which cannot be legislated out of existence, moral agonies which no reason-dictated recipes can soothe, let alone cure. The post-modern mind does not expect any more to find the all-embracing, total and ultimate formula of life without ambiguity, risk, danger and error, and is deeply suspicious of any voice that promises otherwise. The post-modern mind is aware that each local, specialised and focused treatment, effective or not when measured by its ostensive target, spoils as much as, if not more than it repairs. The post-modern mind is reconciled to the idea that the messiness of the human predicament is here to stay.

As a result, postmodernism implies an abandonment of the concepts of 'crime' and 'youth' and the construction of a new language and mode of thought to designate and explore objects of censure and codes of conduct (Hulsman, 1986; De Haan, 1990; Smart, 1990; Sumner, 1994). Henry and Milovanovic (1994, 1996) insist that crime will only stop being a problem once the justice system, media and criminologists stop focusing attention on it. Indeed, they urge us to abandon all grand theory and all established means to understand the phenomenon of 'crime'.

Hunt (1991) is more circumspect. While some criminologists may have left behind a faith in narrowly conceived positivist methods of science, he argues that this should open a space for a more measured assessment of the competing claims to knowledge and facilitate more assured judgements on their relative adequacy. Moreover, a postmodern imagination should alert us to the many ways in which 'youth crime' is 'problematic' – not only in its effects but in its formulation and the ways in which it is so readily framed and understood. Indeed, we may better capture 'youth crime' not by searching for causes, but by using narratives and accounts derived from young people themselves. It is only through a reframing of 'youth' and 'crime' which either removes 'youth' as the key referrent or repositions them as legitimate citizens, that dominant (adult) discourses will be overcome (Brown, 1998, p. 119).

If all of this conjures up contingency, uncertainty and doubt, this should not necessarily be a reason for nihilistic despair. As Morrison (1995, p. 475) concludes, 'doubt is essential to creation' and provides the impetus for 'continual (re)construction'. But exactly what is to be 'reconstructed' often remains unspecified. Intellectual scepticism may be preferable to dogma, but, if ungrounded, can simply produce inertia and political inaction. The continuing problem for radical criminology is to know when detachment or commitment should be prioritized and how (if at all) they can ever be combined (Cohen, 1998).

Summary

An overview of radical and realist theories of crime is given in Table 4.4 below.

Table 4.4 *Radical and realist theories of youth crime*

Theory	Explanation of crime	Key theorists
Neutralization	'Moral holiday'/removal of inhibitions/drift	Sykes and Matza (1957) Matza (1964)
Labelling	Stigma attached to social reaction (moral panic) cements deviant careers. Social control causes crime	Becker (1963) Cohen (1973a) Lemert (1967)
Classical Marxism	Capitalism produces alienation and brutalizing socio-economic conditions	Bonger (1916)
'New criminology'	Lack of tolerance	Taylor et al. (1973)
Critical criminology	Certain populations criminalized through denial of opportunity, social exclusion and crises in hegemony	Chambliss (1975) Hall et al. (1978) Greenberg (1977) Scraton (1987)
Feminist	Patriarchal society encourages 'maverick masculinities'	Smart (1976) Messerschmidt (1993)
Social control	Absence of control (by parents/schools) allows ever present criminal inclinations to be realized. Cultural permissiveness	Gottfredson and Hirschi (1990) Wilson and Herrnstein (1985) Wilson (1975)
Underclass	Illegitimacy, single parenting, welfare dependency	Murray (1990)
Left realism	Relative deprivation	Lea and Young (1984)
Postmodernism	Causal statements impossible to make	Henry and Milovanovic (1996)

Not all of these theories are directed explicitly towards explaining *youth* crime, but all are of relevance. It is noteworthy in itself that a majority of criminological theories have either explicitly or implicitly used 'youth' as a key referent in formulating their notions of 'causation' or 'criminalization'. The key points to emerge from this chapter include the following:

- Rather than refocusing on the illusive search for the *causes* of crime, radical criminologies sought to illustrate how crime was socially constructed through the capacity and ability of state institutions and the political economy of advanced capitalism to define and confer criminality on others.
- This 'radical turn' began with the advent of interactionist and labelling paradigms of the 1960s. Whereas positivism asserted that crime and deviance were a non-rational, determinate product of undersocialization and thus devoid of any human choice, creativity or meaning, interactionism was more concerned to grant authenticity to youth's deviant actions by

recording the motives and meanings of the actors themselves. Labelling developed this position by radically shifting the object of criminological enquiry away from trying to isolate the factors that were presumed to propel a pathological few to break the rules of an assumed social consensus, to an analysis that rested on a conflict or pluralist conception of society in which deviance was ubiquitous and where youthful deviance was constructed through practices of social reaction and social control.

- The 'New Criminology' furthered this process of radicalization by taking the world of personal meanings and social reaction back into a critique of the history and structure of society. This was achieved through locating definitions of crime and modes of control in the precise context of the social relationships and institutional arrangements emanating from particular modes of economic production. What this work advocated was that the key subject of criminology should not be crime and deviance as behaviours, but a critical understanding of the social order and the power to criminalize. Much of this relied on a reworking of the theoretical premises of Marxism coupled with attempts to humanize deviance derived from interactionism and ethnographic research.

- These radical visions surfaced against a political backdrop of the resurgence of a popular law and order politics. On both sides of the Atlantic the rhetoric of the radical right presented a popularly received picture that criminality was voluntaristic – a course of action chosen by pathological individuals with no self control and with the potential for universal moral degeneracy. Within this context, police powers were extended, civil liberties eroded and the use of imprisonment expanded to unprecedented levels. By capitalizing on the fear of crime, the notion of endemic criminality was instilled in communities and enabled the public/political debate to be dominated by images of violent crime, youth lawlessness and a declining morality.

- The new right's capture of almost the whole terrain of law and order politics forced sections of the left to rethink their position and to move closer to the mainstream in an attempt to counter some of its more reactionary policies. With empirical support from a series of victim surveys carried out during the 1980s, left realism claimed that the problem of crime was indeed growing and that in particular property and street crimes were real issues that needed to be addressed, rather than dismissed as simply vehicles of a new right ideology. It claimed that people's fear of crime was rational and a reflection of inner-city social reality. As crime was considered endemic, it needed to be effectively policed; its causes needed to be once more established and theorized, and a social justice programme inaugurated to make the police more accountable to marginal working-class communities.

- However, most of the positivist and realist criminologies take the statistical indices of crime at face value. The continuing contribution of critical criminology is to insist that such indices are in themselves social constructions. When seen in a historical perspective, such theory alerts us to the conditions in which some types of activity come to be defined as punishable in law and the relations of power involved in the framing of such definitions. To understand youth crime, we need also to examine how, why and when the state assumes the power to criminalize.

- A key failing of positivist and most radical criminologies was the absence of any discussion or critical analysis of gender relations and women and crime. Never was it made explicit that the problem of crime may also be one of men, masculinities and patriarchal social relations. The development of feminist inroads into the male bastion of criminology initially took the form of a comprehensive critique of the discipline, first of its neglect even to study women's involvement in crime and criminal justice, and second for its total distortion of women's experiences as essentially biologically driven. Since the mid 1970s a burgeoning literature has demonstrated how criminology is driven by male assumptions and interests, how criminalized women are seen as doubly deviant, and how assumptions about appropriate gender roles mean that women are judged less on the nature of their offence and more on their 'deviant' lifestyle. Some feminists have drawn more on sociologies of gender than on pre-existing criminological knowledge to explore their subject matter. Others have gone further by questioning whether the focus on female law-breakers is a proper concern for feminism and indeed whether a feminist criminology is theoretically possible or even politically desirable.

- This relation between feminism and criminology has been further problematized by a postmodern position that claims that such unifiers as 'women', 'crime', 'criminology' and 'youth' trap any investigation in essentialist categories that obstruct the production of new knowledge. Postmodernism argues against the construction of 'master narratives', claiming that such totalizing accounts lose sight of the multiplicity and diversity of modern power relations. By implication it argues that the *causes* of youth crime have been, and will remain, 'unknowable': that is, its complexities preclude definitive analysis particularly when that analysis is grounded in modernist concerns for capitalism, unemployment, patriarchy, the underclass, permissiveness and so on.

Study Questions

1 What contribution have the radical criminologies made to the youth crime debate?
2 What is the difference between the social causation and the social construction of youth crime?
3 Do realist criminologies add anything particularly new to the youth crime debate or are they simply reworkings of older, positivist theories?
4 Why have some theorists argued that the search for 'a cause' is a misdirected and fruitless activity?
5 'Criminological research is invariably drawn into the political domain.' How far do its agendas and priorities simply reflect prevailing socio-economic and political conditions?

Further Resources

For an informed overview of the diverse and various strands of radicalism and realism, all of the key texts cited in Table 4.4 deserve some attention. A brief overview can be found in the introduction to McLaughlin et al.'s edited collection *Criminological Perspectives* (2003) or in Muncie (1998). Matza's *Delinquency and Drift* (1964) was republished with a new introduction in 1990 and remains a key challenge to positivist notions of causation. Becker's (1963) analysis of marijuana smoking is the classic text on labelling. Hall et al.'s *Policing the Crisis* (1978) shows how labelling can be developed within a critical paradigm to provide some enlightened understanding of how and why particular 'youth crimes' (mugging) are constructed in particular socio-economic conjunctures. One of the best ethnographic studies of this period remains Parker's Liverpool-based *View from the Boys* (1974). For a contrary view of how the study of youth crime can be developed by studying young women using theories that transgress criminology, see Cain's edited collection, *Growing Up Good* (1989). On the relevance of gender, and masculinity in particular, Messerschmidt (1993) is the most useful place to start.

The classic left realist text is Lea and Young's *What Is To Be Done about Law and Order?* (1984), whilst Murray's (1990) increasingly influential analysis of the underclass captures many of the elements of right realism. A critique of both can be found in Scraton (1987). Chapter 12 of Einstadter and Henry (1995) provides an accessible summary of the types of issue that would be involved in deconstructing 'youth crime' from a postmodern perspective, whilst the edited volumes on contemporary critical criminology by Carrington and Hogg (2002) and Walton and Young (1998) continue to reveal the necessity of critical analysis, theoretical innovation and political intervention for a project that will by definition always remain unfinished.

5 Cultural Studies and Cultural Criminology: Youth Cultures, Gangs and Subcultures

Overview

Chapter 5 examines:

- the meaning of 'youth culture', 'youth subculture', 'counterculture' and 'club culture';
- a range of youth styles that have emerged (particularly in Britain) since 1950 and which have attracted adult censure and legal sanction;
- the relationship between youth leisure and (a) processes of consumerism and (b) processes of criminalization;
- strengths and weaknesses of British subcultural theory;
- the relevance of youth leisure pursuits in the construction of 'youth as a social problem';
- the constituent elements of cultural criminology.

Key Terms

bricolage	homology
carnival	imaginary solutions
counterculture	moral panic
cultural criminology	resistance
defusion/diffusion	semiology
difference	style
edgework	subculture
gang	transgression
hegemony	

Unsupervised leisure has almost always been considered a major source of trouble and as posing a threat to young people's moral development. During the sixteenth and seventeenth centuries carnivals were accused of promoting sexual promiscuity and popular ballads were denounced as bawdy and as glorifying criminality. By the nineteenth century, theatre, music halls, dances, penny dreadfuls, street football, gambling and other forms of popular entertainment were all subject to intense campaigns to halt their supposed contamination of youth. In the twentieth century another 'dangerous enemy' was discovered in the new medium of the Hollywood cinema (see Chapter 2). Chapter 5 looks, in some detail, at how youth leisure pursuits from the 1950s on have been subject to adult censure, moral panic and regulation. As will be discussed in Section 5.1, much of this was first encapsulated by the notion of a specific *youth culture* – that is, a way of life shared by young people which is distinct from, and oppositional to, adult culture. By the 1970s this vision of a society primarily stratified by age and generation was challenged by researchers who, in contrast, identified a number of youth *sub*cultures which could be distinguished with reference to their respective class position. And by the 1980s further research also brought attention to significant gender and racial differences in youth subcultural activities. A dominant theme running through all of these studies – summarized in Sections 5.2 and 5.3 – has remained the degree to which 'spectacular' youth subcultures – such as teddy boys, mods, skinheads, punks, hippies, beats and Rastafarians – are inherently deviant and oppositional or simply sites of media and commercial appropriation.

Youth subcultures have always attracted inordinate attention from academics, mass media and politicians, ranging from outright condemnation to commercial popularization. They have *inter alia* been identified as 'folk devils', 'the enemies within', the product of social change, a barometer of future social change and as metaphors for the state of society at any one time. In the tradition of radical youth studies established by the Centre for Contemporary Cultural Studies at the University of Birmingham ('the Birmingham School') in the 1970s, subcultures have also been perceived as sites of resistance to adult authority existing outside of, and in opposition to, the 'mainstream'. In short, subcultures were celebrated as authentic expressions of youthful subversion, particularly in their ability to engender 'moral panic' and adult fear. Section 5.4 offers a critique of this literature by noting how it initially spoke almost exclusively about male forms and largely avoided questions of gender and processes of conformity. Section 5.4 also details how the 'new orthodoxy' of the Birmingham School came to be challenged notably by a revisionist strand of cultural studies in the 1980s but also an emergent postmodern cultural criminology in the mid 1990s.

A long-standing problem had always been the degree to which 'outsider' academics could 'speak for' young people and how far (if at all) the followers of youth styles could recognize and place themselves in the theoretical ascriptions of structure, culture, subculture and resistance that were on offer. What has emerged is a level of analysis that is more flexible, more plural and more attuned to a complex array of subjectivities. Thus the concern is to account for how meaning and identity are *flexibly* constructed within subcultural affiliation (Widdicombe and Wooffitt, 1995); the centrality of pleasure and fun in moments of subcultural transgression (Presdee, 2000) and how youth cultures, because they also tend to be music cultures, exist not as autonomous forms, but are indelibly connected to the media industries (Thornton, S., 1995; Cashmore, 1997). In the apparently 'classless' atmosphere created by the overtly hedonistic style of 'rave culture' in the late 1980s, some researchers have become wary of assigning any specific meaning, fixed structural position or invariable cultural significance to subcultural practice (Redhead, 1990, 1993). Increasingly the boundaries between such opposites as 'culture and crime'; 'resistance and commercialism'; 'opposition and collusion'; 'production and consumption'; and 'subculture and mainstream' have become blurred or dissolved. With the burgeoning of a remarkable diversity and transnationalization of youth styles in the 1990s, the insights initially drawn from the study of local, class-based subcultures in the 1970s have once more been called into question.

Whilst much of this research is usually to be found in cultural studies, it is also notable that youth cultural styles and 'resistances' have frequently been subjected to moral outrage, overt policing and legal challenge. The chapter also reflects how elements of a cultural criminology, with a heritage including the National Deviancy Conferences of the 1970s and interactionism (see Chapter 4.1) now devote a not inconsiderable part of their energy to studying the convergence of cultural and criminal dynamics so that fresh insights can be made into the meaning of rule breaking and how non-conformist styles have been (and continue to be) subjected to criminalization.

Subcultural Theory and Analysis

A Youth Culture?

5.1 The notion of a youth culture was developed from the psychological term 'adolescence' (see Chapters 2.3 and 3.1). Whilst the latter suggested that the key to understanding youthful behaviour lay in physical bodily changes and emotional unheavals surrounding the onset of puberty, the idea of a 'youth culture' suggested that such behaviour was caused by social and economic change. In 1942 the American sociologist Talcott Parsons coined the term 'youth culture' to isolate the supposedly unique and highly distinctive behaviour patterns that were thought to be emerging amongst American 'adolescents'. For Parsons, youth culture emphasized values of hedonism, leisure, consumption and irresponsibility, rather than productive work. He saw the function of youth culture, however, as being to provide a period when young people can break away from dependence on their families and become free to develop a level of autonomy. This was viewed as a purely modern phenomenon and explained with reference to the extended period of training and education afforded to young people in modern industrial societies.

Youth culture, however, was also seen as having dysfunctional qualities. Youth was viewed as belonging to one adolescent subculture which transcended all other cultural attachments to home, neighbourhood or class. As a result young people were placed in an antagonistic relationship to the social order and were the source of major social problems (Parsons, 1942). Such analysis was indicative of a corresponding trend in much sociological enquiry both in America and Britain in the immediate post-war period which declared an end to poverty and heralded the emergence of a new classless society. Youth culture was seen as a classless phenomenon. In Britain, the first influential sociological study of 'youth culture' was Abrams' *The Teenage Consumer*, published in 1959. This book, an empirical survey of a new consumer group, purported to reveal a new culture defined in terms of leisure – milk bars, fashion, clothes, cosmetics, hair styles, rock'n'roll records, films, magazines, dancing and dance halls. This definition of youth as a consumer group implied a classless culture shared by people from different social positions. Abrams' research also revealed – in some contradiction – that the consumer habits of youth were dominated by the interests of working-class males.

One of the earliest challenges to the 'classless teenage consumer' thesis was Willmott's study of *Adolescent Boys of East London*, published in 1966. Following a sample of 246 boys in Bethnal Green, Wilmott discovered that the new teenage leisure culture did not replace existing class-based cultures, but existed alongside them. Despite the fact that the boys had easy access to the growing number of discotheques, beat clubs and boutiques of the West End, they were more likely to use the resources of their locality. He found little sign of what was being referred to as 'the generation gap', as most boys remained with their families and regularly attended school with little or no hostility to their teachers. Willmott's study was important for various reasons. First, it demonstrated that the term 'youth culture' obscured differences within youth. Second, it revealed a marked continuity between youth and adult life. Third, it brought analysis of class divisions into the centre of youth studies.

To varying degrees, Downes's study of corner boy culture in Stepney and Poplar in 1966, Hargreaves' analysis of a secondary modern boys' school in 1967 and Sugarman's study of London schoolboys in 1967 all began to question the classlessness thesis and offer demonstrations of the centrality of class inequalities in structuring both the work and leisure opportunities available to young people. Murdock and McCron's (1973) survey of musical taste substantiated this position. Youths' subcultural identifications, they found, were notably moulded by their social class refracted first through the school and second through the family and neighbourhood. Middle-class pupils were under pressure to pass examinations and only a small minority – the 'scoobies' (a working-class derisory term for students) – took part in a subculture by reading the 'underground press', smoking dope and following the lifestyles of their rock music heroes in their leisure time. Working-class youth, on the other hand, underwent different experiences within the school, community and family which predisposed their brand of 'youth culture' to be more immediate, encompassing values of action, toughness and physical competence. Accordingly the tastes of the 'skins' (working-class skinheads) favoured the potential for dancing and group solidarity offered by amphetamine use, ska and bluebeat. In a later article, Murdock and McCron (1976, p. 24) reiterated the importance of class divisions, but argued that the concern was not simply one of 'substituting class for age . . . but of examining the relations between class and age and more particularly the way in which age acts as a mediation of class'.

Such reasoning was overlooked by many commentators of the counterculture of the late 1960s, who – probably more than most – helped the term 'youth culture' to gain widespread currency. The upsurge of cultural and political radicalism among students and 'drop-outs' in America and Europe in the years 1967–9 convinced such authors as Marcuse (1972) that class and class conflict were now largely redundant and that the more progressive elements in society were to be found in its youth. As the problems facing Western society were analysed in terms of technological dominance and a repressive tolerance in which individual creativity had been suppressed (rather than by reference to poverty, social deprivation and class inequalities), the initial salvation of society was seen to rest primarily with those youths who refused to conform to the dominant needs of repressive society. Youth was viewed as a major source of liberation with potential for the later re-actuation of class conflicts. Roszak (1971) also made great claims for the unification of young people, for with them lay his vision of a viable revolutionary force which would be able to attack the problems of modern 'technocracy' and could transform 'the very sense men have of reality'. However, in Britain at least the counterculture tended to reside within a small minority of the youth population, taken primarily from disaffiliated sections of the middle class. Occasionally they may have spoken for all youth in noting their material and social disadvantages in comparison with their elders (lower rates of pay; prohibitions on property ownership, drinking, driving and marriage; subjugation to adult authority), but their 'revolution' was couched largely in the class-specific goals of individualism, self expression and self discovery.

As a result Brake (1980, p. 8) notes that the concept of *a* youth culture glosses over the existence of 'a complex kaleidoscope of several adolescent and youthful subcultures appealing to different age and class groups, involving different life-styles'. Such class-based analysis, which achieved academic ascendancy in the 1970s, also highlighted how different groups of youth found different solutions to the problems they faced: problems that emanated not only from their respective localized economic and class positions, but also from gender and 'race' relations. Although young people may share certain status attributes simply by virtue of their age, their claims to resources and power are significantly determined by their class, gender, ethnicity and geographical location (see Chapter 1.4).

Gangs and Subcultures

Although groups of youth have long attracted adult condemnation (see Chapter 2), the notion of the 'gang' is peculiar to the twentieth century and largely confined to America. The gang was first defined by Puffer (1912) as 'the play group' existing alongside the family and the neighbourhood. This interpretation was subsequently adopted by Thrasher (1927) in his influential study *The Gang*. Influenced by social ecology theory (see Chapter 3.2), Thrasher estimated that in the 1920s there were over 1,000 youth gangs operating within Chicago's 'zone of transition' alone. Whilst it is clear that this included any number of loose-knit groups, Thrasher's work set the tone for much subsequent gang research in his argument that what begins as a form of play brings youth into conflict with their community and into an environment where a delinquent career progresses. The gang is organized around working-class territorial imperatives and is based on a group solidarity and codes of conduct that are passed down through generations of boys on the streets. The gang provides an alternative refuge and source of belonging and support in otherwise socially disorganized (and largely immigrant) communities: 'a substitute for what society fails to give . . . it fills a gap and affords an escape' (Thrasher, 1927, p. 33). Whyte's (1943) similarly classic study of street corner boys in Boston reiterated many of these themes whilst stressing the importance of a structured (rather than disorganized) environment supportive of long-term mutual obligations. The gang, rather than being in conflict with its community, was viewed as an integral part of the local social order.

By the 1950s the vagaries of what actually constituted 'the gang' were addressed through the alternative concept of 'subculture'. Again American in origin, a theory of *youth subculture* gained sociological prominence through Albert Cohen's (1955) research into the culture of the gang in Chicago. Cohen viewed the gang as a subculture with a value system different from that of mainstream American culture, distinguishable through special vocabulary, shared internal beliefs and specialized ways of dressing and acting. He argued that working-class youth use the gang as a way of reacting against and adjusting to a dominant middle-class society that discriminates against them because of their lower-class position. Their 'status frustration' becomes visible in 'non-utilitarian, malicious, and negativistic' forms of delinquency whereby middle-class ethics of ambition, tangible achievement, deferred gratification, cultivated manners, and respect for property are rejected or reversed.

Similarly, Cloward and Ohlin (1961) explained working-class gang involvement in terms of culturally prescribed high aspirations thwarted by the lack of actual opportunities to afford their realization. They attributed the existence of *different* subcultures to the relative position of sections of youth in the structure of opportunity. All subcultures exist as adjustments made by their members to a lack of access to 'legitimate' middle-class goals. Status is thus achieved via 'illegitimate' and deviant means. Cloward and Ohlin's research concluded that an understanding of the subculture of the gang cannot be divorced from an analysis of youths' position in the labour market and their chances of advancement through the education 'market' (see Chapter 3.1).

However, the sharp separation of delinquent and non-delinquent values on which these studies were based has been heavily criticized, first by Matza (1964) and then by the first British application of American subcultural theory provided by Downes's (1966) study of working-class youths in East London. They mark a shift from concern solely with gang delinquency towards the many attempts to account for the existence and development of youth subcultures in terms of their leisure activities. It is this trend that characterizes the majority of British subcultural studies.

Downes (1966), for example, found little evidence of Cohen's 'status frustration' among the working-class boys of East London, either in school or work. Rather they dissociated themselves from the labour market and deflected their interests, achievements and aspirations into leisure pursuits. Leisure, rather than delinquency, thereby provided working-class youths with a collective solution to their problems. The connection between leisure and delinquency becomes apparent if leisure aspirations also remain unfulfilled. The opportunities for leisure may have increased in the 1960s with an expansive teenage entertainment industry, but access to its commodities involved both expense and a commitment to consumerism. When access was limited because of an inability to acquire the necessary symbols of subcultural leisure – scooter, motorbike, leather jacket, stereo system, and so on – or when the expectation of action was met with 'nothing going on', then some working-class youths reached a 'delinquent solution' by 'pushing the legitimate values of teenage culture to their logical conclusion' (Downes, 1966, p. 134). Whilst there may be some continuation between conventional 'teenage culture' and delinquency, criminal activity is not a key concern. Rather it is argued that leisure and delinquency combine to provide the conditions under which aspects of subcultural behaviour can become *criminalized*. Indeed, in Britain, Downes's study was influential in various respects. Not only did it shift the debate away from discourses of crime and delinquency and towards discourses of leisure and entertainment as a means of securing 'cultural space', but it also recognized how subcultural experiences and opportunities were structured by class-based material and economic conditions.

Neither did Downes (1966) find any evidence of structured gangs in Britain. Whilst Spergel (1992) and Ball and Curry (1995) note that in American research, definitions of the 'gang' are often loose and variable, yet the term implies some form of identifiable leadership, membership criteria and organizational structure, which appear to be lacking in most British youth subcultures. The concept of a youth subculture, then, tends to denote a tacit shared ideology but one that does not depend on face-to-face interaction with, or obligation towards, other members. As a result, Campbell and Muncer (1989) argue that (notwithstanding the British media's continual use of the term) youth gangs rarely, if ever, existed in Britain. As Downes (1966) suggested, the idea of gangs existing in Britain at least in the 1960s was symptomatic of middle-class attempts to impute a structure and organization to working-class groups which they did not possess. America owns the gang, while Britain has traditionally been the home of subcultures.

One of a few British studies which claimed to have discovered the gang was Patrick's (1973) Glasgow research, but, as Campbell and Muncer argue, even though these groups of male youth may have been known by territorial names, they had little internal structure and failed to persist over time. In contrast, the contemporary and classic ethnographic studies of white, black, Chinese and Puerto Rican gangs in America (Thrasher, 1927; Whyte, W.F., 1943; Vigil, 1988; Jankowski, 1991) paint a picture of neighbourhood groups, organized largely along racial lines, with a strong sense of local territory, mutual obligations and, latterly, direct involvement in extortion, trafficking and the drugs trade. As such, Campbell and Muncer (1989) conclude that unlike British subcultures, American gangs are typically not sites of ritual resistance, but alternative business enterprises and communities of identity.

Whilst this may be the case, American gang research in the 1990s has warned of imputing any uniformity to the processes of gang formation and development. Huff (1996) for example, notes that none of the contemporary research on American gangs delivers clear or unequivocal messages. Gangs are diverse and come in a wide variety of forms. Gangs may be joined for protection yet *intra*gang conflict is endemic. They may offer a sense of belonging but many lack stability of membership, cohesion and continuity. Gangs have long been popularly associated with crime, but entire gangs as collectives are rarely involved in its commission. Gang members are not uniformly delinquent. Most violence is internally directed. Gangs are firmly associated with youth, but the age spread of gang members also extends into the forties. There is little evidence that gangs evolve into adult criminal organizations. There may be 'drug crews', 'wilding groups', 'prison gangs', 'gutter punks', 'bikers', 'neo-nazi skinheads' and 'football hooligans' *ad infinitum*. But their differences confound any attempt at definition. Ball and Curry (1995, p. 227) are forced to conclude that most attempts to identify 'the gang' are little more than 'veiled expressions of bourgeois disapproval'.

Indeed, Katz (2000) argues that widely held perceptions of the American gang as rapidly increasing in number, increasingly violent and embedded in drug trafficking are largely driven by news coverage, police recording practices and a popular culture that widely assumes that, but for the existence of gangs, youth crime rates would be substantially lower. Comparing New York and Los Angeles, he contends that gangs, as an interpretive lens for understanding deviance in the American city, appear to rise and fall in relationship to anxieties focused on waves of foreign immigration (Katz, 2000, p. 180). Thus the preoccupation with gangs in New York in the 1950s – subsequently reflected in the play *West Side Story* – coincides with the immigration of Puerto Ricans after the Second World War. The 'gangs problem' in Southern California in the 1980s converges with coterminous initiatives to block immigrants' access to public services. The 'gang' provides a convenient symbol to attach to all forms of youth crime and violence.

So where does this leave 'the gang' in Britain? From the late 1990s it has become increasingly common to assume a proliferation of gang membership and gang-related crime. Under the headline 'GANG MEMBERSHIP SPIRALS AMONG UNDER 16s' (*Observer*, 8 September 2002), it is claimed that there are as many as 30,000 gang members in England and Wales clustered within London, Birmingham and Manchester. Gang culture is also popularly linked to gun crime. A year earlier the same newspaper (*Observer*, 15 April 2001) also claimed that 'GIRLS LEAD THE PACK OF GANGLAND VIOLENCE'. Reality or myth? How far – as Katz might suggest – is contemporary concern with gang violence linked to fears, say, about asylum seekers? Are young women becoming more violent?

It is probably significant that there remains relatively little gang research in Britain. What information we have comes from Home Office projects into particular crime problems. For example, Bullock and Tilley's (2002) research into shootings and violent incidents in Manchester was part of a Targeted Policing Initiative and relies on police data for identifying gang members. Recognizing the problems of definition, it adopted an American description of 'a self formed association, with a name, leadership, geographic territory, regular meetings and collective action to carry out illegal activities'. The research identified four main gangs – Longsight Crew, Pit Bull Crew, Gooch and Doddington – in a small area of South Manchester – each largely made up of black or mixed race males between the ages of 21 and 25. There were relatively few female members. Indeed, the idea of hyper-violent girl gangs so often depicted in the media has been widely dismissed as fanciful (Chesney-Lind et al., 1996; Batchelor, 2001). Members of gangs are involved in a wide range – not simply firearm – offences. Conflict between the four gangs was endemic. The existence of such groups may be beyond dispute. Their permanency is, however, open to debate. The key issue remains why 'the gang' has reached such a level of public concern, particularly when we recall that during the Manchester study, crime rates were declining overall and, whilst shootings fluctuated between

1 and 12 a month between 1998 and 2000, all firearm offences still only accounted for less than 1 per cent of all recorded crime. Moreover nearly half of the shootings did not involve gang members at all. Where there was evidence of gang involvement, the average number of shootings per month increased only from 2.5 in January 1997 to 3 in September 2000.

This of course does not deny that lethal violence is a matter of some concern. However, it calls into question the viability of the convenient academic, political and popular concept of 'the gang'. This problem is exacerbated in any attempt to distinguish the gang from crime firms, organized crime and alternative commercial practices. Fraud and the drug trade, as bootlegging has in the past, often represent a significant blurring of what constitutes legality and illegality (Hobbs, 1997).

Subcultural Resistance

The complex relationship between economic structures, class, culture, leisure, generation and subculture was first examined in detail by the Centre for Contemporary Cultural Studies at the University of Birmingham (the 'Birmingham School') in 1975 (Hall and Jefferson, 1976). On the one hand, the meaning of subcultural style was examined through various ethnographic and semiological analyses; on the other, the political implications of deviance were explored through investigations of the structural and class position of various subcultures and their propensity to engender 'moral panics'.

The analysis of the Birmingham School stemmed directly from Phil Cohen's research (1972) on a succession of working-class youth subcultures in the East End of London during the 1960s. Changes in the mid 1950s in housing, employment and income, it was argued, had caught a majority of the working class in the middle of two dominant but contradictory ideologies: the new ideology of 'spectacular consumption' and affluence on the one hand, and the traditional ideology of work and pride in a job well done on the other. Post-war developments in the local economy served consistently to undermine the solidarity, loyalties and traditions of working-class life. Automated techniques in manufacturing made traditional pride in craftsmanship impossible. The social space of the pub, corner shop and the street was destroyed by high-rise flats. The changes that accompanied 'affluence', then, also threatened the very structure of working-class life.

This predicament was registered most deeply in and on young males as they were forced to travel out of the community to work, or to move away permanently. Those that remained tried – in the form of subcultures – to retrieve those socially cohesive elements that had been destroyed in the parent culture. The internal conflicts of the parent culture came to be worked out in terms of generational conflict. The subcultural styles of the young reflected and acted on these contradictions between traditional working-class puritanism and the new hedonism of consumption. Young people may not have been aware of the origins of such contradictions, but experienced and had to come to terms with them. Those who faced the transition from school to work found themselves in a situation in which they were encouraged, via the media, advertising and consumer industries, to seek immediate gratification, while being constrained by low pay and limited opportunities. Youth styles were thus viewed by Cohen as a 'generational solution' to contradictions facing the working class as a whole.

The Birmingham School refined this approach by drawing on the work of the Marxist author Gramsci (1971). They located subcultures not just in relation to their parent cultures, but also in relation to structures of class conflict. The British working class, it was argued, has developed its own historical cultures and the relations between these and the dominant culture are always negotiable. Working-class culture is always in a position to win 'space', for the hegemony of the dominant culture is never completed. It is always in the process of being contested and fought over. Subcultures contest this space through their 'focal concerns' and in the moments of originality created by the formation of deviant subcultural styles. As a result working-class youth subcultures were considered oppositional forms because of their attempts to 'resist' dominant culture. It is significant that the Birmingham School's major publication was called *Resistance through Rituals* (Hall and Jefferson, 1976). Above all, subcultures were viewed as symbolic representations of social contradictions and as offering a symbolic critique of the established order: they were *oppositional* rather than simply deviant formations.

Both Phil Cohen (1972) and Hall and Jefferson (1976), however, suggested that subcultures offer solutions of a 'magical' rather than of a real nature to contradictions in the socio-economic system. Their 'solutions' were 'imaginary': enacted as play during leisure. Youth styles do not change fundamental class realities. For young people, though, style and leisure allow an expression of identity and self image which helps to counter or deny the contradictions and subordination faced in most other aspects of their lives. Leisure is thus the key area for the creation of distinctive subcultural styles which have not only creative, but also political, potential.

A Matter of Style

While it was recognized that the analysis of style cannot be made in isolation from a subculture's class position and practices, some authors gave privileged attention to a separate line of enquiry concerned primarily with how subcultures selectively appropriated symbolic objects and attached meaning to them. Their attention was so directed because it is in the generation of style that the possibility of resistance and non-ideological political action is thought to be most at work. Clarke (1976), for example, used the cultural anthropologist Lévi-Strauss's (1966) concept of *bricolage* to explain how particular objects can be used by subcultures in such a way as to transform or subvert their original meaning. Thus the 'Edwardian look' of drape jackets was borrowed by the teddy boys of the 1950s and combined with such extraneous items as the bootlace tie and brothel-creepers (suede shoes) to produce a style in antithesis to adult sensibilities. What was involved in this analysis was a *reading* of subcultural style to signify or denote something beyond its surface appearance. Objects are borrowed from the world of consumer commodities and, as they are incorporated into the focal concerns of subcultures, their meaning is reworked. This appropriation of style allows subcultures to express their opposition obliquely or ironically. Hebdige provided the most elaborate analysis of this process in his explanation, for example, of why mods chose to ride scooters, why skinheads wore boots and why punks pushed safety pins through their noses:

> These 'humble objects' can be magically appropriated, stolen by subordinate groups and made to carry 'secret' meanings which express in code a form of resistance to the order which guarantees their continued subordination. Style in subculture is then pregnant with significance. Its transformations go 'against nature' interrupting the process of 'normalization'. As such they are gestures, movements towards a speech which offends the 'silent majority', which challenges the principle of unity and cohesion, which contradicts the myth of consensus. (Hebdige, 1979, p. 18)

For Hebdige, subcultural styles acted as symbolic violations of the social order. Youth styles are not random, but constitute the basis for 'semiotic guerrilla warfare'. In order to explain how certain styles coalesce to create a meaningful subcultural entity, Hebdige borrowed another term from Lévi-Strauss: *homology*. Contrary to popular depictions of subcultures as lawless, Hebdige illustrated how their internal structure was characterized by orderliness; how different elements of style cohered into a meaningful whole (Hebdige, 1979, pp. 113–17). He argued, for example, that there was a homological relation between the spiked hair, the amphetamines, the spitting, the trashy cut-up clothes and the raw and basic music of the punk subculture of the late 1970s. Punk styles fitted together because of their generalized 'anarchy' and refusal to cohere around a stable and permanent set of central values.

Similarly, Willis (1978) and Clarke (1976, p. 179) argued that there existed a homology between the intense activism, physical prowess and love of machines of motorbike boys and their preference for rock'n'roll music, just as there was a homology between the structurelessness, self introspection and loose group affiliation of hippies and their choice of underground or progressive rock music. The concepts of 'bricolage' and 'homology' were thus used to explore how subcultures can alter and subvert normal expectations within a framework of meanings that is both coherent and meaningful. Through these semiotic techniques of analysis, Hebdige was able to view style as a signifier of a unified subcultural practice, rather than as a series of distinct cultural expressions. However, in this concentration on the minutiae of subcultural activities, style is drawn some steps away from its followers' material existence. Whereas for Clarke it is class that is the key to discovering subcultural resistance, Hebdige selects style as the main variable in understanding how such resistance is eventually voiced. The former attempts to relate a set of cultural phenomena to the question of class formations and the construction of hegemony. The latter tries to establish the autonomy of the signifying practices of subcultures from any simple reduction to the interests of any single class. In both accounts, however, the relationship between subculture and leisure remains the dominant theme. It is young people's use of leisure and style which offers possibilities for subcultural resistance. Central to their approach is the assumption that the innovative in style is both rebellious and a form of political protest. Thus the selective use of leisure becomes 'a source of collective power in the struggle with schools or police'.

> In terms of its political content then, we would characterise youth culture as being involved in a struggle fundamental to the social order – that of the control of meaning. Here one can see the significance of the media's stereotyping and thereby redefining of youth cultures. It is an attempt by the dominant culture to reaffirm its own view of society as the only correct one. It is significant that in this struggle for the control of meaning one of the most frequent adjectives used to describe disapproval of behaviour by the young is 'meaningless'. (Clarke and Jefferson, 1973, p. 9)

Recognizing the significance of style was also a key feature of a cultural criminology that emerged some 20 years later (see Section 5.5). Ferrell (1996; 1997) for example, argues that hip hop graffiti writing exists essentially as a 'crime of style' for both its practitioners and the authorities attempting to stop it. Style – particular ways of dressing, talking, walking and so on – is the connecting thread between cultural practice and deviant/criminal identity: as symbols of resistance, indicators of difference and as targets for criminalization.

Alternatively, it has also been argued that oppositional youth styles may be *defused* by transforming them into 'fashionable commodities'. The *diffusion* of ted, punk, mod and hippie styles, for example, through boutique, chain store and recording industry marketing, has also acted to render them 'safe'. In this way symbols of resistance can also become objects simply to be 'displayed' and cease to challenge and disturb the dominant order. They become manufactured products, to be consumed like any other (Clarke, 1976, p. 185).

These analyses of youth subcultures and styles had, by the early 1980s, established the parameters within which a radical vision of youth cultures was contained (see Table 5.1).

Table 5.1 *Key elements of British subcultural theory*

- Situating youthful behaviour in its precise social, economic and historical context
- Locating youth subcultures within the class structure and class conflict of post-war Britain
- Explaining youth style as meaningful and in particular decoding its oppositional qualities
- Examining youth cultures as social processes involved in an ongoing struggle for the 'control of meaning' with other class cultures, dominant culture and the consumer industries

Subcultures and Resistance

5.2 This section offers a brief history of youth subcultures and styles in Britain from the 1950s to the end of the 1970s. It begins by examining how British subcultural analysis was applied to a succession of predominantly working-class, white youth cultures – teddy boys, mods, skinheads, punks – and black youth cultures – rude boys and Rastafarians – in terms that emphasized their oppositional styles and modes of resistance. Section 5.3 goes on to look at how the concept of *counterculture* has been employed to capture the more overt forms of political dissent contained with the beats, CND, 'new left' and hippies of the 1950s and 1960s, the New Age travellers, saboteurs and eco-warriors of the 1980s and 1990s, and the anti-global capitalism movements of the 1990s and 2000s.

Teddy Boys

In the decade 1945–55 British social history was shaped above all by the memory and aftermath of the Second World War. Despite the austerity and rationing which lasted until the mid 1950s, Britain slowly pulled itself towards economic and social recovery, epitomized by the symbolic commitment to creating a welfare state and free state education for all. By the mid 1950s Britain was supposedly riding on a wave of affluence and full employment and was claiming the coming of a classless society. However, affluence also had its price. Inevitably it was those lowest in the social hierarchy – working-class unskilled youths – who found they were excluded from such 'benefits'. The post-war years also saw the 'planning blight' and consequent break-up of many working-class neighbourhoods that had previously existed as close-knit communities. It is against this background that the 'utterly unexpected' rise of the teddy boys has been explained (Fyvel, 1961).

The teddy boy subculture (like a majority of British working-class youth subcultures) was specifically the creation of working-class districts in London. In a period of 'full employment', it was such sections of the population traditionally lacking in power and status who were most likely to find themselves excluded from full-time employment. Faced with an educational system which supposedly provided equal opportunity, it was they who had lost out. In the wake of the new affluence and increasing availability of consumer goods, it was the teds who discovered that there remained a general lack of public provision for leisure for the under-20s. In response they moved into the only space available and made the local 'caff' and the street their 'home'. Identity of self and group was maintained initially by adherence to certain styles of dress – the dandified cut of Edwardian clothes – and later through music – rock'n'roll.

Although the teds, like all other subcultures, attracted a relative minority of youth, it has been argued that the 'nihilist ted spirit' did affect a great many and indeed it was from the rock'n'roll mania of 1956 that the American term 'teenage culture' was imported into Britain (Melly, 1972). Presumably, then, the teds voiced and articulated a disenchantment for which there was a ready, but latent, wider youth market. They responded to their lack of status and 'cultural space' by reaffirming and defending working-class values and defined their particular and separate stance by their choice of dress and music. Their hair, by military, or perhaps more pertinent, by National Service (1947–60) standards, was excessively long and was generally worn with sideburns, a great deal of Brylcreem, some form of quiff at the front and variations of the DA (duck's arse) at the back. Their preferred drug was alcohol. Their clothes were a bastardization of a pseudo-Edwardian style, ironically originally created by Savile Row in the early 1950s for young upper-class men-about-town. It consisted of long 'drape' jackets with velvet collars, tight 'drainpipe' trousers, bootlace ties and thick crêpe-soled shoes. For Jefferson (1976) such style represented an arrogant yet half-conscious parody of the upper classes and also an attempt to glorify the masculinity and slickness of the Hollywood criminal hero. The term 'Teddy Boy' first appeared in print in March 1954 when it was clear that they could no longer be simply referred to as the 'hooligans', 'spivs' or 'cosh boys' of the past (Rock and Cohen, 1970, p. 94).

With the arrival of rock'n'roll, the ted was able to give voice to his disenchantment. Imported from America, rock'n'roll marked an abrupt shift in musical style. Although it was derivative of black blues and white country styles, Melly (1972, p. 36) argues that it was 'a contemporary incitement to mindless fucking and arbitrary vandalism: screw and smash music'. It represented a blatant attack on parental sexual taboo and, for the underprivileged young, became one of the few means whereby self-autonomy could be expressed.

At the showing of the rock 'n' roll film *Blackboard Jungle*, in London in 1956, Britain witnessed its first 'rock riot' (Hebdige, 1988, p. 30). Later Bill Haley's British performances and the first showings of the Elvis Presley films were to be greeted with 'mass hysteria'. They provided a key source of identification not just for teds but for wide sections of working-class youth. Delinquency and 'the teenager' converged. When the adult world wanted order in the cinemas, coffee bars and streets, the teds responded by jiving in the aisles, razoring cinema seats and attacking 'intruders' in their 'territories'. They were assured of a hostile political and media reaction. The *Reynold News* (1 May 1954) described them as a 'grave social evil'; they were demonized as the end result of the importation of an un-British (American) degenerate culture into Britain (Pearson, 1983, p. 19).

However, recording, publishing and film companies gradually realized that there existed a huge market for such interests. The films *The Wild One* (1954), starring Marlon Brando, and *Rebel without a Cause* (1955), starring James Dean, became cult movies in their celebration of teenage lawlessness. The teddy boys' style too began filtering upwards and outwards from south London and underwent significant changes. Leather jackets replaced the drapes, and motorcycles allowed greater freedom and mobility. The 'rocker' style emerged. At the end of 1956 Britain's first home grown rock'n'roll idol, 19 year old Tommy Steele, appeared on the scene. Coupled with skiffle, the possibility of semi-amateur music-making by and for youth became a reality. It was from these origins that in 1957 a group in Liverpool was formed which over the next five years was to evolve into the Beatles. By the late 1950s, the commercial diffusion of 'ted' music and style was such that its oppositional qualities were defused.

Mods

From the late 1950s onwards, British society was being interpreted by many political commentators and sociologists in terms of the earlier prophesied classlessness and embourgeoisement. They argued that post-war affluence had by now eroded differences between middle-class and working-class life chances and styles. Despite contrary empirical evidence of the persistence of the class structure and differential opportunities (Westergaard, 1965), working-class youths of the early 1960s were caught up in the desire to share the fruits of the 'new affluence'. The use of the term 'mod' reflected such contradictions by referring both to the image of a consumer-based 'swinging' London and also to a particular subcultural 'solution'. It was the province of upwardly mobile, working-class youths who had 'made it good' through art school and the commercialization of style – the Beatles, Mary Quant, David Bailey, Jean Shrimpton, Twiggy – and, more precisely, those who found the lower middle-class, non-manual occupations to which they had aspired just as stultifying as the manual jobs they had left behind.

As a subculture, the mods originated from East London and working-class estates in the suburbs of the capital. Typically they were engaged in semi-skilled manual work or basic white collar jobs (van boy, messenger, clerk, office boy, and so on). The mods accepted work in so far as it gave them a greater potential to buy style and status. They lived for nights, weekends and bank holidays. Partly a reflection of their relative affluence and partly an attempt to emulate the cool and slick style of their West Indian neighbours (the 'shades' and pork pie hats), the mod style was characterized by short hair, smart Italian designed suits and an almost narcissistic obsession with neat appearance. Their preferred drug was amphetamine (speed). Mods were the epitome of the conspicuous consumer, whether in clothes, scooters, music or amphetamines. But for Hebdige (1976a) they were never passive consumers. The scooter and clothes were transformed into symbols of solidarity while 'speed' enabled a total commitment to all-night dancing in the clubs and discos. The style they created has thus been 'read' as constituting a parody of the consumer society in which they were situated.

Their leisure was concentrated in the meeting places of music clubs and ballrooms of London's West End, in which American Tamla Motown and Jamaican bluebeat music provided a suitable backcloth. Many of these clubs had previously been exclusively black clubs, and the mods' emulation of black style reveals the extent to which many British subcultures draw on a black heritage for their forms of music and fashion (Hebdige, 1979).

If the mods were something of an apolitical or 'imaginary' reaction against the ideology of classlessness, then they equally reacted against the music and style of the previous decade. Rock'n'roll and the descendants of the teds – the rockers – were dismissed as boorish, out of date and crude. In part this explains the conflict between the subcultures on the beaches at Margate, Brighton and Hastings in 1964. Whether open hatred and violence were continually prevalent between mods and rockers remains open to debate. Certainly Stan Cohen (1973a) offers a convincing argument that our understanding of this phenomenon has been more than tainted by selective and sensational media reporting (see Chapter 4.1).

By 1966 the mod 'movement' in both its middle-class commercial (symbolized by Carnaby Street) and working-class subcultural variants was beginning to wane because of pressures from the media, the market and its own internal contradictions. These two elements of 'mod' never really merged into one and in the following years were to separate further with the coming of the skinheads and the hippies.

Skinheads

Skinheads probably first appeared in East London in early 1968, and were generated from sections of the unskilled working-class community. For Mungham and Pearson (1976) the specific content of their style represented both a 'caricature and [a] re-assertion of solid, male, working-class toughness'. Such an exaggerated reflection of their parent culture was exemplified by their 'uniform' of cropped hair, braces, half-mast trousers and Doc Marten 'bovver boots'. Their association with violence, football hooliganism, and 'Paki' and 'queer' bashing has been viewed as an attempt to recover the cohesiveness of working-class communities and to retain some control over their territory – albeit in its most reactionary form (Hebdige, 1981, p. 40).

Frequently the cause of their anger would be displaced on to the new Pakistani immigrant communities and consequently skinheads were seen as a racist right wing of subcultural style. Despite this, in line with their hard mod ancestors, the skinheads tried to emulate the sharp 'rude boy' of an Afro-Caribbean youth subculture. Accordingly reggae and ska music were adopted for their accessibility and because they enhanced such values as masculinity. But the skinheads steered clear of night clubs, partly because of the expense and partly because they identified more with the traditional working-class activities located around pubs, alcohol, football and the street. They explored avenues that were tainted by the 'work ethic', puritanism and working-class chauvinism. Those who most obviously had dismissed such values – the middle-class hippies – became legitimate targets for their aggression. According to radical deviancy theorists, skinhead culture remained an affirmation of white working-class values (Clarke, 1976; Hebdige, 1981). However, the skinheads were not overtly politically conscious, despite attempts by the National Front and the Socialist Labour League to recruit them. Rather, their subculture filled the gap opened up by the decline of working-class politics and culture – a gap they attempted to defend with their developed sense of 'community' and 'territorality'. As Ian Taylor (1971) noted, such allegiances were frequently centred on the local football team, where traditionally working-class values of collectivity, physical toughness and local rivalry could be acted out.

This attempt to reassert traditional working-class values, Clarke (1976) maintained, was largely of a symbolic nature, finding its expression in the world of leisure, rather than work or community politics. As the style spread outwards from the inner-city areas, it evaporated into groups known as crombies (derived from the crombie coat), smooth-heads and casuals, and the way was open again for consumerism to capitalize on style. Taylor and Wall (1976), for example, emphasize the role consumerism played in taking elements of the skinhead style, fusing it with remnants of the hippie underground and, perhaps for the first time, providing a style (later to be known as 'glam rock') which, they argue, conveyed a sense of classlessness within a now universal manufactured culture. Changes in working-class youth cultures, in this analysis, are thus largely accounted for by manufactured changes and sales potential. Cultural innovations become circumscribed and distorted by the agents of consumerism. But skinhead style has never disappeared. It continually resurfaces – through Oi music, through soccer hooliganism, through the British National Party and neo-Nazi/white supremacist groups particularly in Germany and America and at the harder edge of working-class culture in general.

Punks

The 1960s were a time of relative affluence compared with the 1970s. By the mid 1970s mass unemployment and fascism, coupled with high inflation, had returned. The section of society that suffered most from unemployment was that of the working-class school-leaver, particularly those without any qualifications. It was against this background that punk rock, or as Marsh (1977) termed it, 'dole queue rock' developed.

The formation of a subculture in 1976 was intrinsically tied to the creation of a 'new' musical style. As in the past, the initiating centre was London, the punks gathering in a shop called Sex and a rock club called the Roxy. In contrast to the skinheads, who created a fetishism of their class position, the punks were nihilistic and saw themselves as true outsiders – the blank generation (Hebdige, 1979, p. 120). They saw 'no future' in their own or society's life, and could rely on 'no heroes' from the rock culture of the past. Their attempt to build up an authentic subculture was illustrated by their total rejection of the past (particularly of hippies and rock music) and the formation of small independent record companies to produce their own music. It amounted to a do-it-yourself culture. Any cheap or trashy product was worn as an attack on previous styles. Plastic bin liners, lavatory chains, zips, safety pins, dyed hair, ripped T-shirts, Nazi paraphernalia and defiled school uniforms were valued precisely because of their perversity, abnormality and lack of value. Perversity was symbolically glamorized in the use of rubber wear, fishnet stockings, bondage suits and the 'dirty raincoat'. Punk attempted to undermine and disrupt every pre-existing style, to reduce everything to absurdity. Its music was basic and direct. It didn't matter if this was intended or resulted from a lack of expertise. Everyone could play the guitar. Everyone could write and produce 'fanzines'. Everyone could construct styles of dance or dress. Essentially nothing really mattered, as long as it was seen to be unacceptable to the 'others' (Burchill and Parsons, 1978).

This tendency towards wilful desecration was epitomized by the names of the groups that emerged in 1976 (the Sex Pistols, the Clash, the Damned), their stage names (Poly Styrene, Sid Vicious, Rat Scabies, Johnny Rotten) and their songs ('Belsen Was a Gas', 'Pretty Vacant', 'I Wanna Be Sick on You', and 'Anarchy in the UK'). The Sex Pistols' first album was seized under the 1959 Obscene Publications Act because it had the word 'bollocks' in its title (Cloonan, 1995, p. 351). Punk's language of swear words, with its stress on collective energy and 'the immediate', was decidedly working class, but punks also drew on influences from art school and conceptual art. Thus, in contrast to Marsh's concept of 'dole-queue rock', Frith (1978) argued that punks had connections with middle-class hippies, student anarchists and the avant-garde. Indeed, punks were essentially a stratified subculture made up of both working-class youth, rejecting the wealth and lifestyle of rock superstars, and middle-class art college students attempting to satirize the bourgeoisie. In one sense punk style contained reflections of all major post-war subcultures, but they were presented in a chaotic and distorted manner. If there was any homology within punk style, then it centred on its antithesis to anything orderly, restrained and sacred (Hebdige, 1979). Punk may provide us with an example of the divergence of subcultural politics from subcultural style. Some of the lyrics of punk music – speaking of high-rise flats, dole queues and white riots – appealed to many working-class youths, while others were content to display symbols of revolt without translating them into political action. Punk's political heart was similarity split between the 'cosmetic rage' of anarchism and the stand taken against the National Front by the organization of Rock against Racism concerts and Anti-Nazi League rallies.

The difficulty of distinguishing a unified subculture was exacerbated by early 1977 when punk music was being catered for by the record and leisure industry. Every major record company had a punk band on its books and the King's Road in Chelsea, London, became the centre for punk fashions. Indeed, by March 1978 Frith could describe punk as 'just another form of pop', as dedicated as all other subcultures to orderly consumption.

Rude Boys and Rastafarians

The thesis of the Birmingham School – that subcultural style is evidence of 'resistance' and developed as a response to economic equality – was also applied to the situation of black youth. Indeed, such uniquely black styles as Rastafarianism, reggae and the rude boy have been viewed by Hebdige (1979) as key elements informing some white subcultural practices – both as a means of establishing their own separateness (for example, the mods) or as a vehicle for reaction (for example, the teds). Dominant images of 'youth' and 'black culture' also share many characteristics. Both are routinely demonized as lazy, hedonistic and dangerous (Young, 1971).

In the mid 1960s Afro-Caribbean youth in Britain began to develop a style based on the 'rude boy' subculture of West Kingston, Jamaica. Rudies were 'hustlers' who lived by dope dealing, pimping and gambling. In Britain a style evolved based on self assurance, coolness, 'sharp' clothes and ska music (Hebdige, 1976b). Inevitably, this combination of style, 'race' and petty criminality brought them into conflict with the police. For Sivanandan (1976), the development of these forms of black consciousness amongst 'rebellious black youth' must be placed first in the context of Britain's historical involvement in colonialism and slave trading. As a result of slavery, black people have been living in Britain since the seventeenth century and have consistently been faced with racism and prejudice. For example in Britain's first 'race riot' in 1919, a black seaman was killed following white riots in the Cardiff, Liverpool and Bristol docks. Second, whilst the main period of black immigration to Britain in the 1950s was sponsored as a result of a chronic domestic labour shortage, the black population routinely occupied jobs in the low-status and low-paid service sector. Because such work was only to be found in already overcrowded urban conurbations, black immigrants also came to occupy some of the worst housing in the country. As a result, Sivanandan (1976) has argued, the black population came to constitute a sub-proletariat, separate and different to the indigenous workforce.

The second generation of blacks (British born) then grew up in a situation of social and educational disadvantage, exacerbated not only by growing unemployment but also by a recurring white racism which now manifested itself in the 'race riots' of 1958 in Notting Hill and Nottingham (in which the teds played no small part). As Hall et al. (1978, p. 347) argued, 'race' is the 'principal modality' through which blacks 'comprehend, handle and then begin to resist the exploitation which is an objective feature of their class situation'. 'Race' raises a level of consciousness of structured subordination which is lacking in white working-class youth. The 'resistance' of the 'rude boy' thus occurred in the context of a 'colony' culture: a defensive cultural space enabling the formation of alternative and more explicitly 'oppositional' lifestyles. Moreover the symbolic purchase of the Caribbean and Africa allowed black youth in general to develop styles and a language which were in antithesis to mainstream white sensibilities. As Hall et al. (1978, p. 351) recall:

> Here began the 'colonisation' of certain streets, neighbourhoods, cafes and pubs, the growth of revivalist churches . . . the shebeen and the Saturday night blues party, the construction of the sound systems, the black record shops selling blues, ska and soul – the birth of the 'native quarter' at the heart of the English city.

Behind the swagger, the cool and the hustling of the 'rude boy' lay the more visionary figure of the Rastafarian (Hebdige, 1976b, p. 143). The Rastafarian movement has religious overtones based largely on a reading of Christianity that draws on biblical metaphors to develop a political message. In contrast to the 'rude boy', property, alcohol and gambling are condemned as elements of Babylon (white colonial capitalism) while ganja (marijuana) is believed to be sacred. Although the Rastafarian movement originated in Jamaica, Rastas look to Africa and particularly to Ethiopia for salvation. It was here in 1930 that Ras Tafari was crowned Emperor as Haile Selassie (Lord of Lords and Conquering Lion of Judah). He was acclaimed as the Returned Messiah and Black Christ. The Ethiopian colours of red, green and gold, along with long, uncut hair worn in dreadlocks, became vital symbols for black youth in promoting a positive evaluation of being black (Cashmore, 1979).

By the late 1960s rudies were adopting a Rasta style largely because it provided a way forward from the image of the individual rebel and spoke more explicitly of the development of a black cultural consciousness and the possibility of collective resistance. This was one form of black youths' response to their increasingly strained relations with the British police and the development of Powellism and British Nationalism. As Hall et al. (1978, pp. 357–8) put it:

> In and through the revivalist imagery of the 'dreadlocks', the music of the dispossessed and the insistent, driving beat of the reggae sound systems came the hope of deliverance from 'Babylon' . . . It is the ideological point of origin of a new social movement amongst blacks, the seeds of an unorganised political rebellion. The extent of police supervision of the 'colonies', the arbitrariness and brutality of the hassling of young blacks, the mounting public anxieties and moral panic about 'young immigrants' and crime . . . serve only to reinforce the impression, both inside and outside the colony that, in some as yet undefined way, a 'political' battleground is being staked out.

It is against this background that Hall et al. explain the crisis about mugging in the early 1970s, when a historically recurring form of street crime suddenly became defined as a 'black crime'. The period too is important in marking a fundamental politicization of the 'crime problem': a time when 'black youth' became synonymous with images of urban disorder (Solomos, 1988, p. 96; and see Chapter 1.4).

Yet as Hebdige (1979, p. 44) argues, the sights and sounds of 'the colony' spilt over to inform many of the predominantly white, working-class youth cultures. Black styles were 'a crucial determining factor in the evolution of each youth cultural form'. Elements of the 'rude boy' style were adopted by both mod and skinhead. In 1979 ska music was revived by the Coventry-based Two Tone record label promoting such bands as the Specials, Madness, Selecter and the Beat. In the Anti-Nazi League demonstrations and Rock against Racism concerts of the late 1970s, reggae and punk rock often shared the same stage. As Gilroy and Lawrence (1988, p. 148) argued, 'through reggae, the Rastafarian discourse of "equal rights and justice" provided a political analysis of "police and thieves" for young whites'. Hebdige (1979, p. 45) goes so far as to argue that rather than being culturally distinct, 'black' and 'white' are in continual exchange such that a 'phantom history of race relations' can be read in the succession of post-war British youth cultures. And as Gilroy and Lawrence (1988, p. 127) astutely note, 'it is no accident that moral panics about youth should have occurred at precisely the point where Black cultural forms became incorporated into the subcultures of White, working class youth'.

Countercultures and Dissent

5.3 The decade of the 1960s also witnessed an upsurge in political and cultural protest emanating from middle-class and bohemian subcultures. Unlike the 'imaginary' nature of protest and resistance present in working-class subcultures, sections of middle-class youth have characteristically indicated their own disaffiliation and disillusionment with dominant society by way of political organizations, liberation movements and alternative lifestyles. As a result there is a dominant tendency to view their activities as countercultural rather than simply subcultural. While the term 'subculture' is usually applied to such youth groups as teds, mods and so on to highlight their differences from, and correspondences with, their parent class cultures, the term 'counterculture' has been employed to describe those subcultures that present articulate counter-proposals of how social relations and the social order should be organized and maintained (Yinger, 1960).

In the spate of 'revolutionary' movements of the late 1960s and early 1970s, the term 'counterculture' was notably adopted by such theorists as Marcuse and Roszak. Clarke et al. (1976), however, remind us to be careful in its use. They note that many of its 'radical' notions have been incorporated into the values of dominant culture or indeed owe their existence to those very dominant values which they supposedly counter. In this way the counterculture may be considered as representing a crisis *within* dominant culture, rather than as a conspiracy *against* dominant culture.

The Beats, CND and the New Left

Before the teds and rock'n'roll's arrival in 1953, a section of middle-class youth – the beats – were already indicating their disaffection with post-war society. Rather than having deprivation and poverty imposed on them, the beats voluntarily chose a life of poverty by avoiding work. The 'freedom' that was gained represented a protest against the increasing technological and bureaucratic ordering and impersonality of social life. Faced with an extreme pessimism about the future and the possibilities of progress, the beats lived out the present to the fullest in the style of Woody Guthrie and Dean Moriarty, Kerouac's hero of a life *On the Road* (1957). The American beat scene was best captured in Polsky's (1971) empirical study carried out in Greenwich Village, New York in 1960. It was a scene characterized by anti-politicism rather than apoliticism, by work avoidance rather than inability to work, and by the belief that voluntary poverty was an intellectual gain.

Although the movement was predominantly American, the visual symbols of beat were exported to Britain. Jazz, poetry and marijuana were its hallmarks. The beats' concern for the spontaneous and the creative was mirrored by modern jazz, in which it seemed formal organization was subordinate to improvisation. In Britain, the impact of this music was marginal and was accompanied by a revival of earlier New Orleans and Dixieland styles which eventually were far more successful. Though less 'wild' and more collectively organized, these styles, especially when their folk and blues roots were emphasized, were also capable of attachment to a philosophy of romantic estrangement from society. In Britain this union of jazz with folk and blues styles was to become vital in the origins of skiffle music.

The beat subculture in Britain eventually became one element of a humanist and intellectual rejection of industrialism which found its feet in the Campaign for Nuclear Disarmament (CND). In the mid 1950s, sections of middle-class youth and adults in Britain were concerned with such immediate issues as the coming of the nuclear age, the H-Bomb and the possibility of world peace. Between 1953 and 1957 the dangers of atomic fallout were dominant in the minds of those campaigning for the abolition of nuclear tests. In 1958 the CND organized a protest march to the atomic weapon research centre at Aldermaston and was influential in attracting large numbers of youths to the peace movement. As Parkin (1968) recalls, nominal support for CND was a commonly accepted feature of this youth culture. Whereas working-class political radicalism can be said to be largely geared to economic reforms, the radicalism of these sections of the young middle class was directed mainly to reforms that were basically *moral* in content. CND was thus able to provide a focus for a whole gamut of humanitarian issues coupled with a disenchantment with democratic politics in Britain. It was a vehicle for protest outside class-based politics; accordingly, humanitarian and moral issues, which were marginal to traditional analyses of class politics, became central.

However, CND was far from politically united. It had two important groups of intellectuals – the older generation such as Bertrand Russell, A.J.P. Taylor and J.B. Priestley, who saw CND as providing a moral leadership to the rest of the world, and the 'Angry Young Men', those dramatists and novelists of the late 1950s, such as John Osborne, who were more concerned with the problems of being working class in a so-called middle-class social democracy. There was some discord too over the most appropriate forms of protest: whether they should follow constitutional methods or advocate non-violent civil disobedience. By the early 1960s the anti-bomb movement went into decline and was not revived until the early 1980s when US cruise missiles began to arrive in Britain.

CND, however, had also helped give birth to a movement known as the 'new left'. During the late 1950s and early 1960s the *New Left Review* group constituted the most important theoretical body of dissent in British youth politics. Born from a merger between ex-British Communist Party members (known as revisionists) and university intellectuals, the 'new left' advocated a socialism based not on the Leninist model of centralized political parties, but on a new libertarianism involving Trotskyite principles. After its peak period of influence in the days of the Aldermaston marches, the 'new left' also entered a period of decline. What was to emerge some five years later was a very different protest style, deriving its impetus from the American and European student revolts and from a countercultural 'underground'.

Hippies

The term 'hippie' covers a wide range of bohemian, drug, student and radical subcultures. As with the beats, there was a hard core of artistic-literary intelligentsia; as with the CND movement, there was a strong contingent of anti-war pacifists and radicals. Indeed, the hippie counterculture in Britain was something of a hybrid of CND's liberal humanitarianism and the beats' retreatism. The hippie, like the beat, was deeply critical of the growing dominance of technology and bureaucracy in both capitalist and socialist societies. However, the hippies' withdrawal was not necessarily one of self imposed poverty; it attempted to create a 'new and distinct' way of life which, they hoped, would convert others by example. Neither was the culture manifestly politically orientated. It had no party, no leadership and no manifesto, but lived by its unwritten demands to the rest of society: to seek love rather than violence, and to express oneself freely without fear of social sanctions. Above all, the hippies' alternative lifestyle was aimed at revolutionizing society through peaceful means. As Abbie Hoffman (1968, p. 14) proclaimed, 'Revolution is in your head. You are the Revolution. Do your thing.' For Yablonsky (1968) it was a para-society existing casually beneath the surface – neither subcultural nor countercultural but an attempt to resonate with a deeper reality of cosmic consciousness. It is largely accepted that this particular brand of bohemianism was born in the early 1960s on the West Coast of America, and particularly in the Haight Ashbury district of San Francisco (Wolfe, 1969).

The 'colony' brought with it some of the trappings of the beat subculture. Of note was the use of drugs to explore the limits of imagination and self-expression. A lifestyle developed based on the use of marijuana and particularly lysergic acid diethylamide (LSD or 'Acid') which, because of its hallucinogenic effects, enabled the user to 'trip' through a multitude of distorted ideas, images and actions in rapid succession. The dedicated believed that such an experience enabled reality to become clearer, to be seen free from all preconceptions. The cult was notably spread by Timothy Leary who founded the so-called International Federation for Inner Freedom in 1962 and coined the phrase 'tune in, turn on and drop out' and by Ken Kesey and his group of 'Merry Pranksters'. If Leary's interest was partly scientific and partly tied to religious awakening, Kesey's contribution was to make the acid experience spectacular, wild and playful.

At the beginning of 1967 San Francisco was the setting for the first 'Human Be-In' and by the summer had attracted 100,000 young people into the district. Soon the media discovered the Haight and invented the term 'hippie'. Hippies were soon to attract sympathy for their ideas of love and peace, but were mistrusted for their anti-work, pro-drug and permissive ethos. Drug abuse and permissive morality were to become the main focus for moral panics in the later 1960s. In Britain, LSD was made illegal in September 1966. Regional drug squads were formed in March 1967. Later that year the Rolling Stones were arrested for possession of marijuana. From 1967 to 1969 the offices of the underground newspaper *IT* (*International Times*) were raided by police and its editors imprisoned or fined on charges of obscenity or conspiracy to corrupt public morals (Stansill and Mairowitz, 1971). The underground music clubs, UFO and Middle Earth, were eventually closed after police raids. And in October 1970 the infamous *OZ* obscenity trial began after raids on its offices in June. *OZ*, an underground magazine, was fined £1,000 plus court costs. Prison sentences imposed on its editors, Neville, Dennis and Anderson, were dropped only after a lengthy appeal (Palmer, 1971). Despite the hippies' liberal concerns for peace and individual freedom, their activities were constantly defined as dangerous, whether because of their style of dress, length of hair, drug usage and subversive literature, or merely because of their preference for loud rock music.

'Permissiveness' was assured of an adverse and hostile social reaction. Drug law enforcement in particular developed dramatically throughout the 1960s. During the 1960s and early 1970s there was a marked increase in convictions for possession of marijuana in Britain – from 235 in 1960, to 4,863 in 1969 and 11,111 in 1973. As the 'drug problem' expanded, it took on the appearance of being especially a youth problem. Marijuana remained a vital element in creating a 'moral panic' about youth, even though every major official inquiry from the American La Guardia Report of 1944 to the British Wootton Report of 1969 recommended greater liberality in the treatment of users. The panic culminated in 1971 when the Misuse of Drugs Act was passed. This gave police greater powers to search and hold suspects, and penalties were increased to a maximum of six months' imprisonment or a £400 fine for first offenders.

Political Activists and Anarchism

1968 was a watershed year when bohemian disenchantment was adopted by many student bodies in universities throughout Europe and America as a basis on which a radical political movement could be built. Their contemporary origins lay in the free speech movement and protest at Berkeley, California, in September 1964 when the university authorities tried to ban all political activity on the campus. In the spring of 1965 the movement was fuelled by Lyndon Johnson's order for heavy bombing to start in North Vietnam. The three issues of American imperialism in Vietnam, black civil rights and educational control were to inform the spate of university sit-ins, marches and demonstrations of 1968, in which the strange agglomeration of black militants, students, drop-outs, draft dodgers, mystical hippies and women's liberationists seemed to be momentarily united. In Europe the radical student was particularly motivated by the takeover of the Sorbonne in May by a student/worker alliance and the formulation of an ideology of situationism which emphasized the importance of developing the revolution in everyday life. Reverberations from Paris were felt most in Britain at the London School of Economics and the Hornsey Art College, where students demanded more autonomy in the organization of university education. Similarly, in March and October the Vietnam Solidarity Campaign organized demonstrations outside the American Embassy in Grosvenor Square, London.

At the turn of the decade, the first phase of the counterculture, based on drugs, student activism and mysticism, was superseded by more anarchist political action. The Youth International Party (the Yippies) of America first became widely known in Britain when a group of 20, led by the American Jerry Rubin, disrupted ITV's Saturday night *David Frost Show* in November 1970 (Rubin, 1970). Rubin was quickly deported, but this was only the start of further anarchist activity in Britain. A month later the Angry Brigade came to public attention. Like the Yippies, the Angry Brigade was not an organized group but loosely influenced by French situationism, the Weathermen and Black Panthers in America and the European Red Army Faction and Baader-Meinhof Group. As early as 1968 bombs were planted at targets connected with the American, British and Spanish governments and at the close of 1970 a bomb damaged a BBC van outside the Albert Hall on the morning of the annual Miss World contest. Explosions at the homes of the Attorney-General, the Commissioner of the Metropolitan Police and the Home Secretary, Robert Carr in 1971 eventually broke the previous news silence (Vague, 1997).

The 1960s counterculture was thus a loose affiliation of many disparate radical and libertarian groups. Nevertheless, elements of this 'new radicalism' remained the dominant force in youth culture style until the early 1970s. The counterculture's contribution to youth cultural styles was indeed enormous. Because it encouraged a diverse range of 'alternatives' from Eastern mysticism to Third World revolution, it was able to draw on a multitude of romantic images and symbols (Hall, 1969). Similarly, because the personal and political were fused, all countercultural styles were able to retain an image of being progressive and radical. In music, the acid rock of the San Francisco bands, the progressive and electronic rock of the English Pink Floyd, together with blues and folk revivals, notably from Bob Dylan, achieved ascendancy in music charts worldwide. In fashion, the East was alluded to in the marketing of caftans, incense, Afghan coats and sandals. North American Indian styles – body painting, beads, long hair, headbands – were similarly appropriated in the romanticizing of a simple, primitive and tribal past. In Britain the success of the Beatles' *Sergeant Pepper* album in 1967 led to a craze for old but colourful army costumes or anything considered to be psychedelic and capable of confronting the senses and an outraged adult authoritarian culture (Neville, 1971).

Nevertheless this bohemian 'revolution' was shot through with its own contradictions. Whilst condemning materialism and capitalist enterprise, hippiedom gave birth to numerous small capitalist businesses in T-shirts, pop art, posters, underground newspapers, mail order records and drug-related paraphernalia. Preaching equality, its sexual 'revolution' was also couched in male terms. By the early 1970s, feminists had largely dissociated themselves from the 'global' counterculture and established their own organizations and modes of political action.

DIY Culture: New Age, Sabs and Eco-warriors

During much of the 1970s, middle-class and student radicalism appeared to collapse. However, as McKay (1996) catalogues, it is possible to trace a recurring set of youth and marginal 'cultures of resistance' from the late 1960s to the present.

From the hippie of the 1960s through anarcho punk of the 1970s to the New Age travellers of the 1980s, McKay detects a continuing disillusionment with modernist and rationalist politics and values. Typically such disillusionment has been expressed in retreatism, the occult, mysticism, self sufficiency, grassroots direct action, free festivals and fairs. For example, the annual pilgrimage to Stonehenge to celebrate the midsummer solstice continued unabated from the 1970s to the 1990s despite regular over-reactive policing. 'Peace convoys' continued to travel from festival to festival throughout the summer months in a search for rural authenticity and the utopics of the countryside (Hetherington, 1998). In 1987 thousands gathered at Glastonbury Tor and at other ancient sites throughout Britain (and worldwide) to celebrate the 'harmonic convergence' – a spiritual and planetary realignment predicted in Mayan, Aztec and Hopi writings to be the birth of a 'New Age' (McKay, 1996, p. 51).

By the mid 1980s New Age travellers had come to occupy centre-stage as the new 'folk devils' of British society. When several hundred travellers attempted to hold a free festival in the 'contested space' of Stonehenge in June 1985, English Heritage and the National Trust took out injunctions. Riot police forced the travellers into a field and destroyed many of their vehicles. In the so-called 'Battle of the Bean Field', clubs and batons were freely used by the police. In total, 420 travellers were arrested; their children taken into care. Twenty-four later sued for wrongful arrest, but lost in court. It may have appeared as if a renewed culture of grassroots environmentalism, spirituality, disenchantment with established institutions and a sense of being outside of society (homeless and jobless), had once more come to an end.

However, in subsequent years defiance of materialism, urbanism, consumerism, capitalism and cultural orthodoxy spread out to an amorphous cross-section of marginalized, dispossessed and disillusioned youth. A 'loose network of loose networks' (McKay, 1996, p. 11) was created. Within this DIY culture direct action, pleasure, idealism, creativity, plagiarism, narcissism, indulgence and a simultaneous rejection and embracing of new technologies combined to produce an intuitive liberal anarchism (McKay, 1998). In numerous protests against road building through ancient sites (Solsbury Hill, Twyford Down, Newbury) or the transportation of live animals (Coventry, Shoreham, Brightlingsea), middle-class adult protest emerged alongside that of the radical young. There was a sense of harking back to the English civil war, to the Diggers and the Levellers, and of reclaiming the land for the 'common people'. New Age philosophy was thus instrumental in reawakening new social protest movements – movements that challenged orthodox politics, deliberately lacked traditional leadership patterns and relied on non-violent, but direct forms of action. It was a politics, as Rutherford (1997, p. 124) records, that was 'simultaneously here and not here – ephemeral, transient, disorganized'.

Animal rights movements, poll tax demonstrators, eco-warriors, squatters, new environmentalists, hunt saboteurs and anti-road protesters may indeed appear diverse and disparate groups, but by the mid 1990s many were united in protest against the 1994 Criminal Justice and Public Order Act (CJA). This law effectively attempted to outlaw a way of life. Large gatherings and convoys and camps of more than six vehicles were declared illegal and a new provision of 'aggravated trespass' was aimed at curbing many forms of environmental action, particularly hunt sabotage (see Table 5.2). In October 1994, 100,000 travellers, anarchists, ravers and environmentalists gathered at Hyde Park, London to protest.

Table 5.2   *Public order provisions of the Criminal Justice and Public Order Act 1994*

- Extension of police powers to direct trespassers to leave land and to seize their vehicles. Failure to comply with such directions carries a maximum penalty of three months' imprisonment (sections 61–2)
- New police powers to prevent and stop raves if the playing of amplified music would 'cause serious distress to the inhabitants of the locality'. Maximum penalty three months' imprisonment (sections 63–7)
- A new offence of aggravated and mass trespass carrying a maximum sentence of three months' imprisonment (sections 68–71)
- New criminal sanctions against squatters who fail to leave premises within 24 hours' notice (sections 75–6)
- New powers for local authorities to move on illegal campers and removal of duty of local authorities to provide sites for gypsies (sections 77–80)

The Act also introduced secure training orders for 12–14 year olds, doubled the maximum sentence of detention for 15–17 year olds, allowed juveniles charged with a serious offence to be identified in court and provided for an area by area introduction of curfew orders enforced by electronic monitoring (see Chapters 6 and 7).

In the first few months after the Act over 90 arrests were made, but by 1996 over 200 anti-CJA, 'Right to Party' and 'Reclaim the Streets' groups had been formed and anti-road protests, tree-sitting and disruption of hunt meetings still appeared to be rife: culminating in the treetop and tunnel protest at Manchester Airport in 1997. As Gartside (1997, p. 200) argues, these apparently new, disorganized, ad hoc and carnivalesque forms of protest have broken down traditional conceptions of what constitutes radical politics. The old adages of 'left' and 'right' no longer seem to apply. But the combination of middle-class romanticism, anarchism, tribalism, mysticism, paganism, anti-rationalism, direct action, utopianism and 'opting out' also has clear resonances with the counterculture of some 25 years previously.

Anti-capitalism

If America's military adventures in Vietnam were a major catalyst for worldwide demonstration and protest in the 1960s; at the end of the 1990s it was the activities of the World Trade Organization (WTO), the World Bank (WB) and the International Monetary Fund (IMF).

The anti-capitalist movement in many ways is an attempt to fill a political void following the collapse of communism, and the related increasingly global reach of western neo-liberal economics and multinational corporations (Burbach et al., 1997). Neo-liberal principles of freedom in investment, capital flow and trade underpin a new global economy. Profit for the few is pursued relentlessly without regard to the human and environmental costs. Nation states seem unwilling or unable to counter this realignment of power. The gap between rich and poor is increasing. Orthodox politics are moribund. What is required is a grassroots rebellion – inspired in part by the Zapatista uprising in Mexico in 1994 – which is intent on mobilizing civil society rather than assuming state power. Such readings of global economics and the possibilities of protest have informed a growing number of loose coalitions of anti-capitalist movements. These include *People's Global Action*, formed in Mexico to protest the North American Free Trade Agreement; the environmental pressure groups *Friends of the Earth* and *Greenpeace*; *Earth First!*, a direct action ecology movement; *Globalize Resistance*, a coalition of socialists, anarchists, trade unionists and students; *Reclaim the Streets* and *Critical Mass* best known for campaigns against road building; *Ya Basta!* (Enough!), and *Ruckus Society*, a US-based organization to train activisits in the skill of non-violent civil disobedience, not to mention any number of human rights activists, representatives of indigenous peoples, asylum organizations and environmentalists (Bircham and Charlton, 2001).

London held its first Carnival Against Capitalism in June 1999 (an event predictably depicted by the media as hijacked by violent anarchists) but most analyses of these new anti-capitalist movements begin with Seattle, 30 November 1999 (Harman, 2000). Here 50,000 workers and students converged to force the closing of the second ministerial conference of the World Trade Organization. Protesters held workshops, occupied streets and blockaded the entrance to WTO meetings. The police response was one of imposing curfews and using concussion grenades, plastic bullets and teargas. But the 'Battle for Seattle' witnessed the birth of a new rallying point and international coalition of all those seeking social justice. In April 2000, 30,000 protested at the annual meeting of the World Bank in Washington. In September 20,000 demonstrated at the annual WB/IMF summit in Prague. In April 2001, 80,000 were at the Summit of the Americas in Quebec and many thousands more at the G8 summit in Genoa in July (see Table 5.3). The anti-capitalist movement continues to demonstrate on issues such as third world debt, global warming, genetically modified foods and the economic reasons for war. But neo-liberalism is the underlying target. The common theme is one of self determination and a commitment to cultural diversity. It comprises literally thousands of movements intricately linked via the internet – this medium in itself allowing for mobilization without bureaucracy, hierarchy and leadership. In this way an internationally connected network of local initiatives intent on combating corporate greed and environmental collapse is being built. 'Maybe instead of meeting the proponents of neo-liberalism head on, this movement of movements will surround them from all directions' (Klein, 2001, p. 13).

Table 5.3	*Anti-capitalism: A chronology of protest and criminalization*
Date	**Event**
January 1994	Occupation of the state capital in Chaipas, Southern Mexico, by the Zapatista National Liberation Army in protest at the signing of the North American Free Trade Area. People's Global Action is formed
April 1994	Critical Mass begins its London cycling campaign
May 1996	Reclaim the Streets (RTS) occupies a stretch of motorway in West London
May 1998	First RTS 'global party' with street parties held simultaneously in 17 cities around the world
June 1999	'Carnival against Capitalism' in City of London; mass arrests and 150 injured
November 1999	The 'Battle for Seattle'; paramilitary policing and hundreds of arrests
April 2000	Protest at a IMF/WB meeting in Washington DC; voluntary mass arrest of 600
May 2000	Mayday mass protest in central London; the biggest police operation in the capital for 30 years; 30 arrests
April 2001	Disruption of Summit of the Americas meeting in Quebec City ratifying the Free Trade Area of the Americas; 400 arrests
May 2001	Demonstrations worldwide. In London police detain thousands of peaceful protesters for up to eight hours around Oxford Street
June 2001	European Union summit in Gothenburg; three shot outside building
July 2001	G8 summit in Genoa; one protester shot dead by Italian police, 93 injured, police arrest protesters in hospital
June 2003	G8 summit in Evian; tanks, jeeps and helicopters used for protection. British activitist suing police for attempted manslaughter.
September 2003	Demonstration against WTO summit in Cancun, Mexico; Korean farmer commits suicide
	Demonstration at International Arms Fair in London; Anti-terrorism powers invoked by police

Developments in Youth Cultural Studies

The Invisible Girl

5.4 In the analysis of youth cultures and subcultures, research (at least up to the 1970s) spoke overwhelmingly of *male* youth cultural forms. The significance of culture, class and community, which became well-established parameters in recognizing boys' leisure pursuits, was long ignored in discussions of girls (Dorn and South, 1982). Youth cultures have traditionally been defined in male terms and have been seen as the sole property of young men. If part of youth culture's ability to evoke adult puritanical hostility lies in its explicit male sexuality, Angela McRobbie (1980) argues, this should not be misconstrued as any movement towards sexual liberation on their part. All aspects of youth culture –

from working-class subcultures, black youth cultures and countercultures to the consumer industries – confirm traditional definitions of masculinity and femininity. Thus, whilst Frith and McRobbie (1978) note that women and girls are by no means excluded from some youth cultures, as musical performers they are packaged largely to arouse male sexual fantasy and as consumers they are reduced to a state of non-intellectualism and political passivity. McRobbie and Garber (1976) also argued that girls were not necessarily absent from subcultures, but, because of their different structural position within the home, they were pushed by male dominance to the periphery of social activity. Anne Campbell's (1984) ethnographic study of gangs in New York similarly found that whilst girl gangs existed, they did so as annexes to the male gang. The range of possibilities open to them was dictated by the boys; the sexuality of young women being not only often controlled but also exploited. What such studies concluded is that 'youth culture' is a demonstration of the extent of the victory of those who hold class and sexual power and an affirmation of their ability to retain such power.

Youth cultures do tend to be male-dominated forms concerned with, amongst other things, displays of masculinity. As McRobbie (1980, p. 41) notes in analysing the 'temporary flights' of the teds, mods or rockers, it has been ignored that 'it is monstrously more difficult for women to escape (even temporarily) and that these symbolic flights have often been at the expense of women (especially mothers) and girls'. Moreover boys' peer-group consciousness and pleasure frequently seem to rest on a 'collective disregard for women and the sexual exploitation of girls'. Yet, most of the 1970s studies of youth cultures failed to adopt a critical attitude to the overt sexism of their subjects and unwittingly reinforced stereotypical images of women as passive, dependent and subordinate.

One of the first serious critiques of the Birmingham School's class-based work came from McRobbie's (1978) ethnographic study of 14 and 15 year old working-class girls in Birmingham. She focused on how 'resistance' was generated not through subcultures but through the 'more mundane' contempt for middle-class 'swots' in school and the flaunting of precocious womanhood. But McRobbie remained sensitive to the paradox of these tactics:

> Marriage, family life, fashion and beauty all contribute massively to this feminine anti-school culture and in doing so nicely illustrate the contradictions inherent in so-called oppositional activities. Are the girls in the end not simply doing exactly what is required of them . . . their own culture pushing them into compliance with that role which a whole range of institutions in capitalist society also, but less effectively, directs them towards? (McRobbie, 1978, p. 104)

In addition, girls' potential income and spending power is lower than that of boys. Parents guard girls' leisure time much more closely and, through a variety of moral constraints, their behaviour outside the home is carefully controlled. Much of this is linked to dominant ideologies about women's 'natural' place being in the home, revolving around a culture of domesticity rather than paid employment. As a result, Frith (1983, p. 228) has argued that 'girl culture' becomes a culture of the bedroom, the only place where girls can meet, listen to music, teach each other make-up skills, practise their dancing, compare sexual notes, criticize each other's clothes and gossip. Young women's leisure has operated more within the invisible space of the home than on the streets. Gender divisions within society were simply replicated by youth subcultures. Whatever 'solutions' to class inequalities and deprivation they may have offered to boys, these were certainly not shared by young women.

Conservatism, Consumerism and Conformity

Subcultural styles were typically viewed by the Birmingham School as the basis of new and subversive meanings and as forms of resistance to subordination. There was a tendency to view all deviant activity as some form of political resistance. Style and youth consumption were decoded in terms only of opposition and resistance. The more conservative aspects of subcultural style were ignored (Cohen, S., 1980, p. xii). In the rush to impute political motives, the limitations of, and contradictions within, their modes of protest often became downplayed and obscured.

Most obviously, subcultural protest based on the appropriation and creation of style is limited by its interaction with the consumer and entertainment industries. Revolt based on style becomes restricted because of the ability of the entertainment industry to incorporate and defuse oppositional symbols. Melly (1972, p. 107) calls this the 'castration via trivialisation syndrome' in which 'what starts as revolt finishes as style – as mannerism'. In reviewing 20 years of youth culture 'revolution' in Britain, as voiced through the media of music, fashion, literature and art, he explains how this process operates. Youth's disenchantment with society is typically expressed at a cultural level by questioning the elitism of highbrow culture, the boring nature of work, the meaning of freedom, the constraints of puritanical sexuality and so on. The revolt is, however, short-lived. The consumer industries, eager to market any kind of exploitable 'subversion', move in, offering television appearances, fame and money to the rebellious. Thus, Melly argues that every new youth movement is ultimately packaged, stylized and committed more to the goals of profit than social criticism. Deviant styles must become commercially viable or else vanish into obscurity. In fact the end result is similar in both cases, for commercialism soon ignores 'old' consumer items and looks for new 'deviant' styles to promote in order to keep market demand alive. Subcultures may provide fresh meanings to existing styles or create new styles themselves, but their diffusion is ultimately dependent on marketing and commercial enterprises, over which subcultures have little or no control. The 'anarchy' of punk, for example, was eventually catered for by every major record company in Britain, not as a symbol of working-class resistance, but as yet another youth fashion. In concentrating on moments of authenticity, subcultural theory neglected to view subcultures as also being continually engaged with processes of commercialism and trivialization. Thornton (1995, p. 9) goes further and argues that notions of 'authenticity' are illusory and that the essence of subcultures also lies in how 'media and businesses are integral to the authentication of cultural practices . . . commercial culture and popular culture are not only inextricable in practice but also in theory'.

Similarly, subcultural theory had difficulty in accounting for the processes whereby non-deviant styles were created and gained widespread popularity. The concentration on 'spectacular' subcultures provided an over-politicized analysis of youthful leisure. This opened up the issue of whether the formation of youth subcultures was merely the response of a minority of youth. Because of their dramatic style, media coverage has tended to present the spectacular at the expense of the everyday. But whilst many young people 'follow fashion', they are not necessarily committed to non-conformist lifestyles (Muncie, 1984, p. 103). Most young people accept and use whatever styles are on offer from the consumer and entertainment industries. Their culture may be considered as much manufactured as innovative and rebellious. The major interests of youth thus reflect and correspond to those of the dominant value system and are by no means deviant or in opposition (Murdock and McCron, 1976).

One of a few studies to seriously study the meaning of youth leisure pursuits for young people themselves (as opposed to the deviant/sensational) was Holland's (1995) analysis of the night-time economy in Newcastle. Here he argued that the primary leisure activity of 'going out' was not to get drunk, to find a sexual partner, to rave or to fight (as the media might presume) but the rather more mundane (and obvious?), namely to socialize with friends. Hollands argues that 'going out' provides a space for the construction of identities. It is not simply about hedonism but about regaining 'community' through companionship. Similarly, subcultural 'solutions' themselves are limited because they focus almost exclusively on leisure. Thus in the 1960s and 1970s the dominant order was only occasionally confronted and then in a symbolic fashion whereby youth subcultures were only able to strike 'tangential blows'. As Clarke et al. (1976) acknowledged, there is only compensation for, but no subcultural solution to, the problems of youth unemployment, low pay and compulsory miseducation. Or as McRobbie (1980) has noted, youth cultures almost invariably leave commonsense assumptions about sexuality and gender roles unchallenged.

In a more sophisticated development of such arguments, Willis' (1977) ethnographic study of boys in a Midlands comprehensive school in the 1970s detailed their opposition to authority and conformity in which the lads specialized in a 'caged resentment which always stops just short of outright confrontation'. Their counter-school culture, involving the disruption of lessons and the subversion of school work, was experienced by them as resistance, but ironically contained the seeds of their own downfall. An anti-school culture of chauvinism, solidarity, masculinity and toughness inadvertently prepared them for a life of manual labour. Their symbolic resistance to authority never developed any real power, but instead reinforced the power relations involved in the labour process. The boys colluded in their own domination. Rejecting educational qualifications in preference for 'mucking about' and 'skiving', these working-class 'lads' prepared themselves for a life of resisting boredom by time-wasting on the shop floor. Resistance at school ultimately led to exploitation in the workplace.

The more overt 'political' stance of the 1960s counterculture has also been critiqued because its 'revolution' was largely grounded in the ideologies of passive resistance, dissociation and subjective individualism. In many ways these solutions can be viewed as class specific. Disenchanted with established politics, countercultural protest was based on a romanticism in which expressive values and idealism were seen as an alternative to rationalism. However, this concern for the *quality* of life was possible only for those who did not endure scarcity, poverty and labour alienation in their daily lives. Similarly, the hippies' concern to travel, both geographically and symbolically, via drugs, and to discover new 'realities' can easily be equated solely with hedonism, retreatism and solipsism. In effect, such expressive alternatives allowed them to reassert their own class position as different and liberating. Above all, the emphasis on individual solutions and the belief that freedom could be found 'in your head' denied collective political action (Muncie, 1984, p. 127). The importance given to individualism also created space for hip entrepreneurs to market and perhaps unwittingly defuse the counterculture's 'radical' styles. The swift rise of the underground press, rock music and a drug culture were all a tribute to the ethics of private enterprise and *laissez-faire*. The counterculture's needs were supplied by profit-making organizations, which claimed to support the 'new' community, but performed a role little different to that of any other consumer industry:

> [I]t becomes immediately evident how both the established firms within the entertainment world and a new breed of trendy youth capitalists, sometimes sporting velvet trousers, long hair and tinted spectacles, have sought to exploit every conceivable object for profit, from drugs and pop festivals to Che and revolution. (Jacques, 1973, p. 277)

In this way the cultural radicalism of the 1960s was defused, packaged and merchandised. Much the same ambivalence could be applied to the countercultural revival of the late 1980s and 1990s (Gartside, 1997). Youth have developed into a very definite consumer market. Youth lifestyles seem increasingly constructed through consumption.

While subcultures have been reluctant to attach themselves to established political parties, their history is nevertheless rich in association with numerous political issues. In the late 1950s and again in the early 1980s, sections of middle-class youth were influential in the development of CND. In the mid 1960s many hippies supported the Vietnam Solidarity Campaign. In 1978, black youth and punks came together in the Anti-Nazi League and Rock against Racism carnivals. In 1990 New Age travellers were key players in the environmental protest movement. The tying of youth cultures to particular socialist and libertarian causes may indeed be influential in bringing many young people into a situation in which they may be politicized. But youth cultures are not automatically synonymous with progressive politics. Subcultural style can find its practical expression in support of the right as well as a libertarian left. In particular, the solutions preferred by the teds and skinheads have involved the threatening and attack of immigrant communities. Murdock and Troyna (1981) also catalogued the rise of youth wings within such fascist organizations as the National Front, the British Movement, Column 88 and Viking Youth in the late 1970s. For example, in 1978, 21 per cent of NF supporters were aged between 15 and 20. These organizations might have added a political dimension to some subcultures, but it was a politics embedded in racism.

Subcultural theory might have explained such behaviour as a rational reaction to the 'invasion' of working-class territory, but such analysis tended also to move such problems as 'mugging', 'Paki-bashing' and 'queer-bashing' away from the personal responsibility of the individuals involved. As a result subcultural theory has been critiqued as 'idealist' and 'romanticist' (Young, 1986).

In general it has failed to interrogate the more conservative aspects of subcultural practice. For example, the violence of 'Paki-bashing' was presented mainly in instrumental terms as a means of pursuing such goals as the defence of threatened identities and community homogeneity (Pearson, 1976). The intention, of course, was to demonstrate that violence is not senseless, but is essentially ordered, rational and meaningful. But as a result, subcultural theory tended to underplay the extent of violence in some subcultures and failed to recognize its effects on victims and on vulnerable, particularly immigrant, communities (Lea and Young, 1984). There may indeed be a problem in inferring that such degrees of rationality exist within subcultural violence, especially when the participants would not recognize themselves in the offered explanations (Tierney, 1980).

The terms 'magical', 'symbolic' and 'imaginary' to describe solutions also allowed subcultural theory to infer a potentially infinite range of meanings from subcultural action. While these analyses were certainly imaginative, they also appeared free-floating, unstructured and ambiguous. It was never clear when or how one symbolic interpretation was more adequate than another. This problem was further exacerbated by the concepts of 'bricolage' and 'homology' (see Section 5.1). Rather than providing a fresh understanding of the origins and development of subcultures, they appeared merely as devices to explain away subcultural inconsistencies and to disguise their internal contradictions. British subcultural theory often appeared content to find meanings (magical solution, recovery of community, resistance) quite independent of intent and awareness. The danger indeed, as Cohen (1980, p. xiv) argued, was one of getting lost in the 'forest of symbols'.

Above all there is growing evidence that most young people are deeply conformist. Since Stanley Hall's discovery of adolescence, being young has been generally understood as a time of dramatic emotional upheaval and a period of marked discontinuity in individual development. This has been used as a major factor in explaining troubling aspects of youth behaviour and has acted as a justification for various forms of intervention. However, research published at much the same time as Hall and Jefferson's *Resistance through Rituals* (1976) came to question such assumptions, and to assess how far both the traditional psychologies of adolescence and the radical deviancy theories only helped to create what they described. Rutter et al.'s (1976) questionnaire and interview study of 2,303 14–15 year olds, their parents and teachers on the Isle of Wight, for example, concluded that while there were increases in cases of reported depression, there was little difference in the incidence of psychiatric disorder between 10 year olds, 14 year olds and adults. Difficulties that arose for the first time in adolescence appeared to be related more to stressful circumstances, such as marital disharmony or parental authoritarianism, than to 'adolescence' *per se*. Similarly, parent–child alienation was found to be uncommon, and although peer group influences increased markedly, they did not replace parental influence. Similarly, Coleman (1980) reviewed a range of studies which suggested that differences between young people and parents have been generally overstated both by academics and the media because of their almost exclusive focus on 'bizarre' behaviours or 'spectacular' subcultures. Bandura (1972) argued that the hypotheses of 'storm and stress' and 'resistance' were based on an over-interpretation of superficial signs of adolescent non-conformity. He pointed out that such signs are equally present in both pre-adolescent and adult life. The mass media, he argued, have served to highlight the deviance of young people. This process led to an overemphasis on non-conforming aspects of youth which carried over through stereotyping to inform adult reactions to the vast majority of conforming, untroubled youth. It is a theme that has been reiterated by Miles (2000). Academic, political and media gaze has for so long been focused on the 'melodramatic' and the 'problematic' that the diversity, variability and complexity of young people's lives have been obscured.

Continuity and agreement between the young and adults appear to be far more prevalent than antagonism. A 1982 National Opinion Poll survey of 1,800 15–21 year olds substantiated this premise. Most still lived with their parents, and reported that relations were generally harmonious, 95 per cent getting on well with mothers, 86 per cent with fathers. Moreover, young people were found to be conformist, rather than deviant or radical. Most disapproved of taking drugs, did not drink much alcohol, believed themselves responsible, and mainly turned to 'Mum' when in trouble (cited by Springhall, 1983–4, p. 34). A decade later the *Young People's Social Attitudes* report (Roberts and Sachdev, 1996) similarly found, in contrast to the perennial adult belief that 'kids today just don't know right from wrong', that young people were remarkably honest in financial transactions (e.g. believing it wrong to keep extra money mistakenly given in change) and attracted to religion (e.g. having always believed in God) (Roberts, 1996, pp. 128–40). Above all, the image of 'teenager as rebel' was found to be unsubstantiated: 70 per cent did not smoke, 80 per cent did not go to discos and for 57 per cent the chief worry was about getting a job after their studies. Young people can also be rather more politically conservative than their elders. For example, McNeish's (1996, pp. 71–98) report for the *Young People's Social Attitudes* survey found that 6 in 10 favoured the reintroduction of capital punishment and believed that sending more people to prison would reduce crime. Far from a 'generation gap', the views expressed by young people about crime were very similar to those expressed by adults. A survey of more than 10,000 12–25 year olds conducted by the *Independent* (17 November 1997) concluded that contrary to the popular image of youth as 'ill educated ravers' and 'state spongers', young Britons were more serious minded, hard-working and responsible than any generation since the 1950s.

Post-subcultural Style

Punk's disruption of previous subcultural styles has had some peculiar consequences for subcultural style since the 1980s. Hebdige (1979, p. 26) has argued that because punk contained 'distorted reflections of all the major post-war subcultures' it indirectly led to their revival – at least in stylistic, if not in authentic subcultural terms. During the 1980s a diverse array of teds, scooter boys, suedeheads, bikers, punks, glam revivalists, new romantics, Goths, Rastas and long-haired 'crusties' seemed to coexist on the streets of Britain's inner cities. But the ability of Britain's youth to cause alarm, outrage and fear continued unabated. As the *Daily Express* (8 April 1980) 'explained':

> Who are the teenage rebels? Many are without a cause, whose sole aim is to defy authority of any kind. For others the cause is violence – to rival gangs, to people who don't dress like they do and to innocent bystanders who get in their way. A few belong to mysterious sects who guard their independence by force of arms. But most have one thing in common . . . to engender terror.

Brake (1990, p. 224) offers a more sober assessment of youth cultures in the 1980s. He argues convincingly that they came to be dominated by and replaced by style:

> Youth culture is now expropriated from the young, especially working-class youth, and is consumed by the privileged elite amongst youth. It excuses anything in the name of style, racism, right-wing views, success, consumption, money making and is based on exclusivity and envy . . . the world is a market inhabited by the winners. The losers return to the job centre.

In a similar vein, Roberts and Parsell (1994) conclude, on the basis of a longitudinal survey of 16–19 year olds at the end of the 1980s, that youth cultures have become removed from what were traditionally perceived as predominantly working-class roots. Class-related leisure patterns have become blurred and subject to individualization. If anything, it is middle-class youth that have become ascendant in youth cultural production and consumption, but they found 'no signs of youth cultures expressing class antagonisms or even accentuating class differences' (Roberts and Parsell, 1994, p. 46). Moreover their evidence, in contrast to notions of girls' 'bedroom culture', suggested that whilst young men remained the most committed to leisure, there was little gender difference in participation in out-of-home leisure activities.

At one and the same time these 'readings' of youth cultures suggest that 'things were never the same after punk' (McRobbie, 1994, p. 159). Although there remains a continuing concern for youth as a source of social and political anxiety, youth leisure has evolved into a *mélange* and proliferation of styles that defy any straightforward class-, gender- or 'race'-based analysis. Or as Miles (2000, pp. 159–60) put it, 'young people no longer depend on subcultural affirmation for the construction of their identities (if indeed they ever did) but construct lifestyles that are as adaptable and as flexible as the world around them.'

One of the first traces of such a 'revisionist' cultural analysis of youth can be found in subsequent work produced by the originators of the Birmingham School themselves. In a report prepared for the Sports Council in the late 1970s on the cultural significance of pool, kung fu, discos and skateboarding, a shift from the strictly subcultural to broader notions of youth cultural consumption seemed to force an acknowledgement that

> a fad or fashion within youth culture may be subject to a *range of determinants*, carry a number of *contradictory meanings* and have *variously commercial or autonomously cultural roots* . . . each particular phenomenon needs to be understood in its own *individual complexity*, yet can potentially reveal consistent processes and interrelationships. (CCCS, 1980, p. 10, italics added)

What such a statement seemed to suggest was that youth cultures could be the site of multiple, not simply class-based, meanings. Similarly, Gary Clarke (1990, p. 93), notes that by the 1980s the very diversity of youth styles 'makes a mockery of subcultural analysis' and an 'absolute distinction between subcultures and "straights" increasingly difficult to maintain'. Condemning the Birmingham School as 'essentialist', he argues that more attention should be given to how 'commercial' and 'subcultural' styles make sense to young people themselves. For McRobbie (1980) this necessarily means that such concepts as populism, leisure and pleasure be given as much critical attention as the established triad of class, sex and 'race'.

Such a project has subsequently been realized in a number of ways. In *The Language of Youth Subcultures*, Widdicombe and Wooffitt (1995) draw upon discourse analysis to illustrate how language is used to construct self identities and negotiate the meanings of subcultural involvement. What emerges from their 'conversations' with young people is not a set of 'explanations' (as sought by the social scientist) but a series of 'resources for discursive social action'. As perceived by young people themselves, subcultures are viewed as 'variable commodities' imbued with 'multiple meanings'. Indeed, there is no unitary or fixed meaning to be discovered. Thus the 'nihilism and anarchy' of punk or the 'anti-establishment values' of the hippie are ascriptions imposed by academic analysis and form only one element in how these subcultures are actively 'lived' by those involved.

Paul Willis' *Common Culture* (1990) is a similarly detailed account of the particularities of youth leisure which cannot easily or desirably be generalized. He argues that through leisure, 'young people are all the time expressing or attempting to express something about their actual or potential cultural significance' (Willis, 1990, p. 1). It may be individual or collective, but through language, dress, imagination and 'drama', young people achieve a symbolic creativity in which their identities are forged, remade, lived with and experimented with. Thus it makes little sense to talk of subcultures as in some way authentic, and commercial cultures as imposed and inevitably conservative. Market categories and boundaries are continually being reworked and redrawn, so that it is impossible to predict future developments with any certainty. Moreover the market is an arena that young people are increasingly taking over and transforming for themselves (McRobbie, 1994).

The way in which young people are involved in cultural consumption is also the subject of Thornton's (1995) analysis of club cultures. Again in contrast to the Birmingham School, she argues that the analytical divide between mainstream media and subcultural practice, in which the former is invariably viewed as reactionary (or manufactured) and the latter innovative (or authentic), is a gross oversimplification. Instead the two exist in symbiosis:

> Contrary to youth subcultural ideologies, 'subcultures' do not germinate from a seed and grow by force of their own energy into mysterious 'movements' only to be belatedly digested by the media. Rather, media and other culture industries are there and effective right from the start . . . The Birmingham tradition tended to study previously labelled social types – 'Mods', 'Rockers', 'Skinheads', 'Punks' but gave no systematic attention to the effects of various media's labelling processes. Instead they described the rich and resistant meanings of youth music, clothing, rituals and argot in a miraculously media-free moment when an uncontaminated homology could be found. (Thornton, 1995, pp. 117, 119)

The moral panics associated with youth cultures are not simply generated from outside, nor are they evidence of paranoid adult overreaction. Youth may resent 'the mass mediation of their culture but relish the attention conferred by media condemnation . . . moral panics can be seen as a culmination and fulfilment of youth cultural agendas in so far as negative newspaper and broadcast news coverage baptise transgression' (Thornton, 1995, p. 129). In this way media outrage becomes a part of subcultural practice, self identity and longevity: it legitimates and authenticates youth cultures as different, radical and deviant; it becomes 'the essense of their resistance' (Thornton, 1995, p. 137).

Cultural Exchange and Hybrid Identities

The difficulty of isolating an authentic subcultural practice which is untainted by commercial appropriation has also been raised by numerous studies of patterns of cultural exchange and crossover between African-American, Asian, Caribbean and white cultural and musical styles. In *There Ain't No Black in the Union Jack* (1987b) Paul Gilroy argues that black styles, music, dress, dance, fashion and language are continually being made and remade in the context of new *diasporas* (patterns of dispersal) created by post-colonial migrations. People who have been dispersed from their homelands may retain strong links with their origins and traditions, but are also obliged to come to terms with the new cultures they inhabit without completely assimilating to them. Such people belong to *cultures of hybridity* belonging at one and the same time to several 'homes' but to no one particular 'home'. As Gilroy (1987b, p. 155) claimed, 'The assimilation of blacks is not a process of acculturation, but of cultural syncretism.' Accordingly black expressive cultures and self identities are frequently the result of a fusion of different cultural traditions. Or as Hall (1992, p. 310) puts it: 'Everywhere cultural identities are emerging which are not fixed but poised, *in transition*, between different positions; which draw on different cultural traditions at the same time; and which are the product of those complicated cross-overs and cultural mixes which are increasingly common in a globalized world.'

It is in these terms that Gilroy's *The Black Atlantic* (1993) casts doubt on notions of some 'pure' or 'unified' black culture and notes how by the 1990s, black culture, especially in its musical forms, came to exist as a set of open-ended structures allowing a seemingly endless series of permutations and cultural meanings. In particular, derivatives of reggae – hip-hop and rap music – are described in terms of a 'doubleness' existing 'simultaneously inside and outside the conventions, assumptions and aesthetic rules which distinguish and periodize modernity' (Gilroy, 1993, p. 73). The case of 'gangsta rap' is emblematic. The origins of rap are reputedly in Jamaica, where, in the late 1960s, DJs (rather than musicians) began 'sampling' pieces of previously recorded tracks, playing them repeatedly, or backwards, often with another track playing simultaneously, and adding their own voice or conversation to them. In the 1970s it 'swept through' the black neighbourhoods of New York and New Jersey (Cashmore, 1997, p. 155). By the early 1980s it spread to Los Angeles and in 1986 a rap entitled 'Boyz N the Hood' was recorded by NWA (Niggaz wit' Attitude) – a group consisting of Ice Cube, Easy E, Dr Dre, MC Ren and DJ Yella. This music spoke explicitly of street cultures, gang feuds, black militancy, cop killing, drug dealing and sexual violence. It frequently applauded sadism, misogyny and machismo. Following the release of their first album in 1988, NWA and their song 'Fuck tha Police' were targeted by the FBI for incitement of cop hatred and racial violence. Gangsta rap was widely condemned by US presidents, churches, women's groups and mainstream African-American organizations. Rivalry between LA and New York rappers was reputed to be the source of numerous murders.

In the UK, NWA's 1991 album *Efil 4 Zaggin* (Niggaz 4 Life inverted) was seized under the 1959 Obscene Publications Act (Cloonan, 1995, p. 357). Ten years later So Solid Crew were banned from performing live for allegedly glorifying gun violence. In 2003 the Culture Minister blamed the killing of two black young women on the 'hateful lyrics' of 'boasting macho idiot rappers'. The Home Secretary responded by announcing minimum five-year prison sentences for carrying any illegal weapons (*Guardian*, 6 January 2003). Yet by the early 1990s gangsta rap had already become a multimillion-dollar international industry. The music may have been defiantly black but it also had a huge white following. These contradictions and crossovers have led Rose (1994) to argue that rap is 'a style nobody can deal with': authentic yet commercial (Cashmore, 1997); liberatory (Lipsitz, 1994) yet revolutionary conservative (Gilroy, 1993); confirming white stereotypes of a black criminal 'other', yet symptomatic of the violence, sexism and misogyny of white patriarchal society (hooks, 1994, pp. 115–24). Meanwhile rap music has been adopted and adapted around the world, creating new permutations (such as the peculiarly British jungle and drum 'n' bass as well as numerous crossovers with acid house and rave). Local levels of significance also continually produce diverse and fluid meanings which cannot be reduced to global market considerations (Bennett, 2000; Carrington and Wilson, 2002).

One such notable permutation in Britain has been the fusion of reggae and hip-hop with bhangra. It has long been assumed in Britain that family and informal social controls over 'Asian' youth have been such that distinctive youth styles have never developed. Brake (1980, p. 128), for example, argued that Asian communities were more likely to draw exclusively upon their own historical, cultural and religious traditions and languages, but he also warned that 'as these fail to resolve contradictions, youth subculture will probably arise as a symbol of emancipation from the older generation'. By the mid 1980s there was some evidence that this might be the case. Images of a disaffected South Asian youth first emerged in the early 1980s following disturbances in Bradford and Southall, and achieved national prominence after conflicts with the police in Bradford in 1995 and with the National Front in Oldham, Bradford and Burnley in the summer of 2001. As Malek (1997, p. 141) notes, the contradictory and mythical representations of young South Asians as either assimilated into British society or as violently antagonistic to it dominate public debate, but neither 'captures the complexity of what it means to be young, South Asian and living in Britain'.

Part of the problem is that white ethnocentrism and racism are incapable of recognizing differences within and between 'South Asian' communities and have generally promulgated essentialist notions of 'Asian traits'. In an attempt to overcome dominant discourses that 'Asian', 'Hindu' or 'Islam' are unitary and undifferentiated categories, Webster (1997) constructs a fivefold typology of 'conformists', 'experimenters', 'vigilantes', 'Islamists' and 'ethnic brokers'. Of note are 'experimenters' who 'display a fierce independence from their parent culture' and whose 'cultural preferences and tastes are for those elements of music, magazine and video, culture that emphasize *fusion* and *hybridity*' (Webster, 1997, p. 77). 'South Asian' youth culture is discussed in terms of diasporic and globalized cultural formations in which Hindi films, 'indie' music, bhangra and a pick 'n' mix orientation to drug use have helped to forge a distinctively 'British Asian' set of identities. For example, bhangra, as performed by such artistes as Apache Indian and Bally Sagoo, reveals not only a borrowing of Caribbean sound systems and the soul and hip-hop of black America but also a fusion of Punjabi folk music with reggae. It is a blend which seems to defy unreflective talk about ethnic authenticity. In 1996 Bally Sagoo's 'Dil Cheez' became the first ever song with full Hindi lyrics to enter the top 20 in Britain. It is probably no coincidence that at this very moment of cultural ascendancy, sections of 'South Asian' youth were also being demonized as harbingers of an 'Asian criminality' reputedly linked to organized crime and drug dealing. Islamic fundamentalism and Asian masculinity have increasingly come to be associated with the 'criminal other', promoting – particularly since 9/11 – a criminalization of difference (Goodey, 2001).

However, some analysts have come to question cultural studies' new focus on difference, hybridity, fusions and migrancy. As Ashwani Sharma (1996) argues, these concepts can also act to deny the particularities and authenticities of 'South Asian' youth cultures and to promote a vision of British multi-culturalism which has little basis in reality. The notion of 'hybridity' carries a tendency to erase the 'workings of highly differentiated global capitalism and racism' and leaves 'the subaltern subjects of the "Third World" having no position or location to speak from' (Sharma, 1996, p. 25). Or as Malek (1997, p. 149) concludes, 'the cross cultural locations negotiated by migrant populations are not void of the racial and cultural hierarchies constructed by western racisms'.

As a result a new level of complexity has emerged in the analysis of cultural exchange and hybrid identities. Whilst the categories of 'black', 'Afro-Caribbean' and 'Asian' have been critiqued as a means by which caricatures and stereotypes are maintained and the fluidity, diversity and variety of cultural identities disregarded (Said, 1991), the shift towards viewing 'race' as a social construction has tended to downplay the relevance of continuing racialized forms of power, domination and subordination. In all the talk of 'new ethnicities' (Hall, 1988) and 'the complex internal cultural segmentation [that] has cut through so called Black British Identity' (Hall, 1997, p. 7), there is a danger that 'the valency of "Black" as a political positionality, that strategically unites disparate groups against increasingly organised and vicious manifestations of Euro-racism', will be lost (Sharma et al., 1996, p. 7). The processes of cultural exchange and globalization can be interpreted as polarizing some ethnic identities while simultaneously widening the number of potential hybrid subcultural identities.

Quite clearly, these modes of analysis – despite their internal disputes – allow for more complex and critical analyses of subcultural diversity and processes of resistance. Significantly, in the main, they originated from the early 1980s as a reaction against the essentialism and overdeterminism of class-based analyses (Clarke, G., 1990; Griffin, 1993, Chapter 5). This critique coalesced with the collapse of the 'meta-narrative' or 'single order' means of explanation

Table 5.4   *From subcultures to cultural hybridity*

Subculture	Dominant drug/music/style associations
Differentiated and 'authentic' subcultures 1950s–1970s	
Beats	Marijuana; jazz; college bohemian
Teddy boys	Alcohol; rock 'n' roll; Edwardian
Mods	Amphetamines; soul; Italianate; scooters
Rockers	Alcohol; rock 'n' roll; leathers; motor bikes
Skinheads	Alcohol/amphetamines; ska; working class; boots 'n' braces
Hippies	LSD; underground rock/progressive rock/folk; North American Indian/Eastern
Rude Boys	Marijuana; ska; Jamaican street cool
Rastas	Marijuana; reggae/dub; dreadlocks
Punk and post-punk derivative cultures 1970s–1980s	
Punk	Amphetamines; punk; DIY pastiche
Metal heads	Alcohol; heavy metal; denim
New romantics	Amphetamines; post-punk/retro glam rock; polysexual/androgyny
Diverse hybrid dance cultures 1980s–2000s	
Acid House	
Rave	Ecstasy/poly drug; post-northern soul/Balearic/garage/techno/trance/ambient/
Hip-hop/Rap	Gangsta rap/jungle/drum 'n' bass/speed garage/hardcore/bhangra; casual

characteristic of much social science, whether Parsons' functionalism of the 1940s or the Birmingham School's neo-Marxism of the 1970s. As Scott (1990, p. 4) argued, 'increasing awareness of the complexity of social relations *vis-à-vis* single, coherent, but basically simple, explanatory systems has quite fundamentally altered social theory's conception of its role, and of what it can and cannot be expected to achieve'. So in place of 'grand theory' there has emerged a 'revisionist' analysis which is more attuned to the ethnographic than the structural; to diversity and fluidity rather than determinism; to lifestyle rather than subcultural research; to different subjectivities rather than 'knowable' objective conditions; and to processes of 'becoming' rather than states of 'being'. It is, as Hebdige (1988, p. 207) says, 'a Marxism without guarantees' which is more prone to 'listen, learn, adapt and to appreciate . . . the prospect of new life emerging: a struggling to the light'. It is these forms of analysis that claim to offer fresh insights into the shift from the apparently local, class-based youth subcultures of the 1960s to the transnationalization and hybridity of contemporary youth styles (see Table 5.4). Nevertheless, as Hollands (2002) also usefully reminds us, in all the 'new' talk of 'lifestyle', 'subjectivity' and 'consumer choice', it is vital not to lose sight of ongoing inequalities/divisions of 'race', gender, class and locality which continue to provide important structuring contexts for youth cultural formation.

Cultural Criminology: Explorations in Transgression, Consumerism and the Criminalization of Style

5.5 Emerging from these critiques, analyses of style and leisure matured in the late 1980s. As criminologists become more attuned to the fluid dynamics of representation, image and style, it became possible to sketch out the parameters of a distinctive *cultural criminology* (Ferrell and Sanders, 1995). Its heritage is multifold. It includes the foundational work of interactionism, critical criminology and the Birmingham School but is also deeply inflected with the intellectual insights of postmodernism (see Chapters 4.1 and 4.3). Akin to interactionism, cultural criminology is geared to exploring the multitude of interactions involving the media, the public, rule breakers and control agents through which meanings of crime are collectively constructed and contested. Drawing on anarchist, neo-Marxist and feminist insights, cultural criminology is embedded in critiques of social injustice. Of central influence is the Birmingham School's attention to cultural dynamics and everyday politics and in particular a recognition of the meaning and significance of style. All of this is underpinned by postmodern concerns to be alive to contingencies, hybridities and the way meaning is continually constructed and reconstructed through the discursive connections between subculture, media and crime control. As Ferrell (1999, p. 397) puts it:

[T]he study of crime necessitates not simply the examination of individual criminals and criminal events, not even the straightforward examination of media coverage of criminals and criminal events, but rather a journey into the spectacle and carnival of crime, a walk down an infinite hall of mirrors where images created and consumed by criminals, criminal subcultures, control agents, media institutions and audiences bounce endlessly one off the other.

Cultural criminology then engages with, if not synthesizes, a disparate series of old and new criminologies. Above all it is concerned with unravelling the complex cultural processes through which 'crime' attains meaning. Vital to this is an ethnographic immersion into the cultural and experiential realities of particular events themselves. So it is no surprise that one of its most challenging features remains that of recognizing the participatory pleasure and sheer fun of engaging in criminal(ized) behaviours. Cultural criminology advocates a criminology attuned to the emotions of excitement, humour and desire; to the adrenalin rush of crossing boundaries; to the exhilarations of 'living on the edge'; to the emancipatory power of transgression; and to the liberatory potential of the carnivalesque (see Table 5.5). In essence it encourages cultural studies to recognize 'culture as crime', that is how certain cultural activities – art, music, dance, sex – are also increasingly sites of criminalization; whilst also imploring criminology to recognize 'crime as culture', that is how style and pleasure reside in the continually contested interplay between subcultural, media and political constructs of 'crime' (Ferrell, 1999, pp. 403–6).

Below these intersections of crime and culture are exemplified in the notions of 'style as crime' as applied to the rave and club cultures of the 1980s and 1990s; and to the pleasures of rule breaking as applied to the analysis of the carnival in everyday life.

Table 5.5   *Key features of cultural criminology*

- Explorations of the convergence of cultural and criminal processes and dynamics in everyday life
- A fusion of aspects of cultural studies, postmodernism, critical criminology, interactionism, anarchism and media/textual/discourse analysis
- The use of ethnographic methodologies to reveal issues of meaning and representation
- Investigations of deviant subcultures as sites of criminalization
- Explorations of the role of the emotions of excitement, fun and pleasure in processes of transgression
- Journeys into the spectacle and carnival of crime
- The linkages (and disconnections) between marginality, illegality, media representation and the criminalization of popular culture
- Crime control as a cultural enterprise

Style as Crime: Acid House, Rave and Club Cultures

From modest beginnings on the Spanish Balearic island of Ibiza in 1985, rave has been described as the most 'spectacular' and 'enduring' British youth movement of the twentieth century (Collin, 1997). Rave is essentially a combination of dancing at mass all-night events, synthesized techno music with a heavy repetitive beat and use of the Class A controlled drug, Ecstasy (MDMA).

The all-night, open-air nightclub Hedonism of Ibiza was brought to Britain by a handful of DJs interested in popularizing the intense and collective energy that was generated by acid house music. Initially restricted to such underground clubs as the Hacienda in Manchester and Future, Shoom, Spectrum and The Trip in London, large-scale warehouse acid parties first occurred on the outskirts of London during the second 'Summer of Love' in 1988. In June 1989 over 8,000 young people gathered in a disused aircraft hangar at White Waltham airfield, Berkshire, making history as the largest-ever unlicensed party. By 1992, 20,000–40,000 were to gather over eight days at the Castlemorton Common 'Megarave' in Worcestershire, marking a significant festival/traveller/rave crossover (McKay, 1996, p. 120). Acid house took its name not from the drug LSD but from a musical form based on a 'house' dance style, pioneered in gay clubs in Chicago. Its key characteristic was a heavy four-four beat between 120 and 170 beats per minute. It was delivered through huge sound systems and a vast array of lighting and electronic effects including lasers, smoke machines, strobes, video screens, globes and fireworks. To participate in such parties required a certain degree of affluence – access to a telephone to learn of the latest clandestine venue, a car to travel there and money for the entry fee. Yet it also represented a curiously egalitarian reaction to the final days of Thatcherism. There were no stars or music heroes and whilst previous youth cultures were characterized by clear-cut boundaries of class position and related music or dress codes (or at least this is how they were 'read'), acid house and the warehouse parties seemed to merge all of these into one homogeneous whole. In particular, the Manchester (Madchester) rave scene drew on an earlier Northern Soul scene, all-night dances, African-American music, baggy clothes and amphetamines, and seemed impervious to analyses that insisted that innovation be decoded in terms of resistance (Redhead, 1990).

Rave culture may have smacked of rebellion in that most parties were theoretically illegal and involved numerous circumnavigations of the laws of entertainment, licensing, public order and noise. But it was also a highly organized and commercial endeavour. Tickets sold a day or two before the event gave no indication of the venue. Instead a telephone number was given for further information on the day so that all the sound and light equipment could be set up (on a country estate, in farmers' fields, on airfields, in grain silos, in disused warehouses or wherever) before the police or local residents were alerted. If one venue became impossible, the whole party would simply move to another. Often these were located in the vicinity of the London orbital motorway – dubbed the Magic Roundabout – in order to facilitate ease of access. As Presdee (2000, p. 114) put it:

> Their culture, rather than being a search for the 'authentic' as in modern culture, is an endless search for the 'inauthentic'; that is, a culture that is empty of the authority and the imperatives that come with authenticity. It is this perceived 'emptiness as protest' that prompts panic from 'adult' society.

During the summer of 1989, warehouse parties were each attracting up to 15,000 people, but were also becoming subject to greater police and legal control. By the end of the year a former council youth leader became the first person in Britain to be imprisoned for organizing such parties: he was jailed for ten years on a charge of conspiracy to manage premises where drugs were known to be available. In just two and a half months in 1989–90 the police monitored 249 parties, stopped 44, raided 20 and arrested 267 people on public order and other offences. At one party in Leeds in July 1990 over 800 were arrested by police in riot gear.

In the imagination of the popular press, acid house parties were synonymous with the drug Ecstasy. Described by users as producing rushed feelings of happiness, exhilaration and the 'illusion of an endless present', it also works on the brain in such a way that repetitive rhythmical activity becomes intensified (Keane, 1997). It is reputed to have been patented in Germany in 1914 as an appetite suppressant or for psycho-therapeutic purposes and its use was prohibited as early as 1977. Whilst it is arguable whether the first warehouse parties were indeed full of drug users, by the 1990s it was clear that drug taking had become an integral part of youth culture (see Chapter 1.3). The drug information charities Lifeline and Release estimated that some half a million people a week were taking Ecstasy and attending raves at clubs and parties. Ninety-seven per cent of dance-goers had tried an illegal drug at some time and for 28 per cent this had led to problems with the police (Release, 1997, pp. 10, 25). The users were not simply the disaffected or the marginalized, but overwhelmingly the well-educated and employed. Depictions of drug use as abnormal and unusual became harder to sustain (Hammersley et al., 2002). A 1994 unpublished Home Office report admitted that the elimination of drug use was an unattainable goal (*Guardian*, 1 August 1994). By 2000 even the Police Federation were advocating the downgrading of Ecstasy from a Class A to a Class C drug (*Guardian*, 17 February 2000).

Some time in the early 1990s the commercialization of the dance party movement and the clampdown on unlicensed parties returned acid house and rave to the clubs. First, the Entertainments (Acid House) Increased Penalty Act of 1990 made holding unlicensed 'underground' parties illegal. Second, the 1994 Criminal Justice and Public Order Act outlawed any large gatherings featuring music with 'sounds wholly or predominantly characterized by the emission of a succession of repetitive beats'. Such criminalization was circumvented by entertainment industry entrepreneurs providing permanent venues which were able to meet strict licensing and health and safety regulations. Like all youth cultures before, the 'safe' aspects of acid house and rave were defused by commercial diffusion. Acid house music and its multitude of derivatives – techno, hardcore, garage, trance and ambient – all came to feature in the popular music bestselling charts. It also became a global phenomenon, with raves organized worldwide from San Francisco to Goa in India and Ko Pha-Ngan in Thailand.

In its apparent crossing not only of class but also of national boundaries, rave confounded the neo-Marxist analyses of youth subcultures put forward by the Birmingham School in the 1970s. The multitude of different dance cultures appeared as neither simply oppositional nor commercial; neither authentic nor manufactured; neither marginal nor mainstream. Rave culture has thus been viewed by some from a postmodern and cultural criminology perspective as something disparate and diffuse: as a 'sea of youth styles' continually (recirculating) in the pursuit of 'hedonism in hard times' (Redhead, 1993, p. 4). Nevertheless, Sarah Thornton (1995, p. 25), whilst admitting that rave 'may have involved large numbers of people and they may have trespassed on new territories', argues that it retained distinct demographics – 'chiefly white, working class, heterosexual and dominated by the lads'. Similarly, Angela McRobbie notes that young women appear to be less involved in the cultural production of rave than their male counterparts, but she also detects in rave changing modes of femininity and masculinity. As dance is a key rationale for rave, it 'gives girls a new-found confidence and a prominence' and because the drug Ecstasy encourages an atmosphere of unity, traditional laddish aggro tends to be replaced by more sensuous and less threatening displays of masculinity (McRobbie, 1994, pp. 168–9).

In these ways the phenomenon of rave appeared to disrupt many of the traditional assumptions and expectations about subcultures that circulated around youth cultural studies (Bennett, 1999). In contrast to the Birmingham School, what seemed to be required was a 'revisionist' analysis that was capable of, on the one hand recognizing 'different youthful subjectivities' and on the other accounting for an increasing globalization of youth culture made possible by satellite communications and the transnational marketing and cultural exchange of musical forms and cultural vocabulary. By the early 1990s, for the first time it became possible to talk of a 'global' dimension to many youth styles and cultures (Osgerby, 1998, p. 200). The phenomenon of rave also clearly illustrates how certain musical and cultural styles, when viewed as oppositional and threatening, activate 'criminalizing crusades' against large numbers of young people. Yet all attempts to regulate leisure, pleasure and desire only succeed in producing yet more transformations of the carnivalesque. Raoul Vaneigem (2001, p. 35) expressed the sentiment clearly enough by claiming there is always a world of pleasure to win 'and nothing to lose but boredom'.

Seizing Pleasure: Edgework, Transgression and the Politics of Carnival

Whilst much of criminology is content to construe crime as rational action inspired by opportunity and lack of control, cultural criminology points to a wide range of crime – from writing graffiti, joyriding and vandalism to murder – that is clearly expressive rather than simply instrumental. Cultural criminology stresses the existential motives for breaking rules, taking risks and challenging authority. That this recognition of the pleasure of crime has only begun to be seriously interrogated in the last decade is something of a surprise given that any cursory glance at television programme listings, the contents of mass circulation newspapers or bookshop shelves instantly confirms the extent to which audiences perceive crime not just as a social problem but as a major source of amusement and diversion. Cultural criminology challenges us to accept that the pleasures of creating harm, doing wrong and breaking boundaries is also part of the equation.

The starting point is Jack Katz's (1988) seminal work on the 'seductions of crime'. Here he maintains that individual emotions, such as excitement, are central to the criminal event. Deviance offers a means of 'self transcendence': a way of overcoming the mundanity, banality and predictability of everyday life. Katz applies this analysis to shoplifting, robbery and murder but it surely has clear resonance in a whole series of criminal(ized) activities such as vandalism, car theft, drug use, joyriding, fire starting, car racing, hooliganism, gang fights and so on that we usually associate with youth. Each speaks of the thrill of 'taking it to the limit'; of gaining moments of control; and of being seduced by the existential pleasures of transgressive acts.

Lyng's (1990) work on voluntary risk taking continued this theme by introducing the concept of 'edgework'; a term borrowed from Hunter S. Thompson's journalistic descriptions of his anarchic – usually drug-induced – experiences. Whilst not specifically addressing youthful deviant behaviours, Lyng's analysis of edgework in high-risk and dangerous 'extreme' activities such as sky diving, hang gliding, car racing, test piloting and fire fighting, had clear resonances for anyone interested in the expressive aspects of crime. 'Edgework' neatly captures the spontaneous creative and intrinsically rewarding aspects of self actualization that are otherwise thwarted in a highly regimented, trivialized and degraded world of labour. Edgework provides an illusion of control in an alluring space of 'experiential anarchy in which the individual moves beyond the realm of established social patterns to the very fringes of ordered reality' (Lyng, 1990, p. 882).

Drawing on the insights of 'seduction' and 'edgework', O'Malley and Mugford (1994) have argued that a new phenomenology of pleasure is needed if we are to recognize 'crime' as *transgression* from the impermissible and as *transcendence* from the mundane. Moreover the notion of 'escape from the routine' provides one explanation for many forms of urban youth crime: as attempts to achieve some control within an otherwise insecure and alienating world. Transgression offers a mode of being in which individuals take control through a 'controlled loss of control' (Hayward, 2002, p. 87). In turn the 'grasping of such moments' inevitably interacts with cultures of crime control. As Ferrell's (1996; 1998; 2001) ethnographic excursions into the Denver hip-hop scene, street busking, BASE jumping and gutter punks have established, when such activities become progressively more policed, outlawed and criminalized, the more 'edgy excitement' they are capable of providing, and the more the pleasure of insubordination can be realized.

These intersections of culture, crime and control are also the subject of Presdee's (2000) analysis of crime as carnival. Rules are transgressed because they are there; risk is a challenge, not a deterrent. Increases in control provoke further transgression rather than conformity. Presdee explores the paradox that as the state attempts to impose a greater regulation over the minutiae of everyday life, it produces not only a greater compliant rationality but also higher degrees of resistant emotionality. The pursuit of pleasure becomes in itself antagonistic to the state. Presdee neatly captures this entwining of regulation and pleasure through the notion of 'crime as carnival'. Carnival is a site where the pleasure of playing at the boundaries is clearly catered for. Festive excess, the mocking of powerful and 'irrational' behaviour, have long been temporarily legitimated in the moment of carnival. Now as the possibility of such moments recede (and with them sources of joy, humour and celebration), as the consumer industries commodify pleasure and as the state attempts to stamp down on the 'anti-social', the spirit of carnival is expressed in numerous on the edge and spontaneous activities such as SM, raving, joyriding, computer hacking, Reclaim the Streets parties, recreational drug use and extreme sports. But not being part of the project of scientific rationalism renders such activities as 'irrational' and the resulting behaviour becomes rapidly criminalized: 'in other words everyday life is subjected to a creeping criminalization process where the carnival of crime becomes a necessity in our lives' (Presdee 2000, p. 160).

It is this sense of a spiralling process of regulation . . . consumerism . . . transgression . . . pleasure . . . criminalization . . . that cultural criminology offers. It may be accused of an excessive romanticizing of the (male) deviant but yet it is a mode of analysis that does more than most to open up the transgressive immediacy of youth lifestyles to an otherwise blinded criminological gaze. For Young (2002, p. 271) it once more offers an opportunity for critical criminology to keep in mind 'the urgency of opposition, yet with an eye for irony imbued as always with a sense of fun'.

Summary

- A routine element of popular notions of 'problem youth' is concern over unsupervised leisure, gangs and 'spectacular' subcultures. Structured gangs are more an American phenomenon; Britain has historically been the source of less organized youth subcultures. The 'deviant' qualities of British subcultures are to be found less in criminal or delinquent behaviour and more in non-conformist lifestyles. As a result much of the research into this area has traditionally emanated from cultural studies, rather than from criminology *per se.*

- Cultural criminology marks a significant emergent paradigm in investigating the convergence (and contestation) of cultures, crimes and crime control. Not only does it fuse cultural studies and critical criminology but through its preferred concepts of transgression, edgework and carnival, it is able to unravel the complex circuitry through which the meaning of crime is constructed, lived, enforced and resisted.

- The terms in which academics have tried to make sense of youth cultures have shifted markedly over the past 50 years. In the 1950s the dominant discourse was of a homogeneous *youth culture* which was believed to transcend all other social divisions. In the 1960s this was substantiated by notions of a *youth counterculture,* assumed to be in direct opposition to dominant culture. Such visions were first critiqued by the Centre for Contemporary Cultural Studies in Birmingham ('the Birmingham School') in the 1970s who identified a series of *youth subcultures,* differentiated by their respective class positions. By the 1980s feminist researchers pointedly argued that class-based analyses ignored or misrepresented gender divisions in subcultural formation. Coupled with a growing acknowledgement of the importance of black youth cultures, by the 1990s radical youth studies had moved to a more complex position capable of recognizing *hybridity, difference* and *diversity* in all youth cultural practices. Ethnographic studies alive to flexible subjectivities have come to challenge theories based to differing degrees on the principles of structural determinism.

- In some respects these theoretical shifts have mirrored shifts in youth cultural styles. Whilst clear working-class origins could be assigned to the teddy boys and skinheads, yet punk, and in particular rave culture, appeared either to transcend class boundaries or to be a reflection of individual consumer choices and styles. Class, gender and 'race' have all weakened as predictors of style and identity *on their own.* Increasingly they have been viewed as imposed categories which are unable to capture the fluidity of cultural practices.

- In the 1970s a class analysis challenged individualized accounts of adolescent pathology or rebellion, by identifying subcultural practice and style as forms of 'resistance'. But by the 1990s the boundaries of 'resistance' and 'conformity' had become blurred. Media saturation has made it difficult to draw distinct lines under moments of subcultural authenticity or consumerist manufacture. To a significant degree, style has replaced youth cultures. Subcultures have dissolved under the weight of an increasingly individualist and consumer-based society.

- Nevertheless, the 'deviant' and the 'different' continue to evoke adult condemnation. Non-conformity remains subject to criminalization. Certainly the 'threat' of youth continues to maintain a high public profile – particularly in matters of public order. 'Fighting crews' attached to certain football clubs, Reclaim the Streets parties, clandestine rave parties, fears of heroin, crack and Ecstasy 'destroying young minds', 'lager louts' at home and abroad, 'Asian' gangs and New Age travellers, all suggest both moral panic and a continuing disaffection of some sections of the youth population. None is amenable to traditional criminological or essentialist class-based subcultural analyses. They appear as disparate, fragmented and transient forms of action which repeatedly cross class and 'race' boundaries. Frequently it seems their notoriety is achieved as much through the political concern to impose more forms of rigid regulation, dependency and control as because of any 'new' and 'more alarming' behaviour patterns of young people themselves.

Study Questions

1   Why is unsupervised youth leisure a social problem?
2   How far are youth cultures able to challenge dominant culture?
3   How far do youth cultures represent an oblique form of acquiescence to dominant culture?
4   How useful are the twin concepts of *resistance* and *subculture* in explaining youthful behaviour?
5   How does cultural criminology reuse the concepts of 'crime' and 'culture' to provide fresh insights into the meaning of youthful transgression?

Further Resources

The key texts in cultural criminology are Ferrell and Sanders' edited collection (1995) and Mike Presdee's eminently readable *Cultural Criminology and the Carnival of Crime* (2000). Ferrell (1999) provides a good exposition of cultural criminology's theoretical and methodological underpinnings whilst acknowledging its heritage in 1970s British subcultural theory. Here the original key text in the analysis of youth subcultures in Britain is the Centre for Contemporary Cultural Studies' collection of working papers published in summer 1975 and reissued by Hutchinson as *Resistance through Rituals* (Hall and Jefferson, 1976). The book comprises a theoretical introduction followed by a number of case studies of ted, mod, skinhead, Rasta and girl subcultures. A similar set of case studies is contained in *Working Class Youth Culture* edited by Mungham and Pearson (1976). The significance of style, particularly within punk, is given more detailed attention by Dick Hebdige in *Subculture: The Meaning of Style* (1979). Steve Redhead's analysis of acid house and rave in *Rave Off* (1993) remains one of the few serious attempts to explore the politics of 1990s youth culture. Thornton's *Club Cultures* (1995) provides a convincing argument for viewing processes of subcultural authenticity and manufacture as inseparable. McKay's edited collection *DIY Culture* (1998) is a useful overview of cultural politics and lifestyle politics in the 1990s.

For more detailed analysis of black youth see Solomos' *Black Youth, Racism and the State* (1988) and Gilroy's '*There Ain't No Black in the Union Jack*' (1987b). For analysis of gender see Chapter 5 of Brakes' *The Sociology of Youth and Youth Subcultures* (1980), Sue Lees' *Losing Out* (1986) and the collection of articles by Angela McRobbie in *Feminism and Youth Culture* (1991).

Osgerby's (1998) social history of popular and youth cultures in Britain is an informed and readable overview of the shifts in style, politics and social reaction from the 1940s to the mid 1990s. A useful overview of how and why academic discourses about youth (which focuses on labour markets, crime, and sexuality as well as leisure) were challenged and reformed during the 1980s can be found in Griffin's *Representations of Youth* (1993). Gelder and Thornton's (1997) edited collection *The Subcultures Reader* reproduces many of the key traditional and contemporary 'readings' of subcultures and begins to give coherence to this 'relatively unexcavated discipline'. For anyone coming new to the area this is probably the best place to start.

6 Youth and Social Policy: Control, Regulation and Governance

Overview

Chapter 6 examines:
- the ways in which the everyday lives of young people are subject to particular forms of social regulation;
- various 'sites' of youth regulation including housing, welfare benefits, training schemes, crime prevention and the policing of public space;
- the relationship between criminal justice and social policy;
- the politics of social control and notions of a disciplinary or carceral society;
- how the concept of 'social control' has been utilized in various criminological theories;
- new modes of youth governance in the twenty-first century.

Key Terms

'anti-social' control	social control
carceral society	social crime prevention
dispersal of discipline	social exclusion
governmentality	state control
marginalization	transcarceration
risk society	zero tolerance
situational crime prevention	

This chapter explores the control and regulatory effects of welfare and social policy in Britain. Social policy has traditionally been viewed as an ostensibly progressive series of social arrangements concerned with the distribution of resources in order to meet individual and social needs. Yet, since the nineteenth century, social welfare provision has also had at its centre the themes of regulation and discipline. Whilst problems of control and order have always lain at the heart of discussions of youth justice and penal policy, it was only from the late 1950s that any sustained attempt was made to apply such concepts to the apparently benign implementation of social policies in such areas as health, education, housing and employment. One of the earliest contributions was Saville's (1957) Marxist argument that the welfare state arose largely out of capitalist self interest: in order to increase social stability, secure a compliant workforce and ensure the financial gain of the few. Any progressive elements in social policy were portrayed as a series of concessions, just sufficient to blunt working-class resistance to the structures of their exploitation and powerlessness. Such lines of argument have been significantly developed since the 1960s. For some radical criminologists (notably Stan Cohen), a major concern has been to examine how the 'exceptional' and 'exclusionary' interventions of criminal justice intersect with the continuum of 'everyday' and 'inclusionary' interventions to be found in education, social work, employment and leisure.

This chapter assesses the ways in which the everyday lives of young people are regulated by examining developments in youth training, welfare entitlement, housing policy, crime prevention and policing from the 1980s to the present. Whilst Chapter 7 examines the relationship between young people and formal agencies of control, this chapter looks at the different ways in which social policy and policing establish a structuring context in which 'what it means to be young' has become more tightly defined and increasingly regulated. Social policy development in Britain since the 1980s has been dominated by the neo-liberal objectives of economy (reducing public expenditure), efficiency (reliance on market forces) and effectiveness (enhancing consumer choice). Yet it has also been influenced by a neo-conservative authoritarianism in which the imperatives of order and control have dominated. The contradictions have played themselves out in the identification of social exclusion as both the cause and product of crime. Successive Labour governments since 1997 have prioritized work and family morality as key targets in tackling the causes of crime. As a result an eclectic series of concerns – from truancy, poverty, homelessness, worklessness to teenage pregnancy – have been identified, in the process drawing social policy and criminal justice agendas closer together.

The chapter begins by examining how these developments in problem identification, social policy and welfare reform have been (or can be) conceptualized by critical studies in social control. It assesses how far such concepts as 'state control', 'surveillance', 'discipline', 'carceral society', 'transcarceration' and 'governance' are able to capture the often hidden and diverse ways in which the regulation of the many is achieved.

Theorizing Control, Regulation and Governance

6.1

The term 'social control' is notoriously difficult to pin down. In functionalist sociology the concept appears as a neutral term to describe a variety of social processes – from infant socialization to incarceration – that induce social order, and to explain how conformity is maintained in pluralist democracies. Within interactionism the focus is somewhat narrower, but similarly concerned with how co-operation and social integration are achieved, usually without recourse to coercive and authoritarian discipline. Interactionists broadly conclude that the key to the maintenance of social order lies in the realm of informal and primary socialization processes through which core social values are transmitted and internalized. Such benign readings of 'social control' as a functional necessity and as essentially apolitical were mirrored in traditional positivist criminology whose key concern, at least up to the 1950s, remained one of developing 'scientific', pragmatic and institutionally based policies for the individualized control of offenders. As Cohen and Scull (1983, pp. 5–6) recall, the standard definition of 'social control' is rooted in a social psychological perspective and is used as a term first simply to describe all the means and processes through which social conformity is achieved and second, to construct a hierarchy of such means ranging from primary socialization, through informal mechanisms (such as peer group pressure) to formal methods associated with the police and the legal system. Within all such readings it is widely assumed that a consensus exists in society; that primary socialization is largely successful in achieving a widespread and uncontested conformity; and that external agencies are only called upon to 'mop up' those deviants who have suffered a failure or lack of adequate socialization.

It was not until the late 1960s that an alternative view of social control, as organized repression, came to the fore. Generated by the protest movements in America (civil rights, Vietnam, counterculture) and the emerging utopian and personal politics of the 'new left', arguments concerning the essential consensual nature of society became harder to sustain. In particular the labelling perspective asserted that society was made up of a number of diverse groups in which actions defined as deviant by some would be viewed as normal by others. The identification of the deviant and the criminal was thus an intrinsically political process through which, for example, capitalist institutions and the ruling classes were able to impose their will on the exploited and the powerless (see Chapter 4.1). In this formulation, social control was conceptualized not simply as a reactive and reparative exercise, but as an active force in the identification and creation of the deviant. As Chunn and Gavigan (1988, p. 109) note, 'the concept of "social control" as "doing good" had become the concept of "social control" as "doing bad"'. Or as Lemert's original formula described it:

> Older sociology tended to rest heavily upon the idea that deviance leads to social control. I have come to believe that the reverse idea (i.e. social control leads to deviance) is equally tenable and the potentially richer premise for studying deviance in modern society. (Lemert, 1967, p. ix)

Such a premise did indeed become influential in critical readings of a wide range of purportedly reformist and welfare-related practices. For example, the coercive – but often hidden – aspects of control entailed in the professional practices of youth training, social work, law, probation, medicine, schooling and psychiatry were highlighted and analysed as part of a burgeoning social control culture. In turn an image of society as moving incessantly towards more sophisticated means of repressive control was created. The intrusion of the state into the private and familial; the capacity for behaviour to be continually subjected to surveillance, monitoring and regulation; and the spectre of mind control – all these constructed a powerful portrayal of a one-dimensional society (Marcuse, 1964) in the image of George Orwell's *Nineteen Eighty-Four* (1949) and Aldous Huxley's *Brave New World* (1932). As Cohen (1985, p. 6) explained:

> Social control has become Kafka-land, a paranoid landscape in which things are done to us, without our knowing when, why or by whom, or even that they are being done. We live inside Burroughs' 'soft machine', an existence all the more perplexing because those who control us

seem to have the most benevolent of intentions. Indeed, we ourselves appear as the controllers as well as the controlled.

Moving the concept of social control from its benign underpinnings, this new interpretation maintained that social control, whether weak or strong, informal or formal, remained all-pervasive. There was very little that remained that could not be seen as an instrument of social control (Stedman-Jones, 1977). The key neglected issue – particularly within labelling – was how and why such control operated differently in different social contexts. Lacking any precise definition and consistent use, the concept was aptly described by Cohen (1985, p. 2) as 'Mickey Mouse' and by Lowman et al. (1987, p. 4) as 'a skeleton key opening so many doors that its analytic power has been drained . . . a spectral category which becomes all things to all theorists'.

From Social Control to State Control

In the 1970s the answer to such ambiguities lay in situating particular processes of social control in their precise socio-structural and historical settings. The emerging Marxist criminology and sociology of law, for example, placed a theory of the state centre-stage in the analysis of how control was exercised in twentieth-century capitalist societies (see Chapter 4.1). Thus Hall et al. (1978, p. 195), whilst acknowledging the theoretical importance of labelling's identification of centres of power (the ruling classes; the professions) and of its questioning who has the power to label whom, eventually found the *control culture approach* to be ahistorical and too imprecise for an adequate understanding of processes of conformity, legitimation and, most significantly, opposition, in the class-structured democracies of 'late capitalism'. In particular, the control culture approach did not locate centres of power historically and thus was unable to account for moments of shift and change; it failed to differentiate between different types of state and political regime; and did not specify the type of social formation which requires a particular form of legal order. Above all, it adopted a predominantly coercive view of power and legal relations. Simply substituting coercion for the functionalist notion of consensus failed to identify how the exercise of power was often legitimized. The complex combination of processes of social regulation and civil liberties; of naked force and willing consent; and of resistance and deference was, quite simply, lost in a perspective that caricatured all police, social workers, teachers, philanthropists and reformers as unconscious agents of socio-cultural repression (Hall and Scraton, 1981, p. 470). Hall et al. (1978, p. 195) argued for the abandonment of the term 'social control' (except for 'general descriptive purposes') and its subjugation to that of 'state control', in which it is recognized that the production of consent is achieved not simply through coercive measures, but through state leadership, direction, education and tutelage. Chunn and Gavigan (1988, p. 120) reached a similar conclusion, again by stressing the ahistorical nature of 'social control' and by arguing that critical scholars should be searching for alternative concepts that are 'attentive to the dynamic complexity of history, struggle and change'.

Feminist research has also alerted us to significant gender-based differences in the operation of social control (Heidensohn, 1985). Disobedient or runaway young women and the 'unfit' teenage mother are far more likely to be candidates for intervention than disobedient, runaway or sexually active heterosexual young men. Moreover many social and employment policies have traditionally tended to be predicated on assumptions of female dependency and male independence. Systems of social control impact differently on different subject populations. A state-centred perspective may be able to recognize how 'social control' produces (rather than simply prohibits) certain behaviours, but on its own is unable to capture the nuances of control afforded by a 'gendered lens' (Walklate, 1995). In addition, some feminist authors have argued that the extension of control in some areas, rather than being dangerous, is urgently required in order to protect women from male domestic and street violence. As Smart (1989) argues, the law can be used not simply for disciplinary purposes, but also as a means to pursue a discourse of 'rights'.

Foucault on the Carceral Society

Following the work of Foucault (1977), the term 'social control' was resurrected as a means through which analytical justice could be done to the complex and contradictory means by which order is achieved in democratic societies. Foucault's critique of 'power as state centred' and the shift towards acknowledging the role of processes of diffuse societal power (or the 'microphysics of power') significantly broadened the concept of social control to include not only state and institutional practices but also the realms of discursive construction, ideology and the production of meaning.

Foucault refers to a continuous *disciplinary discourse*, in which no one source is given privileged attention, which informed and was intertwined with all forms of social control in the late eighteenth century. The reform of prisoners, confinement of the insane and supervision of industrial workers, as well as the training and education of children, all formed part of an emerging *carceral society*, in which it was not only deviance or crime that was controlled, but also every irregularity or the least departure from the norm.

> [I]t was no longer the offence, the attack on common interest, it was the departure from the norm, the anomaly; it was this that haunted the school, the court, the asylum or the prison . . . [I]t is not on the fringes of society that criminality is born, but by means of ever more closely placed insertions, under ever more insistent surveillance, by an accumulation of disciplinary coercion . . . By operating at every level of the social body and by mingling ceaselessly the art of rectifying and the right to punish, the universality of the carceral lowers the level from which it becomes natural and acceptable to be punished. (Foucault, 1977, pp. 299, 301, 303)

The carceral discourse, it is argued, is so pervasive that ultimately it affects our very vision of the world: it enters the human soul. The power of the prison, and in particular the juvenile reformatory (see Chapter 2.2) in the 1840s, is less explicable in terms of penal philosophy, or as a success or a failure, than it is by the 'power of normalization' that operates simultaneously and to varying degrees in the school, the hospital and the factory. This power emanates not simply from the state or a mode of production but, for Foucault, from forms of knowledge that inform all social relations. The emergence of the reformatory was but one reflection of the diffusion of new forms of knowledge grounded in positivism and the human sciences which first began to surface in the late eighteenth century. The aim was to produce a new kind of individual subjected to habits, rules, orders and an authority that is 'exercised continually around him, and upon him, and which he must allow to function automatically in him' (Foucault, 1977, p. 129).

Foucault's initial investigation of penal reform thus becomes a means of exploring the wider theme of how domination is achieved and how individuals are socially constructed in the modern world. It is because of this broad canvas, on which images of regulation, discipline, surveillance, consent, normalization and coercion are constructed, that Foucault's work remains influential in historical and contemporary readings of social control. For example, it has enabled criminology to study the way in which various welfare state institutions are deeply implicated in the 'regulation of life'. But it also allows for a greater sensitivity to the interrelations of social structure with processes of power, knowledge and governance. It is at once attuned to processes of domination *and* enablement; of constraint *and* resistance (Lacombe, 1996).

Donzelot (1979), for example, has argued that from the mid nineteenth century onwards 'expert knowledges', whether emanating from welfare agencies, the school or the juvenile court, have continuously devised remedies for the 'aberrant' which have penetrated deep into the everyday life of the urban working classes. Psychologists, paediatricians, social workers, teachers and health visitors formed a 'tutelary complex' to 'watch over' not only the young but also their families. This was achieved not by overtly coercive means but by persuading the family of its social responsibility to others and to its own members. Familial autonomy, or government *by* the family, was replaced by government *through* the family. The aim was to govern society by delegating legitimacy to professionals empowered to nurture individuals into social citizenship. Such programmes had as much to do with the governance of particular moral and social orders as they had explicitly to do with crime and disorder. Every departure from the norm comes under scrutiny to be monitored and regulated not simply through formal criminal justice legislation but through an ever-expanding range of familial and social policy interventions. Moreover as these interventions can act anywhere along a disciplinary/enabling continuum, they are difficult to characterize as either one or the other. Rather they are progressively internalized such that citizens come to unreflectively make and remake their own conceptions of themselves within a disciplinary discourse.

Foucault and Donzelot's work clearly avoids any ready identification with 'grand' theoretical paradigms and thus more readily escapes the critique of essentialism so often directed at general theory. Indeed, Garland (1990, p. 154) concludes that, as a result, there is now 'a much greater sensitivity to the nuances of penal measures and to what they can tell us about the regulatory means through which we are governed and the forms of subjectivity (or objectivity) into which offenders are pressed'. Terms such as 'regulation', 'knowledge', 'normalization', 'governmentality' and 'discipline' have come to hold a central place in this 'revisionist' literature of social control. The key elements of Foucault's argument are summarized in Table 6.1.

Table 6.1 *Foucault's* **Discipline and Punish**

- The punitive techniques of supervision and surveillance first formulated in the prison have penetrated the whole of society.
- Punishment is aimed not at the body, but towards training the human soul.
- Such techniques are directed not only towards offenders, but to all departures from the norm.
- Disciplinary networks become natural, legitimate and 'normalized' elements of the social landscape.
- Social control becomes diffuse, hidden and dispersed.
- Social control is exercised not simply through the state but through power-knowledge strategies. As a result control may be pervasive but is always contingent. It produces resistance as well as subjugation.

Cohen on the Dispersal of Discipline

Stanley Cohen's (1979, 1985, 1987) 'dispersal of discipline' thesis reworks that of Foucault to contend that as control mechanisms are dispersed from custody into the community, they penetrate more deeply into the social fabric. A blurring of boundaries between the deviant and non-deviant, the public and the private occurs. A 'punitive archipelago' is expanded as new resources, technology and professional interests are applied to a growing number of 'clients' and 'consumers'. Entrepreneurs are drawn into the control enterprise in search of profits. Communities are mobilized to act as voluntary control agents in their own right. But, throughout, the growing invisibility and diversification of the state's role do not mean it has withered away. The prison remains at the core of the system. The rhetoric of community control continues to camouflage what is really going on: 'The price paid by ordinary people is to become either active participants or passive receivers in the business of social control' (Cohen, 1985, p. 233).

The end result of drawing law and order agendas into social policy for youth has meant that any progressive elements have become obscured by ambivalence and ambiguity. Alternatives to prison (such as electronic monitoring) and crime prevention (rather than law enforcement) policies have failed to reduce the reach of criminal justice and tend to draw more young people into the mesh of formal controls. Such reforms have also been supported for non-progressive reasons, as, for example, 'solutions' to the fiscal crises of the state, rather than as determined responses to youth marginalization or exclusion. Cohen summarizes the final outcome of this 'dispersal of discipline':

- The weak, pathetic and sick are subject to too little 'control'. Neglected and deprived of help, treatment and services, they are left to suffer silently or to be exploited by commercial interests.
- The petty or 'potential' delinquents are subject to more intrusive and disguised control in the name of diversion or prevention.
- The hardcore, serious criminals are subject to further degradation. As the soft end of the system appears more and more benign, so the hard core criminals appear more hopeless and become easy targets for policies such as selective incapacitation.
- The powerful remain free to carry out their depredations with impunity.
- The ordinary population are subjected to further and more subtle involvement in the business of social control. Everyday life becomes 'controllized' by Crime Prevention through Environmental Design, informers, new systems of surveillance of public space, and databanks. Whole populations are made the object of preventive social control before any deviant act can take place.' (Adapted from Cohen, 1987, pp. 363–4)

Lowman et al. (1987, p. 9) argue that these developments can best be captured in the concept of *transcarceration*. They argue that as the old institutions of control remain and the new are created, we are now confronted with a

peno-judicial, mental health, welfare and tutelage complex . . . [F]or delinquents, deviants and dependants this means that their careers are likely to be characterized by institutional mobility as they are pushed from one section of the help-control complex to another. For control agents, this means that control will essentially have no locus and the control mandate will increasingly entail the 'fitting together' of subsystems.

In congruence with Foucault's thesis, this formulation of control continues to acknowledge its versatility: infiltrating many levels of discourse and 'arenas of action' and serving and constituting a diversity of interests. Of particular note is how, by the 1990s, much of this control became privatized – that is, removed from direct state control and activated by communities, voluntary agencies and private security companies. It is in this context that Cohen (1994, p. 74) can begin talking of social control as a commodity: as something to be purchased and sold.

Rose on Governance

To make sense of these shifts in crime control and social regulation, numerous authors have increasingly turned to the concept of 'governance'. Derived from Foucault's (1991) brief writings on 'governmentality', 'governance' (though often used in an eclectic fashion) refers to any act, means or tactic through which conduct is regulated. These might range from state-sponsored techniques of domination to techniques of self government. Governance means something more than state government. It is also concerned with the tactic of using particular knowledges to arrange things in such a way that populations accept being governed and begin to govern themselves through 'the conduct of conduct'. This is never simply a matter of state coercion. Rather 'to govern' acknowledges an autonomy and freedom of the governed; such capacities are not crushed but worked with and utilized to achieve particular modes of governance. As Rose (1999, p. 5) put it:

> The investigations of government that interest me here are those which try to gain a purchase on the forces that traverse the multitudes of encounters where conduct is subject to government: prisons, clinics, schoolrooms and bedrooms, factories and offices, airports and military organizations, the market place and shopping mall, sexual relations and much more . . . . They focus upon the various incarnations of what one might term 'the will to govern' as it is enacted in a multitude of programmes, strategies, tactics, devices, calculations, negotiations, intrigues, persuasions and seductions aimed at the conduct of the conduct of individuals, groups, populations – and indeed oneself.

In this analysis the state is relocated as one element in 'multiple circuits of power' connecting a diversity of authorities, forces and complex assemblages. The subjects of government are not simply 'members of a flock to be shepherded, as children to be nurtured and tutored' but are 'citizens with rights, rational, calculating individuals whose preferences are to be acted upon' (Rose, 2000, p. 323).

How can this help us to understand the regulation of young people? Rose (1989, p. 121) contends that it allows us to realize how childhood has, over the past 200 years, become 'the most intensively governed sector of personal existence'. The continual casting of children in a double bind of in need of support and control has enabled virtually every aspect of their lives to be subject to inspection, surveillance and regulation. Of course the means through which this is achieved has been subject to historical change. Governance theory then is also intent on accounting for how broad historical shifts in political rationalities have impacted on the governance of youth.

Rose (1996b) has identified three modes of governance that have dominated since the eighteenth century: the 'liberal', the 'welfare liberal' and the 'advanced liberal'. Following Foucault (1977; 1991), classical liberalism is depicted as allowing individuals the freedom to govern their own lives. The disciplinary logic of the reformatory, for example, is to produce the subjective conditions of self regulation necessary for the governance of a society of free and civilized individuals. Governance is achieved through 'authorities of expertise'. Rose contends that, by the twentieth century, this liberal project had failed, as evidenced in greater social fragmentation and individualization. Increases in crime and unemployment attested to the dangers of *laissez-faire*.

Penal-welfare emerged as one formula for reorganizing social, political and economic affairs. The state took on a greater responsibility for guaranteeing not only individual freedom but also collective security. Social insurance and social work were its hallmarks: both ostensibly inclusionary by guarding against the economic vagaries of systems of wage labour, whilst establishing the parameters of 'correct' behaviour in return. Security and protection were provided in return for social obligation and social responsibility. However, since the 1960s this penal-welfare framework has been systematically undermined by the development of forms of neo-liberal (or in Rose's more generic term 'advanced liberal') governance. This can be broadly characterized as placing less emphasis on social contexts, state protection and rehabilitation and more on prescriptions of individual responsibility, an active citizenry and governing at a distance. Welfare liberalism was increasingly critiqued for encouraging state dependence, overloading the responsibilities of the state, and undermining the ability of individuals to take responsibility for their own actions. For Rose (1996a), a 'death of the social' is evident in the transformation of 'old' notions of *social* engineering, *social* solidarity, *social* benefits, *social* work and *social* welfare to create responsible (that is, not welfare-dependent) citizens.

This has involved a break-up of 'top down' forms of bureaucracy and a move towards network-based and indirect forms of control. Self governance and public participation are encouraged, albeit within performance measures set by policy makers. The state governs 'at a distance', relying on 'joined-up' partnerships rather than traditional command and control structures. It steers rather than controls (see Table 6.2).

Table 6.2   *New modes of governance*

- Replacing the command and control structures of government by 'governing at a distance'.
- Building partnerships and networks across the public, private and voluntary sectors to achieve 'joined-up' governance.
- Devolving responsibility for government to individuals, families and communities.
- Creating the 'active citizen' and 'negotiated self governance'.
- Opening up decision making to greater public participation and the individual desire to govern their own conduct with freedom.
- Involving civil society in the process of governance.
- Privatizing the state sector.
- Promoting the role of government as steerer and co-ordinator rather than as controller.
- Regulating devolved governance through 'risk rationalities, fiscal accounting, audit and evaluation research.

Sources: Newman (2001, p. 24); Muncie and Hughes (2002, p. 3); Dean (1999 p. 135)

This analysis helps us to make sense of many of the reforms ushered in by both the Conservative Right and New Labour in the past decade. It expresses a preference for free market solutions, deregulation, privatization and workfare (where any benefit entitlement is conditional upon acceptance of work) in a climate where risks are to be calculated and outputs are to be managed through continual performance measures and where policy is justified through recourse to 'scientific' evaluations of 'what works'. Above all a multiplicity of modes of governance is created: authoritarian at one time, welfarist at another; delivering discourses of responsibility as well as rights; and driven by a deeply imbued moralization as well as pragmatism (Stenson, 2000; Muncie and Hughes, 2002).

Governance theory, to date, has mainly been concerned with unravelling the processes through which we are governed, but it also marks a significant theoretical step in understanding the detailed nuances and contradictions of reform. Foucault and Cohen clearly broadened the traditional subject matter of the criminology of youth by blurring the boundaries of social policy and criminological knowledges. Their strength lay in identifying major trends in 'the disciplinary' and 'the carceral'. Governance theory goes further by also alerting us to the 'heterogeneity, contestability and mobility in practices for the government of conduct' (Rose, 2000, p. 323). Rights-based social movements, local initiatives and the intrinsic spaces for resistance opened by neo-liberalism's commitment to self governance all suggest possible avenues for a reconstitution of 'social' modes of government. Indeed, Stan Cohen (1987) and such authors as Cain (1985) and De Haan (1990) have come to argue that the inclusionary principles, values and ideals that inform some social policies should not be abandoned, but resurrected within agendas of social justice, rather than criminal justice. For them, informalism, mutual aid and community control remain the preferable goals: 'the further away we move from the discourse of criminal justice, the more likely are we to find the conditions for realizing those values . . . [T]o be realistic about law and order must mean to be unrealistic (that is imaginative) about the possibilities of order without law' (Cohen, 1987, p. 374). The evolving of contradictions between centralization, devolution, fiscal crises and community responsibility will continue to open up spaces in which more progressive and emancipatory forms of politics and penality can be pursued (De Haan, 1990, p. 166; Cohen, S., 1994, p. 85; Muncie and Hughes, 2002, p. 16).

The remainder of this chapter examines how the concepts of social control, regulation and governance have been (or can be) utilized to shed light on the rationale and discursive practices of youth training, housing policy, policing and crime prevention.

Youth Training and the Labour Market

6.2 This section explores how young people's lives have become increasingly constrained within the relationship between education, training, entry to the labour market and unemployment. Characteristically, research in this area has tended to view the process as an orthodox linear transition from school to work and has failed to recognize its social control implications. Any deviation from an 'ideal' progression from full-time education to full-time employment is perceived in negative terms: as a 'broken' transition, as a 'failure' of certain young people to adjust to the demands of the labour market. Such concern is of course by no means new. The vagaries of the youth labour market vexed many a Victorian reformer and the problems of dead-end jobs, prolonged unemployment, 'wasted potential' and 'idle hands' were uppermost in the minds of the founders of the welfare state after the Second World War. During times of relatively full employment the transition from school to work has been viewed as non-problematic. But, as Coles (1995) has argued, the traditional 'careers' of young people – leaving school and finding employment, leaving families of origin and forming their own, and leaving the family home and living independently – rest crucially not only on personal decisions, but also on prevailing social and economic contexts. In the 1970s most young people seemed to manage these transitions with relative ease. A majority left school at 16 and within six months 90 per cent had secured employment (Coles, 1995, p. 30). By 1980, this picture had changed dramatically.

Triggered by economic recession and a restructuring of the labour market which reduced the demand for young unskilled labour, the numbers of unemployed school leavers rose dramatically from the mid 1970s. In September 1973 there were 14,000 school leavers (under-18s) without a job. By July 1980 this figure had risen to 368,000. This almost 26-fold increase took place despite higher numbers of young people avoiding the labour market by going into higher and further education. The unemployment rate of 18–25 year olds was even greater: in July 1982 some 926,499 were registered as unemployed – almost one in six of this section of the population. A quarter of a million had been out of work for a year or more; over 75,000 for over two years and almost 20,000 for three years. Overall some 30 per cent of the unemployed were under 25. The situation was even more acute for black youth. In November 1982, the Commission for Racial Equality reported that 60 per cent of young Afro-Caribbeans who were available for work in the 16–20 age group were without a job. At that time some 40 per cent of young whites and Asians were also out of work. The spectre of unemployment has continued to face young people. Every rise in adult unemployment since the 1960s has been accompanied by a greater rise in the youth rate. At its peak in 1983 (when it was still possible to use official statistics as a reliable indicator of real unemployment), the rate for all ages was some 12 per cent, but for under-18s it was over 50 per cent. Regional unemployment was even more substantial. In Liverpool where overall unemployment was 20 per cent, in 1983, under-18 year old unemployment was nearly 90 per cent.

It was in this context that New Labour announced a range of 'welfare to work' initiatives prior to the 1997 election. It estimated at the time that there were still a quarter of a million 18–24 year olds experiencing long-term unemployment. In 1998 the New Deal for Young People effectively abolished youth unemployment at a stroke by compelling those not in work to take up a number of education, training or subsidized work options. However, it was still estimated that half a million 16–24 year olds (around 10 per cent) were unemployed in 2002 (www.poverty.org.uk).

YOP, YTS and YT

Since 1975 when youth unemployment first became a major political issue, governments have poured resources into various job creation, work experience and training schemes. In 1976 the then Prime Minister, James Callaghan set the tone by blaming young people for not having the skills that the economy required of them. He further blamed education for not teaching students what was required of them by the business community. The bulk of subsequent reforms were initially directed towards 16 year old school leavers. This was not unsurprising. In the early 1980s nearly 50 per cent of Britain's 16 year olds still left school to find work. In July

1983 over half of these were either unemployed or on a government-sponsored training scheme.

In 1978 the Youth Opportunities Programme (YOP) was launched by the Labour government under the guidance of the Manpower Services Commission (MSC). Initially some 86,000 school leavers were involved and 69 per cent of YOP trainees later found full-time employment (Forester, 1981, p. 96). In 1981 the scheme was expanded to provide places for 180,000 young people. YOP consisted of four different elements: Work Experience on Employers' Premises (WEEP); Community Projects (Community Service Schemes); Training Workshops (manufacture of consumer products from wood, metal or fabrics); and various kinds of work preparation courses. Its aim was to prepare young people for work by making them more acceptable to employers. This was to be achieved by providing not only work experience but also 'life and social skills' related to work discipline, appearance and punctuality. The basic premise of the programme was that youth unemployment had risen because of a sudden failure of youth to be suitable candidates for employment. In effect it promoted a 'blame the victim' ideology. As Phil Cohen argued, the aim of the programme could not realistically be on expanding job opportunities as these depended on an uplift in the market economy:

> [I]ts real effect is limited to ideology – to represent youth employment as a problem of faulty supply rather than demand; a failure of the educational system rather than capitalism; a personal problem of joblessness due to lack of motivation, experience or skill, rather than the position youth occupies in the market economy. (Cohen, P., 1982, p. 45)

Indeed, as the YOP expanded, its 'success rate' noticeably declined. By 1981 the numbers of trainees subsequently finding full-time employment fell to about 36 per cent. By far the largest element in the YOP was the WEEP scheme, which accounted for three-quarters of YOP places. It was also the element that received most criticism. Rather than providing secure future job opportunities, the scheme artificially created a demand for youth labour which in market terms was no longer profitable. Trainees worked for up to six months with one employer, often in unskilled, repetitive and menial jobs for which they were paid a minimal allowance by the government. The scheme was cheap to run but clearly lent itself to the possibility of employers replacing paid employees with a succession of YOP trainees. By 1981 the MSC conceded that one in three of the positions created had cost a permanent worker a job. Above all, the scheme was used not so much for the training, but for the vetting of youth by employers. The MSC's booklet *Instructional Guide to Social and Life Skills* emphasized the need 'to adjust trainees to normal working conditions', to check for 'signs of alienation in matters of time keeping, discipline etc.' and 'any unsatisfactory relationships' (cited by Morgan, 1981, pp. 105–6). Essentially, the young unemployed were viewed as deviants who needed 'treatment' in the form of work discipline, regulation and surveillance. As Morgan concluded:

the Youth Opportunities Programme offers a chance to experience the discipline of work without being allowed any of the advantages that go with it . . . [Young people] are, through the 'training programme' encouraged to believe that it is their personal inadequacies which create unemployment. They are in effect, less powerful and more atomised on the programme than off it. (Morgan, 1981, p. 109)

In this way YOPs also acted as a form of social control, by attempting to reassert the value of the work ethic to those who found work unavailable. Such a benefit came to be lost on the young and unemployed. For a majority, WEEP only provided a temporary respite from the dole queue. Many learnt that because of low allowances they were as well, if not better, off receiving supplementary benefit than a YOP allowance. Others questioned the dubious amount of training they received as cheap labour in menial jobs. Indeed, there is no evidence that the YOP made any difference to the amount of regular employment available to school leavers. But the programme did have two clear political attractions: it helped to keep some 300,000 people every year off the official unemployment register and also off the streets. The social order implications of high youth unemployment were noted as early as 1978. A minister at the DES in the last Labour government warned that, without jobs,

a growing number of youngsters are bound to develop the feeling that society has betrayed them. Such feelings can very easily lead to crime and even more sinister, can provide a fertile ground for the breeding of various kinds of political extremism. I do not think it is exaggerating to suggest that these factors pose a threat to the fabric of society potentially as serious as that of armed conflict between nations. (Cited by Loney, 1981, p. 11)

It was thus partly in response to questions of social order that in 1983 a Conservative government unveiled its new Youth Training Scheme (YTS) as a 12-month training programme directed at *all* 16 and 17 year old school leavers. It aimed to provide a permanent bridge between school and work by requiring *all* young people under the age of 18 either to continue in full-time education or to enter a one-year period of post-school work experience combined with related training and education. Intended as a comprehensive scheme covering some 460,000 employed and unemployed school leavers, it sought to influence the way industry trained its own workforce as well as providing a scheme to cope with the unemployed. From its inception, however, YTS came under fire for being unlikely to solve some of the problems of YOP. Like YOP it was open to abuse by employers and its acceptance by employers and trainees depended on the level of grant both parties eventually received from the government. There was no guarantee that all young people would receive a similar 'training'. Rather, 'training' was determined by regional location and the short-term preferences of employers.

In essence YTS was an attempt to provide a permanent structural resolution to the crisis of youth unemployment by tightening the control over school leavers. As Finn (1983, p. 22) concluded: 'state agencies are increasingly going to determine what it means to be young'. In 1985 YTS was extended to a two-year programme and came to cater for more than a quarter of all school leavers. From 1988 it was administered by employer-dominated Training and Enterprise Councils (TECs) in England and Wales and Local Enterprise Councils (LECs) in Scotland. In 1990 it became known simply as Youth Training. But in all these forms it continued to interpret the problem of employment *for* young people, as a problem *about* young people. By insisting that the young working class had special developmental needs, their exclusion from the labour market, their redefinition as trainees and their exposure to new forms of educational experience were all spuriously justified. Indeed, YTS's primary fallacy lay in its premise that a programme of vocational preparation would enable the young to be better equipped to compete for jobs, without actually expanding real job opportunities. Even if youth were to be persuaded to accept their status as a new client group in need of a protracted period of education and training, at the end of each scheme, trainees would face the same future as most YOP graduates – the dole. As Stafford (1982, p. 77) warned, this form of integrating youth into the labour market would depend on their willingness to accept any alternative to the dole. As such it would be 'precarious and rests on a promise which must surely turn sour'. Similarly, Finn (1987, p. 190) concludes that the aim of YTS was essentially contradictory: 'to produce a generation of young people who are basically skilled and willing to work, but who can also maintain these qualities in suspended animation through any periods of unemployment'.

Deregulation

By 1988 the option of the dole was also removed when the Conservative government abolished income support benefit for all 16 and 17 year olds, other than for a small majority who could plead 'severe hardship'. By now 16 year olds were faced with a limited range of options: to continue with schooling or further education; to accept a place on a government-sponsored training scheme; or, if unemployed, to stay dependent on their families. As a result it has been widely acknowledged that the period of adolescence has been formally extended, with any possibility of independence removed for the vast majority (Furlong and Cartmel, 1997, p. 43). In 1989 18 per cent of minimum-age school leavers entered the labour market; by 1994 this had been reduced to 9 per cent. Conversely the proportion of 16 year olds in full-time or part-time education rose to 80 per cent (*Observer*, 23 July 1995).

Those entering the labour market in the 1980s also faced a series of additional hazards. Since the nineteenth century a political consensus had ensured that young people were given some protection from market exploitation, but in the 1980s market deregulation meant that restrictions on hours and conditions of work and rates of pay were removed. The problem of youth unemployment, it was claimed, was one of young people being too expensive to employ. As Roberts (1995, p. 15) records, Young Workers' Schemes offered subsidies to employers only on condition that they hire young people at rates of pay below the average for the age group. In 1986 the protection of Wages Councils was also removed. The jobs available to 16 year olds increasingly became low paid and insecure: 'the type of dead end juvenile jobs that had existed before the Second World War, but which had been driven off the labour market in the subsequent conditions of full employment, began to be recreated in the 1980s' (Roberts, 1995, p. 17).

Those entering youth training fared little better. At its peak, in 1989, the YTS route accounted for 27 per cent of young men and 20 per cent of young women school leavers, but rapidly contracted in the 1990s as educational participation grew. Despite government claims that YT was designed to improve skills and subsequent employability, the schemes were consistently critiqued by young people themselves as 'slave labour' with employers operating 'try-out schemes' in which young people's work performance was assessed and only the best retained (Coffield et al., 1986). For many, YT was also an exercise in 'warehousing' in which no long-term career benefits were forthcoming (Banks et al., 1992). Mizen's (1995) equally critical, empirical study of school leavers and trainees' experiences and accounts in Coventry painted a picture of YT 'more as an extension of pre-existing forms of discipline and control than as the beginning of a new and welcome chapter in the lives of many working class young people'.

As the new vocationalism was experienced as an 'alienating and negative experience' imposing low-skilled work experience, with poor rates of pay and with no eventual promise of a job, it was received by young people with a (realistic) combination of resistance, denial and ambivalence (Mizen, 1995, pp. 197–202). Indeed, in 1994 only 56 per cent of ex-trainees were in jobs six months after completing their schemes. Moreover, particularly for working-class trainees and members of ethnic communities, it was argued that training took place in a labour market context in which the chances of employment were virtually nil (Furlong and Cartmel, 1997, p. 32).

The experience of training was also fragmented and individualized. With the onset of YT geared more directly to employers' immediate needs, a bewildering array of schemes offered by different sponsors, employers and managers emerged. Their relative value came to be recognized hierarchically, the most sought after (those more likely to lead to employment) being provided by employers; the least sought

---

Table 6.3   *Youth labour markets in the 1980s and 1990s*

- Shift from manufacturing to service sector
- Decline in demand for unqualified 16 year old school leavers
- Growth in part-time, temporary, low-paid and lower-tier employment
- Deregulation of markets prioritizes increased training, flexibility and low labour cost
- Decline in trade union membership and influence – reinforced by legislation
- Restricted access to income support and unemployment benefits
- From 1989 an increase in unemployment – disproportionately for young men and blacks
- Growth in numbers remaining in full-time education and/or training
- Complex maze of 'transitions' and multiple routes from school to work – 'transitions' extended, fragmented, fractured and individualized
- Maintenance of regional, class, gender and 'race' based structures of opportunity and disadvantage
- Conditions of uncertainty, risk and disaffection exacerbated

Source: Derived from Furlong and Cartmel (1997, Chapter 3)

after, those offered by local authorities and training centres. Experiences of youth training also remained stratified by class, gender and 'race'. The most disadvantaged and those from ethnic minorities tended to be concentrated in schemes with low rates of subsequent employment. The promised new opportunities failed to materialize, with the vast majority of schemes reinforcing and reproducing gender stereotypes in their provision of 'suitable' work for young men and women (Griffin, 1985; Cockburn, 1987; Wallace, 1987). Table 6.3 summarizes this parlous state of the labour market for young people in the 1990s.

One of the most palpable consequences of a contracting and deregulated youth labour market was the expansion of what Furlong and Cartmel (1997, p. 17) described as 'an army of reluctant conscripts to post-compulsory education'. In the mid 1970s a third of 16 year olds stayed on at school; 20 years later it was nearer 80 per cent. A range of vocational courses (BTEC, NVQ and GNVQ) have been introduced in schools and colleges of further education, though arguably these have been mainly directed at lower-attaining, working-class pupils and have little affected the traditional academic routes followed by the middle classes. Moreover the 'careers' of young people in further education often remained precarious. About a third of those starting a full-time post-16 course left early or failed the relevant examinations. The concepts of 'career' and 'transition' seemed particularly irrelevant for such young people. Instead their lives were characterized by a *mélange* of training courses, part-time, low-paid work (as low as 33 pence per hour – *Guardian*, 11 February 1998) and unemployment. Here the sensitizing concepts of 'drift', 'normalized dislocation' and 'structured aimlessness' may better capture a sense of youth's uncertain futures in an unstable market, than those of 'transition' or 'marginalization' (Fergusson et al., 2000).

Indeed, as Brinkley (1997) records, the free market logic of deregulation did not help young people back into work, despite their being cheaper to employ. Demand in industrialized economies for skilled workers meant that the young – especially those without qualifications – were left behind. Between 1979 and 1997, 31 changes were made to how youth unemployment figures were officially arrived at. But using data from Department of Employment Labour Force Surveys, Brinkley suggests that in 1996 the unemployment rate for under-25s was 14.8 per cent; almost twice the national average. Unemployment has always hit the young hardest, particularly so for ethnic minorities. Thus whilst in 1995 15 per cent of white 16–25 year olds were estimated to be unemployed, this compared quite favourably to the 51 per cent of Afro-Caribbean young men, 41 per cent of Afro-Caribbean young women, 34 per cent of Pakistani/Bangladeshi young men and 30 per cent of Indian young men (*Runnymede Bulletin*, No. 292 February 1996, pp. 6–7). But these estimates also missed a sizeable number of the population. Wilkinson's (1995) Sunderland-based study found that between 5 and 10 per cent of 16 and 17 year olds were neither in education or training nor in employment, nor did they have any access to income support. Officially, they did not exist. This could amount to some 100,000 young people nationally who occupied what Williamson (1997) controversially, but perceptively, called 'Status-Zero'.

The New Deal for Young People

The New Deal for Young People (NDYP) was introduced nationally by New Labour in April 1998 after being piloted for just four months. It was part of a broader 'welfare to work' initiative aimed at encouraging lone parents back to work, reducing levels of state dependency, tackling social exclusion and encouraging individual responsibility. The NDYP, according to the Department of Work and Pensions, is here to stay as a key element in preventing 'a life on benefit' (*Guardian*, 26 March 2003). But does it offer anything more than the failed programmes of the past?

The New Deal is aimed at unemployed 18–24 year olds who have been claiming Jobseeker's Allowance for six months or more. In 1997 New Labour made their electoral claim that by 2002 the NDYP would get 250,000 young people off benefit and into work, education and training. To do so, young people first enter a Gateway period where for four months they receive support and guidance from a personal advisor initially designed to help find any (unsubsidized) employment. If this fails there are five New Deal options: subsidized employment, full-time education and training, work in the voluntary sector, work with an Environment Task Force or self-employment. 'A life on benefit' is not an option. The New Deal is mandatory. Sanctions, in the form of cutting benefits, are applied to those who fail to co-operate. For some this smacks of US-inspired workfare, where almost all benefit entitlement is entirely conditional upon the acceptance of work (Fergusson, 2002). As such whilst NDYP may hold inclusionary and developmental claims, its underlying rationale remains one of discipline. It is a continuation of the 'welfare bad; work good' ethic which underlay the Conservatives' introduction of the Jobseeker's Allowance. No effort is made to address structural problems of inequality and dead-end jobs in the youth labour market. Explanations of unemployment remain fixed in a skills-deficit model (Jeffs and Spence, 2000; Tonge, 1999; Hyland and Mussan, 2001). The talk is not of full employment but of 'individual employability' (Mizen, 2003).

The success or otherwise of the NDYP has been subject to numerous official evaluations. Their findings are at best ambiguous. New Labour met its target of removing a quarter of a million from benefit as early as 2000. By the end of 2001 it was estimated that around 40 per cent of participants had found unsubsidized jobs. But a further 30 per cent had left for unknown destinations. The impact of NDYP was believed to have in reality reduced youth unemployment by some 35,000 whilst only creating some 15,000 new jobs (NAO, 2002). As with previous employment initiatives, job creation relies on demands in local economies rather than as something amenable to state engineering. Many participants would have found work anyway. Percy-Smith and Weil (2002) maintain that there is little evidence to suggest that the scheme has produced any tangible benefits in job security, conditions and future prospects. All that has been created is an endless roundabout of multiple moves in and out of training, paid work, unemployment, voluntary work: an intensifying of churning and instability (Fergusson, 2002). Further, the element of 'compulsory inclusion' treats lack of commitment as a 'punishable offence rather than an opportunity for learning' and only ensures integration into a world of inequalities and labour exploitation (Percy-Smith and Weil, 2002, p. 125). Much of this seems borne out by participants' perspectives. Ritchie (2000) for example, reports that nearly two-thirds leave NDYP in the initial Gateway period in order to avoid any of the compulsory (and unattractive) placement options. Avoiding sanctions inevitably means accepting low-paid, low-quality, short-term jobs (which in turn of course keeps wage inflation low). Kalra et al. (2001) report that non-participation and drop-out is driven by poor experiences of the programme and the sense that it would not deliver a decent job, particularly for minority ethnic young people.

The political rationale for youth training and employment schemes lies elsewhere than in the creation of jobs. Indeed, NDYP has been expressly identified as an anti-crime as much as an economic policy (Straw, 1998, p. 12). Yet, if NDYP is a vehicle for crime reduction then non-participation is likely to be interpreted as placing young people 'at risk'. This logic has also informed a raft of 'inclusionary' measures aimed at a younger 13–19 age group. Notable is the Connexions initiative of 2001. This is a universal service of advice and guidance but geared to that 9 per cent of 16–18 year olds not in education, training or work. Significantly, Connexions is about providing mentors in schools and colleges drawn from a range of agencies, but whose chief preoccupations are those of inducting young people into the labour market and monitoring those at risk of becoming disconnected from the education/training/work complex. It involves establishing a database on all 13–19 year olds with information flowing from one agency to another. For Garrett (2002) it amounts to a 'new regime of virtual control'. The issuing of a Connexions Card to 2.4 million young people effectively allows their levels of 'participation' to be continually tracked and monitored. Much of this of course easily resonates with the themes of 'active citizenship', 'governing at a distance', 'joined-up governance', 'individual responsibility' and 'state steering' to be found in New Labour's Third Way modes of governance (see Section 6.1 above).

Above all, historically, the young and unemployed working classes have been understood as both a potential threat to the social order and, partly as a consequence, in need of special provision from, and direction by, that same social order if they are to assume their role as the next generation of adult workers. Youth training has always been a vocational fallacy. It has always been a means through which working-class identities can be reworked and remade; providing a cultural, rather than vocational, apprenticeship in working-class expectations of work (Hollands, 1990). In this context, training policies display a Janus face, where what is altruistically proclaimed to be meeting 'needs' also acts to constrain and remake working-class identities. The social order consequences of youth unemployment is one underlying factor in this succession of educational and training initiatives. The fear is never far from the surface that if young people fail to gain experience of a market-based work ethic at an early age, then they will never acquire the 'appropriate' attitudes necessary for the establishment of a flexible, disciplined and compliant citizenship. It is a discourse that has become cemented in New Labour's insistence that waged work is the prime route through which young people can be rescued from 'passive dependency' and social exclusion.

Homelessness and the Housing Market

6.3 Measuring the extent of youth homelessness is largely guesswork. In the mid 1990s voluntary organizations estimated that between 150,000 and 250,000 young people became homeless every year (*Guardian*, 16 September 1996). Such estimates are usually based on enquiries or agency referrals to campaigning organizations such as Shelter. Official estimates based on local authority housing department records put the figure substantially lower. This is largely because a number of criteria have to be met before a person is officially *accepted* as homeless. For example, they must show that they are not intentionally homeless and that they have a 'priority need', such as being at risk of sexual or financial exploitation. Both estimates are likely to greatly underestimate the extent of homelessness among women and black youth who for different reasons tend to seek temporary accommodation with friends. The issue is also clouded by the lack of a precise definition of homelessness. It may, or may not, include any of the following: sleeping rough, newly arrived migrants, runaways, people in hostel/bed and breakfast accommodation, people with temporary and insecure tenures, squatters, travellers, people leaving care or prison, and people in involuntarily shared or unsatisfactory accommodation.

Nevertheless it is widely regarded that the issue – once a key concern of nineteenth-century reformers – only resurfaced in many Western industrial countries in the 1970s and 1980s. In media and political discourse the issue has characteristically been phrased in behavioural terms for which the young homeless themselves must take responsibility. As Margaret Thatcher opined in 1988: 'There is a number of young people who choose voluntarily to leave home and I do not think we can be expected – no matter how many there are – to provide units for them' (*Hansard*, 7 June 1988, vol. 134). In contrast a number of structural arguments have been forwarded which suggest that homelessness has been generated by changes in housing, social security and local taxation, as well as labour market policies. 'Young runaways' have become an express target of New Labour's Social Exclusion Unit, which claims that 5,000 children a year survive by stealing, begging, drug dealing and prostitution (SEU, 2002).

The Withdrawal and Reconstitution of State Welfare

A key cause of youth homelessness has always been a lack of affordable accommodation. In the 1980s access to such accommodation was further limited as a result of Conservative policy which severely reduced council house building from 125,000 in 1969 to 8,000 in 1991 (Hutson and Liddiard, 1994, p. 47). This decline was compounded by the 1980 Housing Act which instituted a 'right to buy' policy for existing council house tenants, thus removing 1.5 million residences from the social housing sector. Restrictions were also placed upon local authorities to use no more than 25 per cent of the revenue from sales to provide accommodation for the homeless. The end result has been a decline in publicly rented housing from 32 per cent to under 22 per cent of the total housing stock. Privately rented housing also fell by a half to less than 8 per cent of the total stock. Young people found themselves excluded from local authority housing (being deemed 'low priority') and from private rentals (due to cost, declining supply, unemployment and a fall in real incomes). Whilst an expanding gap between demand and supply came to be widely recognized, the Conservative government was content to let the voluntary sector and housing associations fill this space, yet by 1991 the latter accounted for just over 3 per cent of the housing market (Hutson and Liddiard, 1994, p. 50). The commitment was clearly one of forcing young people to stay at home. The scale of the problem was provided by an opinion poll commissioned by Shelter in 1987. Twenty-four per cent of 15–25 year olds were found to have personally experienced difficulty in finding housing. A third of these were still living with their parents. As Killeen (1992, p. 192) argued: 'this stressful situation could apply to as many as 1.5 million young people in Britain. Youth homelessness is one of the consequences which occurs when families can no longer tolerate this stress.'

The 'crisis' has been exacerbated by consistently restricting young people's access to benefits. In 1985 limits were placed on payments for board and lodgings, following a media campaign against young unemployed who were living on the 'Costa del Dole' in seaside towns. Claimants could claim full board allowances only for short periods and no longer than eight weeks. They were then required to leave the area and not return to claim benefit for six months. In 1988 – following the 1986 Social Security Act – a new era of 'repressive disciplinary welfare' (Carlen, 1996, p. 44) was initiated with abolition of all benefits for most 16 and 17 year olds and a gradated level of benefit introduced for those under 25. *Age*, rather than *need* became the chief determinant of benefit entitlement. Before the Social Security Act, housing benefit to pay for rent, household rates and water rates was available in full for the unemployed with no income. From 1988, however, all claimants had to pay at least 20 per cent of their rates (subsequently the poll tax, the community charge and then Council Tax) from their income benefit. As Hutson and Liddiard (1994, p. 55) explain, because those under 25 were already on lower benefit rates, these young people found they were required to pay a larger proportion of their income on rent than their older contemporaries. The result was failure to meet rent costs and frequent eviction. And the knock-on effect of having to pay part of the community charge was that increasing numbers failed to register as electors for fear that this would make them more easily traceable. In fact more than a million potential first-time voters did not register in 1992 and 2.5 million, or 40 per cent of 18–24 year olds, did not vote in that election: 'The consequences of this trend in terms of future participation in democratic processes are not difficult to predict' (Killeen, 1992, p. 194). In addition supplementary benefit, housing benefit and income support have gradually been removed for those in further and higher education. Dependency on loans and/or families has been institutionalized.

Since 1997 New Labour has reconstituted the issue of homelessness as one element in an array of 'risk factors' of social exclusion. 'Rough sleepers' are targeted as a key area for intervention – along with truancy and teenage pregnancy – in its 2001 report *Preventing Social Exclusion*. The Rough Sleepers Unit established in 1999 is specifically designed to act on routes into homelessness (such as young people leaving care) and does so through 'joined-up' working with health, employment and education programmes. The main policy recommendations tend to remain at this level of providing integrated support and advice agencies. The lack of affordable housing, high rents, the impact of benefit policies and shortage of social housing are rarely officially alluded to (Kemp and Rugg, 2001). The 2002 Homeless Act does, however, require all local authorities to develop and publish strategies of how they intend to *prevent* homelessness; though again certain conditions such as 'priority need', 'local connection' and 'unintentionally homeless' have to be met. Whilst 16 and 17 year olds are accepted as 'priority need', being the subject of an anti-social behaviour order, for example, may be deemed to have contravened the 'unintentionality' condition. All of these reforms continue to be legitimized in the name of tackling a so-called 'dependency culture' which, it is argued, inflates the costs of social security and actively supports a permanently out-of-work underclass (see Chapter 4.2). Table 6.4 summarizes some of the most important reforms since 1983 in benefits, employment and housing.

Table 6.4   *The withdrawal and reconstitution of state welfare, 1983–2004*

1983	Unemployed 16–17 year olds living at home lose contribution to board
1984	Extended to 18–20 year olds
1985	Limits on length of time under-25 year olds living away from home can receive financial assistance towards board and lodging
1986	Young people's wages removed from Wages Council regulations
1987	No supplementary benefits for students during short vacation
1988	Income support withdrawn from most 16 and 17 year olds and reduced for under-26s
	Changes to housing benefit rules lead to relatively higher cost of rent for some under-25s in employment or on a training allowance
	Discretionary Social Fund replaces Exceptional Needs payments
	Compulsory payment of at least 20 per cent of Community Charge
1989	Employment Act repeals restrictions on hours of work for 16–18 year olds
1990	Students lose housing benefit. Student loans introduced
1991	No income support for students in long vacation
1996	Jobseeker's allowance replaces unemployment benefit
1996	Housing benefit for under-25s reduced to cover cost of a room in shared accommodation only: the 'single room rent' rule
1997	All benefits dependent on adherence to 'Welfare to Work' principles
	Social Exclusion Unit established
1998	Introduction of tuition fees for students
	National minimum wage introduced, but excludes 16–18 year olds
	Introduction of New Deal for Young People (NDYP) in 18–25 age group
	Withdrawal of Jobseeker's Allowance for those failing to take NDYP options
1999	NDYP benefit sanctions increased
	Rough Sleepers Unit established
	Piloting of Education Maintenance Allowances (EMA) to encourage 16–19 year olds to stay in full time education/training: contingent on signing a 'learning agreement'
2001	Establishment of Connexions service to guide and track progress of all 13–19 year olds
2004	National roll-out of EMAs

Sources: Roberts (1995, p. 16); Land (1997, pp. 104–7); Mizen (2004, pp. 147–71)

Criminalization, Survivalism and Risk

Reviewing shifts in policy up to the mid 1990s, Carlen is led to conclude that there is now 'a much strengthened disciplining of pauperised and redundant youth *independently of the criminal justice and/or penal systems*' (1996, pp. 46–7, italics in original) and that when young people are 'outwith the protection of employment, family and welfare they are most likely to adopt one of the transient lifestyles which may well bring them into conflict with the law'. Such a possibility has become a reality. A ready connection between homelessness and crime – shoplifting, petty theft, begging, prostitution, drug taking – is widely assumed, so that the homeless are more likely to be criminalized through police harassment and extra police surveillance. For 'homeless' travellers and squatters the 1994 Criminal Justice and Public Order Act effectively limited their ability to live within the law. In 1994 John Major, then Prime Minister, launched an attack on 'offensive beggars' – claiming that 'it is not acceptable to be out on the street' and 'there is no justification for it these days' (*Guardian*, 28 May 1994). He urged more rigorous application of the law – begging is an offence under the 1824 Vagrancy Act and sleeping rough is punishable by a £200 fine. A year later the then shadow Home Secretary, Jack Straw, echoed such sentiments by calling for the streets to be cleared of the 'aggressive begging of winos, addicts and squeegee merchants' (*Guardian*, 5 September 1995). As part of a crackdown on 'anti-social' behaviour, in 2003 David Blunkett, Home Secretary, announced that begging would be a recordable offence (*Sunday Times*, 26 January 2003; *Guardian*, 13 March 2003). Reflecting the multiple agendas of social exclusion, youth homelessness is increasingly officially researched and understood in the context of other problems such as drug use (Wincup et al., 2003). Beggars face the prospect of being viewed solely as a criminal nuisance rather than as victims. Ironically, criminalization is known to further increase the risk of homelessness. If apprehended, lack of a fixed address ensures that the homeless are less likely to be given bail and more likely to be remanded in custody. On release, a known criminal record makes the chances of accessing rented or hostel accommodation that much more difficult. A third of young people leaving custody are likely to be homeless or at risk of being so. Criminalizing the young homeless only ensures that a vicious circle ensues (Hutson and Liddiard, 1994, p. 66).

In contrast to such authoritarian 'solutions' based on images of a 'feckless criminal and dangerous underclass', Carlen's (1996) interviews with 150 homeless young people in Manchester, Birmingham, Stoke-on-Trent and rural Shropshire led her to argue that the real issue was not one of homelessness, but of the denial of citizenship rights to those who already face destitution. Her conclusions are worth quoting in full:

1   Young homeless people do not constitute an underclass with moral values different to those held by any other cross section of society – though their struggles to survive unpromising childhoods may have made them cynical about the extent to which those moral values have ever had (or ever will have) any political effects.

2   Young homeless people are a threat to society not because of their minor lawbreaking activities but because the economic, ideological and political conditions of their existence are indicative of the widening gap between the moral pretensions of liberal democratic societies and the shabby life chances on offer to the children of the already poor.

3   The crimes of 'outcast youth' in general should be understood neither in relation to motivational factors, nor in relation to social control, but in relation to 'anti-social' controls which, having deliberately excluded certain young people from citizen rights and citizen duties, in turn furnish the state with further justifications for abrogation of its own obligations to a youth citizenry denied. (Carlen, 1996, p. 124)

Taken collectively these shifts in employment, welfare and housing policy have created a situation in which young people have to negotiate a set of risks unknown to previous generations. Furlong and Cartmel (1997) draw on Beck's (1992) and Giddens's (1991) notion of a 'risk society', to explore this changing context. Here, it is suggested that Western industrial societies are undergoing a dramatic transformation in which the old and predictable structures of labour markets and welfare systems are being dismantled and replaced by a series of uncertainties and contingencies. As Beck (1992, p. 23) claimed, *social risk positions* in some dimensions 'follow the inequalities of class and strata positions but they bring a fundamentally different distributional logic into play . . . they contain a *boomerang effect* which breaks up the pattern of class and national society.' People's lives have become orientated towards the identification, negotiation and management of risk. With the break-up of old solidarities, perceptions of risk become increasingly individualized. Crises and setbacks are responded to as personal shortcomings rather than as events beyond the individual's control. Nowhere is this more keenly felt than in the youth labour and housing markets. However, Furlong and Cartmel's (1997) review of youth policy leads them to conclude that, whilst risks have clearly increased, they continue to be distributed in a way that reflects established social divisions of class, gender and 'race'. Although the 'collective foundations of social life have become more obscure, they continue to provide powerful frameworks which constrain young people's experiences and life chances' (Furlong and Cartmel, 1997, p. 109).

Policing, Prevention and Social Exclusion

6.4 Tony Blair first coined the 'realist' slogan 'Tough on Crime, Tough on the Causes of Crime' in January 1993 in an attempt to wrestle the law and order agenda away from the Conservatives. Since then New Labour has continually promised that its policies would be based on recognition of the underlying causes of crime which could then be addressed by a raft of social and economic, as well as legal measures. These 'causes' were first spelt out in detail in the consultation document *Tackling the Causes of Crime* (Straw and Michael, 1996). The key social and economic conditions of crime were then considered to be parenting, truancy, drug abuse, lack of facilities for young people, homelessness, unemployment, low income and recession. However, a year later when the White Paper *No More Excuses* was published, these 'causes' were significantly contracted to provide a more limited focus on parenting, truancy and peer groups. Now the key factors were deemed to be: being male, being brought up by criminal parents, living in a family with multiple problems, poor parental discipline, school exclusion and associating with delinquent friends (Home Office, 1997e, p. 5).

The emergent strategy to deal with these issues was first formalized in the 1998 Crime and Disorder Act which prioritized the principle of preventing offending by children and young people. This was the first piece of criminal justice legislation in England and Wales (at least since the Vagrancy Statutes of the early nineteenth century) to act explicitly against moral/social transgressions as well as law breaking. The prevailing contention was that crime runs in certain families, that the quality of parent–child relations is a key 'risk factor' and that *anti-social behaviour* in childhood is a predictor of later criminality. Such notions opened the door to a range of legislative initiatives targeted at 'disorderly' as well as criminal behaviour. It was also capable of drawing children below the age of criminal responsibility into formal networks of social control. Much of this pre-emptive early intervention became justified through notions of 'child protection' or 'nipping crime in the bud'. In tandem the Social Exclusion Unit was established in 1997 to 'join up' policy initiatives in such diverse areas as neighbourhood deprivation, unemployment, drug use, teenage pregnancy, truancy and school exclusion. It is this seemingly expansive range of conditions that apparently constitutes the 'causes' of crime. The following six years witnessed a succession of initiatives – some old, some new – in an effort to prevent the onset of offending. These have included:

- proactive policing of public space;
- zero tolerance policing of incivilities;
- the targeting of anti-social behaviour;
- the targeting of 'dysfunctional' families;
- expansion of CCTV surveillance;
- preventing social exclusion through employment/training;
- delivering basic minimum standards;
- establishing crime reduction and community safety partnerships.

All of this can be considered to have significantly blurred the boundaries between traditional social policy and criminal justice agendas.

Policing Public Space

Public space, and particularly the street, has always provided one of the main arenas for youth leisure. Public space provides one of the few sites in which young people can 'hang out' relatively free of direct adult supervision. Yet it is on the streets that troubling aspects of their behaviour are at their most visible and where crucial elements of the relationship between young people and the police are forged. As

Corrigan's (1976, 1979) conversations with 'the boys' from Sunderland revealed, alternative sites for leisure are rejected because they 'are not open to the boys as real choices'. The cinema, disco, dance hall and clubs were frequently too expensive. Home was constrained by parents. Youth clubs were bypassed because of the need for compliance with their rules and regulations. As Loader (1996, p. 50) put it, 'the routine use of public space is not altogether a meaningful choice. Rather it is one consequence of an age-based exclusion from both autonomous private spaces and cultural resources of various kinds.' As a result certain local places and spaces – the street corner, the city centre, the shopping mall, the precinct – take on a special significance, arousing emotional attachments and cementing a sense of territory and identity. According to Keith (1993, p. v), social relations are '*inscribed* in space'. Empirical studies in Belfast (Jenkins, 1983), Sunderland (Callaghan, 1992), Manchester and Sheffield (Taylor et al., 1996), Edinburgh (Loader, 1996) and Brighton (Measor and Squires, 2000) have all demonstrated the centrality of localized existences in framing the 'cognitive maps' of young people.

Keith's (1993) study of the policing of black communities also reveals how particular parts of cities – notably the 'Front Lines' of All Saints Road, Railton Road and Sandringham Road in London – came to signify the very nature of police/black relations in Britain. They are the spaces in which notions of 'normal behaviour' for black youth and police alike are continually recreated, contested and renegotiated (Keith, 1993, p. 161). In popular discourse much is made of the street as a site of inter-area rivalries and conflict, but for Corrigan's 'boys', their main street activity was 'doing nothing'. Yet 'hanging about' still offered the most potential for something exciting *to* happen:

> given nothing to do, something happens, even if it is a yawn, or someone setting down on somebody else's foot, or someone turning over an old insult or an old injury and it's this in the context of 'nothing' that leads to fights – something diminutive and unimportant outside the context of 'doing nothing' yet raging and vital within that context. (Corrigan, 1979, p. 133)

'Doing nothing' though may be interpreted by external observers as 'loitering with intent'. It is an apparent lack of productive activity that inspires a hostile reaction. The boys' experience of leisure was likely to attract the attention of the police at some time. This was how they got into trouble:

> The boys see trouble as something connected purely with the police, or other social control agents; one cannot get into trouble without the presence of one of these groups. At no stage do they perceive it as doing wrong or breaking rules . . . What wrongs are they doing if they just walk around the streets and the police harass them? The reasons for the harassment lie with the police, and *not* inside any rule that the boys are breaking, since for the boys the streets are a 'natural' meeting place. (Corrigan, 1979, p. 139)

Similarly, Loader's (1996, p. 78) interviews with police officers in Edinburgh show that one of their most prominent views is that young people hanging about in groups are either directly or indirectly involved in criminal behaviour. Their objection is largely to the 'collective use of public space irrespective of whether or not others find it unsettling'. The issue here is essentially the historically recurring concern of 'who controls the streets', in which the imaginary connection between a 'dangerous' place (the street) and a 'dangerous' time (youth) is constructed and maintained (Cohen, P., 1979, p. 128). In the Brighton study (Measor and Squires, 2000), the act of congregating, gathering or hanging out in public places was essentially for the purposes of socialising, to do the things adults did when they got together – eat, drink, talk, flirt. Despite the fears expressed by welfare professionals and local inhabitants such gatherings may be noisy but are largely harmless. They are as much the province of girls as of boys; of high achievers as well as the 'excluded'. These are not 'youth out of control' but moments of socialisation afforded by the relative freedom of the street.

However, histories of police–youth relations are replete with examples of the proactive policing of young people's use of public space. In a study in Edinburgh, 44 per cent of a sample of over 1,000 11–15 year olds had been 'moved on or told off', 13 per cent had been stopped and searched and 10 per cent had been arrested or detained in a police station in the previous nine months (Anderson et al., 1994, p. 130). The police response varies according to the 'race' and status of the young people with whom they come into contact. Afro-Caribbean and homeless youth are especially vulnerable to police surveillance and harassment. Under powers governed by the Police and Criminal Evidence Act, which requires police to have reasonable suspicion, Afro-Caribbeans are eight times more likely than whites to be stopped. However, under section 60 of the Criminal Justice and Public Order Act 1994 police can stop people if they believe there is a serious risk of violence. This power is 18 times more likely to be used against Asians than whites and 27 times more likely to be used against Afro-Caribbeans (*Guardian*, 21 April 2003). The police were also given new powers in 1996 to use 'reasonable force' to confiscate bottles and cans of alcohol from under-18 drinkers on the street (*Guardian*, 7 September 1996) and in 1998 to stop children in the street if they were believed to be truanting (*Guardian*, 10 May 1998).

Coupled with these legal and discretionary powers there has been a significant contraction of spaces deemed to be 'public'. More malls and shopping centres have become semi-privatized, employing security guards to deter 'undesirables' and those who do not conform to images of the ideal consumer. As White (1990) argues, from the point of view of 'consumption', unemployed and dispossessed youth are 'virtually worthless'. Their presence is viewed as a threat to the normal course of commerce. Presdee (1994, p. 182) captures this sense of dislocation in his notion of young people as the 'space invaders' of modern shopping centres:

> Young people, cut off from normal consumer power, invade the space of those with consumer power. They have become the 'space invaders' of the 1990s, lost in a world of dislocation and excitement; a space where they should not be. Modern consumerism demands that they look, touch, and take, or appropriate.

In these circumstances, consumption, desire, excitement and pleasure converge with exclusion to create new conceptions of 'doing wrong' (see Chapter 5.5). Young people using the mall as a meeting place are, quite literally, rendered 'out of place' (Sibley, 1995, p. xii).

The planning and design of urban space has increasingly been informed by wider concerns for population control and surveillance. In 2003 plans were announced to close certain alleyways and footpaths on the grounds that they encourage anti-social behaviour (*Guardian*, 7 May 2003). The CCTV camera, along with gates, locks and alarms, has become a familiar sight in many public areas and is becoming so on housing estates and in rural villages. By 2001 there were at least 2.5 million cameras across the country giving the UK the highest density of 'eyes on the street' in the world. Pioneering research on three such schemes by Norris and Armstrong (1999) found that those targeted for surveillance were disproportionately young, male and black. They were targeted not because of their involvement in crime but for 'no obvious reason' and on the basis of 'categorical suspicion' alone. In Los Angeles, Mike Davis (1990) has recorded how areas of commerce and affluent neighbourhoods are relying on a fortress mentality of gated communities and private armed response patrols to insulate themselves from the 'outside' and from 'outsiders'. In these ways the new technologies of surveillance render certain sections of the population both 'out of time and out of place'. They also fuel the demand for ever more sophisticated means of profiling, monitoring and tracking entire populations through smartcards, mobile phone alerts, eyescans, facial recognition and so on (McLaughlin and Muncie, 1999). In 2003 police loaded the two-millionth genetic profile onto the UK's national DNA database (*Guardian*, 15 July 2003).

Situational Crime Prevention and Community Safety

All of these measures are legitimized in the name of situational crime prevention. This strategy assumes that most youth crime is opportunistic and that crime rates can be effectively reduced through environmental design, target hardening and situation management. In Britain its impetus stemmed from a Home Office research study, *Crime as Opportunity* (Mayhew et al., 1976), which showed that certain crimes (for example, car theft) could be reduced by the fitting of security devices (such as steering wheel locks). In the following years a series of studies concluded that personal security could be improved by a vast array of risk avoidance measures. But it was not until the early 1980s that the concept of situational prevention was fully realized in practice and political discourse. The reasons for its re-emergence were myriad – the most significant being the clear failure of law enforcement policies to have any effect on crime rates. In England and Wales recorded crime had continued to grow at the rate of about 6 per cent per annum. The rhetoric of 'getting tough' began to look increasingly thin. In tandem, rapidly escalating costs to administer expanded criminal justice systems appeared to deliver a poor cost-effective return.

Such 'failure' was a severe embarrassment to the Conservative government which was elected in 1979 on a law and order ticket (an embarrassment which continued to grow through three successive re-elections). The response from the right was to broaden its intervention by arguing that criminal justice policy and practice could only have a limited impact on crime control. The sources of crime and also the means for its control were deemed to lie in the actions of individual citizens and their local communities. Thus public responsibility became pivotal in such schemes as the 'target hardening' of homes, businesses and personal possessions and through the assumed greater security offered by membership of Neighbourhood Watch. It was this ideological shift which opened the door to strategies of prevention, and to the recruitment of a whole number of central government departments, local authorities and voluntary agencies to the business of crime control.

Whilst this logic of crime prevention is primarily 'watch' based, it has also characteristically addressed environmental issues, such as the redesign of public transport facilities in order to improve surveillance of passengers, the redesign of coin-operated telephones and fuel meters to discourage theft and vandalism and dramatic increases in CCTV surveillance of roads and public places. More recently, the success of cross-political parties' attempts to persuade the 'community' to take such responsibility for crime control has resulted in the paradoxical development of private (or local council) security patrols in residential areas where householders are able and prepared to meet such costs and a rise in vigilantism in areas where they are not. Both can be viewed as symptomatic of a radical redefining of the limits of the state's core responsibility for law enforcement.

Despite apparent successes in some areas (see Forrester et al., 1988; Clarke, 1992), the dangers of hardening specific crime targets remain those of: the development of a fortress mentality in which homeowners become obsessed with physical security and fear of crime and youth disorder increases, rather than reduces; the displacement of offences to other areas or to other targets; and greater criminal sophistication in methods of theft, burglary and robbery. Above all the situational approach does not necessitate any radical rethinking of youth and crime policy on the part of governments. Rather it allows evasion of responsibility for the failure of law and order measures, prolongs the disavowal of the social causes of crime and, in particular, helps to deny any acknowledgement that social and economic policies, which have helped to generate youth unemployment, homelessness and reduced state welfare or urban decay, might in any way be related to increases in recorded rates of crime. It has 'no strategy for progressive social change and no concern for the overcoming of social divisions' (Garland, 1996, p. 466) and is concerned solely with techniques of risk management (Feeley and Simon, 1992). Youth crime can simply be defined in the neo-classical terms of low self control and lack of individual responsibility embedded in a feckless 'underclass' (see Chapter 4.2).

Nevertheless the impetus given to 'prevention' in the early 1980s gathered strength through the decade. The recognition that situational measures needed the compliance and participation of a wide range of public and private institutions and central and local decision-making bodies and could be carried out through a variety of voluntary agencies and individual action, opened another door for notions of *community crime prevention* to enter the political arena. In England and Wales an interdepartmental circular of 1984 was issued by central government and sent to all chief constables and local authority chief executives encouraging them to co-ordinate their resources in the prevention of crime. Through this initiative the concept of *inter-agency co-operation* was realized. Once more, central government was attempting to distance itself from its traditional role as the natural provider of public services. Now responsibility was firmly placed on the shoulders of 'communities'. Whilst the precise constitution of 'communities' remained unclear, the involvement of non-criminal justice agencies had the potential to broaden the concept of prevention to include such elements as housing allocation, welfare rights, employment opportunities, informal social control mechanisms and the provision of diversionary activities for young people. Community crime prevention in England first materialized in the 1986 Five Towns initiative, the 1987 Safer Cities programme, and in 1991 was redefined as *community safety* through the influential Home Office report *Safer Communities* (the Morgan Report). This was given statutory footing in the 1998 Crime and Disorder Act which places a duty on local authorities, the police, health authorities and probation to work together to reduce problems of crime and disorder in their area. As Hughes (2002) records, the rise of community safety has been exponential and raises the possibility of moving from narrow law and order agendas to more generalized visions of 'harm reduction' in the pursuit of social justice. Yet the vagary of all such terms – crime prevention, crime reduction, community safety, harm reduction – renders the field open to a continually contested politics. It is as yet a poor relation to the dominance of technological surveillance measures which suggest an 'anti-social' world of fortified exclusionary spaces. It also has to work within an authoritarian climate in which recourse to overtly punitive measures of control seem to be increasingly sought after. Finally, an obsession with 'prevention' may simply act to draw all manner of 'unwanted acts' under official gaze (Hughes et al., 2002).

Policing the 'Anti-social': Zero Tolerance and Curfews

'Zero tolerance' refers to intensive community policing strategies that were introduced in New York in 1994. The strategy is based on the principle that by clamping down on minor street offences and incivilities – begging, under-age smoking and drinking, unlicensed street vending, public urination, graffiti writing – and by arresting aggressive beggars, fare dodgers, squeegee merchants, hustlers, abusive drunks and litter louts, many of the more serious offences will be curtailed. In part the strategy is based on Wilson and Kelling's (1982) right realist theory which claims that if climates of disorder are allowed to develop, then more serious crime will follow in their wake. Merely leaving a broken window unrepaired, they argued, will quickly encourage outbreaks of vandalism. Failure to combat vandalism will see an escalation in the seriousness of crimes (see Chapter 4.2). In practice, zero tolerance was the brainchild of William Bratton, Police Commissioner of the NYPD, who reorganized New York policing strategies by making each precinct commander accountable for monitoring and reducing *signs of* crime, as well as crime itself (Dennis, 1997). Primary emphasis was placed on crime prevention and disorder reduction.

It was heralded as a great success, particularly in reducing the number of firearms offences and rates of murder. New York, once synonymous with urban violence, fell to the 144th most dangerous in an FBI comparison of crime in America's 189 largest cities. Even though the precise reasons for such a decline remain disputed – over the same period many American cities witnessed a fall in their crime rates without the introduction of zero tolerance; it was also part of a longer trend in the decline of violent offences associated with the trade in crack cocaine – the idea of creating environments which discourage offending and incivility was imported into Britain in 1995 as part of New Labour's campaigning agenda. In Britain, the concept was also appropriated from the 'presumption to arrest' policies advocated by anti-domestic violence initiatives. Limited experiments in zero tolerance policing were first pursued by the police in King's Cross, London; Middlesbrough; Hartlepool; Birmingham; Shoreham; and Glasgow in 1996. In Glasgow, for instance, Operation Spotlight was specifically targeted at after-hours revellers, groups of youths on the streets and truants. As a result, charges for drinking alcohol in public places increased by 2,240 per cent, dropping litter by 320 per cent and urinating on the street by 140 per cent. It was also claimed that such initiatives had led to an overall fall in the local crime rate of some 15 per cent (*Guardian*, 13 January 1997). But they have not always been assured of a positive response.

> The New York style of policing – targeting groups of people in a personal and adversarial way – not only creates scapegoats, but risks sparking confrontation . . . the point is that whenever one group is targeted and blamed for the ills of society, they are likely to interpret this as dismissal from the mainstream . . . The danger is that certain sections within the community, resentful and locked into a spiralling cycle of blame and retribution, will withdraw their consent from the law completely. (Charles Pollard, Chief Constable Thames Valley Police, cited in NACRO *Criminal Justice Digest*, April 1997, p. 18)

Nevertheless low-level disorder and incivilities have always been a major New Labour target. One of the most radical initiatives of its reforming agenda was the availability of new civil orders and powers that can be made other than as a sentence. This 'civilianization of law' is both welfarist and moralizing in tone (Hughes, 2002, p. 129). Child safety orders, local child curfews and anti-social behaviour orders for example, do not necessarily require either the prosecution or indeed the commission of a criminal offence. *Child safety orders* can be made by a family proceedings court on a child below the age of criminal responsibility if that child is considered 'at risk'. Justified as a 'protective' measure, it places the child under the supervision of a social worker or a member of a youth offending team for a period of up to 12 months. The court can specify certain requirements such as attending specified programmes or avoiding particular places and people. Breach may result in the substitution of a care order under the powers of the 1989 Children Act. In addition local authorities can, after consultation with the police and local community, introduce a *local child curfew* to apply to *all* children under the age of ten in a specific area. This places a ban on unsupervised children being in a specified area between 9 p.m. and 6 a.m. The reach of such curfews was extended to 15 year olds in 2001, although it remains significant that by 2003 no local authority had ever evoked such a power. The police attempted to do so in Corby, Northants in 2003 but failed to get local authority backing.

Similarly, an *anti-social behaviour order* (ASBO) is a civil order that can be made by the police/local authority on anyone over the age of ten whose behaviour is *thought likely* to cause alarm, distress or harassment. The order lasts a minimum of 2 years and breach is punishable by up to 5 years' imprisonment. It has been subject to a barrage of criticism such as its merging of civil and criminal law, its criminalization of incivility and its exclusionary effects (Ashworth et al., 1998). Though initially justified as a means to control 'nuisance neighbours', there is increasing evidence that ASBOs are primarily targeted at youthful 'rowdy and unruly' behaviour. In Campbell's (2002) review 74 per cent were made on under-21s. The 'anti-social' is often synonymous with police perceptions of problems with young people (Bland and Read, 2000). There is also evidence to suggest that ASBOs, though a civil measure, may accelerate routes into custody. In 2000 over half of those sentenced in court for breach received a custodial sentence (Campbell, 2002). Further some local authorities have begun experimenting with *Acceptable Behaviour Contracts* (ABCs) directed at low-level incivility. If so identified, a young person must agree to undertake activities to change their behaviour, as formulated by a local youth offending team (YOT) and their parents. Breach can lead to the imposition of an ASBO. The 2003 White paper – *Respect and Responsibility: taking a stand against anti-social behaviour* (Home Office, 2003a) – extends police and local authority powers to confiscate stereos, to criminalize begging, to give fixed penalty fines for 'disorderly' 16 and 17 year olds and to ban the sale of spray paints and fireworks to those under 18 (see Table 6.5). Significantly, it grants groups other than the police, including private security guards, the power to issue fines. In September 2003 the first national census of anti-social behaviour was launched with numerous agencies from police to street cleaners required to record any 'undesirable' behaviour. Within 13 broad headings the 'anti-social' included a diverse array of behaviours from

---

Table 6.5   *Powers of the Anti-social Behaviour Act 2003*

- Fixed penalty fines for a wide range of low-level disorders including insulting behaviour, graffiti, fly-posting, litter and wasting police time. The power to fine held by community safety officers, street wardens, private security guards and others, as well as the police
- Powers to confiscate noisy stereos and televisions
- Police power to disperse groups of 2 or more young people on the street
- Fines and parenting orders for parents of disorderly or truanting children
- Begging a recordable offence
- Ban on airguns and replica guns
- Ban on selling spray paint to under-16s
- Local authority powers to close noisy pubs and clubs
- Media allowed to name 'anti-social' children
- Closure of 'crack houses' within 48 hours

prostitution and vandalism to littering, noise, swearing, begging and street drinking (*Guardian*, 10 September 2003). All of these measures might be described as 'defining deviance up', but with the paradoxical result that public tolerance to incivility is progressively lowered and public fear of young people significantly increased (Young and Matthews, 2003).

'Giving the concept of zero tolerance teeth': this is how a Home Office source first described such proposals to impose curfews, exclusion zones and other restrictions on vandals, persistent offenders and drug dealers (*Sunday Times*, 22 June 1997). In fact a 'night restriction order' was included in the Criminal Justice Act 1982 as a means of strengthening the conditions which a court could impose as part of a probation or supervision order. It was rarely used due to the reluctance of social workers and probation officers to police it. And in 1991 the Criminal Justice Act had already introduced a new sentence: that of 'curfew orders' for offenders aged 16 and over. These required offenders to remain at a specified place for specified periods of between 2 and 12 hours per day for up to six months. Such orders could also be enforced by electronic monitoring arrangements. The idea of a curfew is by no means unprecedented.

What was novel about the renewed interest in curfews in 1997 was their application to children under the age of ten and on the *presumption*, rather than committal, of crime. Again the notion has American origins. San Diego first introduced a juvenile curfew in 1947, but it was only in the 1980s and 1990s that the policy took off as politicians sought to 'act tough' on crime. By 1995 juvenile curfews were routinely used in at least 146 of America's 200 largest cities. Typically aimed at those 17 and under, they usually run from 10.30 p.m. to 6.30 a.m. but a growing number also operate during school hours. President Clinton, in 1996 pre-election mode, advocated curfews for all teenagers by 8 p.m. on school nights on the grounds that it will help people to be better parents. Violators can be fined, or can face community service and probation, or their parents can be fined. Again the policy has been lauded as a great success. In Phoenix, for example, juvenile crime is believed to have dropped by 26 per cent since a curfew was introduced in 1993; in Dallas serious offences fell by 42 per cent; while New Orleans claimed a 29 per cent fall in auto theft and 26 per cent fewer murders.

However, curfews are notoriously difficult to enforce and are likely to be implemented in a highly selective way in which all manner of myths and stereotypes about 'troublesome' people and places are likely to come into play. Nevertheless, in October 1997, Strathclyde Police became the first in Britain to 'pilot' a dusk to dawn curfew on under 16 year olds on three estates in Hamilton, east of Glasgow. They were empowered to escort children home or to the local police station if they had no 'reasonable excuse' to be on the streets – playing football, meeting friends – after 8 p.m. It was legitimized as a caring service to protect children and address public fears of harassment (*Guardian*, 4 October 1997). But its main impact appears to have been one of raising unnecessary fears amongst the elderly population and increasing parental insecurity about the safety of their children (*Guardian*, 11 April 1998; Waiton 2001). On the grounds of civil liberties, Jeffs and Smith (1996, p. 11) argue that curfews are discriminatory and fundamentally wrong: 'Wrong because they criminalize perfectly legal and acceptable behaviour on the grounds of age . . . to select young people and criminalize them for doing what the rest of the population can freely do is doubly discriminatory.' Or as Ferrell (1997, p. 27) put it, 'curfews protect symbolic constructions of adult authority by patrolling the cultural and temporal space of kids . . . they work to unravel the nocturnal cultures and alternative spaces that kids have built around coffee houses, raves, music and style'. In so doing, positive communication between the generations is lost.

Family Remoralization

'Parental responsibility' became something of a watchword in many aspects of British social policy in the 1980s and 1990s (Allen, 1990). Whilst notions of 'good' and 'bad' parenting have informed much of youth justice reform since the nineteenth century, an image of wilfully negligent parents colluding with or even encouraging misbehaviour was popularized by the Conservatives in the 1980s as the inevitable result of a 1960s permissive culture. The breakdown of the nuclear family unit, high divorce rates and increases in single parenting, it was argued, were the root causes of moral decay epitomized by increased crime rates, homelessness and drug taking. In addition excessive welfare dependency had encouraged families to rely on state benefits rather than on each other, and in this process children's moral development had been eroded (Murray, 1990; Dennis and Erdos, 1992).

As a result, since the early 1980s successive governments have introduced a series of legal measures to enforce parents to bring up their children 'responsibly' (Mooney, 2003). The 1982 Criminal Justice Act ordered parents or guardians to pay a juvenile offender's fine or compensation. The 1991 Criminal Justice Act empowered the court to bind over parents to care for and control their children. Parents are liable to forfeit up to £1,000 if the child reoffends. The 1994 Criminal Justice and Public Order Act extended the bind over provisions to include ensuring compliance with a community sentence. In 1998 Labour introduced the parenting order to require the parents of convicted young people to attend counselling and guidance classes and to comply with specified requirements, such as ensuring regular school attendance. In 2001 a new offence of 'aggravated truancy' was created carrying a fine or a 3-month prison sentence for parents who seemed to condone truancy. Ninety million pounds was given to schools to develop the electronic tracking of pupils. In May 2002 a mother in Oxfordshire was given a 60-day jail sentence for failing to ensure her daughters attended school. In July of the same year parents in London were fined £4,000. In December plans were announced to give head teachers the power to issue fixed penalty fines for failing parents (*Guardian*, 13 December 2002).

Whilst such notions of 'responsible parenting' and the dangers of a 'parenting deficit' might be usually associated with Conservative ideologues, on coming to power Tony Blair argued:

We cannot say we want a strong and secure society when we ignore its very foundations: family life. This is not about preaching to individuals about their private lives. It is addressing a huge social problem . . . Nearly 100,000 teenage pregnancies every year; elderly parents with whom families cannot cope; children growing up without role models they can respect and learn from; more and deeper poverty; more crime; more truancy; more neglect of educational opportunities, and above all more unhappiness. Every area of this government's policy will be scrutinized to see how it affects family life. Every policy examined, every initiative tested, every avenue explored to see how we strengthen our families. (*Guardian*, 1 October 1997)

Six years later it was reiterated that 'strong families are the centre of peaceful and safe communities. Respect is all-important and this is missing in families that behave dysfunctionally' (Home Office, 2003a, p. 8). In this rhetoric strong families fit the traditional image of conjugal, heterosexual parents with an employed male breadwinner. Single parenting, teenage mothers and absent fathers are key harbingers of social disorder. Indeed, one of Labour's key formative influences in defining a 'third way', Etzioni's communitarian agenda, also emphasizes that the root cause of crime lies within the home and that it is in the domestic sphere that the shoring up of our moral foundations should begin (Etzioni, 1995, p. 11). It is such a communitarianism which speaks of parental responsibility and moral obligation that continually resurfaces in the reforming agenda of the twenty-first century (Hughes, 1996, p. 21).

The 'weak family' is viewed as the key driver of crime. 'Weak families' are those with poor parenting skills, teenage pregnancies, single parenting and 'broken homes'. In this way New Labour continues to promulgate a discourse of individual and family responsibility and to formulate interventions based on developmental psychology which push structural explanations and material contexts further to the background. Above it reveals a growing tendency to use authoritarian youth (criminal) justice agencies to tackle issues of family support and failures in welfare services (Goldson and Jamiesen, 2002).

Tackling Social Exclusion

'Social exclusion' is a relatively new term in British social policy. It has been officially defined as 'what can happen when people or areas suffer from a combination of linked problems such as unemployment, poor skills, low incomes, poor housing, high crime, bad health and family breakdown' (Social Exclusion Unit, 2001, p. 1.1). The Social Exclusion Unit (SEU), set up in 1997, had by 2002 identified and reported on five issues: neighbourhood renewal; rough sleeping; teenage pregnancy; school exclusion and truancy; and young people not in education/training/employment. Clearly it is not just crime, but youth and crime, which is driving this agenda. The discovery that child poverty had trebled between 1979 and 1995, that Britain has more children growing up in unemployed households than anywhere else in Europe, that it has the highest teenage pregnancy rate, and that 80 per cent of rough sleepers use drugs, encouraged something of a move to a holistic approach to tackling the 'problem of youth'. The SEU is – along with the Children and Young Persons Unit established in 2000 – designed to co-ordinate policy making across government, businesses, voluntary agencies, schools and communities. A plethora of initiatives have followed including: *Sure Start* to encourage young parents back into work through provision of nursery places; *Quality Protects* to provide sex education for those in care; *Positive Activities for Young People* (PAYP) and *Splash Schemes* to provide leisure activities for those 'at risk' during school holidays; *Education Action Zones* to reduce truancy; *Neighbourhood Renewal Funds* to improve local services; *Youth Inclusion Projects*, targeting 'high-risk' 13–16 year olds, as well as the *New Deal* and *Connexions* (see Section 6.2 above) and numerous advice and mentoring schemes which in turn all connect with the work of crime reduction partnerships and the Youth Justice Board (see Chapter 7). All of this is directed at a perceived excluded underclass believed to be responsible for most crime. They have all been justified as 'ways of helping to tackle the roots of juvenile crime' (Home Office, 1997c, p. 10). Needless to say, some have been widely condemned by those on the right for rewarding troublemaking and in the case of PAYP, of providing a 'perverse incentive to offend' (*Sunday Times*, 10 August 2003).

At first sight these initiatives do seem to reveal some long-term, enlightened and structural responses to youth crime. Pitts (2001, p. 147), however, argues that they only offer a partial understanding and only deal with superficial aspects of the economic and political problems that lie at the heart of social exclusion. First, the dynamics of exclusion result from market *forces* which generate economic insecurity and from market *values* which promote individual adaptations rather than fundamental reform. For Young (1999), we have witnessed a shift over the past half century from an inclusive society based on incorporation and full citizenship to a society organized around the material and cultural ramifications of *exclusivity*. Unless real opportunities are opened up through the advancement of a 'radical meritocracy', he argues, then little will be achieved either to facilitate inclusion or dismantle the structures of exclusion. Or as Currie (1985, p. 225) has argued, in order to tackle the roots of the crime problem 'we must build a society that is less unequal, less depriving, less insecure and less corrosive of cooperative values'.

Second, the very concept of 'exclusion' promotes a view of inequality as something peripheral; existing only at the margins of society. Labour's attempts to reintegrate 'the excluded' fails to acknowledge that their inclusion would only be to a world dominated by market exploitation, discrimination and a widening gap between rich and poor. As Levitas (1996, p. 7) put it:

> it is a discourse unable to address the question of unpaid work in society (work done principally by women) or of low paid work and completely erases from view the inequality between those owning the bulk of productive property and the working population, as well as obscuring the inequalities among workers.

Social exclusion implies minimal reform. It stresses that it is the responsibility of individuals to accept the structures of their own dominance. It centres only a puritanical work ethic as the route to inclusion, denying other forms of reciprocity and solidarity. It allows a benevolent view of society to be maintained even whilst levels of inequality multiply (Levitas, 1998).

Third, social exclusion individualizes social problems by identifying those 'at risk'. The key issue is then transformed into how risks can best be managed. The problem is defined as inadequate management rather than structural inequality; response becomes managerial rather than transformative (McLaughlin et al., 2001; Young and Matthews, 2003).

Finally the inclusionary policies of the SEU are also frequently underpinned by coercive measures. Forcing young people into the labour market on poverty wages, for example, may indeed be viewed as *promoting* exclusion rather than moving to its abatement. Targeting 'at risk' populations may simply exacerbate negative perceptions of particular areas or groups and accelerate their criminalization. Above all the talk is of economic and moral inclusion. The issue of *political* inclusion, through which communities might be empowered and full citizenship achieved, is largely overlooked (Percy-Smith, J., 2000). Indeed, exclusionary processes may stem more from an 'overclass' intent on protecting their own political and economic interests than from an 'underclass' in whose name the SEU seeks to govern.

Criminalizing Social Policy

A major preoccupation with the family and anti-social behaviour has dominated Labour's legislative initiatives and has opened the door to a range of legislative initiatives targeted at 'nuisance' and the 'disorderly' as well as criminality. It has also drawn numerous aspects of social policy – housing, income support, youth inclusion programmes, family support, New Deal employment schemes and Sure Start nursery programmes – into a broader criminal justice agenda. As a result children below the age of criminal responsibility have been drawn into formal networks of social control. For example the Youth Justice Board announced in 2002 that new *youth inclusion and support panels* will target those as young as 8 if they are considered 'at risk of offending'. In response to the torture and murder of 8 year old Victoria Climbie, in 2000, the Laming Inquiry eventually recommended that every child in England be given an ID number to track when they became known not only to education and social services but also to police and youth offending teams (*Guardian*, 9 September 2003). Issues of child protection are merged with those of anti-social behaviour (Home Office, 2003b). Whatever the welfare rationale of such programmes, they are also delivered through justice agencies. In this way social policy and welfare are becoming indistinguishable from criminal justice.

Much of this early intervention is justified through notions of 'child protection' or 'nipping crime in the bud' or 'zero tolerance'. Discourses of 'prevention', it seems, are insatiable in identifying 'risk conditions' and targets ripe for intervention. Further access to welfare resource often appears dependent on there being some assumed crime prevention pay-off. There is clearly a danger when the provision of financial and other resources depends on the prior identification of delinquent or 'at risk' bodies. The tendency is for all aspects of social policy to become governed by an overriding concern for risk management. Social policy becomes crime led, incorporated as another element of criminal justice policy and with youth workers, in particular, redefined as adjuncts of the criminal justice system (Stenson and Factor, 1994, p. 1). When young people are considered as 'at risk' of offending behaviour, either for the first time or for a repeated occurrence, it is a status that is likely to bring them further to the notice of formal agencies of control. The danger exists that those who 'fail to respond' to a particular preventive setting become all the more vulnerable to an escalation in penalties or, as Tony Blair put it, we should not be surprised if 'the penalties are tougher when you have been given the opportunities but don't take them' (cited in Vaughan, 2000).

A problem for much social exclusion work, therefore, is that their operations are simply grafted onto the operations of the criminal justice system, rather than remaining independent with no formalized connections to the police, courts or corrections. Moreover the consistent danger of developing quasi-welfare and community-based initiatives lies in the long recognized contradiction that if a young person is eventually sentenced to an institution, then that person will be seen as having already 'failed' elsewhere (Krisberg and Austin, 1993). It is in such circumstances that the labels of 'persistent offender', 'hard core' and 'intractable' can be readily applied and exclusion encouraged. As Muncie et al. (1995) claimed, the benefits of a preventive approach based on principles of social inclusion ultimately require a commitment to long-term change which cannot simply be measured by a reduction in all the costs of crime and crime control, or by managing 'risks', but by improving the quality of life for all young people.

> The absence of any integrated, and potentially challenging, set of policies focusing on young people and their social, economic and political conditions has led to a range of fragmentary initiatives, of which concern with youth crime prevention is but one example. Current emphasis on this issue carries the danger of it leading the agenda, of absorbing all other potentially progressive interventions into its terms of reference. 'Crime prevention' by current definition is about reducing or rectifying troublesome behaviour. By default it has a disturbing tendency to establish the boundaries of policy for all young people. In the process, notions of positive and creative citizenship are de-emphasized through a myopic focus on troublesome behaviour. (Muncie et al., 1995, p. 356)

It is clear that any number of inclusionary and exclusionary practices can be legitimated within the general rubric of 'crime prevention and community safety'. Criminal justice is being increasingly turned to for the resolution of social problems. New Labour has ultimately conspired to promulgate the familiar story that crime, however complex, is to be blamed on the moral failure of culpable individuals, families and communities. An obsession with risk factors and evidence-based analysis fails to address the complex inter-related problems of child poverty, urban degeneration and social inequality. It continually seeks new disciplinary techniques rather than developing a political commitment to forge new routes to an active citizenship based on tolerance, mutual respect, empowerment and entitlement (Pitts, 2001; Hill and Wright, 2003). As a result, whilst there have been important shifts in discourse and practices, the dominant terms of the political debate over 'the problem of youth' have not been disrupted. In many respects New Labour's 'modernization' of youth policy amounts to an 'institutionalization of intolerance' (Muncie, 1999a). Reform has been legitimated in the name of opportunities, support and community empowerment. In reality it is the state that has greatly increased its power and its reach. Intensive schooling, employer-led training, the diminution of welfare, family dependency, the resort to the rule of law: all of these attest to the conditions of being young, becoming 'a much more arduous state to be' (Mizen, 2004, p. 183). Or as Lee Bridges (2003) has concluded, it is those very same children and their families in disadvantaged communities that already endure the greatest victimization that now face the brunt of the new authoritarianism.

Summary

This chapter has stressed the importance of how youth governance is achieved not simply through formal legal controls, but by processes of inclusion, integration and discipline. It has sought out some of the linkages between various social policies and between social policy and criminal justice policy. By drawing on Foucault's notion of a 'carceral society' and Cohen's 'dispersal of discipline' thesis, it has illustrated one way in which the often separate analyses of youth training, housing, crime prevention, policing and public space can be brought together and adequately theorized. A number of key critical and explanatory themes have been identified:

- Social policy for young people is generally constructed around three competing discourses: young people as *either* the producers of 'trouble' for others *or* as vulnerable and in need of protection *or* as deficient and in need of supervision and training.
- Anxieties concerning youth are realized in a growing multitude of welfare, educational, employment, crime prevention and policing programmes which serve to control and shape young people's lives by lengthening the period of family dependency and by moulding petty details of the domestic lives of their parents. In this way discipline is dispersed.
- State agencies act to tighten conceptions of 'normality' (as in youth training), but in other arenas state intervention is withdrawn (as in welfare support). Such withdrawal is legitimized by 'multi-agency partnership' and 'community responsibility'. The state has initiated ways of acting at a distance, of activating 'private' agencies and co-ordinating sectors of social policy to reorder all aspects of youths' everyday lives.
- Economic contingencies provide the parameters in which any social reform is entertained (e.g. housing policy, community crime prevention, youth labour markets). Youth is generally perceived as lasting longer. Pathways to adulthood are broken, non-linear and individualized.
- Class/gender/'race' relations are reproduced through systems of discipline and surveillance (e.g. in employment policy, routine policing).
- Certain languages and classifications legitimize institutional practice and are exemplars of power in their own right (e.g. 'individualized risk', 'social exclusion' and 'blaming the victim' discourses).
- Social policy has its own propensity to create conditions of exclusion and 'risk' (e.g. housing and homelessness; labour market and unemployment) in which alternative survivalist 'careers' may be initiated.
- It is indisputable that since the 1970s more areas of young people's lives have been subject to surveillance, monitoring and institutionalized regulation. In the process, more and more elements of youthful behaviour have either become heavily circumscribed or subjected to criminalization. Social control has moved from a reactive to a proactive pre-emptive force – identifying the 'anti-social', anticipating disorder and criminalizing 'nuisance'.

Study Questions

1   How did social policy reform in Britain in the 1980s and 1990s affect young people?
2   Does New Labour's emphasis on social exclusion represent a break from or a continuation of past failures?

3   How do employment, welfare and housing policies encourage a protracted adolescence?
4   In what ways can it be argued that social policy and policing do not alleviate or control crime, but actively create it?
5   What are the future prospects for a 'carceral society'?

Further Resources

There is no existing work which *explicitly* draws on theories of social control and governance to explore the regulatory practices embedded in social policy for young people, but Mizen's *The Changing State of Youth* (2004) is an authoritative overview of how recent reforms in education, training, work, social security and youth justice continue to centre 'youth' in the political management of capitalist societies. For an empirical overview of how various youth policies in the 1990s (education, training, housing and criminal justice) fermented poverty and disaffection amongst the young, see Williamson (1993). Coles' *Youth and Social Policy* (1995) and Furlong and Cartmel's *Young People and Social Change* (1997) cover much the same ground and in more detail, the former working with the concept of 'career', the latter with the concept of 'risk'. See Taylor (1999, Chapter 3) for an insightful analysis of how the material outcomes of market societies regulate the social circumstances and behaviours of the young. Hughes (1998) and Hughes et al. (2002) provide the most comprehensive and critical mappings of the field of crime prevention and give the debates a much needed theoretical grounding. For the most incisive critical analyses of the concept of social exclusion, see Youngs' *The Exclusive Society* (1999) and Levitas' (1998) *The Inclusive Society?* For those interested in sociologies of social control, the 'dispersal of discipline' thesis and theories of governance, Foucault's *Discipline and Punish* (1977) and Cohen's *Visions of Social Control* (1985) are the obvious places to start.

To keep abreast of policy developments, Social Exclusion Unit publications can be accessed on www.socialexclusionunit.gov.uk. The intention to join up services is evident in the Children and Young Person's Unit at www.cypu.gov.uk. Statistics on child poverty, youth unemployment and so on can be found at www.poverty.org.uk. The web sites of The Joseph Rowntree Foundation, Child Poverty Action Group and NCH Action for Children also provide useful commentaries. The journal *Youth and Policy* provides a useful critical analysis of most of the relevant issues.

---

7 Youth Justice Strategies: Compromise and Contradiction

Overview

Chapter 7 examines:

- major developments in youth justice (focusing initially on England and Wales and Scotland) from the second half of the twentieth century to the present;
- the impact of welfare-based initiatives in delivering a separate justice system for juveniles and young people;
- the nature, and limitations, of the welfare vs. justice debate;
- challenges to welfarism from advocates of custodial punishment, legal rights, risk management and diversionary strategies;
- contradictions between child protection and strategies aimed at making communities, families and individuals responsible for offending behaviour;
- the interrelationship between political ideologies and reform of the youth justice system;
- international developments, global trends and national/regional/local configurations in youth justice reform.

Key Terms

actuarialism	net widening
adulteration	punishment in the community
bifurcation	rehabilitation
corporatism	reparation
diversion	responsibilization
doli incapax	restoration
globalization	retribution
intermediate treatment	welfare model
justice model	youth custody
managerialism	

Youth justice in the twenty-first century has evolved into a particularly complex state of affairs. It is designed to punish the offender whilst keeping their welfare paramount. It is at one and the same time about crime prevention and retribution. It makes claims for restoration and reintegration whilst seeking some of the most punitive measures of surveillance and containment in custodial and community settings. It targets those believed to be 'at risk' as well as the convicted. It is delivered by an ostensibly joined-up series of agencies concerned with health and education as well as criminal justice. It is clouded in layers of rhetoric whereby locking up the young is for their training or controlling their 'cultural space' is for their welfare.

Above all it is the gradual accretion of numerous initiatives that have emerged over two centuries.

But the 'new' never replaces the old. In the twenty-first century discourses of protection, restoration, punishment, responsibility, rehabilitation, welfare, retribution, diversion, human rights and so on exist alongside each other in some perpetually uneasy and contradictory manner. It is not hard to realize why. From the early nineteenth century, when the troubled and troublesome among the youth population were first thought to require a different response to that afforded to adults, the history of youth justice has been riddled with ambiguity and unintended consequences. In the 1830s a liberal approach to young offenders first took the form of establishing specialized prisons for the young (such as that at Parkhurst on the Isle of Wight). The dominant strategy was one of *punishment*, but in segregated institutions where the 'vulnerable' young would not be contaminated by contact with older and more experienced offenders. By the 1850s, however, this approach was challenged by the reforming zeal of philanthropists and 'child savers'. In that era, young people were believed to be in need of treatment within moral re-education programmes designed to both deter and prevent offending. 'Justice' was offered to young people in the form of reformatories, which in the twentieth century evolved into approved schools and latterly community homes. Intervention was couched in a language of care directed not only towards the offender, but also towards those thought likely to offend – the orphan, the vagrant, the runaway, the independent and those with a 'deviant' street lifestyle. The emergent strategy was one of *treatment* within institutions (see Chapter 2.2).

A century later this 'progressive' approach to young offenders once more took a significant turn. Institutions were criticized as stigmatizing, dehumanizing, expensive, brutalizing and as criminogenic rather than rehabilitative agencies. 'Justice' for juveniles was now to be offered through the abolition of custody and the establishment of a range of treatment units located in the community. The care and control of young offenders were to be handed over to social service professionals. Intervention was couched in the language of *welfare* rather than correction and expanded to include younger and less or non-delinquent populations (see Chapter 2.4). By the 1980s, however, with the re-emergence of a justice-based philosophy, support for the rehabilitative ideal was relegated to the search for the most efficient ways of delivering *punishment in the community*. Initially this appeared to be successful. From the mid 1980s, the numbers sent to custody were dramatically reduced, while informal cautioning and the use of intensive supervision burgeoned. However, 'justice' took a decisively retributive turn in the early 1990s when custody was once more promoted with the slogan 'Prison Works'. The dominant strategy became that of *punishing all young offenders*, whether in community or institutional settings.

By the late 1990s youth justice discourse had shifted once again. The incoming Labour government placed youth justice reform at the top of its agenda. It attempted to overcome, or bypass the philosophical disputes of welfare/punishment by reformulating the purpose of youth justice in England and Wales to that of '*preventing* offending by children and young people' in which there would be 'no more excuses'. The sheer volume and speed of pilot schemes and legislative activity since 1997 have indeed been remarkable. This includes a raft of initiatives targeted at disorderly and anti-social behaviour as well as the criminal. It has deliberately drawn many aspects of social, health and employment policies into a crime reduction agenda (see Chapter 6.4). Collectively these initiatives have been heralded as marking the most radical 'shake-up' of the youth justice system in a century. As a result youth justice now circulates around a complex series of modes of governance (Muncie and Hughes, 2002).

For ease of reference this chapter condenses this complexity into four – seemingly distinct, but in practice overlapping – strategies for dealing with young offenders. These are:

1 *welfare-based interventions* designed to help young people in trouble and to secure their rehabilitation and reintegration into mainstream society;
2 *justice-based interventions* designed to give young people the same legal rights as those afforded to adults and divert them from the damaging effects of court and custodial processing;
3 *risk management interventions* designed to identify those 'at risk of offending' and secure their 'restoration' through pragmatic, cost-effective and proven methods;
4 *authoritarian interventions* designed to punish offenders and prevent further offending through punitive deterrence.

The relative impact that these competing strategies have made on youth justice practice is assessed, focusing in particular on developments since the 1960s. Whilst the chapter recalls this history in something of a chronological fashion, it also stresses how these strategies have, in some form, always coexisted and continue to do so. What follows then is predominantly a history of political and professional debate, in which the diverse and competing discourses of welfare, justice, risk management and punishment have come to do battle over their respective places in the governance of the 'delinquent body'.

Welfare

7.1 The key formal principle underlying all work with young offenders is the ensuring of their general welfare. The Children and Young Persons Act 1933 established that all courts should have primary regard to the 'welfare of the child' and this was bolstered by the 1989 Children Act's stipulation that a child's welfare shall be paramount. Similarly, the UN Convention on the Rights of the Child requires that in all legal actions concerning those under the age of 18, the 'best interests' of the child shall prevail (Association of County Councils et al., 1996, p. 13).

Whilst the principle of welfare in youth justice has proved to be consistently controversial, since the early nineteenth century most young offender legislation has been promoted and instituted on the basis that young people should be protected from the full weight of the criminal law. It is widely assumed that under a certain age young people are *doli incapax* (incapable of evil) and cannot be held fully responsible for their actions.

Doli Incapax

The age of criminal responsibility differs markedly across Europe. In Scotland the age of criminal responsibility is 8, in England and Wales 10, in France 13, in Germany 14, in Norway, Denmark, Finland and Sweden 15 and in Belgium and Luxembourg 18. How certain age groups – child, juvenile, young person, adult – are perceived and constituted in law is not universally agreed upon (see Table 7.1).

Table 7.1 *Ages of criminal responsibility in Europe*	
Austria	14
Belgium	18
Denmark	15
England and Wales	10
Finland	15
France	13
Germany	14
Greece	12
Ireland	12
Italy	14
Luxembourg	18
Netherlands	12
Northern Ireland	10
Norway	15
Portugal	16
Scotland	8
Spain	14
Sweden	15
Turkey	12

Each age group is a socially and historically specific concept and as such is also liable to review and change. For example in Ireland the age of responsibility was raised from 7 to 12 in its Children Act of 2001. In England and Wales, whilst the under-10s cannot be found guilty of a criminal offence, for many years the law also presumed that those under 14 were also incapable of criminal intent. To prosecute this age group the prosecution had to show that offenders were aware that their actions were 'seriously wrong' and not merely mischievous. During the mid 1990s, however, the principle of *doli incapax*, which had been enshrined in law since the fourteenth century, came under attack from both the left and right. The doctrine was placed under review by the Conservative government following a High Court ruling in 1994 that it was 'unreal, contrary to commonsense and a serious disservice to the law'. Three years later, the Labour Home Secretary announced that the ruling would be abolished in the Crime and Disorder Act 1998 in order to 'help convict young offenders who are ruining the lives of many communities', on the basis that 'children aged between 10 and 13 were plainly capable of differentiating between right and wrong' (*Guardian*, 21 May 1996, 4 March 1997). This was in direct contradiction to United Nations recommendations – first made in 1995 and repeated in 2002 – that the UK give serious consideration to *raising* the age of criminal responsibility and thus bring the UK countries in line with much of Europe. Somewhat perversely, New Labour's Crime and Disorder Act 1998 has moved in the opposite direction. It gives no specific direction to the courts or to the newly established youth offending teams that child welfare should be of primary consideration. Instead its reform programme presents this 'adulteration' and erosion of civil liberty as an enabling new opportunity and, even more paradoxically, as an 'entitlement' (Haydon and Scraton, 2000). In the 1997 White Paper, *No More Excuses*, and in response to the UN Committee on the Rights of the Child in 1999, Labour has claimed that:

> Children need protection as appropriate from the full rigour of the criminal law. The United Kingdom is committed to protecting the welfare of children and young people who come into contact with the criminal justice process. The government does not accept that there is any conflict between protecting the welfare of the young offender and preventing that individual from offending again. Preventing offending promotes the welfare of the individual young offender and protects the public. (Home Office, 1997e, para 2.2)

> [I]f a child has begun to offend they are entitled to the earliest possible intervention to address that offending behaviour and eliminate its causes. The changes will also have the result of putting all juveniles on the same footing as far as the courts are concerned, and will contribute to the *right* of children appearing there to develop responsibility for themselves. (UK Government, 1999, para 10.30.2, italics added)

The abolition of *doli incapax* removes an important principle which (in theory at least) had acted to protect children from the full rigour of the criminal law. As Bandalli (2000, p. 94) argues, it reflects a steady erosion of the special consideration afforded to children, extends the remit of the criminal law to address all manner of problems which young people have to face, and is 'symbolic of the state's limited vision in understanding children, the nature of childhood or the true meaning of an appropriate criminal law response'.

Welfare Legislation

The argument that first surfaced in the nineteenth century that age and the neglect and vice of parents should be taken into account when adjudicating on juveniles opened the way for a plethora of welfare-inspired legislation in the twentieth century. As Clarke (1975, p. 12) argued, it created a hole in the principles of traditional punitive justice 'through which subsequent armies of psychiatrists and social workers have run and thoroughly confused the law's focus on criminal responsibility'. Whilst the goal of 'delivering welfare' through the 'personal influence' of 'professionals' – as established by the 1933 Children and Young Persons Act – was heralded as an important victory for the welfare lobby, it was to provide the juvenile justice system with a fundamental contradiction which is still being grappled with today. The two philosophies of criminal justice and welfare remain incompatible, because while the former stresses full criminal responsibility, the latter stresses welfare and treatment to meet the *needs* of each individual child. The defining of what constitutes 'need' was, and remains, problematic. Welfarism, it seems, is just as capable of drawing more young people into the net of juvenile justice as it is of affording them care and protection. Moreover the very existence of a system legitimized by 'welfare' is always likely to come under attack from those seeking a more retributive and punitive response to young offending.

By the 1950s these disputes and contradictions were reflected in a system whose remit stretched from dealing with the neglected by way of some form of welfare assistance, such as receiving children into local authority care, to providing attendance centres (run by local authorities and the police) and to establishing detention centres (run by the prison service) expressly designed to 'retrain' the offender through hard labour and punitive military drill (empowered by the Criminal Justice Act 1948).

Such confusion was to become most prominent in the spate of committees, recommendations and Acts concerned with the control and treatment of juveniles that characterized the 1960s. These culminated in the highly controversial 1969 Children and Young Persons Act in England and Wales and the 1968 Social Work Act in Scotland. Both advocated a rise in the age of criminal responsibility and sought alternatives to detention by way of treatment, non-criminal care proceedings and care orders. It was one element in the Labour Party's vision of a society based on full employment, prosperity, expanded educational opportunities and an enlarged welfare state which would overcome social inequalities and thus remove a major cause of young offending (Pitts, 1988, p. 3). The prevailing political view of the late 1960s was that young offending was largely trivial and transient in nature and above all was so commonplace that the full weight of the law was unjustified and counterproductive. In England the 1968 White Paper *Children in Trouble* argued that:

> It is probably a minority of children who grow up without ever behaving in ways which may be contrary to the law. Frequently such behaviour is no more than an incident in the pattern of a child's normal development. (Home Office, 1968, pp. 3–4)

In Scotland, the Kilbrandon Report described delinquency as a 'symptom of personal or environmental difficulties' (cited by Morris and McIsaac, 1978, p. 26). Young offending was seen as an indication of maladjustment, immaturity or damaged personality: conditions which could be treated in much the same way as an illness or disease. Reflecting such a philosophy, the White Paper advocated a range of interventions to deal with offenders through systems of supervision, treatment and social welfare in the community rather than punishment in custodial institutions. The Kilbrandon Report advocated the abolition of the juvenile court and its replacement by a welfare tribunal. Central to both was the increased involvement of local authority social workers. Their role was to prevent delinquency by intervening in the family life of the 'pre-delinquent', to provide assessment of a child's needs, and to promote non-custodial disposals. A significant reduction in the number of young people appearing before the courts was envisaged, with offenders, in the main, being dealt with under care and protection proceedings or informally. The perceived need was to divert young people from court and custodial processing. When court action was unavoidable, civil proceedings leading to care orders implemented by the local authority were to replace criminal proceedings leading to custodial orders. Attendance centres and detention centres were to be phased out in favour of either community-based intermediate treatment (IT) schemes, which would offer supervised activities, guidance and counselling or residential care in local authority-run community homes with education. Magistrates were no longer to be involved in detailed decisions about appropriate treatment; again this was to be the province of social workers and social service professionals (Morris and McIsaac, 1978, p. 25).

These proposals – which were to inform much of the Children and Young Persons Act 1969 and the Social Work (Scotland) Act 1968 – were thus quite explicitly based on a social welfare approach to young offenders. Authority and discretion were notably shifted out of the hands of the police, magistrates and prison department and into the hands of the local authorities and the Department of Health and Social Security. As Thorpe et al. declared, 'the hour of the "child-savers" had finally arrived' (Thorpe et al., 1980, p. 6).

However, in England and Wales during the 1970s vital elements of the Children and Young Persons Act 1969 were never implemented. The Act had consistently attracted criticism during its White Paper stages for being too welfare minded and permissive (Bottoms, 1974). The new Conservative government elected in 1970 almost immediately declared it would not implement those sections of the Act that were intended to raise the age of criminal responsibility from 10 to 14 years and to replace criminal with care proceedings. The Conservatives essentially objected to state intervention in criminal matters through a welfare rather than a judicial body. Likewise magistrates and the police responded to the undermining of their key positions in the justice system by becoming more punitively minded and declining the opportunity to use community-based services on a large scale. Above all, rather than replacing the old structures of juvenile justice, the new welfarist principles were grafted on to them. The treatment–punishment continuum was merely extended. Intermediate treatment was introduced but detention centres and attendance centres were not phased out. Community homes with education (CHEs) arrived but retained the character of the old approved schools. Care proceedings were made in criminal cases but, as it was still possible to take criminal proceedings against children under 14, the former were used only occasionally (Thorpe et al., 1980, p. 22). When care orders were used, they were largely targeted at young women, on the grounds of 'moral danger' and for 'status offences' – running away from home, staying out late at night and so on – which would not be punishable by law if committed by an adult and rarely considered as 'serious' if committed by boys.

In practice traditional principles of punitive justice were never seriously undermined by the 1969 Act. These remained largely intact, with welfarist principles merely being added to the range of interventions and disposals available to the court. In practice, the new welfare elements of the system were generally employed with a younger age group of, for example, low school-achievers, 'wayward girls' and truants from 'problem' families designated as 'pre-delinquent' (the social workers' domain), while the courts continued their old policy of punishing offenders (the magistrates' domain). Although ideologically opposed, 'the two systems have in effect become vertically integrated and an additional population of customer-clients has been identified in order to ensure that they both have plenty of work to do' (Thorpe et al., 1980, pp. 22–3).

Children's Hearings

In Scotland a different outcome was reached from the welfare/punishment debates of the 1960s. The sheriffs, probation officers and police associations gave way to the advocates of reform largely because Kilbrandon's brand of welfarism was grounded in notions of social education which appealed to a strong Scottish identity with educational processes (Whyte, 2000). The 1968 Social Work (Scotland) Act established new social work departments, gave local authorities a general duty to promote social welfare for children in need and established the children's hearings system (which came into operation in 1971). Children's hearings are not a criminal court but a welfare tribunal serviced by lay people from the local community. They deal with those deemed in need of care and protection as well as those involved in offending on the grounds that their similarities far outweigh any differences (Lockyer and Stone, 1998). Cases are initially referred to a reporter from a range of bodies including education authorities, social work departments, the police and procurators-fiscal. The role of the reporter is to sift referrals and decide on a future course of action. Around 60 per cent of all referrals are considered unworthy of future action. Some 10 per cent are referred to social work departments. The grounds for referral to a children's hearing, as established by the Children (Scotland) Act 1995, are:

- being beyond the control of parents;
- falling into bad associations and being exposed to moral danger;
- lack of parental care, causing suffering or ill health;
- having committed an offence;
- having been the victim of a sex or cruelty offence;
- living in a household where there is, or is likely to be, the perpetrator of such an offence;
- having failed to attend school regularly;
- misuse of alcohol or any drug.

On its inception a majority of the grounds for referral were for offences. However, by the 1990s non-offence grounds made up about a third, reflecting a rise in the number of girls referred for care and protection reasons. Reporters are thus endowed with considerable discretionary power. Initially they do seem to have been influential in reducing the numbers facing processing and adjudication. Between 1969 and 1973 a reduction of 39 per cent was achieved, whereas in England and Wales the numbers considered by the juvenile court increased by 4 per cent (Morris and McIsaac, 1978). However, rates of referral have increased in the 1990s (McGhee et al., 1996, p. 62); the most common reason for referral now being non-attendance at school (Scottish Consortium, 2000).

When a case reaches a hearing it is deliberated upon by three lay members of a panel, the parents or guardians of the child, social work representatives and the child itself. Representation is encouraged but not necessarily legal representation. Legal aid is not available, making the procedure at odds with the UN Convention on the Rights of the Child (Norrie, 1997). Safeguarders may be appointed but rarely are so. The hearing cannot proceed unless all parties understand *and* accept the grounds for referral. The hearing does not determine guilt or innocence (it can only proceed if guilt is admitted) and is solely concerned with deciding on future courses of action. Before reaching any decision, reports on the child from the social work department are heard, thus granting the social worker a more pivotal role than in the English juvenile courts. In a review of the hearing's more positive features, Dickie (1979, p. 68) concludes:

> The system encourages communication and collaboration between the relevant professions and permits a flexibility in the provision of services appropriate to the child's changing needs. Above all, perhaps, is its capacity to focus on the interests of the individual child and to tackle problems in a manner which encourages the family to participate and retain its self respect . . . a system which has such inherently strong welfare values must appeal to social workers.

A hearing has no powers to imprison or impose community penalties. Its powers are limited to one of three decisions: discharge, supervision order or residential supervision order. The most frequent (and increasing) disposal is a social work supervision requirement. About 15 per cent result in residential supervision. This usually involves committal to a list D school (the equivalent of an English community home with education). However, it is also worth remembering that whilst over 15,000 children are referred to a hearing each year, there is also a minority whose offences are considered so 'serious' that the hearings system is bypassed and referred directly to the adult Sheriff and High Court system (Gill, 1985). In 1995 213 and in 1997 148 under-16s were charged in an adult criminal court (Whyte, 2000). In this respect Scottish welfarism is reserved for less serious offences and some routes into adult justice have remained unchallenged. Moreover the hearings system only deals with those up to the age of 16. Whilst in Scotland there are almost no penal options for those under the age of 16, there remains a continuing presence of custodial institutions for older children whose regimes are far removed from the promotion of welfarism. In 1985 the only custodial centre for young people, at Glenochil, Alloa, came under criticism following a sequence of suicides unparalleled in the custody of young people. As in England, some of Scotland's most punitive systems still appear to be reserved for its young. Prior experience of the hearings system may lead to especially severe interventions in the adult system (Waterhouse et al., 2000). And welfarism always remains prey to shifts in the broader political climate. As McGhee et al. (1996, pp. 68–9) noted, during the 1990s there was something of a shift from notions of a 'child's best interest' to that of 'public protection':

> Nearly 25 years later the gap Kilbrandon tried to close between the needs of children in trouble with the law and children in need of care is beginning to open . . . [T]his change in outlook is reflected both in the United Kingdom and abroad and is likely to pose a serious challenge to the philosophy which lies behind the Children's Hearings System. Increased public pressure to make children accountable for wrongdoing, plus a growing concentration on the needs of victims, have contributed to the public focus shifting from the welfare of the child to offending behaviour and its consequences.

Nevertheless the Scottish hearing system is frequently evoked as a model for the reform of judicial-based systems, such as in England (e.g. ADSS, 1985). It is said to have informed some of the aspects of restorative justice introduced to the English system in 2002, with the advent of referral orders and the establishment of youth offender panels to hear all first-time offenders (see Section 7.3). Conversely in 2003, Scotland, in an attempt to deal with a newly identified group of persistent offenders (but also one suspects from pressure to overcome the anomaly that Scotland is the only country in Europe to routinely deal with 16 and 17 year olds in adult criminal courts), decided to experiment with re-establishing youth courts for this particular age group (Audit Scotland, 2002; Scottish Executive, 2003). However, the youth court pilot got off to less than an auspicious start when on its first day only three cases were due to be heard, one accused failed to turn up and the court session was terminated after 10 minutes (*The Herald*, 3 June 2003). In addition in 2003 plans were announced to give the hearings new powers to electronically tag under 16 year olds and to force their parents to take responsibility for their offending. The Scottish Communities Minister clouded these authoritarian shifts in a welfarist discourse by claiming that 'We are not helping young people at all if we don't try to deal with their behaviour' (*Guardian*, 23 June 2003). As in England, Scotland it seems, is witnessing a dramatic repoliticization of youth justice.

'In a Child's Best Interests?'

Welfare in youth justice is predicated on the assumption that all intervention should be directed to meeting the *needs* of young people, rather than responding to their *deeds*. Historically it has tended to see little differentiation between offending and non-offending troublesome behaviour: both are symptomatic of a wider deprivation, whether material neglect, lack of moral guidance or a 'parenting deficit'. As a result it is capable of drawing many more young people into its remit than if it were simply concerned with matters of guilt or innocence. Remarking on the impact of the 1933 Children and Young Persons Act, Springhall (1986, p. 186) argues that there is 'abundant evidence' to show that rather than diverting youth from court, it actively encouraged them to court. Because of the 'welfare' focus of the Act, there was a greater willingness to prosecute on the assumption that care and treatment would follow. Similarly, because delinquency is ill defined, there is little or no control over who might be considered deserving of intervention.

The persistent critique of welfarism (which gathered pace in the 1970s – see Section 7.2) is that its rhetoric of benevolence and humanitarianism often blinds us to its denial of legal rights, its discretionary and non-accountable procedures and its ability to impose greater intervention than would be merited on the basis of conduct alone. As Hudson (1987, p. 152) put it: 'identifying needs amounts to listing reasons for intervention', often drawing young people into the justice system at an earlier age and for relatively innocuous offences. In particular welfarism seems to encourage greater intervention into the lives of young women and very young children on the grounds of 'moral danger' and on the presumption that they are 'at risk'. 'Wayward girls', for example, may find themselves committed into the residential care of the local authority, and thence into stigmatizing institutions, without having committed an offence at all (Gelsthorpe, 1984, p. 2). A summary of the key assumptions of welfarism is given in Table 7.2.

Table 7.2   *Assumptions of welfarism*

- Delinquent, dependent and neglected children are all products of an adverse environment which at its worst is characterized by multiple deprivation. Social, economic and physical disadvantage, including poor parental care, are all relevant considerations.
- Delinquency is a pathological condition, a presenting symptom of some deeper maladjustment beyond the control of the individual concerned.
- Since people have no control over the multiplicity of causal factors dictating their delinquency they cannot be considered responsible for their actions or be held accountable for them. Considerations of guilt or innocence are, therefore, irrelevant and punishment is not only inappropriate but is also contrary to the rules of natural justice.
- All children in trouble (both offenders and non-offenders) are basically the same and can be effectively dealt with through a single unified system designed to identify and meet the needs of children.
- The needs or underlying disorders, of which delinquency is symptomatic, are capable of identification and hence prevention, treatment and control are possible.
- Informality is necessary if children's needs are to be accurately determined and their best interests served. Strict rules of procedure or standards of proof not only hinder the identification of need but are unnecessary in proceedings conducted in the child's best interests.
- Inasmuch as need is highly individualized, flexibility of response is vital. Wide discretion is necessary in the determination and variation of treatment measures.
- Voluntary treatment is possible and is not punishment. Treatment has no harmful side-effects.
- Child welfare is paramount, though considerations of public protection cannot be ignored. In any event, a system designed to meet the needs of the child will in turn protect the community and serve the best interests of society.
- Prevention of neglect and alleviation of disadvantage will lead to prevention of delinquency.

Source: Adapted from Black Committee Report, 1979 (Belfast, HMSO) cited by Stewart and Tutt (1987, p. 91)

Justice

7.2 During the 1970s, faith in social work's ability to diagnose the causes of delinquency and to treat these with non-punitive methods increasingly came to be questioned. Discretional social work judgements were viewed as a form of arbitrary power. Many young people, it was argued, were subjected to apparently non-accountable state procedures and their liberty was often unjustifiably denied (Davies, 1982, p. 33). Social work involvement not only preserved explanations of individual pathology, but also undermined a young person's right to natural justice. It may also have placed young people in *double jeopardy* – sentenced for their background as well as for their offence – and unintentionally accelerated movement up the sentencing tariff. Based on the experience of the 1970s, in which the numbers of custodial sentences increased dramatically, a new justice-based approach argued that a return to notions of due process and just deserts was called for.

The Opposition to Welfare

The critique of welfare had three main elements, which came from markedly divergent political positions. From the right, welfare and rehabilitative systems were condemned as evidence that the justice system had (once again) become too 'soft on crime'. Second, radical social workers argued that the 'need for treatment' acted as a spurious justification for placing considerable restrictions on the liberty of young people, particularly young women, which were out of proportion either to the seriousness of the offence or to the realities of being 'at risk'. Third, civil libertarians and liberal lawyers maintained that welfarism denied young people access to full legal rights and that their 'cause' would be better served by restoring due process to the heart of the justice system.

Political Opposition

In England and Wales during the 1970s the numbers sent to youth custody increased dramatically. This was in direct contradiction to the intentions of the 1969 Act. The recommitment to custody was based on the three main factors. First was the popular belief that the 1970s had witnessed a rapid growth in juvenile crime, characterized by a hard core of 'vicious young criminals'. The second factor was a tendency on the part of magistrates to give custodial sentences for almost all types of offence, particularly if the offender was already subject to a welfare-based care or supervision order. The third factor was the role of welfarism in drawing juveniles into the system at an increasingly early age.

Rather than acting as a check on custodial sentencing, these developments collectively accelerated the rate at which a young person moved through the sentencing tariff. As a result, the number of custodial orders rose dramatically. A 1981 Department of Health and Social Security report concluded that the number of juveniles sent to borstal and detention centres increased fivefold between 1965 and 1980. Less than a fifth of this rise could be attributed to increased offending; instead, it was believed to reflect a growing tendency on the part of the courts to be more punitive (DHSS, 1981). The intermediate treatment schemes introduced by the 1969 Children and Young Persons Act in England and Wales initially acted less as an alternative to custody and more as a means of drawing younger and 'pre-delinquent' children into the 'net' of the youth justice system. For Cohen (1985, p. 37) and Austin and Krisberg (1981) the real effect was to increase the reach and intensity of state control. They list a catalogue of 'failure':

- the youth justice system expanded and drew more people into its reach (*net widening*);
- the level of intervention, involving individualized treatment and indeterminate sentencing, intensified (*net strengthening*);
- institutions were rarely replaced or radically altered, but were supplemented by new forms of intervention (*different nets*).

In addition, as Bottoms (1974) argued, it is important to recognize that the 1969 Act was never implemented in full, being opposed by the 1970–4 Conservative government, the magistracy, the police and some sections of the probation service on the grounds that it undermined 'the due process of law'. The underlying social welfare philosophy of the Act was quashed. While the legislation stressed the importance of fitting appropriate care and treatment to each individual child, the values held by the police and magistracy tended to stress punishment to fit the crime. Mandatory consultation between the police and local authority social service departments did not come into operation, so a common view of child protection was never developed.

Between 1971 and 1977 there was a 225 per cent increase in sentences to detention centres and a 70 per cent increase in attendance centre orders. The numbers of males aged 14–16 sent to custody increased from 3,200 in 1971 to 7,700 in 1981. Much of this new authoritarianism coalesced with a highly politicized debate about the supposed criminality of black youth and their involvement in such street crimes as 'mugging' (Hall et al., 1978). At the time Landau and Nathan's (1983) study of the Metropolitan Police area, for example, showed that for some offences – violence, burglary, public order – black youths were more likely to be charged immediately rather than have their cases referred to a juvenile liaison bureau for a decision about whether to caution or not. In the early 1980s Afro-Caribbeans made up about 5 per cent of the population in London, but 17 per cent of the people arrested (Smith and Gray, 1983). In court black youth were less likely to be given non-custodial sentences and received longer custodial sentences despite having fewer previous convictions. As a result, in the borstals and detention centres of the south of England, black youth often constituted over a third of the inmates (Kettle, 1982, p. 535).

While magistrates were committed to incarcerating the young offender, social workers extended their preventive work with the families of the 'pre-delinquent'. Ironically, this development meant many more children were under surveillance, the market for the courts was widened and more offenders were placed in care for relatively trivial offences. In practice, preventive work meant that children were being sent to institutions at a younger age. As in the past, new institutions which were supposed to reform youth instead created new categories of delinquency. As Thorpe et al. remarked, the liberalism of the 1969 Act produced a judicial backlash in which popular wisdom about juvenile justice and its actual practice became totally estranged:

> The tragedy that has occurred since can be best described as a situation in which the worst of all possible worlds came into existence – people have been persistently led to believe that the juvenile criminal justice system has become softer and softer, while the reality has been that it has become harder and harder. (Thorpe et al., 1980, p. 8)

Welfare and Young Women

Such arguments appeared all the more pertinent when applied to the situation of young women. Young women were frequently brought into court for offences that might be dealt with informally or ignored if committed by adults or young men. Often their offences were (and remain) related to behaviour regarded as sexually deviant and promiscuous or to a perceived need for their 'protection'. Here a moral evaluation of what constitutes 'need' is much greater. Whilst cultural codes of masculinity, toughness and sexual predation are the norm for young men, there is little or no conception of 'normal' exuberant delinquency for young women. When young women appear before the court, they are likely to be viewed as 'abnormal' – breaking not only the law, but also the 'rules' of how they should behave. Because of the statistically exceptional nature of their criminality, female delinquency tends also to be seen as a perversion of, or rebellion against, 'natural' feminine roles. As Hudson (1988, p. 40) argued, a predominantly treatment- and welfare-focused paradigm adjudicated as much on questions of femininity as it did on matters of guilt or innocence:

> [W]hen white male youth commit criminal offences they are not usually seen as intrinsically challenging normative expectations about behaviour for young and adult men . . . rarely is there any suggestion that male delinquency is incongruent with masculinity . . . Young women, however, are predominantly judged according to their management of family, sexual and interpersonal relationships . . . [T]hey are subject to a double penalty: firstly because they have broken the law and secondly because they have defied social codes which prescribe passivity for women. (Hudson, A., 1988, pp. 39–40)

The end result of such gender-specific modes of social control was that young women were (and continue to be) drawn into the justice system for reasons wholly unrelated to the commission of offences (Casburn, 1979); they were less likely to be fined and more often placed on supervision or taken into care than young men (May, 1977); and they were more likely to be committed to approved schools on 'care, protection and control' rather than 'offence' grounds

(Shacklady Smith, 1978). As Harris and Webb (1987, p. 154) concluded,

[W]hether the overt intent of the courts and the experts is to monitor girls' behaviour or whether such monitoring is rather the effect of an almost complete dearth of ideas as to what is to be done, the effect of these processes is a disproportionate exercise of power over girls.

'Nothing Works'

The critique of the gender-specific nature of youth justice coalesced with a critique of welfare and rehabilitation in general. In Britain, Clarke and Sinclair (1974, p. 58) argued that 'there is now little reason to believe that any one of the widely used methods of treating offenders is much better at preventing reconviction than any other'. They questioned the notion that delinquency and crime were symptoms of individual pathology and instead advocated interventions based on the assumption that crime was a *rational* action performed by ordinary people acting under particular pressures and exposed to specific opportunities. Crime, it was argued, could best be controlled by making targets harder (e.g. through improved security measures) than by trying to identify and tackle any presumed underlying causes. The most devastating critique of welfare, however, came from Martinson's (1974) analysis of 231 studies of treatment programmes in the USA. He concluded that 'with few and isolated exceptions the rehabilitative efforts that have been reported so far have had no appreciable effect on recidivism' (Martinson, 1974, p. 25). This conclusion was widely received as 'nothing works': that it was a waste of time and money to devote energy to the rehabilitative treatment of (young) offenders.

'Back to Justice'

Finally, liberal lawyers and civil libertarians maintained that welfare, rather than being benevolent, was an insidious form of control. Young offenders were considered to need protection not only from punitive justice, but also from welfare's 'humanitarianism' (Cohen, S., 1985). As Taylor et al. noted:

Under English law the child enjoys very few of the rights taken for granted by adults under the principles of natural justice. The law's reference to the child's 'best interests' reflects the benevolent paternalism of its approach. Essentially as far as the courts are concerned, the 'best interests' principle empowers social workers, psychologists, psychiatrists and others to define on the basis of their opinions what is good for the child . . . [The law] does not require that the experts should substantiate their opinions or prove to the court that any course of action they propose will be more effective in promoting the best interests of the child than those taken by the parent or by the child acting on his own behalf . . . a child may find that his/her arguments against being committed to care are perceived as evidence of their need for treatment, as a sign, for example, that they have 'authority problems'. (Taylor et al., 1979, pp. 22–3)

Similarly, Morris, commenting on the Scottish hearing system, argued:

> Euphemisms are frequently used to disguise the true state of affairs, to pretend that things are other than they are. Courts become tribunals, probation becomes supervision and approved schools are renamed residential establishments. But few are deceived by these verbal devices. (Morris, 1974, p. 364)

Underlying this critique was a scepticism about the value of treatment, welfare and therapy and their ability to provide justice for children. For example, the introduction of compulsory treatment measures, Morris argued, was purchased at the expense of other values such as individual liberty, natural justice, due process and fairness. The Kilbrandon Report made extensive use of such medical terms as 'symptom' and 'diagnosis' and compared its own recommendations to those of medical practice. The implications of this approach to understanding delinquency are far-reaching. In particular, Kilbrandon assumed that the causes of delinquency lay primarily within the individual and his or her family. The 'problem' was defined in terms of pathology and maladjustment (emanating from individual positivism – see Chapter 3.1) rather than, for example, as arising out of the social, economic and political condition of young people (factors such as unemployment, irrelevant schooling, urban deprivation, lack of recreational facilities). As a result, juvenile justice in Scotland in particular became dominated by the jargon and practices of the child-saving ideology – 'at risk', 'prevention', 'disturbance', 'deprivation', 'personality disorder', 'treatment', 'cure' – which acted to reconstitute a child's identity as deviant and pathological. Such 'character assassinations', it was argued, legitimized greater incursion into young people's lives than could be provided by simply concentrating on the circumstances of the act of misconduct (Morris et al., 1980).

The Justice Model

In the wake of these wide-ranging criticisms of welfarism, a new justice-based model of corrections emerged. Its leading proponent in America, Von Hirsch (1976), proposed that the following principles be reinstated at the centre of criminal justice practice:

- proportionality of punishment to crime, or the offender is handed a sentence that is in accordance with what the act deserves;
- determinacy of sentencing and an end to indeterminate, treatment-oriented sentences;
- an end to judicial, professional and administrative discretion;
- an end to disparities in sentencing;
- equity and protection of rights through due process.

Proponents of 'back to justice' argued that determinate sentences based on the seriousness of the offence, rather than on the 'needs' of individual offenders, would be seen as fair and just by young people themselves. A greater use of cautions by the police for minor offences would, they argued, help to keep young people out of the courts. When in court, closer control over social workers' social inquiry reports would ensure that intermediate treatment (IT), care orders or other forms of welfare intervention would be used only in the most serious of cases. In this way most offenders would either not be prosecuted at all or at least would not be subject to social work surveillance. The role of social work, it was maintained, would be to offer supervision schemes only in those cases when custody was being suggested. Social work should only be involved at the 'heavy end' of offences. Above all, a greater promotion of community-based interventions by government and social service departments should be promoted.

Leading proponents of this philosophy, such as Morris et al. (1980) and Taylor et al. (1979), maintained that a social work understanding of delinquency, given its dominant grounding in psychoanalytical theories, does not necessarily lead to the more equitable exercise of justice. They condemned the fact that since the 1908 Children Act, the fate of juvenile offenders had increasingly become dictated by the discretionary and arbitrary powers of individual social workers and magistrates. Children's rights, they argued, would be better upheld by returning to the principles of equality before the law.

In some respects such arguments marked a return to early nineteenth-century principles of viewing the juvenile as a young adult. The approach, however, was complemented by proposals for law reform which would decriminalize such juvenile crimes as drinks and drugs offences, homosexual or heterosexual behaviour under the age of consent, and remove the force of law from misdemeanours such as truancy and running away from home. In this way it became possible to raise the issue of the 'rule of the law' as a progressive demand. Taylor et al. (1979), for example, argued for the right to legal representation and legal aid in the juvenile court and for it to be accepted that the proceedings were injurious. Rather than viewing the reforms of the past century as progressive, they argued that they had consistently served to erode the rights of children. For example, the child's 'best interests' were usually determined by such 'experts' as social workers, psychologists and psychiatrists by way of social inquiry reports. In court these assumed an authority greater than the definitions of 'best interest' made by the parent or by the child acting on his or her own behalf. Moreover such reports were not automatically available to the child, the parents or the child's lawyers. Any adult appearing before a court expects to know beforehand the full case to be answered. In the juvenile court this right was not always deemed to be in the child's 'best interests'.

The 'back to justice' approach thus advocated reform of both the English and Scottish systems of youth justice whereby the court's role as an administrator of *justice* would be reinstated. The assumptions of the justice model are outlined in Table 7.3.

Table 7.3   *Assumptions of the justice model*
• Delinquency is a matter of opportunity and choice – other factors may combine to bring a child to the point of delinquency, but unless there is evidence to the contrary, the act as such is a manifestation of the rational decision to that effect.
• In so far as people are responsible for their actions, they should also be accountable. This is qualified in respect of children by the doctrine of criminal responsibility as originally evolved under common law and now endorsed by statute.
• Proof of commission of an offence should be the sole justification for intervention and the sole basis of punishment.
• Sanctions and controls are valid responses to deviant behaviour both as an expression of society's disapproval and as an individual and general deterrent to future similar behaviour.
• Behaviour attracting legal intervention and associated sanctions available under the law should be specifically defined to avoid uncertainty.
• The power to interfere with a person's freedom and in particular that of a child should be subject to the most rigorous standard of proof, which traditionally is found in a court of law. Individual rights are most effectively safeguarded under the judicial process.
• There should be equality before the law; like cases should be treated alike.
• There should be proportionality between the seriousness of the delinquent or criminal behaviour warranting intervention and the community's response; between the offence and the sentence given.
Source: Adapted from Black Committee Report, 1979 (Belfast, HMSO) cited by Stewart and Tutt (1987, p. 92)

The Welfare vs. Justice Debate

The justice model in turn attracted its fair share of criticism. As Clarke (1985b) pointed out, the staking out of 'justice' as a strategy for reform is always liable to allow proponents of law and order to recruit the arguments of 'natural justice' for their own ends, even though the former is more concerned with retribution and the latter with judicial equality and consistency. In the political climate of the 1980s, notions of 'justice' and 'anti-welfarism' were indeed politically mobilized by the right. The ability of the 'back to justice' movement to reorganize this arena politically came into doubt. In these circumstances it was not surprising to find that some political credibility returned to those who wished to reinforce the principle of welfare in the processing of young offenders.

Davies (1982), for example, argued that the failures of welfare were due in the main to partial implementation and lack of financial backing. Whilst the call for greater judicial safeguards for young people in court was lauded, it was argued that this should not preclude a determined defence of welfarism's central 'caring' practices. Similarly, Cullen and Gilbert (1982) maintained that welfarism remained the only route through which the state can be forced to recognize that it has an obligation to care for the offender's welfare and needs. Expunging it completely from the system will only produce more repressive and punitive outcomes.

In these ways a welfare vs. justice debate dominated the 1970s and 1980s but it also came to be viewed as particularly sterile. Asquith, for example, argued tellingly that the 'back to justice' conception of law as due process makes it inattentive to the inequalities that are built into the formulation of law and its operation in a class and racially stratified society:

> Policies which ignore the social and economic realities in which children find themselves, while promoting greater equality and justice within formal systems of control, may not only ignore, but may compound the structural and material inequalities which have been historically associated with criminal behaviour. (Asquith, 1983, p. 17)

Similarly, Hudson contended that

> By disclaiming any reformative function of the law, by accepting that the most that can be done is punish fairly according to present definitions of crime and seriousness, the justice model colludes with establishment definitions of what are real problems. By abstracting crime from its social context, by abstracting individuals from their collectivities, by abstracting the administration of criminal justice from the wider field of political struggle, the justice model thus inextricably allies itself with the use of the legal system as an important part of the apparatus of repression. (Hudson, 1987, p. 166)

To those who advocated welfarism as a solution to these problems, Thorpe et al. had this to say:

> Rather than arguing about the relative merits of 'justice' and 'welfare' we ought perhaps to take a step backwards and survey the framework which effectively supports them both. The beads may be of different colours and situated at opposite ends. But they are on the same thread. (Thorpe et al., 1980, p. 106)

The welfare vs. justice debate may now be considered to be particularly moribund, especially as neither model has been fully realized in practice. However, the remnants of the debate remain with us. Youth justice has evolved into a complex patchwork of processes and disposals, drawing upon welfare, justice, retribution, rehabilitation, treatment, punishment, prevention and diversion. Each has a constantly shifting presence as political priorities, central directives and local initiatives veer from one position to another.

Progressive Justice: Diversion and Decarceration

The practical result of a resurgence of legalism and 'back to justice' in the 1980s was predictably complex and contradictory. On the one hand, it seemed to play into a retributivist discourse intent on making all offenders responsible for their actions and seeking their punitive just deserts; on the other, it opened the door to such notions as 'minimum intervention', 'maximum diversion', 'due process' and dealing with offences rather than offenders in which the reach of juvenile justice was to be reduced rather than increased.

In 1979 the Conservatives launched a strong attack on delinquency in the run-up to the general election and throughout the early 1980s condemned the 'soft' way that 'dangerous young thugs' were dealt with. Through the liberal use of terms such as 'wickedness' and 'evil', delinquency once more became a moral issue. Much of this approach rested on many Conservatives blaming the supposed permissiveness of the Children and Young Persons Act 1969 and liberal child-rearing practices of the 1960s for the increase in delinquency (Morgan, P., 1978). Margaret Thatcher, the incoming Prime Minister, attacked those who had created a 'culture of excuses' and promised that her government would 're-establish a code of conduct that condemns crime plainly and without exception' (Riddell, 1989, p. 171). The search for individual or social causes of crime – personality, unemployment, deprivation, lack of opportunity – was to be abandoned. The rhetoric of treatment and rehabilitation was to be replaced by the rhetoric of punishment and retribution. Welfarism was to be replaced by the rule of law. The language of 'rights' was appropriated by one of self responsibility and obligation (Anderson, 1992, p. xviii). Hall (1980) captured this mood by arguing that Britain was in the throes of a 'deep and decisive movement towards a more disciplinary, authoritarian kind of society' in which a 'regression to stone-age morality' was being realized in 'a blind spasm of control'. In October 1979 it was announced that new 'short, sharp, shock' regimes would be introduced into detention centres. In 1982 a new Criminal Justice Act gave magistrates powers to sentence directly to youth custody centres (previously they were limited to making recommendations to the Crown Court for borstal training). Those parts of the 1969 Act which had advocated a phasing out of custody were officially abandoned. It seemed as if there was going to be a considerable increase in the number of juveniles 'tasting porridge' (McLaughlin and Muncie, 1993, p. 176).

However, contrary to the 'net widening' and 'net strengthening' predictions of many commentators, both the youth crime rate and the youth custody rate declined dramatically during the course of the 1980s. Indeed, the mid to late 1980s has been heralded as amounting to a 'successful revolution' in criminal – particularly juvenile – justice policy (Allen, 1991) or at least as 'a delicately balanced consensus' in which all elements of the youth justice system (for different reasons) appeared to support the principles of diversion, decriminalization and decarceration rather than the 'futile and counterproductive' outcomes of custody (Goldson, 1997b). According to the criminal statistics released by the Home Office, the numbers of young people aged 17 or under convicted or cautioned decreased from 204,600 in 1983 to 129,500 in 1993. The number of young offenders sentenced to immediate custody was also significantly reduced. In 1983 a total of 13,500 14 to 17 year old males were sentenced to immediate custody for indictable offences compared to 3,300 in 1993. This represented a fall from some 15 per cent of all court dispositions to 11 per cent.

The precise reasons for these dramatic reductions (and largely unexpected given that the political climate was dominated by Thatcherism) remain in debate. However, a number of key elements can be noted:

- *Demographic change.* There was a 19 per cent fall in the overall juvenile population in this period.

- *Diversion.* One of the foundational elements of youth justice has always been that young people should be protected from the full rigours of adult justice. This has meant that a range of diversionary strategies have always retained some presence in the form of:
  - *Diversion from crime* – typically this involves various methods of crime prevention which can range from target hardening to skills training and education (see Chapter 6.4);
  - *Diversion from prosecution* – from the early 1970s to the mid 1990s the police increasingly adopted a system of cautioning minor offenders through formal warnings rather than seeking prosecution;
  - *Diversion from custody* – whilst alternatives to adult prisons have existed since the mid nineteenth century, the notion of custody, in any form, being harmful and counterproductive regained prominence in the mid 1980s. Community-based programmes were increasingly promoted as viable alternatives to custody.
- *Experiments in decarceration.* The epitome of diversion was the decision in Massachusetts USA to close all state-run facilities for juvenile delinquents in 1970. Jerome Miller, Head of the Department of Youth Services, adopted a strategy of closing all the state's youth training schools (akin to the English borstal) prior to establishing any community-based alternatives. Enlisting government and media support, the Department was able to portray juvenile institutions as destructive places, and by speeding up parole and through a number of novel administrative devices, all such schools were closed by 1975. This commitment to decarceration survived, despite political pressure, until the early 1980s. Since then, however, it is generally acknowledged that slippage has occurred due to an increasing use of secure units and transference of juvenile cases to the adult courts (Rutherford, 1986, pp. 67–107). Nevertheless the Massachusetts experiment revealed to many policy makers and practitioners that decarceration was not an impossible goal.
- *Cautioning.* Attempts to divert offenders from court, encouraged by the 1969 Children and Young Persons Act, first took the form of juvenile liaison panels in which the police, together with social workers and teachers, decided whether or not to prosecute apprehended youths (Hudson, 1987, p. 145). Other schemes were entirely police run and developed cautioning rather than prosecution for first-time or minor offenders. Nationally in 1970, 35 per cent of those under 17 were cautioned, but by 1979 this had increased to 50 per cent (Gelsthorpe and Morris, 1994, p. 968). By the 1990s about 60 per cent of young offenders were dealt with in this way, although there were wide and fluctuating regional variations. Home Office circular 14/1985 furthered this process by encouraging the police to use 'no further action' or 'informal warnings' instead of any formal action (until a reversal of the policy in 1994). This again seemed to have a major diversionary effect. In Northamptonshire, for example, in 1985, 86 per cent of juveniles who came to the notice of the police were either prosecuted or formally cautioned; but by 1989 this had been reduced to 30 per cent (Hughes et al., 1998). A recurring criticism of cautioning has been its potential to administer a punishment, particularly in caution-plus schemes which combine a warning with reparation such as gardening and house cleaning, without any judicial hearing (Ditchfield, 1976). However, in the late 1980s at least they did seem capable of significantly reducing prosecutions.
- *Legislative restrictions on custody.* The 1982 Criminal Justice Act may have extended magistrates' custodial powers but it also built in a series of conditions that had to be met before this could happen. First the use of 'criminal' care orders was significantly curtailed. As a result there was a massive contraction of the residential care sector with the number of young people

in community homes with education (CHEs) declining from 7,500 in 1975 to 2,800 in 1984 and the numbers of CHEs falling from 125 to 60. By the late 1980s the use of care orders in criminal cases had become so insignificant that it was repealed. It no longer became possible to commit offenders to residential care on the grounds that they were in 'need' of welfare. Courts were also required to specify the criteria under which custody was being recommended. Legal representation for juveniles was introduced. Community service orders were made available for 16 year olds. The 1988 Criminal Justice Act further tightened the criteria before custody was to be considered. The 1991 Criminal Justice Act cemented this process by arguing that prison was 'an expensive way of making bad people worse' and by establishing a proliferation of 'community sentences' within the broader philosophy of 'punishment in the community' (Home Office, 1990, para 2.7 and see Section 7.4 below).

- *Intensive intermediate treatment.* In 1983 the Department of Health and Social Security's Intermediate Treatment (IT) Initiative financed the establishment of 110 *intensive* schemes in 62 local authority areas explicitly to provide alternatives to custody (Rutherford, 1989, 1992). Intermediate treatment practitioners were required to evolve 'new justice-based styles of working' which focused less on the emotional and social needs of juveniles and more on the nature of the offence. IT was to be restricted to those who were at serious risk of custody. Through such means it was hoped that magistrates would be persuaded that IT was no longer a 'soft option' but a 'high tariff' disposal. As McLaughlin and Muncie (1993, p. 178) have recorded, a strong 'alternatives to custody' ethos was developed within many social work departments and supported by the campaign groups of NACRO, the Children's Society and the Association for Juvenile Justice. Many agreed with the criticisms of the welfare approach and the coercive role that social workers played previously and developed a justice-based approach as self-styled *youth justice* workers:

  > The position extends beyond a refusal to recommend custodial sentences in the courts, encompassing a broad campaigning role with respect to the abolition of custody. The once ambiguous, if not ambivalent, attitudes about custody held by social workers during the early 1980s have been replaced by unequivocal opposition. (Rutherford, 1989, p. 29)

  Many social services departments began to construct their policies premised on the notions of minimum intervention, maximum diversion and underpinned by justice as opposed to welfare principles. By the mid 1990s, Martin (1997) was able to catalogue over 150 diversionary community programmes operating in England and Wales designed to address offending behaviour through victim awareness, anger management, drug awareness and positive leisure schemes.

- *Multi-agency collaboration.* A new localized *systems* approach emerged to operate these programmes drawing on social services, probation, the police, education, local authorities and numerous voluntary and charitable bodies. Youth justice teams came to be committed to creating 'custody-free zones' in their areas. Of crucial importance was the fact that this approach had the full backing of the Magistrates' Association. Hence those working in the juvenile justice system began to act in tandem: a stark contrast to the inter-agency conflicts and rivalries which were characteristic of the 1970s and early 1980s.

- *Expense* and *effectiveness.* In 1990–1, it was estimated that keeping an offender in custody for three weeks was more expensive than 12 months of supervision or community service. In addition 83 per cent of young men and 60 per cent of young women leaving youth custody were reconvicted within two years; the reconviction rate of those participating in community-based schemes was assumed to be substantially lower. NACRO's (1993) monitoring of the Intermediate Treatment Initiative indeed found reconviction rates of between 45 per cent and 55 per cent, and even though subsequent research funded by the Home Office and the Department of Health could find no clear evidence to suggest that community penalties held more than a modest advantage over custody in preventing reoffending (Lloyd et al., 1994; Bottoms, 1995), a major stimulus to community-based corrections had been born.

As a result of all of these factors it appeared as if justice-based principles of proportionality in sentencing or 'just deserts' was capable of providing a more visible, consistent and accountable decision-making process which, despite the law and order rhetoric, was also able to make a significant impact on the numbers of young people in custody.

Institutional Injustices

It is notable that the successes of the 1980s were not equally shared by all. Numerous studies in the 1980s found that Afro-Caribbean youth, in particular, were dealt with more harshly than whites at every stage of the judicial process – from arrest to sentencing (see Table 7.4). In 1987, 9.8 per cent of the under-18s received into custody were from ethnic minorities compared to their representation in the general population of no more than 5 per cent (Children's Society, 1989, p. 10). Whether such disparity occurs because of direct discrimination has remained stubbornly immune to statistical verification. As Asquith (1983) suggested, formal justice may simply reflect a wide range of legal *and* non-legal factors associated with criminality. So the over-representation of black youths may be explained by such

---

Table 7.4   'Race', youth and criminal justice

- Afro-Caribbean youth are especially likely to be stopped by the police and to be arrested. The rate for 'Asians' is lower than or equal to that of whites (Walker et al., 1990).
- Once arrested, Afro-Caribbeans are less likely to be cautioned than whites, and more likely to be prosecuted (Landau and Nathan, 1983; CRE, 1992; Goldson and Chigwada-Bailey, 1999).
- Afro-Caribbeans are more likely to be charged with indictable-only offences (Hood, 1992).
- Afro-Caribbeans are more likely to be remanded in custody, awaiting trial, rather than released on bail (Shallice and Gordon, 1990; Hood, 1992; Goldson and Peters, 2000).
- Afro-Caribbeans are subsequently more likely to be acquitted, either because they tend to be tried in Crown Court (where acquittals are higher), or because they tend to plead not guilty, or because they are more likely than whites to have been charged with crimes of which they are innocent (Walker, 1988).
- If found guilty, Afro-Caribbeans are more likely to be given a custodial sentence and for longer periods than whites (Hudson, A., 1989). They are also less likely to receive probation (Brown and Hullin, 1992).

Sources: Developed from Fitzgerald (1993) and Bowling and Phillips (2002)

factors as *age* (on average the Afro-Caribbean population is younger than the white and thus a higher proportion falls within the peak age of offending), *employment status* (Afro-Caribbean unemployment rates are consistently higher than for whites or Asians), *homelessness* (which may influence decisions about whether to grant bail) and *court of trial* (Afro-Caribbeans tend to plead not guilty and fail to benefit from a 'discount' afforded to those who plead guilty).

Arguably, it is the accumulation of such factors – the 'multiplier effect' (Goldson and Chigwada-Bailey, 1999) – which acts to discriminate against young blacks, rather than overt judicial racism. Hood's (1992) study of four Crown Courts (where offenders can be committed for sentence if aged 15 or over) concludes that whilst discrimination clearly occurs, because sentencing disparities cannot be accounted for by crime rates or by previous criminal records, it is not systematic. Disparities in sentencing were most marked for offences of medium seriousness, where, arguably, judicial discretion is at its highest, and also varied markedly between different courts and judges. All of this suggests that formal justice is not immune to producing discriminatory outcomes. As Goldson (1997b) records, 'the "justice" that prevailed was permeated with institutional injustices'. Within 'back to justice' and 'due process' strategies, the continuing social basis of law (and its interpretation and implementation) remained hidden by a liberal rhetoric of equality and rights.

Moreover as 'back to justice' entered the 1990s, early warnings of its possible appropriation by those more interested in retribution seemed to be more than credible. Indeed, the period 1991–3 may well go down in the chronicles of youth justice as yet another watershed when the public, media and political gaze fixed on the perennial issue of juvenile crime and delivered a familiar series of knee-jerk and draconian responses. This time, it was renewed images of the 'repeat' or 'persistent' young offender and the atypicality of the Bulger murder which provided the rationale for another U-turn in youth justice policy (see Chapter 1.1). By 1993 the Home Secretary's notion that 'prison works' was to lead to a further reinvention of the young offender and a corresponding increase in the use of youth custody (see Section 7.4).

Risk Management

7.3 Despite the 'successes' of the late 1980s in reducing youth custody, New Labour's 1998 Crime and Disorder Act promised to break with 'past failures' and to open up a new era in youth justice based on the primary aim of *preventing crime and disorder*. In doing so, Goldson (2000b) has argued that diversion has been replaced with a pre-emptive early intervention, heralding a significant increase in the intensity and reach of the youth justice system. The system may still make claims for welfare and justice but they have tended to be submerged within the rather less philosophically defensible aim of preventing offending by any pragmatic means possible. In place of the pessimistic 'nothing works' paradigm, evidence-based research and the fiscal audit were turned to reveal interventions that might 'work'. Moral debate about the purpose and *process* of intervention seemed to be shifted to the sidelines in the search for 'value for money' and cost-effective, measurable *outputs*. Young offending simply became another risk to be managed (Muncie, 2002).

Corporatism, Managerialism and Partnerships

As early as the late 1980s some commentators had come to argue that it made little sense to talk of youth justice in terms of offering either welfare and/or justice. Pratt (1989), for example, detected a newly developing *corporatist* strategy which removed itself from the wider philosophical arguments of welfare and punishment. This was characterized by administrative decision making, greater sentencing diversity, the construction of sentencing 'packages', centralization of authority and co-ordination of policy, growing involvement of non-juridical agencies and high levels of containment and control in some sentencing programmes (Pratt, 1989, p. 245; Parker et al., 1987). The aim was not necessarily to deliver 'welfare' or 'justice' but rather to develop the most cost-effective and efficient way of *managing* the delinquent population. The issue came to be defined in scientific and technical terms; the political/moral debates about the causes of offending and the purpose of intervention were shifted to the sidelines (Pitts, 1992, p. 142). Youth justice was reconceptualized as a delinquency management service in which the hard core were still locked up, whilst an expanding range of statutory and voluntary community-based agencies tailor-made non-custodial sentences which, they hoped, would be stringent enough to persuade magistrates not to take the (more expensive) custodial option.

By the 1990s such corporate, multi-agency strategies were to become subsumed within a much broader process of public sector managerialization. This, as Clarke and Newman (1997) have catalogued, has generally involved the redefinition of political, economic and social issues as problems to be managed rather than necessarily resolved. When the Conservatives came to power in 1979, management was identified as the key means through which the public sector could be rid of staid bureaucratic structures and entrenched professional interests and transformed into a dynamic series of organizations able to deliver 'value for money'. The neo-Taylorist vision of rationalized inputs and outputs being employed to reduce the costs of public services, became embedded in the drive to impose the three E's of *economy*, *efficiency* and *effectiveness* on all aspects of public provision. Social issues were depoliticized. Policy choices were transformed into a series of managerial decisions. Evaluations of public sector performance came to be dominated by notions of productivity, task remits and quantifiable outputs.

Whilst the full impact of such managerial missions came relatively late to criminal justice, by the 1990s the 'mean and lean' and 'more for less' mentalities gradually opened up law and order to a series of investigations from the Public Accounts Committee, the National Audit Office and the Audit Commission. Their recommendations have overwhelmingly been in support of subjugating professional skills and autonomy to management ideals of 'what works', of attaching resources to certifiable 'successful' outcomes and of devolving responsibility for law and order from a central state to a series of semi-autonomous local partnerships, voluntary agencies and privatized bodies. It is an agenda that has increasingly crossed party-political boundaries precisely because it *appears* apolitical. The removal of such 'transformative' issues as individual need, diagnosis, rehabilitation, reformation and penal purpose and their replacement by the 'actuarial' techniques of classification, risk assessment and resource management shifts the entire terrain of law and order from one of understanding criminal motivation to one of simply making crime tolerable through systemic co-ordination. As Feeley and Simon (1992, p. 454) have argued, 'by limiting their exposure to indicators that they can control, managers ensure that their problems will have solutions'. Managerialism represents a significant lowering of expectations in terms of what the youth justice system can be expected to achieve. Evaluation comes to rest solely on indicators of internal system performance (McLaughlin et al., 2001).

In 1996 the Audit Commission published its first report on the youth justice system in England and Wales. Noting that the public services (police, legal aid, courts, social services, probation, prison) spent around £1 billion a year processing and dealing with young offenders, it argued that much of this money was wasted through lengthy and ineffective court procedures. The thrust of the report was a need to shift resources from punitive to preventive measures. It was particularly critical of youth courts: the process of prosecution taking on average four months, costing £2,500 for each young person processed and with half of the proceedings ultimately discontinued, dismissed or discharged. The system, it was argued, had no agreed national strategies and local authorities acted more as an emergency service than as a preventive one. The report recommended the diversion of a fifth of young offenders away from the courts altogether and into programmes such as Northamptonshire's Mediation and Reparation schemes – thus saving £40 million annually on costs. In short the Audit Commission argued that:

> [T]he current system for dealing with youth crime is inefficient and expensive, while little is being done to deal effectively with juvenile nuisance. The present arrangements are failing young people – who are not being guided away from offending to constructive activities. They are also failing victims – those who suffer from some young people's inconsiderate behaviour, and from vandalism, arson and loss of property from thefts and burglaries. And they lead to waste in a variety of forms, including lost time, as public servants process the same young offenders through the courts time and again; lost rents, as people refuse to live in high crime areas; lost business, as people steer clear of troubled areas; and the waste of young people's potential. (Audit Commission, 1996, p. 96)

The Commission's priority was clearly one of diversion: partly on the grounds of 'value for money' and partly because of the lack of effectiveness of formal procedures. In congruence with a corporatist model, it advocated the development of multi-agency work with parents, schools and health services acting in tandem with social services and the police. In line with managerialist objectives, the

Commission argued that these goals could only be met by a clearer identification of objectives, more rigorous allocation of resources and the setting of staff priorities. The aim was to build a pragmatic strategy to prevent offending rather than wed the system to any particular broad philosophy of justice or welfare. The issue of the causes of offending was side-stepped by the identification of 'risk conditions' (factors that correlate with known offending) such as inadequate parental supervision, truancy, lack of a stable home or use of drugs. In the guise of 'modernization' welfare, justice and rights have been eclipsed by the 'imprecise science' of risk assessment and the statutory responsibility to meet performance targets. A performance management agenda prioritizes cost-effective measures for the realization of specific outputs (rather than outcomes). This is neatly captured in the promotion of what is termed 'SMART' targets, that is targets which are 'specific', 'measurable', 'achievable', 'realistic' and 'time-tabled' (Audit Commission, 1999).

Much of this was subsequently reflected by the statutory duty, imposed by the 1998 Crime and Disorder Act, for local authorities to establish youth offending teams (a partnership of social service, police, probation, education and health authorities) which formulate and implement youth justice plans, setting out how youth justice services are to be provided, monitored and funded and how targets for crime reduction are to be met in each local authority area. The Act also established a Youth Justice Board to monitor the operation of the system, promote good practice and advise the Home Secretary on the setting of national standards. In particular it initiated one of Labour's five key election pledges to introduce *fast-track punishment* for persistent young offenders, by insisting that the time between arrest and sentencing be cut by half. Here Labour was clearly responding to one of the repeated concerns of the Audit Commission (1996, 1998) for more streamlined procedures, better case management and time limits for all criminal proceedings involving young people. The aim was to develop a system that was not only more efficient, but also more cost-effective.

By the late 1990s all local authorities in England and Wales were given the *statutory* duty to 'prevent offending by young people'. All aspects of their work have become infused with crime prevention and crime reduction responsibilities. For example, by 2000 all 154 local authorities had formulated and implemented an annual Youth Justice Plan, setting out how youth justice reform was to be funded and put into operation, and had established a YOT (youth offending team), consisting of, on a statutory basis, representatives from each of social services, probation, police, health and education authorities. These agencies are designed to 'pull together' to co-ordinate provision, to ensure each agency acts in tandem and to deliver a range of interventions and programmes that will ensure that young people 'face up to the consequences of their actions'. What were formerly youth *justice* teams (designed to divert young people from court and custody) have been replaced by youth *offending* teams (designed to directly intervene in all aspects of criminal, anti-social and disorderly behaviour). In effect the YOT displaces the statutory child care operations of social services departments (Goldson, 2000b). But each YOT plan also has to be submitted to a national body – the Youth Justice Board – for approval which, by 2000, had formulated a set of practice criteria to act as national standards (Youth Justice Board, 2000). Moreover, their work is constantly scrutinized through budgetary planning and auditing for cost and effectiveness. The Youth Justice Plan enables local agencies to be held to account for their 'success' or 'failure'. Discourses of 'best value', 'fiscal responsibility' and 'cost-benefit' proliferate within performance targets, audits and statutory limits (Vaughan, 2000; Muncie, 2002).

These developments suggest a wholesale dehumanization of the youth crime issue, such that the sole purpose of youth justice becomes one of simply delivering a cost-effective and economic 'product'. Its 'success' is measured more by what it does than by what it achieves (McLaughlin and Muncie, 1994, p. 137). Key elements of New Labour's 'managerialization' of youth justice are given in Table 7.5.

Table 7.5 New Labour, new managerialism and youth justice

- Recasting the past as 'failure' in order to clear the ground (despite the 'successes' of the late 1980s in reducing youth crime and custody rates)
- Identifying risk conditions rather than causes of youth crime
- Setting statutory time limits from arrest to sentence
- Establishing performance targets for YOTs
- Discovering 'what works' via evidence-based research
- Establishing Youth Justice Board as a central body
- Establishing YOTs to 'join up' local agencies
- Establishing statutory obligation on local authorities to 'prevent offending by young people'
- Establishing means of standardizing risk conditions (e.g. by formulating ASSET assessment tools)
- Disseminating efficient practice via communication.

Source: Muncie and Hughes (2002, pp. 5–6)

However, whatever the rhetoric of government intention, the history of youth justice is also a history of active and passive resistance from pressure groups and from the magistracy, the police and from youth justice workers through which such reform is to be effected. At one level this is reflected in the continuing wide disparities between courts in the custodial sentencing of young people. These range from 1 custodial sentence for every 10 community sentences in the South-West to 1 in 5 in the West Midlands and the North-West. On another level it is reflected in the haphazard implementation of national legislation and youth justice standards in different localities (Holdaway et al., 2001). Indeed, Cross et al., (2003) have begun to detect divergences between policy and practice in Wales and in England. Significantly the Welsh Assembly decided to locate youth justice services in the portfolio of Health and Social Services rather than Crime Prevention, thus prioritizing a 'children first' rather than an 'offender first' (as in England) philosophy. There is also always a space to be exploited between written and implemented policy. The translation of policy into practice depends on how it is visioned and reworked (or made to work) by those empowered to put it into practice. As a result youth justice practice may well continue to be dominated not by *national* homogeneity but by a complex of *localized* rehabilitative 'needs' and responsibilized 'deeds' programmes. The key question remains how far pragmatic and managerial partnerships are capable of challenging and overcoming the persistently recurring appeals for custody that surface in popular and political discourse (see Section 7.4).

The 'What Works' Paradigm

The emergence of the terms 'risk management' and 'prevention' in the field of youth justice also reflects the growing importance of what has been termed a new penology of 'actuarial justice'. This shift first took place in the USA in the 1980s in response to demands for more accountability and rationality in correctional policy. Transformative and rehabilitative rationales of correctionalism have been increasingly challenged by an actuarialist language of calculating risk and the statistical probability of reoffending. Appropriate interventions are then modelled on psychological profiling and an assumed level of 'risk'. As Kempf-Leonard and Peterson, (2000, p. 78) explain:

> Often called risk and needs classification instruments, these measures are used to assign points to various characteristics of the youth and his or her alleged offense. The points are typically derived from statistical models that identify the relative importance of each characteristic in predicting the policy outcome of interest . . . much in the manner of insurance tables which predict the likelihood of having an automobile collision, house fire or serious illness. The guidelines then provide a classification grid that identifies the suggested juvenile justice intervention within each category of scores.

Preventing Reoffending

Offender profiling and risk classification have been eagerly turned to as a means of overcoming the 'nothing works' pessimism that had pervaded youth justice and probation for two decades. Gradually the case has been made that *some* forms of intervention can be successful in reducing *some* reoffending for *some* offenders at *some* times. Much of this was based on Ross et al.'s (1988) research on a cognitive skills training programme developed for high-risk *adult* probationers in the USA. In a meta analysis of over 400 research studies on the effectiveness of such 'treatments', Lipsey (1995) claimed that when intervention is focused around behavioural training or skills issues and sustained over a period of at least six months, then a 10 per cent reduction in reoffending can be expected. Focused and structured supervision programmes combining behavioural and skills training, training in moral reasoning, interpersonal problem solving skills training and vocationally oriented psychotherapy have all been cited as 'successful' (McGuire, 1995). Reports of other initiatives in mediation, caution-plus and reparation schemes have also claimed positive outcomes. For example Northamptonshire's Diversion Unit of the 1990s, which dealt with young offenders who had already been cautioned and which brought offender and victim together to discuss compensation, recorded substantially lower reoffending rates than for similar offenders who had been sent to youth custody (Hughes et al., 1998). The HALT programme in Holland has been another key referent for would-be reformers. There cautioning is supplemented with work relevant to the offence, payment of damages and an educational component. Aylesbury's Restorative Justice Scheme, based on the Maori conception of bringing offenders face to face with their victims, also claimed a dramatic reduction in reoffending (see below). The Youth Justice Board (*YJB News* Issue 13, 2002) has claimed that the introduction of final warnings (instead of cautions) in 2000, which also require some structured intervention, has resulted in a 15 per cent reduction in reoffending.

In general a new orthodoxy has emerged which claims that intensive, highly structured programmes that address offending behaviour are capable of success. As a result there has been something of a renaissance of interventionist (rather than diversionary) approaches, justified by reference to the 'proven' capacity of such treatments to 'work' in risk management terms (see Table 7.6).

Table 7.6   *The principles of 'what works'*

- Attempt a risk classification and target more intensive programmes at high risk offenders.
- Focus on the specific factors associated with offending.
- Use a structured learning style that requires active participation on the part of the offender.
- Develop high programme integrity.
- Match the level of risk, based on offending history, with the level of intervention.
- Use cognitive-behavioural interventions which help to improve problem solving and social interaction, but which also address and challenge the attitudes, values and beliefs that support offending behaviour.
- Base interventions in the community to facilitate 'real life' learning.

Sources: Derived from Audit Commission (1996); McGuire (1995); Goldblatt and Lewis (1998)

Preventing Youth Crime

Farrington (2000) is the leading proponent globally of the theory and practice of youth criminality prevention, focusing on the risk factors at play in the aetiology of delinquency. Based on research into the backgrounds and attitudes of future offenders, Farrington (1996) has identified poor child rearing, hyperactivity, low intelligence, harsh or erratic parental discipline, divorce, low family income and poor housing as the major risk factors (see Chapter 1.3). Numerous authors (Farrington, 1996; Utting, 1996; Sherman at al., 1997; Graham, 1998) have claimed that the 'most hopeful' methods to tackle crime and anti-social behaviour (derived from experimental research in the USA and Canada) are those which involve:

- home visiting by health professionals to give advice on infant development, nutrition and alcohol and drug avoidance in order to reduce parental child abuse;
- pre-school 'intellectual enrichment' programmes in nurseries to stimulate thinking and reasoning skills in young children (based on the High/Scope Perry Pre-School Program in Michigan);
- parenting education programmes;
- cognitive and social skills training to teach children to consider the consequences of their behaviour;
- teacher training and anti-bullying initiatives in schools.

These projects tell us that if we grant the necessary educational and economic resources to socially deprived families, then their children are likely to benefit. However, when attached to a preoccupation with law and order, they are read as the need to discipline 'failing families' (Pitts, 2001, p. 97). The biggest appeal of this risk factor paradigm of prevention lies not in its scientific rigour but in its fit with prevailing ideological imperatives and its pragmatic orientation for both identifying the interrelated risk factors behind anti-social behaviour and 'curing' or managing the problem by means of specific targeted prevention techniques. At its core is the claim that the approach is 'evidence led' and predicated upon the credo of 'what works'. A burgeoning growth industry in psychological risk profiling is indicative of much contemporary theory and practice in youth crime prevention, which combines the techniques of risk calculation with a continuing 'rehabilitative' commitment to 'changing people'. Rehabilitation and treatment programmes are now much more focused on 'what works' and on 'offender accountability' in an attempt to escape the populist condemnation that they are 'soft on crime'.

Nevertheless this 'new' paradigm has not been without its critics. Smith (2003, p. 137) has in particular queried the Youth Justice Board's claims of success. He detects a relative decline in such 'lenient' disposals as final warnings and fines in favour of community sentences coupled with dramatic rises in custody. Identification of those 'at risk' has simply contributed to a criminalization of younger and relatively minor offenders against which previously no formal action might have been taken. Above all Smith casts doubt on the reliability of the statistical reoffending data presented by the YJB. Like is not compared to like and the difficulty remains of isolating any effect specific to a particular intervention without acknowledging wider demographic and socio-economic contexts. It is for this reason that attempts to replicate 'success' from one locality or from one jurisdiction to others have generally failed because the dynamic processes and interactions of change have been overlooked (Crawford and Jones, 1996).

The 'what works' ethos has been more broadly challenged on a number of levels. Tilley (2003) warns of the methodological and scientific shortcomings of evaluations based on experiments and which are then uncritically employed to inform policy. He suggests the quest for a universal 'what works' solution is misguided and unachievable. A more 'realist' approach would be to ask the rather more complex and contingent question: 'What works for whom in what circumstances, and how?' Even then we should not expect replicability across time and space. What works today may not tomorrow. What works with some people in some places will not with others. Pitts (2001) condemns the 'what works' industry as the subordination of science to governance. Research is used selectively and only when it seems to confirm predetermined governmental policies. This view seems to be reinforced in the way that New Labour has often 'rolled out' pilot programmes before any evaluation has been able to report (Wilcox, 2003). Either way, actuarial assessments tend to focus on that which can be measured easily (such as the time interval between arrest and court appearance). That which eludes quantification (such as histories of multiple disadvantage) is ignored. Practice becomes geared to meeting (and manipulating) internal targets rather than responding to the needs and circumstances of offenders (Jones, 2001). Formulaic service delivery negates professional autonomy and traps decision making within an inflexible 'technocratic framework of routinized operations' (Webb, 2001, p. 71). It suggests that youth justice work can be value free and objective, existing in some vacuum outside of social relationships and cultural formations.

Evaluation, too, is never a pure science. Most commissioners of evaluation research might want the 'facts', but facts do not speak for themselves. The unpredictability and variability of local contexts and the complexity of the social and the political in general militate against standardization and uniformity. There are no law-like, universal 'best practices' (Goldson, 2001). The search for the consistently efficient and cost-effective means that the personal and cultural dynamics of youth justice work are overlooked. Further the clamour for the pragmatic 'quick fix' precludes not only critical research but also policy proposals which might look to the long term and the more fundamentally transformative (Muncie, 2002).

Finally the discourse of 'what works' is deceptively benign, practical and non-ideological. How could anyone claim to act otherwise and advocate policies that are demonstrable failures? Yet youth justice reform is also clearly driven by assessments of what is electorally popular. In practice 'what works' is not just a rational, objective and neutral process, it is also driven by political, institutional and economic imperatives.

Restorative Justice

Much has been made of the principles of restorative justice – and its potential for restitution, reparation and reconciliation – that ostensibly underpin some of New Labour's legislative initiatives. Within restorative justice the talk is less of formal crime control and more of informal offender/victim participation and harm minimization. Formal processes are seen as inimical to the resolution of conflicts because they neutralize the emotional and social dynamics of criminality and victimization. Formal processes 'steal' the conflict from those most directly involved (Christie, 1997). Advocates of restorative justice instead look to traditional forms of dispute resolution reputedly to be found in the informal customary practices of Maori, Aboriginal and Native American indigenous populations. The prominence of faith-based ideas and communitarianism is also much in evidence.

According to its proponents, restorative justice holds the potential to restore the 'deliberative control of justice by citizens' and to restore 'harmony based on a feeling that justice has been done' (Braithwaite, 2003, p. 57). It has come to find practical expression in various forms of family group conferencing in Australasia, in healing circles in Canada and in community peace committees in South Africa. Both the United Nations and the Council of Europe have given restorative justice their firm backing for its potential to achieve participative justice and to reduce the recourse to youth imprisonment. There is little doubt that restoration holds the potential for a fundamental overhaul of policy and practice (see Table 7.7). Some radical advocates, for example, speak of replacing legal definitions of crime and formal procedures with processes of reconciling conflicting interests and of healing rifts (De Haan, 1990; Walgrave, 1995).

Table 7.7   *Key elements in restorative justice*

- Crime is fundamentally a violation of people and interpersonal relationships
- Restoration is a continuum of responses to the needs and harms experienced by victims, offenders and communities
- Maximization of public participation, especially of victims
- Providing offenders with opportunities and encouragement to understand the harm caused and to make amends
- Maximization of voluntary participation; minimization of coercion and exclusion
- Community responsibility to support victims and integrate offenders
- Mutual agreement and opportunities for reconciliation/negotiation take precedence over imposed outcomes
- The prioritization of healing, recovery, accountability and change over punishment.

Source: Derived from Zehr and Mika (1998)

The often quoted reference point is the experience of Family Group Conferences (FGCs) pioneered in New Zealand in 1989 and based on traditional systems of conflict resolution within Maori culture. FGCs involve a professional co-ordinator, dealing with both civil and criminal matters, who calls the young person, their family and victims together to decide whether the young person is 'in need of care and protection' and, if so, what should be provided. The key element of progressive restorative practice is that the offender is not marginalized but accepted as a key contributor to decision making. Moreover in New Zealand FGCs are not simply involved in trivial cases but also serious offences involving burglary, arson, rape and so on. It is claimed that their introduction has resulted in an 80 per cent reduction of those in care for welfare or criminal reasons (Morris and Maxwell, 2001). Nearly all FGCs are able to reach agreement and advise an active penalty – usually community work, apologies or reparation. Further, it is argued they act as an effective vehicle for enabling the participation and strengthening of families while respecting the interests of victims (Hudson et al., 1996, p. 234).

Restorative principles are also said to have informed the police-led cautioning scheme for juveniles established in the Wagga Wagga police district in New South Wales, Australia. There the restoration of juveniles was said to be achieved through processes of 'reintegrative shaming' (Braithwaite, 1989). It was this model that was first imported to England through the establishment of a Restorative Cautioning Unit by Thames Valley Police in Aylesbury in 1995. Two years later it was claimed that of 400 offenders involved, reoffending rates had fallen to as low as 4 per cent, compared to 30 per cent for those who had only received a caution (*Guardian*, 18 October 1997). Young and Hoyle's (2002) subsequent evaluation cast doubt on these figures as no reliable data existed for reconviction following 'old style' cautioning in Aylesbury. Nevertheless they concluded that exposing offenders to the emotionally charged views of those whom they most care about, such as parents and friends, helped to reduce the likelihood of re-sanctioning by about half. Moreover most offenders, victims and their respective supporters were generally satisfied with the fairness of the process.

Further grounding of elements of restoration in English youth justice has been made possible through the introduction of reparation and action plan orders in the 1998 Crime and Disorder Act and the introduction of referral orders and youth offender panels following the 1999 Youth Justice and Criminal Evidence Act. The Northern Ireland criminal justice review (O'Mahony and Deazley, 2000) also advocates youth conferencing to be at the heart of its new approach to juvenile justice. Referral orders are a *mandatory*, standard sentence imposed on all offenders, no matter how relatively minor the offence, as long as they are under 18 years old, have no previous convictions and plead guilty. Following pilots in 11 areas, they went national in 2002. Offenders are referred to a youth offender panel (made up of local volunteers) to agree a programme of behaviour to address their offending. There is no provision for legal representation. It is not a formal community sentence but does require a contract to be agreed to last from a minimum of 3 months to a maximum of 12. The programme may include victim reparation, victim mediation, curfew, school attendance, staying away from specified places and persons, participation in specified activities, as well as a general compliance with the terms of the contract for supervision and monitoring purposes. Through such measures it has been claimed that youth justice is in the midst of a potentially radical shift from being exclusionary and punitive to becoming inclusionary and restorative (Crawford and Newburn, 2003).

Critical perspectives on restorative justice have however begun to emerge from a number of different avenues. Evaluations of the referral orders, for example, have lauded the more positive lines of communication that have been opened up between offenders, parents, victims and communities, but have lamented its coercive nature, problems of low victim participation, blurred lines of accountability and a general failure to provide offenders with the socio-economic resources necessary for them to develop a 'stake-hold' in community life (Crawford and Newburn, 2003; Gray, 2003). Gelsthorpe and Morris (2002) contend that restorative principles are additions to, rather than core defining components of, a system that remains built around, and continues to act upon, notions of just deserts, punishment and retribution. Restorative processes simply deal with low-level offenders who, through a combination of New Labour's other measures in crime prevention and pre-emptive early intervention, are being sucked into the system at an increasingly early age. Neither does restorative justice offer any challenge to managerialism and risk management strategies. Rather it may serve an integral role in sorting the 'high risk' from the 'low' (Cunneen, 2003).

A danger also remains that any form of compulsory restoration may degenerate into a ceremony of public shaming and degradation, particularly when it operates within a system of justice whose primary intent is the infliction of further harm. Within restorative programmes the burden tends to remain on individuals to atone or change their behaviour, rather than on the state to recognize that it also has a responsibility (within UN conventions and rules – see Section 7.4) to its citizens. Notions of individual responsibility rather than those of community empowerment, social inclusion and 'restorative *social* justice' tend to proliferate (White, 2003). Restorative justice accepts at face value that the police and the state can be impartial arbiters of conflicts and ignores the 'hidden injuries' endured by the workless, the marginalized and the homeless, who are the most likely to be the subjects of its gaze. It has tended to be introduced for financial, electoral and administrative reasons rather than as a systemic alternative to otherwise retributive systems. Further, international evaluation research has cast some doubt on whether restorative justice 'works' to reduce recidivism. The results tend to be mixed, but with some reductions in reoffending for young violent offenders. All of this encourages a degree of scepticism and ambivalence towards the claims made for restoration and its future potential to overhaul the injustices of retribution (Daly, 2002). As Cunneen (2003, p. 191) concludes:

> [Restorative justice] might prove positive from a technocratic view, but still fail to ensure equitable or just outcomes for particular groups of people. Conversely we might support some programmes from a human rights perspective although in terms of measurable outcomes they rate much the same as traditional court-based forms of interventions.

Authoritarianism

7.4   Whatever the progressive intent of welfare, justice, restorative and risk management strategies, there is contrary evidence to suggest that they have always been embedded in deeper punitive and authoritarian motives. Even at moments of penal reductionism, the young offender institution, detention centre, youth custody centre, borstal, approved school, reformatory or youth prison has formed the cornerstone of youth justice against which all other interventions are measured and assessed. There has also persisted a strong law and order lobby which has forcibly argued that youth crime is caused by simple wickedness and that the only real punishment is that which involves incarceration. As a result every decarcerative reform has been subject to either judicial or political backlash. Governments and policy makers, it seems, are only prepared to sanction non-custodial options as long as custody is retained for particular groups of young offenders (Pratt, 1989, p. 244).

The Custodial Sanction

From Borstal to YOI

When the first specialized detention centre for young offenders was formally set up by the Crime Prevention Act of 1908 at Borstal in Kent, it was heralded as a major liberal breakthrough. The separation of the under-21s from adults in their own closed institutions was seen as a major step towards the training of the young criminal. In the spirit of rehabilitation, borstal 'trainees' could be held for at least a year and no more than three years; the regime was based on strict discipline, hard work and drill; it was directed not at the 'incorrigible' but those of 'criminal habits and tendencies' or those associating with 'persons of bad character'. From the outset it attracted criticism for instituting long periods of confinement – up to three years for offences that would not ordinarily attract more than six months (Radzinowicz and Hood, 1990, p. 389). However, it also claimed a remarkable success in preventing reoffending. The first survey in 1915 reported reconviction rates as low as 27 to 35 per cent.

In 1961, the Criminal Justice Act reduced the minimum age for borstal training to 15, and made it easier to transfer young people from approved schools and integrated borstals into the prison system. This integration meant that the training component declined and their regimes became more punitive. The role of borstal as an alternative to prison was undermined, and it was turned instead into a primary punitive institution which acted as a funnel into the prison system. Taylor et al. (1979, p. 65) argued that 'younger and less difficult young people' were increasingly subject to 'tougher punishment'. Partly as a consequence, the reconviction rate which had stayed at 30 per cent throughout the 1930s increased to 70 per cent, suggesting that borstal accentuated forms of behaviour it was designed to suppress. Taylor et al. (1979) described how offers of help were provided inconsistently and arbitrarily withdrawn. Physical and verbal abuse by officers and other inmates was not uncommon. A picture emerged of largely punitive regimes in which retraining was minimal and the possibility of being permanently institutionalized forever present: 'Common humanity, statistical evidence and above all commonsense demand the abolition of the Borstal institution' (Taylor et al., 1979, p. 71).

In 1982 borstals were renamed youth custody centres and in 1988 were included in a wider network of young offender institutions (YOIs). In many respects they now act as mirror images of adult prisons for the young. Following the 1994 Criminal Justice and Public Order Act, the maximum sentence of detention in a young offender institution was increased from 12 to 24 months. The same Act also introduced secure training orders for 12 to 14 year olds who had been convicted of three or more offences which would be imprisonable in the case of an adult. By 2003 three such centres were available.

The 1998 Crime and Disorder Act, abolished these separate sentences and replaced them with a generic detention and training order (DTO). This came into force in April 2000. A DTO can be given to 15 to 17 year olds for any offence considered serious enough to warrant a custodial sentence; and to 12 to 14 year olds who are considered to be 'persistent offenders'. The orders are for between 4 and 24 months. Half of the order is served in the community under the supervision of a social worker, a probation officer or a member of a youth offending team. A custodial sentence of detention (without the training component) is now restricted to those aged 18, 19 and 20. However, for 'grave' crimes, the youth court can pass its jurisdiction to the Crown Court. Under sections 90–92 of the Powers of Criminal Courts Act 2000 (which consolidated those of section 53 of the 1933 Children and Young Persons Act), a 10–17 year old can be detained for a longer period than the normal maximum of two years, at the discretion of the Home Secretary, either in a local authority secure unit or a prison service establishment. The numbers caught in these powers increased from some 100 in 1992 to over 600 in 1999. In addition the Criminal Justice and Police Act 2001 extended the reasons for giving custodial remands from 'protecting the public from serious harm' to 'preventing the commission of future imprisonable offences'.

Conditions in young offender institutions have been a recurring cause for concern. Goldson (1997a, p. 83) argues that not only are they 'unsuited to guaranteeing basic standards of safety and welfare, but each day is characterized by a culture of bullying, intimidation and routine self harm'. Between 1990 and 2000, 134 15 to 21 year olds committed suicide in prison. Rates of self harm have escalated with 1,173 recorded instances in 1996/7 alone (Goldson, 2002b, p. 60). The average assault rate in YOIs is over 34 per cent (Prison Reform Trust Press Release, 10 September 2001). As Liebling (1992) established, young offenders are particularly vulnerable to the degrading and debilitating conditions of imprisonment. Young prisoner suicides tend to occur within one month, or at most one year of reception into custody; often when they are on remand, awaiting sentence. Young Offender Institutions also appear to be riddled with individually and institutionally racist practices. The Commission for Racial Equality (2003) discovered high levels of intimidation, discrimination and failure to protect black prisoners epitomised by the murder of 19 year old Zahid Mubarek in 2000 by his cell mate who was known to the authorities to be a violent racist. In one of the first ethnographic pieces of research to test the impact of the Prison Service's anti-racist policies specifically in YOIs, Wilson and Moore's (2003) interviews of 45 teenage boys vividly describe a daily routine of prison officer verbal abuse. Terms such as 'chimp', 'golliwog' 'nigger' and phrases such as 'when I wipe my arse it looks like you' reveal a deeply imbued racism. Yet each of the three YOIs in this study had officially met their performance targets in race relations. For the boys the work of race relations liaison officers and management teams was an irrelevance. None felt racist incidents were worth reporting, if not for fear of retaliation then because none would be taken seriously.

A report by the Howard League (1995, p. 67) concluded in much the same terms as Taylor et al.'s (1979) condemnation of the borstal system: 'an approach which concentrates on incarcerating the most delinquent and damaged adolescents, in large soulless institutions under the supervision of staff with no specialist training in dealing with difficult teenage behaviour, is nonsensical and inhumane.' In 2003 the privately run YOI at Ashfield was condemned as the worst jail in Britain with bullying endemic and staff having lost effective control (*Guardian*, 5 February 2003). Goldson's (2002c, pp. 159–60) research of the experiences of those subjected to secure and penal regimes, whether in the name of welfare or criminal justice, led him to conclude:

> locking up children is spectacularly ineffective . . . children invariably leave prison not only more damaged but also more angry, more alienated, more expert in the ways of crime and more likely to commit more serious offences – in fact more of everything that the children themselves and the community need much less of.

Such an argument appears all the more pertinent when applied to girls. There are no dedicated young offender institutions for under 18 year old women. Holding girls in wings of adult prisons has long been condemned but despite repeated promises over 25 years to remove all girls from prison service accommodation, the practice continues. Ironically, it is their small number that means that they appear 'tacked onto' the rest of the system. There is little specialist staff training. Because of the few facilities available, girls are often held further from home, again undermining the possibility of restoring family and community ties. In 1999 86 girls were held in prison; by 2002 there were 120 (NACRO, 2001; Howard League, Press Briefing, 2003). The counterproductive nature of imprisoning children is well known and widely shared. Yet it barely figures in any discussion of a youth justice system which claims to be acting solely on the basis of 'what works'.

Detention Centres and Boot Camps

Detention centres were introduced by the Criminal Justice Act of 1948 and enabled the courts to sentence offenders aged 14–21 to short periods of an explicitly punitive regime. Again this was justified on the grounds that sending young offenders to prison only helped to cement criminal careers, but there is strong evidence that their introduction was also a result of a quid pro quo for the abolition of corporal punishment (Muncie, 1990). Detention centres were established as an 'experiment', but lasted 40 years. Throughout they were dogged by a lack of any precise definition of purpose. Despite significant opposition the only detention centre for girls was opened at Moor Court, near Stoke-on-Trent in 1962. It was closed seven years later because military drill and physical education were not considered appropriate in the 'training' of young women.

Whilst detention centres always promised the delivery of a 'short, sharp, shock', in the 1950s and 1960s their regime was not that far removed from that of borstals. In the 1970s, in an effort to appease those who viewed the entire juvenile justice system as too soft, the Home Secretary announced the establishment of two 'experimental' regimes in which 'life will be constricted at a brisk tempo. Much greater emphasis will be put on hard and constructive activities, and discipline and tidiness, on self respect and respect for those in authority . . . These will be no holiday camps' (Whitelaw cited in Thornton et al., 1984, para. 1). The regimes were subsequently evaluated by the Home Office's Young Offender Psychology Unit, which concluded that they had 'no discernible effect on the rate at which trainees were reconvicted' (Thornton et al., 1984, para. 8.21). At one centre (Send, for 14–17 year olds) reconviction rates were 57 per cent both before and after the experiment; at the other (New Hall, for 17–21 year olds) the rate rose from 46 to 48 per cent. Doubt was also expressed as to whether the new tougher regimes were actually experienced as more demanding. Indeed some of the activities, such as drill and physical education were comparatively popular; more so than the continuous chore of the humdrum work party which they replaced.

Despite such findings, the tougher regimes were not abandoned but *extended* to all detention centres. In 1985 the rhetoric and political expediency of the 'short, sharp shock' appeared to take precedence over research evaluation or practical experience (Muncie, 1990, p. 61). The political demand for repressive penal policies repeatedly overshadows logical argument. As Harris (1982, p. 248) commented, 'punitive and liberal legislation are judged by different criteria, the latter being immediately at risk when it fails to reduce recidivism, but the former, however ineffective, appearing to a society in which to punish wrongdoing seems natural, to contain an intrinsic logic.'

The experiments in 'short, sharp shock' were formally abolished in 1988 but it took only another eight years for their revival. The introduction of American-styled boot camps in 1996–7 ignored all the lessons learnt in the previous 50 years. The origins of the boot camp lie in survival training for US military personnel during the Second World War. They were introduced in the US from 1983 in response to prison overcrowding and a belief that short periods of retributive punishment would change or deter offending behaviour: 'typically detainees might face pre-dawn starts, enforced shaved heads, no talking to each other, being constantly screamed at by guards, rushed meal times, no access to television and newspapers and a rigorous and abusive atmosphere for 16 hours a day' (Nathan, 1995, p. 2). Such regimes have consistently failed to live up to expectations: the deterrent effect of military training has proved negligible; the authoritarian atmosphere has denied access to effective treatment; there have been occasional lawsuits from inmates claiming that elements of the programme were dangerous and life threatening; they have failed to reduce prison populations; they distract attention from other policies that may work better; and their popularity relies more on an emotive nostalgia for some mythical orderly past than on effectiveness (Parent, 1995; Simon, 1995).

Despite such warnings, the British government decided to go ahead. The first boot camp was opened in 1996 at Thorn Cross Young Offenders Institution in

Cheshire. But instead of a military-based regime, it employed a 'high-intensity' mixture of education, discipline and training. A second camp, opened at the Military Corrective Training Centre in Colchester in 1997, promised a more spartan regime. Aimed at 17–21 year olds, its open prison conditions, however, excluded the most serious of offenders. The notion, too, of handing criminal cases over to a military authority provoked an avalanche of complaints from virtually all sides of the criminal justice process. Each place cost £850 per week compared to £250 per week in other young offender institutions. Despite these misgivings the New Labour government of 1997 was initially reluctant to move for their abolition for fear of being seen to have gone 'soft' on crime. But eventually pressure from the prison service – on grounds of cost, if not effectiveness – was successful in shutting down the Colchester camp barely 12 months after its opening and when only 44 offenders had gone through its regime. Meantime the high-intensity training regime at Thorn Cross continues.

Custodial Remands

If an offender under 17 is remanded in custody awaiting trial, then that person should be placed in the care of the local authority. However, if they are deemed unruly, then guardianship is passed to the prison department. As a result whilst no person under 17 can be sentenced to imprisonment as such, the number of juveniles locked up in adult prisons and remand centres has long been a cause for concern. In 1990 15 year old Philip Knight hanged himself in Swansea Prison while awaiting sentence for stealing a handbag. The outcry that followed forced the government to introduce legislation to end such remands, but in 1995 about 1,500 15 and 16 year old boys were still being held in adult prisons: an *increase* of 72 per cent since 1992. Of those 1,500, more than half did not eventually receive a prison sentence. The practice also appears to be significantly racialized. In 1995, in London, 53 per cent of those sent to Feltham Remand Centre were from ethnic minorities, in Birmingham it was 51 per cent, and Manchester 43 per cent (*Independent*, 5 July 1995). In response, the 1998 Crime and Disorder Act placed a statutory duty on local authorities to provide bail support schemes so that juveniles might be removed from the 'corrupting influence' of prison service custody. However, in 2001 the rules governing custodial remand were relaxed to cover persistent minor offending as well as public protection. In September 2002 the total remand population in the juvenile secure estate stood at 653 (NACRO, 2003b, p. 10).

Secure Units

Young offenders may also find themselves subject to incarceration in local authority or privately run secure accommodation. During the 1970s almost 500 secure units were introduced in community homes with education, youth treatment centres and in assessment centres. The major argument for expanding prison-like conditions within such settings was that their referrals were more difficult than in the past. Millham et al. (1978) and Cawson and Martell's (1979) research, however, concluded that there was no such significant change. Moreover, because at the time the numbers sent to borstal had increased, those in the residential care system were arguably *less* difficult than previously. Confusion also existed over whether the role of a secure unit was to punish or treat or both, or whether they existed simply because no other 'suitable' disposal was available. Harris and Timms (1993) described the situation as one of 'persistent ambiguity'.

In congruence with other custodial disposals, the rate of reoffending was high. Experience of a secure unit also appeared to increase the chance of reoffending for younger children and for those who had not committed offences prior to going in. During the 1980s a number of authorities closed their units partly because of over-provision and partly because of more rigorous conditions attached to gaining a DHSS licence (Harris and Timms, 1993, p. 76). Nevertheless the provision of secure accommodation, not only for offenders but also for runaways, prostitute children and abused suicidal children, rose again in the 1990s to near 300. As Harris and Timms (1993, p. 169) concluded: 'the most potent predictor of high usages of secure accommodation is a local authority's possession of a secure unit'. Any increase in places simply attracts more young people who are considered to be in need of such means of control/protection. Added to this was the proposal, first formally proposed in 1993, just days after the murder of James Bulger, to build five secure training centres for 12–14 year olds to tackle the presumed 'epidemic' of persistent offending, at a cost of between £2,000 and £3,000 per week per child.

Whilst in opposition Labour had been unequivocal in condemning such centres as both expensive and ineffective but the first was opened in Kent in April 1998 as the custodial element of a new secure training order. It was run by a subsidiary of the private security firm Group 4. In the following five years two more units were established, all provided by the private sector. The Youth Justice Board plans to purchase a further 400 places from the private sector by 2005. The existence of such places is widely assumed to be the root cause of an 800 per cent rise in under 15 year olds being sent to custody between 1992 and 2001 (NACRO, 2003b). However there is little evidence of their success. Research at one centre (Medway) found that nearly all children reoffended or breached the conditions of the community part of their secure training order (Hagell et al., 2000).

New Labour; New Punitiveness

The 1998 Crime and Disorder Act may have promised to break with 'past failures' but the evocation of prevention is present not only in such programmes as parenting classes or drugs education but also in containment in secure environments. As a result despite the (re)emergence of restoration and tougher community penalties, there is also contrary evidence to suggest that the custodial function of youth justice has never been seriously questioned. An ideology of 'popular punitiveness' holds sway, emphasizing the importance of punishing the offender for their wrong-doing in the name of retribution. This strategy of crime control is reflected in the doubling of the numbers of young people incarcerated over the past decade. England and Wales now lock up more young people than any other country in Europe: four times the rate in France, 12 times that in the Netherlands and 160 times that in Norway, Sweden and Finland (Muncie, 2003a and see Section 7.5); and often in conditions condemned by the Chief Inspector of Prisons as 'utterly unsuitable' and as 'unworthy of any country that claims to be called civilised' (Children's Rights Alliance, 2002). With reconviction rates of ex-prisoners as high as 88 per cent and increasing evidence of inappropriate and brutalizing regimes characterized by racism, bullying, self harm and suicide, it is clear that child incarceration is an expensive failure but nevertheless continues apace (Goldson and Peters, 2000). As a result a compelling case against youth custody has been repeatedly made (see Table 7.8).

Table 7.8   *The case against custody*

- Custody fails to prevent reoffending or to act as an individual deterrent. Over 80 per cent of those sent to youth custody reoffend within a two-year period following release.
- The value of custody as a more widespread deterrent is doubtful. Custody is a fairly remote concept for most young people. Paradoxically it is those who know friends who have been in custody who seem most likely to follow suit. Increasing the rate of custody has practically no impact on crime rates.
- A juvenile in custody is making no restitution or reparation to the victim or to the community at large.
- Whilst prisons provide society with immediate 'protection' from the offender, the great majority of juveniles sentenced to custody pose no serious risks to the community. Indeed, they may become a significantly greater danger on their return.
- Over half have prior experience of care or social services involvement. Penal custody exacerbates broken links with family, friends, education, work and leisure, and causes stigmatization and labelling. Rather than reintegrating young people into the communities where they must learn to live, custody results in further social exclusion. Many are discharged without anywhere to live.
- Custody diverts valuable resources from community-based measures of protection and prevention which, in many cases, appear more successful at preventing reoffending.

Sources: Derived from Children's Society (1989, pp. 12–13; 1993, pp. 45–51); Goldson (2002b); NACRO (2003b); Monaghan et al. (2003)

The juvenile (under 18) prison population rose from 1,328 in June 1992 to 2,615 in June 2002 driven by a growing tendency to incarcerate the under-15s, ethnic minorities and young women. There was a 175 per cent increase in the use of custody for young women between 1992 and 1996 alone (Worrall, 1999). During the 1990s the average sentence length for 15–17 year olds doubled. Ironically such expansion has been explained not only by a greater willingness for magistrates to resort to custody and with longer sentences as a response to the prevailing climate of popular and political punitiveness (*Independent*, 18 June 2003) but also because the introduction of the DTO with its training component persuaded them this might be a progressive disposal. By making custody appear less harsh, its greater use is encouraged (Goldson, 2002b).

Community Surveillance and Punishment

The anti-custody ethos of the 1991 Criminal Justice Act (implemented in October 1992) was justified through the promise of more rigorous community disposals. These were not to be considered as alternatives to custody, but as sentences in their own right. This did not necessarily imply a slackening of control or the reawakening of welfarist principles. *Punishment* in the community was to be achieved through attaching conditions to supervision in the form of electronic monitoring, curfew, community service or residence requirements (Worrall, 1997). This required a change in focus for the juvenile court and in the practices of probation and social work agencies. For the latter it meant a shift in emphasis away from 'advise, assist, befriend' and towards tightening up the conditions of supervision and surveillance. For the former it meant the abolition of the *juvenile* court (which had previously dealt with criminal and care cases) and the creation of *youth* courts and 'family proceedings' courts to deal with such matters separately. As a result the goal of welfare was effectively removed from youth criminal justice policy.

Community-based interventions have, however, long been criticized as failing to impact on custodial populations. Scull has argued that they are driven more by financial imperatives than from any enlightened desire to decarcerate. The move towards community punishment has been generated by a growing *fiscal crisis* within welfare capitalism:

> [T]he continuation of an increasingly costly social control policy which in terms of effectiveness, possesses few advantages over an apparently much cheaper alternative becomes ever more difficult to justify; and the attractiveness of that alternative to governments under ever greater budgetary pressures becomes steadily harder to resist. (Scull, 1977, p. 139)

Community-based interventions have also been critiqued for accelerating routes into custody. In a Canadian study, Hylton (1981) examined the effects of community corrections programmes introduced in Saskatchewan from 1962 to 1979. He concluded that not only did these fail to reduce the size of the prison population, but they actually resulted in a threefold increase in the proportion of persons under formal state control. In the USA, the National Evaluation of the Deinstitutionalization of Status Offenders project reported that the programmes were so clearly biased to heighten the intake of less serious offenders, that many more were caught up in the referral network than if the project had not been established (Kobrin and Klein, 1983). As Hudson (1987, p. 149) commented, it seems as if 'each time a law was reformed or a policy innovation implemented, it came as an addition to the system. New forms of treatment were added; old forms of punishment were retained.'

The existence of 'alternatives' also has the effect of instigating a policy of *bifurcation* in which security at the institutional end of the system is hardened and maximized (Bottoms, 1977). The incarcerated come to be viewed as having failed all attempts to reintegrate and are seen as constituting a new hardcore, intractable and dangerous element of the population. In tandem, higher security within penal establishments is legitimized. Pursuit of correctional programmes into the community also extends the means of coercive control into non-justice agencies such that probation, housing, education, employment and family services all have a role to play in an extended correctional continuum (see Chapter 6.5). Such practices led Stanley Cohen (1985, p. 62) to ask, 'When do the confines of custody end and those of the community begin?' A blurring of boundaries not only draws social workers, probation officers and community service personnel into a more overtly controlling function, but ultimately widens the net of social control so that it becomes capable of ensnaring us all.

Nevertheless, in 1989, England began experimenting with such US-inspired schemes as electronic monitoring. Despite a faltering start, such schemes have proliferated (Nellis, 1991). Further in 1995 a Green Paper continued to advocate the further 'strengthening' of the conditions of *punishment* in the community such that they represented physical hard labour (Home Office, 1995), despite the fact that such a 'strengthening' had already been legislated for in the 1991 Criminal Justice Act. The 1993 Criminal Justice Act almost immediately overturned some of the decarcerative principles of the 1991 Act, while the 1994 Criminal Justice and Public Order Act doubled the maximum sentence of custody within young offender institutions. In addition the 1997 Crime (Sentences) Act introduced mandatory minimum sentences for certain offences, extended electronic monitoring to the under-16s as part of a curfew order, and for the first time allowed convicted juveniles to be publicly named if the court was satisfied that it was in the interests of the public to do so. Youth justice once more turned full circle, away from diversion and decarceration and back to an emphasis on punitive custody. The 'actual and real context of juvenile crime was lost within reactionary histrionics and authoritarian frenzy' (Goldson, 1997b, p. 131).

Despite the formal emphasis on crime prevention, the 1998 Crime and Disorder Act has done little to challenge this punitive mood. Rather it significantly added to the reach and intensity of community-based sentences. New Labour, for example, remains committed to the use of electronic tags to enforce curfews and in 2002 further extended their reach to include 10–15 year olds as part of youth bail conditions or to monitor the community part of a detention and training order. But, as Whitfield (1997) has warned, young people generally have the lowest rates of compliance with tagging orders, and in any event the tag may be used as a status symbol to 'impress friends' rather than acting as a deterrent. In June 1998 magistrates were rebuked by Jack Straw for *not* having used extensively enough the power granted in 1997 to name and shame young offenders by releasing their identities to the media (*Guardian*, 12 June 1998). In 2001 'community service' was renamed as 'community punishment'. The entire purpose of probation has been transformed from one of social work informed assistance to one of risk management and surveillance (Nellis, 2002). Intensive supervision and surveillance programmes were also launched that year as part of a pilot 'zero tolerance of yob culture' campaign, largely aimed at those 15 and 16 year olds with a prior record of offending and as a last community-based resort before custodial sentencing. They are not a court order as such but can be added to a supervision order, community rehabilitation order or to bail. They typically involve 24 hours a day electronic monitoring together with training, offending behaviour work and reparation. In 2003 a further intensive control and change programme for 18–20 year olds was unveiled combining tagging, curfew, unpaid community work, compensation and work with an assigned mentor. The Director of the National Probation Service enthusiastically declared it to be 'the most restrictive and intensive penalty that probation has yet rolled out. We have very high hopes for this' (*Guardian*, 3 April 2003). Again in 2003, 'intensive fostering' was proposed for those released on bail. The full range of disposals available to police, local authorities and the courts in England and Wales in 2003 is listed in Table 7.9.

Successive Home Secretaries have sought to gain law and order credibility by claiming that existing levels of community supervision and surveillance are a 'soft option'. Custodial and community punishment appear to exist in some symbiosis. If magistrates are to be persuaded to use the non-custodial options, it is widely believed that their conditions must be made consistently more punitive. The danger, as frequently voiced, lies in up-tariffing and net widening. If this is the case, then punishment in the community ironically serves to fuel an increase, rather than decline, in the use of the custodial sector.

The Abrogation of Rights

In 1989 the United Nations Convention on the Rights of the Child established a near global consensus that all children have a right to *protection*, to *participation* and to basic material *provision*. The only countries not to have ratified are Somalia and the USA. The Convention built upon the 1985 UN Standard Minimum Rules for the Administration of Youth Justice (the Beijing Rules) which recognized the 'special needs of children' and the importance of dealing with offenders flexibly. It promoted diversion from formal court procedures, non-custodial disposals and insisted that custody should be a last resort and for minimum periods. In addition the Rules emphasized the need for anonymity in order to protect children from lifelong stigma and labelling. The Convention cemented these themes in the fundamental right that in all legal actions concerning those under the age of 18, the 'best interests of the child shall be a primary consideration' (Article 3.1). Further it reasserted the need to treat children differently, to promote their dignity and worth with minimum use of custody and that children should participate in any proceedings relating to them (Article 12).

In 1990 the UN guidelines for the Prevention of Juvenile Delinquency (the Riyadh guidelines) added that youth justice policy should avoid criminalizing children for minor misdemeanours. The European Convention on Human Rights first formulated in 1953 provides for the due process of law, fairness in trial proceedings, a right to education, a right to privacy and declares that any

Table 7.9   *The range of 'youth disposals' available to police, courts and local authorities in England and Wales in 2003*

Pre Court
Reprimands and final warnings (replaced cautions in 1998)

Civil Orders
Child safety order for under-10s (family proceedings court)
Local child curfew (initially for under-10s and extended to 15 year olds in 2001)
Anti-social behaviour order
Acceptable behaviour contract
Sex offender order

Youth Court Orders
Discharge
Conditional discharge (largely made redundant by the introduction of referral orders)
Referral order (introduced in 1999)
Bind over of offender
Bind over of parent or guardian
Parenting order (introduced 1998)
Fine
Fine of parent or guardian
Compensation order
Reparation order (introduced 1998)
Attendance centre
Action plan order (introduced 1998)
Exclusion order – with or without electronic monitoring (introduced 2000)
Drug treatment and testing orders (introduced 1998)
Community rehabilitation (prior to 2001 known as 'probation' for those aged 16 or over)
Community punishment (prior to 2001 known as 'community service' for those aged 16 or over)
Combination order (community rehabilitation and community punishment)
Curfew order (with or without electronic monitoring)
Supervision order (for those aged 10–17)
Supervision order with conditions (e.g. intensive supervision and surveillance introduced 2001)
Detention and training order – a generic sentence combining detention in a young offender institution (if aged 15 or over) and the secure training order (for those aged 12–15) (introduced in 1998; in force 2000)
Detention under sections 90–92 of the Powers of Criminal Courts (Sentencing) Act 2000 such that for 'grave crimes', magistrates can commit 10–17 year olds for trial to the Crown Court (formerly Section 53 of the 1933 Children and Young Persons Act)

deprivation of liberty (including curfews, electronic monitoring and community supervision) should not be arbitrary or consist of any degrading treatment. It was incorporated into British law following the 1998 Human Rights Act and implemented in 2000.

Yet as Freeman (2002) notes, the implementation of these directives has often been half-hearted and piecemeal. For example, in the gamut of New Labour youth justice reforms, no directive has ever been given to the courts or youth offending teams that child welfare should be of 'primary consideration'. As we have noted the UN has, first in 1995 and again in 2002, advised the UK to raise its age of criminal responsibility but New Labour has stubbornly refused to do so (see Section 7.1). England and Wales, Northern Ireland and Scotland have the lowest ages of criminal responsibility in Europe (see Table 7.1). The UN Convention stipulates that children should be protected from custody whenever possible and when deprived of liberty should be treated with humanity. In England age reductions in the detention of young people coupled with increases in maximum sentence appear directly at odds with the UN Convention on the Rights of the Child. This states at Article 37 that imprisonment of a child 'shall be used only as a measure of last resort and for the shortest appropriate period of time'. Moreover as there are no separate young offender institutions for girls, they are held in adult prisons often sharing the same facilities as adults. Again this is in contravention of the UN Convention that states that 'every child deprived of liberty shall be separated from adults unless it is considered in the child's best interests not to do so' (Howard League, 1999). The Home Office response has been to claim that such arrangements are beneficial because older women 'tend to mother the youngsters' (cited by Toomey, 2002). The UN's 2002 observations on the UK's implementation of the Convention repeated the concerns over non-compliance: increasing numbers of children in custody (despite decreases in the crime rate); at earlier ages for lesser offences and for longer periods (not as a 'last resort'); custodial conditions that do not adequately protect children from violence, bullying and self harm (failure to accord with 'best interests') (Monaghan et al., 2003).

Article 6 of the Human Rights Act provides for the right to a fair trial with legal representation and a right to appeal. The introduction nationwide of referral orders with lay youth offender panels deliberating on 'programmes of behaviour' with no legal representation would appear to be in denial of such rights. Article 8 confers the right to respect for private and family life and protects families from arbitrary interference. Parenting orders, child curfews and anti-social behaviour orders, in particular, would again appear to be in contempt (Freeman, 2002). Curfews override parental discretion and also seem incompatible with Article 11 of the European Convention on Human Rights, which affirms the right to freedom of peaceful assembly, and Article 14, which bestows such a right to all irrespective of age (Walsh, 2002). Just as seriously, many of the principles of restorative justice that rely on informality, flexibility and discretion sit uneasily against legal requirements for due process and a fair and just trial (Ashworth, 2003). This is compounded by preventive early interventions directed at those calculated to be 'at risk'. Prevention seems to have no boundaries and makes the system insatiable (see Chapter 6). There are other grounds for considering that the rights of children and parents are being bypassed. New Labour claims to be supportive of parents and protective of children but its preventive rhetoric is backed by coercive powers. Civil orders are backed up by stringent criminal sanctions. By equating 'disorder' with crime, the reach of youth justice is broadened to take in those below the age of criminal responsibility and the non-criminal as well as the known offender.

Clearly it is possible to claim an adherence to the principle of rights whilst simultaneously pursuing policies that exacerbate structural inequalities and punitive institutional regimes. New Labour consistently claims it is acting in children's best interests whilst simultaneously dismantling many of the distinctions between youth and adult justice. The development of a positive rights agenda remains at best limited, at worst non-existent (Scraton and Haydon, 2002).

Comparative Youth Justice

7.5 There are relatively few rigorous comparative analyses of youth justice. In many respects this is not surprising. Comparative research is fraught with difficulties (Nelken, 1994). The classification and recording of crime differ, and different countries have developed different judicial systems for defining and dealing with young offenders. What is classified as penal custody in one country may not be in others though regimes may be similar. Not all countries collect the same data on the same age groups and populations or within the same time periods. Linguistic differences in how the terms 'minor', 'juvenile', child' and 'young person' are defined and operationalized further hinder any attempt to ensure a sound comparative base. Nevertheless comparative study is becoming more of a necessity, not simply to learn from the experiences of others or to appreciate cultural difference but to recognise the increasing impact of policy transfer, international treaties and economic globalization on national sovereignty (Pakes, 2004; Muncie, 2004).

Globalization

The globalization thesis suggests that shifts in political economy, particularly that of capital mobility, across advanced industrialized countries are progressively eroding the foundations of redistributive welfare states and severely constraining the range of strategic political strategies and policy options that individual states can pursue (Beck, 2000; Bauman, 1998). The concept of globalization suggests two interrelated transformations of interest to youth criminology. First that youth justice policies are converging worldwide (or at least across Anglophone countries). A combination of macro socio-economic developments, initiatives in international law and accelerations in processes of policy transfer and diffusion can be viewed as symptomatic of a rapid convergence and homogenization. The necessity of attracting international capital compels governments to adopt similar economic, social and criminal justice policies in part aided by geo-political mobility and subsequent policy transfer, diffusion and learning. Second this homogenization, it is contended, is underpinned by a fundamental shift in state/market relations. A loss (or at least a major reconfiguration) of the social is evidenced in the processes whereby neo-liberal conceptions of the market and international capital encourage the formulation of policies based less on principles of social inclusion and more on social inequality, deregulation, privatization, penal expansionism and welfare residualism. In effect, the thesis presages the decline of social democratic reformist politics and projects worldwide (Mishra, 1999).

This fundamental change in youth justice has been broadly characterized as placing less emphasis on the social contexts of crime and measures of state protection and more on prescriptions of individual/family/community responsibility and accountability (see Chapter 6.1). It suggests that a number of interrelated – sometimes contradictory – criminal justice processes have occurred to varying degrees across neo-conservative and social democratic neo-liberal states. These include the privatizing of the state sector and the commodifying of crime control; the widening of material inequalities between and within states thus creating new insecurities and fuelling demands for centralized authoritarian law and order strategies; the devolving of responsibility for government to individuals, families and communities (as captured in the notion of the 'the active citizen'); and the espousing of scientific realism and pragmatic 'what works' responses to crime and disorder in the hope that an image of an 'orderly environment' can be secured which in turn will help to attract 'nomadic capital'.

Numerous authors have remarked upon the impact that these processes have had in a growing homogenization of criminal justice across Western societies, driven in particular by the spread of punitive penal policies from the USA (Wacquant, 1999; Jones and Newburn, 2002). In youth justice these shifts are recognized in a general diminution of a welfare-based mode of governance in favour of various 'justice'-based responsibilization and managerial strategies (Muncie and Hughes, 2002). Six recurring and interrelated themes can be identified (diminution of welfare; adulteration; risk profiling and prevention, responsibilization; actuarialism; and penal expansion) which appear to have some global resonance (for the USA, see Krisberg and Austin, 1993; for Canada, see Smandych, 2001; for England and Wales, see Goldson, 2000a; for Australia, see Cunneen and White, 2002).

Collectively these processes suggest an acceleration of the governance of young people through crime and disorder (Simon, 1997). The continual reworking and expansion of youth justice systems; a never-ending stream of legislation apparently dominating all other government concerns; the political use of youth crime as a means to secure electoral gain; the excessive media fascination both as news and entertainment with all things 'criminal'; and the obsession with regulation whether through families, schools or training programmes all attest to the disorder attributed to young people as a central motif of governance. Such readings of contemporary youth justice lend weight to the primacy of ascribing the multivariate modes of youth governance to neo-liberal rationalities and technologies (Muncie, 2004). These broad trends, recognizable in many Western youth justice systems, lie at the heart of a neo-liberal version of the globalization thesis.

National Diversity

However, even a cursory look at some of the most basic statistical data highlights national diversity rather than global similarity.

The UK countries stand out as having some of the lowest ages of criminal responsibility in the European Union. Of the statistical data that are available, most are directed at recording head counts and rates of youth custody. The Council of Europe (1998), for example, has recorded that in 1996, with the exception of Ireland and Turkey, England and Scotland had the highest percentage of their prison population under the age of 21, with Scotland at 18.8 per cent; England 17.8 per cent; France 10 per cent; Italy 4.5 per cent; and Finland 3.6 per cent. There seems to be something of a correlation here: those countries with the lowest ages of responsibility also have more of their prisons filled with young people. Data derived from the International Centre for Prison Studies (2002) are again partial and range across some four years, but reveal the remarkable extent to which England and Wales lock up more young people than any of their European neighbours. Figures are not available for the same dates, but it is notable that in September 2002 there were over 3000 under 18s in prison in England and Wales compared to some 800 in France in May 2002. At the other extreme, in Norway, Denmark, Finland and Sweden in 2000 the numbers were all below 20 (Muncie, 2003a). Further breakdowns of penal populations from the United Nations Survey on the Operation of Criminal Justice Systems (2002) provide rates of juvenile imprisonment per 100,000 of population. These statistics show a rate of 38.40 per 100,000 in the USA and 18.26 per 100,000 in England and Wales compared to 0.11 in Denmark, 0.07 in Norway and 0.02 in Belgium (see Figure 7.1).

Figure 7.1   *Rate of convicted juveniles admitted to prison: selected countries 1994/1997/1998/2000*

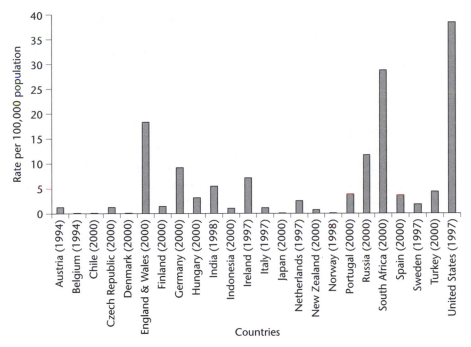

Source: United Nations Office for Drug Control and Crime Prevention (2002)

Any such basic comparative analysis cannot help but point up the atypicality and exceptional nature of such countries as the USA and England and Wales. Not only has youth justice in England and Wales become more complex, but there can be no doubt that it has also become more punitive. As we have noted (see Figure 1.1), the number sentenced to youth custody has almost doubled since 1993 and this has occurred despite the fact that the recorded youth crime rate has been declining, not rising over the period. Indeed, international research has consistently found that there is no correlation between crime rates and custody rates (Council of Europe, 2000). Locking up young people is driven by something other than crime. The use of custody appears politically, rather than pragmatically inspired: prison 'works' at a political and symbolic level even when it is a demonstrable failure.

This begs the question as to why some nation states, such as England and Wales, are so markedly different? How has the majority of Europe seemingly been able to develop more imaginative and less harmful responses to youth offending? The clues to address these questions are part ideological, part cultural and part political. Whilst it may be impossible to present a typology of European youth justice systems, five contrasting features might be developed (Muncie, 2004). These are the relative import of the welfare principle, tolerance, republicanism, restoration and repenalization, discussed below. All suggest widely divergent future directions for youth justice in Europe (and possibly elsewhere).

The Welfare Principle

Belgium and Scotland stand out as examples where the primacy of the welfare principle remains the fundamental rationale for youth justice. In Belgium special youth brigades exist in most police forces, often staffed by officers holding social work diplomas. All judicial interventions are legitimated through an educative, rather than punitive, responsibilizing discourse. Whilst in practice some welfare measures are backed by punitive and coercive powers, it remains impossible to impose legal penalties on those aged under 16 (Walgrave and Mehlbye, 1998).

Scotland abolished the juvenile court in 1968 and has been operating with a welfare tribunal for the majority of under 16 year old offenders for the past 30 years. It has not been without its critics, not least because of the lack of legal safeguards and the apparent tendency for the adult courts to deal with those aged 16 and over with undue severity. Scotland continues to have a high percentage of its prison population aged under 21 years. Nevertheless the hearings system ensures that child welfare considerations hold a pivotal position for younger offenders and provides a credible alternative to the punitive nature of youth justice pursued in many other jurisdictions (McAra and Young, 1997; Smith, 2000; Whyte, 2000 and see Section 7.1).

Tolerance

In Holland, youth prison populations were reduced in the 1970s by limiting penal capacity, emphasizing rehabilitation and supporting a culture of tolerance (Downes, 1988; Komen, 2002). HALT projects begun in Rotterdam in 1981 and various other social crime prevention initiatives appear to have had an impact on vandalism, truancy and shoplifting by replacing judicial intervention with reparation schemes and advice agencies to improve youth's 'survival skills'. In Finland the young offender prison population has been reduced by 90 per cent since 1960 without any associated rise in known offending. This was achieved by suspending imprisonment on the condition that a period of probation be successfully completed. Immediate 'unconditional' sentencing to custody is now a rarity (National Research Institute, 1998; Kuure, 2002). The Norwegian criminologist Nils Christie has argued that this dramatic shift has been made possible by a conscious effort on the part of successive Finnish governments to formulate a national identity closer to that of other Scandinavian states (Christie cited in Karstedt, 2001). It is reflected in the promotion of a 'good social development policy is the best criminal policy' ethos (NACRO, 2003b, p. 5).

In Trondheim, Norway, in 1994 a 5 year old girl was murdered by two 6 year old boys. The exceptionality of this case mirrored that of the murder of James Bulger by two 10 year old boys a year earlier in England. In the seven subsequent years public, media and political outcry remained unabated in the UK, continually dwelling on the 'leniency' of their sentence, their 'privileged' access to specialized rehabilitation and their eventual 'premature' release under a cloak of fearful anonymity. In Norway the murder was always dealt with as a tragedy in which the local community shared a collective shame and responsibility. The Norwegian boys were never named and returned to school within two weeks of the event (see Chapter 1.1).

Republicanism

In France in the 1980s the Mitterand government responded to a series of violent disturbances in Lyon and Marseilles, not by implementing more authoritarian measures, but by developing means of education and vocational opportunity and avenues for local political participation and incorporation. The Bonnemaison initiative involved the recruitment of older youth (*animateurs*) to act as paid youth workers with youngsters in the ghetto suburbs. These were connected with residents and local government officials to form crime prevention committees designed to address issues of citizenship and urban redevelopment as well as those of security. It is widely assumed that such strategies, based on local democratic representation rather than repression, were at least initially successful in achieving a greater integration particularly for children of North African origin (King, 1988, 1991; Pitts, 1995, 1997).

Since the 1980s however there is compelling evidence of a greater convergence of French and English crime prevention strategies made up of a patchwork of zero tolerance policing and of situational and social methods (Crawford, 2001; Roche, 2002). In particular the right-wing government of Alain Juppe from 1993–7 provided no new dynamic for a social crime prevention policy, instead it prioritized a zero tolerance, police-led approach. It is a policy that has been continued by the left-wing Jospin government. The socio-economic conditions that produce youth marginalization and estrangement are no longer given central political or academic attention (Bailleau, 1998). Nevertheless writers such as Pitts (2001) continue to maintain that a culture of French *republicanism*, driven by notions of social *solidarity* and *integration*, ensures a more lasting rejection of American punitiveness than seems to be possible or politically acceptable in countries such as England.

In Italy, judges have an additional power to grant a 'judicial pardon' which, together with a policy of '*liberta controllata*' (a form of police supervision), means that young people are incarcerated only for a few serious and violent offences (Ruxton, 1996; Dunkel, 1991). For Melossi (2000) this is driven by an Italian cultural tradition of soft paternal authoritarianism linked to low levels of penal repression. Comparing penal policy in Italy and the USA, Melossi is drawn in part to the relative impact of Catholic paternalism and radical Protestantism in informing each country's cultural repertoire. This 'cultural embeddedness' may not determine penal policy but it provides the parameters in which the purpose and meaning of punishment are understood.

Restoration, Reconciliation and Conflict Resolution

There has been a substantial growth in interest in restorative justice across Europe in the past 20 years. The Council of Europe has recommended to all jurisdictions that mediation should be generally available, that it should cover all stages of the criminal justice process and that it should be autonomous to formal means of processing. Weitekamp (2001) argues that its influence has been particularly strong in those jurisdictions with no prior provision for victim support. Austria is often cited as being at the forefront of such developments. Following its 1989 Juvenile Justice Act, 50 per cent of cases suitable for prosecution were resolved by out-of-court mediation and by informal negotiations between offender, victim and mediator to achieve reconciliation (Justice, 2000).

Repenalization

Notwithstanding these developments, reform in most countries of the global north seems to be progressively underpinned by versions of neo-liberal politics and strategies of responsibilization. In the past decade many European countries have reported a distinct hardening of attitudes and criminal justice responses to young offending, driven in part by the growth of right-wing politics throughout Europe. For example, there was a dramatic reversal in Dutch penal policy from the mid 1980s onwards. Once heralded as a beacon of tolerance and humanity, Holland embarked on a substantial prison building programme linked to a tendency to expand pre-trial detention and to deliver longer sentences on conviction (Pakes,

2000). The conditions governing the possibility of transferring juvenile cases to an adult court have also been relaxed. For Junger-Tas (2002) these shifts are driven by neo-liberal market reform, mass immigration, changes in the labour market and a related lowering of the tolerance level for crime and violence. Fear and insecurity fuel demand for a 'norm enforcing system' that is both retributive and interventionist.

Tham (2001) reports similar shifts in the 1990s across many European social democracies, including Italy, Germany and the Scandinavian countries. In Denmark penalties have been explicitly increased for crimes committed by young people, whilst in Sweden policies of rehabilitation have been replaced by 'just deserts' and an expansion of penal legislation. Whilst this has yet to produce any notable expansion in prison populations, Tham (2001) detects a break-up of social democratic welfare humanitarianism and the emergence of a new moralism of 'zero tolerance' associated with the disciplinary techniques of the free market. Social democratic governments are increasingly turning to law and order as a means of providing symbols of security and to enhance their own chances of electoral support. Such analysis clearly resonates with the expansion of interventionist and authoritarian policies ushered in by New Labour in England. But here they have been employed with a much greater punitive effect (Goldson, 2000a, 2002b; Muncie, 2002). Whilst many European countries may have added punitive elements to their legislation in the 1990s, none has moved to such a dramatic repenalization of young offending as that witnessed in the USA and in England and Wales. The philosophy of child protection continues to hold sway in most European countries.

These brief case studies provide various important clues about why there are marked variations in youth justice policy and youth custody, not only across Europe but worldwide. The answer seems to lie primarily with securing the political will to experiment with alternative forms of conflict resolution, coupled with a cultural sensibility that imprisoning young people is not only harmful but also self defeating. To understand more fully the atypical American and English cases, we need to look more closely at what drives their recurring punitive mentality: at the levels of public fascination with all things criminal, with a media that consistently mobilize around law and order, and with political parties of all persuasions that seem incapable, even in an era of 'what works', to rise above popular punitiveness.

Summary

Contemporary policies and practices of youth justice are complex and complicated. This chapter has provided a framework of welfare, justice, risk management and authoritarianism in order to disentangle some of the system's contradictory aims and outcomes, but it could just as easily be seen as the accretion of numerous levels of discourse (see Table 7.10).

Table 7.10 Youth justice discourses	
Welfare-paternalism	Youth as deprived. Care, guidance and supervision as the 'paramount consideration'. Focus on needs. Rationale to respond to individual needs.
Liberal justice	Youth as rational actors. The erosion of age considerations by focusing on the gravity of the offence and formulating a proportionate response. Rationale to ensure due process and fairness.
Neo-conservative remoralization	Youth as immoral. Risk assessments to act on the possibility of future crime and on the non-criminal as well as the criminal. Legitimated as crime prevention via early intervention. Rationale to compel social inclusion.
Neo-liberal responsibilizatoin	Youth as irresponsible. Certain individuals, families and communities have a responsibility to transform themselves, increase informal controls and reduce criminal opportunities. Rationale to devolve state responsibility for crime control.
Neo-conservative authoritarianism	Youth as dangerous. The resort to overtly punitive measures to respond to and channel perceptions of public punitiveness for short-term political expediency and electoral gain. Rationale to protect the public.
Managerialism	No particular or specific 'reading' of youth. The rewriting of the purpose of youth justice to achieve measurable and cost-effective outputs that are amenable to audited accounting. Internal system coherence. Rationale to achieve a pragmatic implementation of policy.
Human rights	Youth as vulnerable to adult power and under-protected. Challenging youth justice to recognize that children can and should participate directly in decisions affecting their lives. Rationale to alleviate harm, abuse, exploitation and social marginalization.

As youth justice has developed in response to increases in the influence of those professionals working in the system and also to changes in the broader political climate, it has evolved in a state of constant flux. No one of these approaches has achieved ascendancy. Instead, youth justice has expanded and oscillated to meet a variety of different demands and aspirations:

- The concept of 'need', associated with welfare models of intervention, attempts to address problems either of destitution and delinquency through moral reformation (the nineteenth-century version) or perceived psychosocial disorders through counselling and social work (the 1960s version). It also surfaces obliquely in the alleviating of 'risk conditions' through retraining, restoration and reparation (the current version).
- In contrast, justice-based models stress the importance of rights (the liberal version) or self responsibility (the conservative version). In both, intervention is aimed at tackling the offence, rather than its mitigating circumstances.

- Neither welfare (meeting needs) nor justice (responding to deeds) is ever present in pure form. The youth justice system contains elements of both, thus ensuring that a complex, ambiguous and confused *mélange* of policies and practices exists at any one time. Both also have unintended consequences: welfarism leading to over-regulation (particularly of girls); justice leading to the abandonment of 'meeting individual needs' (particularly as appropriated by the right in the 1990s). However, whilst the welfare versus justice debate may provide a useful starting point to understand the youth justice system, it restricts analysis to the internal machinations of the system itself. We can question how far either ideal can be realized when both remain absent from, or are peripheral to, social relations elsewhere.

- Youth justice has evolved as a complex object incorporating elements of welfare, restoration, punitive justice and liberal justice. Multi-agency work has drawn many aspects of public service into its remit. Wider goals of welfare or justice have become submerged in a more pragmatic and managerial assessment of 'what works'.

- Diversion has had a recurring presence in youth justice for at least the past 30 years. But it is a concept with multiple meanings. In the 1960s and 1970s diversion largely meant developing cautioning as an alternative to prosecution and developing community-based treatments as an alternative to custody. By the mid 1980s dramatic reductions in youth custody were achieved. By the mid 1990s multi-agency diversion schemes came to be lauded not only as effective but also, importantly, as more economical. Corporatist and managerial strategies emerged which were less interested in 'best interests' or 'protecting rights' and more concerned with achieving pragmatic and tangible outcomes. This entailed drawing educational, health and social services into the business of youth crime control. To this extent, many aspects of social policy have become thoroughly 'criminalized' (see Chapter 6.5). In the twenty-first century diversionary strategies have been eclipsed by those of pre-emptive early intervention.

- Progressive practice is forever prey to reactionary overhaul when 'get tough on crime' agendas achieve ascendancy. By the mid 1990s the climate for such practices as diversion became decidedly chilly with a reassertion that 'prison works' and that specialized detention facilities (secure training centres and boot camps) should be expanded. By 1994 it was noticeable that the numbers in youth custody had once more started to rise: a rise that has continued through to 2003 despite Labour's newfound commitment to crime prevention and restoration.

- Managerial discourses have come to occupy a central place in youth justice. New Labour's project of modernization rests on an evidence-led, 'what works' logic in which outputs are to be continually monitored, audited and evaluated. However, this pragmatism coexists with persistently recurring appeals to custody. A constellation of the managerial and the authoritarian is one of the defining fault-lines of twenty-first century youth justice.

- Comparative research points to some fundamental global shifts in youth justice, such as the emergence of justice-based principles in the 1970s, risk management in the 1990s and the increasing importance of international conventions and rules. However, it also reveals England and Wales to be an atypical European case.

- Youth justice reform is not simply driven by an increase in crime. It is also a reflection of sudden and volatile shifts in political mood in which short-term political gain and the need for the state to assert itself can override all other concerns. The study of youth justice ultimately tells us more about social order, the state and political decision making than it does about the nature of young offending and the most effective ways to respond to it.

Study Questions

1 What is the purpose of youth justice?
2 How far is New Labour's package of reforms driven by inclusionary or exclusionary motives?
3 Is there any place for welfare in youth justice systems?
4 Why do welfare, restorative and diversionary reforms always appear to be partial, ambiguous and politically contested?
5 How has a discourse of risk management impacted on the delivery of contemporary youth justice?

Further Resources

The Home Office (www.homeoffice.gov.uk) and the Youth Justice Board (www.youth–justice–board.gov.uk) websites will keep the reader up to date on statistical and official readings of contemporary issues in youth crime and youth justice in England and Wales. For Scotland and Northern Ireland see www.scotland.gov.uk and www.nics.gov.uk respectively. The articles in the journal *Youth Justice* (2001 onwards) will encourage a more critical and reflective understanding of these developments.

Goldson's edited collection *The New Youth Justice* (2000), Pitts' *The New Politics of Youth Crime* (2001) and Smith's *Youth Justice* (2003) provide some of the most incisive critiques of New Labour's reform programme. There are numerous reviews of post-war developments in juvenile and youth justice in England and Wales: Harris and Webb (1987), Gelsthorpe and Morris (1994), Pitts (1988) and Frost and Stein (1989) are all well worth consulting. Hudson's *Justice through Punishment* (1987) provides a radical critique of both welfare and justice strategies. The Audit Commission's report *Misspent Youth* (1996) is the clearest example of how managerial solutions can be embedded in youth justice. Muncie et al.'s edited collection *Youth Justice: Critical Readings* (2002) brings together many of the classic texts with contemporary commentaries.

There is now a burgeoning literature on restorative justice. Johnstone's (2002) *Restorative Justice: Ideas, Values, Debates* is a comprehensive introduction and the edited collection by McLaughlin et al. (2003) *Restorative Justice: Critical Issues* reproduces many of the formative texts. The edited collections by Morris and Maxwell (2001) and Bazemore and Walgrave (1999) offer commentaries on its application to youth justice across numerous jurisdictions.

However, there are few comparative texts which venture far beyond the descriptive. Winterdyk's edited collection (2002) is probably the most comprehensive in terms of world coverage whilst Walgrave and Mehlbye (1998) is a collection of contributions from nine European countries. An initial attempt to develop a comparative youth justice in the context of globalization has been made by Muncie (2004). www.un.org is the search site for United Nations publications. To initiate more general searches it is of interest in itself that the phrase 'juvenile justice' will open more doors than the term 'youth justice' currently favoured in England, or for that matter the term 'child criminal justice' employed by the United Nations.

Glossary of Key Terms

(A fuller exposition of most of these terms can be found in McLaughlin and Muncie's *The Sage Dictionary of Criminology*, published by Sage in 2001.)

Actuarialism – the classification of populations according to their assumed level of risk of offending/reoffending (Feeley and Simon, 1992).

Adolescence – a term originating in the eighteenth century to describe the special status of young people undergoing extended periods of educational training. Widely popularized in the twentieth century as a period of emotional upheaval and 'storm and stress' which affects all young people (G.S. Hall, 1905).

Adulteration – a dissolving of distinctions between juvenile (child/youth) justice and adult justice.

Aetiology – a term derived from medicine which suggests that the specific causes of crime and deviance can be identified, in much the same way as causes of disease and illness.

Anomie – a social state of 'normlessness' induced when aspirations are incapable of being met because of restricted opportunities (Durkheim, 1897; Merton, 1938).

'Anti-social' control – whereas legitimate social control sets limits to individual action in the interests of the collective, anti-social control mechanisms (such as the deregulation of the market and the curtailing of trade union activity in the 1980s) act to increase social and economic inequality (Carlen, 1996).

Bifurcation – a policy of separating out the treatment of serious offenders from that of minor offenders, with the end result that 'tough' offenders are dealt with by overtly punitive means (Bottoms, 1974).

Bricolage – the reordering and recontexualization of objects to communicate fresh meanings (Lévi-Strauss, 1966).

Carceral society – the notion that, as systems of surveillance increase, forms of control pioneered in the nineteenth-century prison are replicated throughout the social order (Foucault, 1977).

Carnival – the performance of transgression and excess as a part of everyday life and as resistance to conformist rationality (Presdee, 2000).

Causal analysis – the proposition that certain antecedent individual and social factors will invariably and unconditionally have a certain effect.

Child savers – a term used to describe nineteenth-century philanthropists and reformers who were ostensibly working to remove children from adult forms of criminal jurisdiction (Platt, 1969).

Classical Marxism – a theory of history which views social change and social relations (including crime) as the working out of fundamental conflicts between classes rooted within particular economic modes of production (Marx, 1859).

Corporate crime – offences committed by business corporations in the furtherance of their own profits.

Corporatism – forming one body with common aims and objectives from previously separate agencies and organizations. Used to describe teams of youth justice workers that emerged in the late 1980s (Pratt, 1989).

Correlation – a statistical technique pioneered in the early twentieth century for quantifying the degree of association between variables.

Counterculture – a term used to describe those youth subcultures which formulate counter-proposals of how the social order should be organized. Usually applied to the protest movements emanating from middle-class, student and bohemian sources in the 1960s (Yinger, 1960).

Crime – conventionally described as a violation of the criminal law, but contested (by some) to include all social injuries and social harms (Michael and Adler, 1933; Hulsman, 1986).

Criminalization – the application of the criminal label to particular 'deviant' behaviours or groups.

Critical criminology – a school of criminology that emerged in the 1970s which examines the deficiencies, absences and closures in existing theories and modes of understanding the concept of 'crime' (Taylor et al., 1975).

Cultural criminology – the study of everyday existences, life histories, music, dance and performances to discover how and why certain cultural forms become criminalized (Ferrell and Sanders, 1995).

Dangerous classes – a nineteenth-century term applied with fear and disgust to those members of the working classes who seemed to pose a threat to order.

Defusion/diffusion – the weakening of subcultural opposition through commercial appropriation (Clarke, 1976).

Delinquency – a term, loosely used, to refer to any kind of youthful misbehaviour.

Depravation – a term used to describe the young as morally corrupt and wicked.

Deprivation – a term used to describe the young as lacking in moral guidance.

Determinism – the proposition that people have no control over their actions and that human action is determined by external forces.

Deviance – a social rather than legal concept to delineate rule-breaking behaviour.

Deviancy amplification – the proposition that many of the means designed to control deviant behaviour have the obverse effect of increasing it (Wilkins, 1964).

Difference – a concept used to capture a sense of cultural diversity and variability; avoiding the moral connotations of describing any behaviour as deviant, but retaining a tendency to set boundaries between patterns of behaviour in which certain groups can readily be identified as 'differing' from some presumed norm.

Differential association – the principle that criminal behaviour is learnt when individuals are exposed, socially and culturally, to pro-criminal rather than anti-criminal values, patterns and association (Sutherland and Cressey, 1970).

Discourse – personal, media, political or academic 'talk' and 'writing' about a subject in which knowledges are organized, carried and reproduced in particular ways and through particular institutional practices (Clarke and Cochrane, 1998).

Dispersal of discipline – the proposition that means of control pioneered in the prison are now to be encountered in more apparently benign community settings.

Diversion – strategies developed in the youth justice system to prevent young people from committing crime or to ensure that they avoid formal court action and custody if they are arrested and prosecuted.

Doli incapax – a principle dating back to the fourteenth century which assumes that under a certain age children are incapable of knowing right from wrong and therefore cannot be held criminally responsible for their actions.

Drift – the proposition that juvenile delinquents are not committed to anti-social behaviour but oscillate between conformity and delinquency (Matza, 1964).

Edgework – intense moments of pleasure which accompany the danger and skill of risk taking and breaking boundaries (Lyng, 1990).

Essentialism – the belief that social behaviour is determined and driven by some underlying process or 'essence' as in *genetic determinism* or *positivism* or *classical Marxism.*

Ethnographic research – research which is directed towards in-depth and detailed understandings of the lives and personal meanings of subjects.

Eugenics – a doctrine promoting rejuvenation of the physical stock and moral character of the population by demanding that social undesirables should be isolated or sterilized.

Extroversion – the proposition that an unreserved or impulsive personality correlates with a higher propensity for criminal behaviour (Eysenck, 1964).

Folk devil – an individual or group who, through stereotyping and scapegoating, comes to be represented as the embodiment of social problems (Cohen, 1973a).

Gang – variously defined, but usually connoting a group of people who persist over time, have rules of membership and an identifiable leadership.

Genetic determinism – a theory which proposes that certain inherited traits predispose certain people towards criminality. Criminals are born (Lombroso, 1876).

Globalization – a contested term but one that draws attention to an increasing homogeneity and convergence of social/criminal justice knowledge and policy and driven in the main by multinational, neo-liberal economics and technologies (Bauman 1998; Beck, 2000).

Governmentality – the proposition that social order is achieved not through a 'disciplinary society' or by state coercion, but through dynamic relations of power and knowledge to be found in a multitude of institutions (Foucault, 1977).

Hegemonic masculinity – the configuration of gender practice which embodies and guarantees the dominant position of men and the subordination of women (Connell, 1995).

Hegemony – the cultural dynamic by which a group claims and sustains a leading position in social life (Gramsci, 1971).

Hidden crime – those crimes that are not recorded by the official criminal statistics.

Homology – the selection of objects through which style is generated in order to ensure that they 'fit' and form some coherent ensemble (Lévi-Strauss, 1966).

Idealist history – a view of historical change which emphasizes the place of ideas and good intentions and which equates progress with benevolent and humanitarian reform.

Imaginary solutions – the means by which youth subcultures overcome the structural problems of unemployment and disadvantage by expropriating and fetishizing consumption and style.

Interactionism – a school of social science which focuses on the shared meanings that members of a society develop.

Intermediate treatment – a diverse range of community programmes in England and Wales designed to keep young offenders out of court or out of custody. Originating in the early 1970s they were first directed at those considered 'at risk' of offending. By the mid 1980s, 'intensive' forms were developed as alternatives to custody.

Justice model – the proposition that the principles of proportionality, due process, determinant sentencing and non-discretional decision making should be the central elements of systems of youth justice (von Hirsch, 1976).

Labelling – a sociological approach to crime and deviancy which focuses on the processes whereby social reaction (stereotyping, scapegoating) causes (rather than curtails) further offending (Becker, 1963).

Left realism – a school of criminology that emerged in Britain in the 1980s which claimed to take people's fear of crime seriously. In contrast to critical criminology, it advocates social democratic means of crime control (Lea and Young, 1984).

Managerialism – a cultural formation and set of ideologies and practices which suggest that the organization of public services is best served by managers, rather than professionals or bureaucrats. It assumes that a pragmatic and performance-centred management will prove an economic, effective and efficient means to solve a wide range of social and economic problems (Clarke et al., 1994).

Marginalization – the proposition that changes in the labour market have acted to push some young people on to the periphery of the social order by preventing their transition to social and economic independence.

Maternal deprivation – a theory that proposes that juvenile crime is caused by the separation of children from their mothers (Bowlby, 1946).

Modernity – a period from industrialization to the 1970s in which it was assumed that social problems could be addressed through positivist science and rationality.

Moral panic – a concept that implies that the social reaction to certain phenomena is out of proportion to the scale of the problem, but performs a vital function for the state in distracting attention from more deep-seated problems and in acting as a means by which moral boundaries can be reactivated (Young, 1971; Cohen, 1973a).

Net widening – the process whereby attempts to prevent crime inadvertently draw more subjects into the criminal justice system (Austin and Krisberg, 1981).

Official statistics – statistical data compiled by the police and the courts and routinely published by the Home Office as indices of the extent of crime.

Persistent offending – the recurring notion that a small group of offenders make up a disproportionate part of the 'crime problem'.

Positivism – a theory that emerged in the early nineteenth century which argues that social relations can be studied scientifically using methods derived from the natural sciences. In criminology it straddles biological, psychological and sociological disciplines in an attempt to isolate key causes of crime.

Postmodernism – an intellectual movement which challenges faith in science as a foundational principle for the structuring of society and is sceptical of any grand theory's attempt to discover the 'truth'. In contrast to modernism it is prepared to accept doubt, uncertainty and relativism.

Protracted adolescence – the notion that as periods of education and training are extended (as in the 1990s), then a state of adolescence will persist to at least the mid-twenties.

Punishment in the community – a strategy developed in the 1980s, that community-based sentences would only be effective (popularly and politically) if they became more punitive.

Racialization – a process whereby specific groups of people are construed as a 'type' by referring to a limited number of their physical or cultural attributes.

Rational choice – in contrast to positivism, the proposition that has come to some prominence since the 1980s that offenders make rational decisions about which crimes to commit and where, according to the available opportunities (Cornish and Clarke, 1986).

Recording of crime – the selective act of the police making a record that a crime has occurred.

Reformation – the reform of offenders through punishment in the hope they will come to realize their own moral shortcomings.

Rehabilitation – the reform of offenders through various treatment methods whereby they can be retrained and re-educated.

Relative deprivation – a concept, latterly associated with left realism, by which it is argued that it is not absolute deprivation or poverty that causes crime, but perceptions of deprivation or injustice (Lea and Young, 1984).

Reparation – a strategy employed in the criminal justice system whereby an offender pays compensation to, or acknowledges their wrongdoing in the presence of, the victim.

Reporting of crime – the selective act of the public informing the police that a crime has been committed.

Representation – the process whereby knowledge and understanding of social phenomena are constructed by how they are (re)presented by public bodies and institutions (media, governments, academics).

Rescue – part of the rhetoric of nineteenth-century juvenile justice: the intention of removing children from the 'vices' of the street.

Resistance – the means by which subordinate cultures and youth subcultures are able to 'win space' from a hegemonic dominant culture (Clarke et al., 1976).

Responsibilization – strategies for holding offenders responsible for their own actions and for encouraging communities to be more active in crime control (Garland, 1996).

Restoration – a philosophy and practice of bringing offenders, victims and communities together in order to repair harms, reconcile conflicts and heal rifts (Zehr and Mika, 1998).

Retribution – the philosophy that vengeance should be sought and offenders punished for acts they have committed in the past.

Revisionist history – in contrast to *idealist history*, revisionist history analyses historical change not as progress but as evidence of a strengthening of state power through which 'problem populations' can be identified and criminalized.

Right realism – a school of criminology that emerged in the 1970s which was less interested in discovering the causes of crime and more in developing effective means for its control (Wilson, 1975).

Risk society – the proposition that in the late twentieth century the certainties of industrialism and science have collapsed and been replaced by a series of local, global and individualized conditions of risk (Beck, 1992).

Self reports – a means of assessing the extent of crime by asking people directly whether they are perpetrators.

Semiology – a branch of linguistics concerned with the 'reading' of signs and symbols.

Situational crime prevention – a policy of preventing crime by making targets harder to hit, such as improving household security, redesigning housing estates and increasing means of surveillance.

Social constructionism – a perspective that begins with exploring assumptions associated with the labelling of things and emphasizes the importance of social expectations in the analysis of taken-for-granted and apparently natural social processes (Clarke and Cochrane, 1998).

Social control – an ill-defined term which has been used to describe all means through which conformity might be achieved – from infant socialization to incarceration (Cohen, 1985).

Social crime – the proposition that some crime is committed simply for self and family survival.

Social crime prevention – a policy of preventing crime by targeting anti-social behaviour and those considered 'at risk' as well as known offenders. Includes programmes to open up educational opportunities, improve parenting skills and provide wider access to sports/leisure facilities.

Social disorganization – a concept that implies that certain communities have no stable values and lack effective means of social control (Shaw and McKay, 1942).

Social exclusion – a broad concept that refers not simply to the way in which the poor are marginalized from the economic mainstream, but which emphasizes isolation from relationships and sources of identity.

Somatotyping – a means of measuring variations in body types according to which certain physiological features have been claimed to be causative of delinquency (Sheldon, 1949).

State control – a radical perspective on social control which contends that the primary source of control lies within the state and that all forms of deviancy control have become increasingly centralized (Cohen, 1985).

Status frustration – the end result of judging working-class children by middle-class standards. Working-class youth who find themselves at the bottom of the status hierarchy find a 'solution' to their lack of formal status by achieving status through delinquent means (Cohen, A., 1955).

Status offence – violation of formal or informal rules which are applied only to certain sections of society. The focus is less on the offence itself and more on who commits it. In the USA such status offences as being incorrigible, truant or sexually precocious apply only to children.

Strain – a social structural condition whereby certain pressures are exerted on people to engage in non-conformist behaviour, for example because of disjunctures between culturally defined goals and available means to achieve such goals (Merton, 1938).

Style – the means by which subcultures are able to express their 'resistance' (Clarke, 1976).

Subculture – first used by anthropologists, Cohen (1955) applied it to the study of delinquency to connote a set of values that differed from the mainstream or dominant culture. Subsequently used by Clarke et al. (1976) to explore correspondences and divergencies between youth and their class-based 'parent' cultures.

Transcarceration – a reworking of Foucault and Cohen's radical perspective on social control, to stress the fluidity of the correspondences between, and the cross-institutional dynamics of, the help-control complex, whereby delinquents are constantly shifted between agencies of correction, probation, welfare and mental health (Lowman et al., 1987).

Transgression – a preferred term to 'deviance' to signify elements of boundary crossing and transcendence in rule breaking.

Underclass – first used in America to describe the economically marginalized. Subsequently reworked to describe those who are dependent on state benefits, either as morally bankrupt, work-shy scroungers and thus 'undeserving' (Murray, 1990) or as the victims of recession, deprivation and political marginalization (Mann, 1991).

Victim surveys – a means of measuring the extent of crime by asking the public to recall any crimes committed against them which may not have been recorded in the official statistics.

Welfare model – the proposition that the principles of meeting needs, wide judicial discretion, informalism and treatment should be the central elements of systems of youth justice (Cullen and Gilbert, 1982).

Youth – an ill-defined and variable period of the life-span between infancy and adulthood.

Youth custody – a variety of institutions designed for the reform and/or punishment of children, juveniles and young people, ranging from the reformatories, industrial schools and Parkhurst prison of the nineteenth century; the borstals, approved schools, community homes, detention centres, youth custody centres, secure units and boot camps of the twentieth century; to the young offender institutions and secure training centres of the twenty-first century.

Zero tolerance – an intensive community policing strategy pioneered in New York in the mid 1990s whereby minor offences and incivilities are targeted, on the assumption that more serious offending will be curtailed as a result (Dennis, 1997).

References

Abrams, M. (1959) *The Teenage Consumer*, London, Press Exchange.

ADSS (Association of Directors of Social Services) (1985) *Children Still in Trouble*, London, ADSS.

Agnew, R. (1992) 'Foundation for a general strain theory of crime and delinquency', *Criminology*, vol. 30, no. 1, pp. 47–87.

Ahluwalia, S. (1991) 'Currents in British feminist thought: the study of male violence', *Critical Criminologist*, vol. 3, no. 1, pp. 5–6, 12–14.

Aichhorn, A. (1925) *Wayward Youth*, reprinted 1955, New York, Meridian.

Ainsworth, P. (2000) *Psychology and Crime: Myths and Reality*, London, Longman.

Alcock, P. and Harris, P. (1982) *Welfare, Law and Order*, London, Macmillan.

Allen, R. (1990) 'Punishing the parents', *Youth and Policy*, no. 31, pp. 17–20.

Allen, R. (1991) 'Out of jail: the reduction in the use of penal custody for male juveniles 1981–88', *Howard Journal*, vol. 30, no. 1, pp. 30–52.

Anderson, D. (ed.) (1992) *The Loss of Virtue: Moral Confusion and Social Disorder in Britain and America*, London, Social Affairs Unit.

Anderson, S., Kinsey, R., Loader, I. and Smith, C. (1994) *Cautionary Tales: Young People, Crime and Policing in Edinburgh*, Aldershot, Avebury.

Ariès, P. (1962) *Centuries of Childhood*, London, Cape.

Ashworth, A. (2003) 'Is restorative justice the way forward for criminal justice?', in McLaughlin et al. (eds) *Restorative Justice: Critical Issues*, London, Sage.

Ashworth, A., Gardner, J., Morgan, R., Smith, A., Van Hirsch, A. and Warik, M. (1998) 'Neighbouring on the oppressive: the government's Anti-Social Behaviour Order proposals', *Criminal Justice*, vol. 16, no. 1, pp. 7–14.

Asquith, S. (1983) 'Justice, retribution and children', in Morris, A. and Giller, M. (eds) *Providing Criminal Justice for Children*, London, Edward Arnold.

Asquith, S. (1996a) *Juvenile Justice and Juvenile Delinquency in Central and Eastern Europe*, University of Glasgow, Centre for the Child and Society, http://eurochild.gla.ac.uk.

Asquith, S. (ed.) (1996b) *Children and Young People in Conflict with the Law*, London, Jessica Langley.

Association of County Councils, Association of Metropolitan Authorities, Association of Directors of Social Service, National Association for the Care and Resettlement of Offenders and Association of Chief Officers of Probation (1996) *National Protocol for Youth Justice Services*, London, Association of Metropolitan Authorities.

Audit Commission (1996) *Misspent Youth: Young People and Crime*, London, Audit Commission.

Audit Commission (1998) *Misspent Youth '98: The Challenge for Youth Justice*, London, Audit Commission.

Audit Commission (1999) *Safety in Numbers: Promoting Community Safety*, London, Audit Commission.

Audit Scotland (2002) *Dealing with Offending by Young People*, Edinburgh, Auditor General.

Auletta, K. (1982) *The Underclass*, New York, Random House.

Aust, R., Sharp, C. and Goulden, C. (2002) *Prevalence of Drug Use: Key Findings from the 2001/2002 British Crime Survey*, Findings, no. 182, London, Home Office.

Austin, J. and Krisberg, B. (1981) 'Wider, stronger and different nets: the dialectics of criminal justice reform', *Journal of Research in Crime and Delinquency*, vol. 18, no. 1, pp. 165–96.

Aye Maung, N. (1995) *Young People, Victimization and the Police*, Home Office Research Study no. 140, London, HMSO.

Back, L. (1996) *New Ethnicities and Urban Culture*, London, UCL Press.

Bagguley, P. and Mann, K. (1992) 'Idle, thieving bastards? Scholarly representations of the underclass', *Work, Employment and Society*, vol. 6, no. 1, pp. 113–26.

Bailey, S., Thornton, L. and Weaver, A. (1994) 'The first 100 admissions to an adolescent secure unit', *Journal of Adolescence*, vol. 17, pp. 207–20.

Bailey, V. (1987) *Delinquency and Citizenship: Reclaiming the Young Offender 1914–1948*, Oxford, Clarendon.

Bailleau, F. (1998) 'A crisis of youth or of juridicial response?', in Ruggiero, V., South, N. and Taylor, I. (eds) *The New European Criminology*, London, Routledge.

Ball, R. and Curry, D. (1995) 'The logic of definition in criminology: purposes and methods for defining "gangs"', *Criminology*, vol. 33, no. 2, pp. 225–45.

Bandalli, S. (1998) 'Abolition of the presumption of *Doli Incapax* and the criminalisation of children', *The Howard Journal*, vol. 37, no. 2, pp. 114–23.

Bandalli, S. (2000) 'Children, responsibility and the New Youth Justice', in Goldson, B. (ed.) *The New Youth Justice*, Lyme Regis, Russell House.

Bandura, A. (1972) 'The stormy decade: fact or fiction?', in Rogers, D. (ed.) *Issues in Adolescent Psychology*, 2nd edn, New York, Appleton.

Banks, M., Bates, I., Breakwell, G., Bynner, J., Emler, N., Jamieson, L. and Roberts, K. (1992) *Careers and Identities*, Buckingham, Open University Press.

Barry, A., Osborne, T. and Rose, N. (eds) (1996) *Foucault and Political Reason*, London, UCL Press.

Batchelor, S. (2001) 'The myth of girl gangs', *Criminal Justice Matters*, no. 43, pp. 26–7.

Bauman, Z. (1993) *Postmodern Ethics*, Oxford, Blackwell.

Bauman, Z. (1997) *Postmodernity and its Discontents*, Oxford, Blackwell.

Bauman, Z. (1998) *Globalization: The Human Consequences*, Cambridge, Policy.

Bazemore, G. and Walgrave, L. (eds) (1999) *Restorative Juvenile Justice: Repairing the Harm of Youth Crime*, Monsey, NY, Criminal Justice Press.

Beck, U. (1992) *Risk Society: Towards a New Modernity*, London, Sage.

Beck, U. (2000) *What is Globalization?*, Cambridge, Polity.

Becker, H. (1963) *Outsiders*, New York, Free Press.

Becker, H. (1967) 'Whose side are we on?', *Social Problems*, vol. 14, no. 3, pp. 239–47.

Beinart, S., Anderson, B., Lee, S. and Utting, D. (2002) *Youth at Risk? A National Survey of Risk Factors, Protective Factors and Problem Behaviour among Young People in England, Scotland and Wales*, London, Communities That Care/Joseph Rowntree Foundation.

Beirne, P. and Messerschmidt, J. (1991) *Criminology*, Fort Worth, TX, Harcourt Brace Jovanovich.

Bell, V. (1993) 'Governing childhood: neo-liberalism and the law', *Economy and Society*, vol. 22, no. 3, pp. 390–403.

Belsey, A. (1986) 'The New Right, social order and civil liberties', in Levitas, R. (ed.) *The Ideology of the New Right*, Cambridge, Polity.

Belson, W.A. (1975) *Juvenile Theft: The Causal Factors*, London, Harper & Row.

Bennett, A. (1999) 'Subcultures or neo-tribes? Rethinking the relationship between youth, style and musical taste', *Sociology*, vol. 33, no. 3, pp. 599–617.

Bennett, A. (2000) *Popular Music and Youth Culture: Music, Identity and Place*, New York, St Martins Press.

Bennett, T., Holloway, K. and Williams, T. (2001) *Drug Use and Offending: Summary Results of the First Year of the New-ADAM Research Programme*, Home Office Research Study no. 236, London, Home Office.

Bircham, E. and Charlton, J. (eds) (2001) *Anti-capitalism: A Guide to the Movement*, London, Bookmarks.

Blagg, H. (1987) 'Social crime prevention and policies for youth in England', *Research Bulletin*, no. 24, Home Office Research and Planning Unit, London, HMSO, pp. 16–19.

Blagg, H. (1997) 'A just measure of shame?: Aboriginal youth and conferencing in Australia', *British Journal of Criminology*, vol. 37, no. 4, pp. 481–501.

Blanch, M. (1979) 'Imperialism, nationalism, and organised youth', in Clarke, J., Critcher, C. and Johnson, R. (eds) *Working Class Culture*, London, Hutchinson.

Bland, N. and Read, T. (2000) *Policing Anti-social Behaviour*, Police Research Series no. 123, London, Home Office.

Bonger, W. (1916) *Criminality and Economic Conditions*, Chicago, Little, Brown.

Boswell, G. (1995) *Violent Victims*, London, Prince's Trust.

Bottomley, K. and Pease, K. (1986) *Crime and Punishment: Interpreting the Data*, Milton Keynes, Open University Press.

Bottoms, A. (1974) 'On the decriminalization of the juvenile court', in Hood, R. (ed.) *Crime, Criminology and Public Policy*, London, Heinemann.

Bottoms, A. (1977) 'Reflections on the renaissance of dangerousness', *Howard Journal*, vol. 16, no. 2, pp. 70–96.

Bottoms, A. (1983) 'Neglected features of contemporary penal systems', in Garland, D. and Young, P. (eds) *The Power to Punish: Contemporary Penality and Social Analysis*, Aldershot, Gower.

Bottoms, A. (1995) *Intensive Community Supervision for Young Offenders*, Cambridge, Institute of Criminology.

Bottoms, A. and Wiles, P. (1992) 'Explanations of crime and place', in Evans, D.J., Fyle, N.R. and Herbert, D.T. (eds) *Crime, Policing and Place*, London, Routledge.

Bowlby, J. (1946) *Forty-four Juvenile Thieves*, London, Baillière, Tindall and Cox.

Bowling, B. (1999) *Violent Racism: Victimisation, Policing and Social Context*, revised edn, Oxford, Oxford University Press.

Bowling, B. and Phillips, C. (2002) *Racism, Crime and Justice*, London, Longman.

Box, S. (1981) *Deviance, Reality and Society*, 2nd edn, London, Holt, Rinehart & Winston.

Box, S. (1983) *Power, Crime and Mystification*, London, Tavistock.

Box, S. (1987) *Recession, Crime and Punishment*, London, Macmillan.

Braithwaite, J. (1989) *Crime, Shame and Reintegration*, Cambridge, Cambridge University Press.

Braithwaite, J. (2003) 'Restorative justice and a better future', in McLaughlin, E. et al. (eds) *Restorative Justice: Critical Issues*, London, Sage.

Brake, M. (1980) *The Sociology of Youth and Youth Subcultures*, London, Routledge.

Brake, M. (1990) 'Changing leisure and cultural patterns among British youth', in Chisholm, L., Büchner, P., Kruger, H-H. and Brown, P. (eds) *Childhood, Youth and Social Change*, London, Falmer.

Brake, M. and Hale, C. (1992) *Public Order and Private Lives*, London, Routledge.

Brantingham, P.J. and Brantingham, P.L. (1984) *Patterns of Crime*, New York, Macmillan.

Bray, R.A. (1911) *Boy Labour and Apprenticeship*, London, Constable.

Bridges, L. (2003) 'New Labour and new authoritarianism in criminal justice', www.irr.org.uk/2003/January.

Bright, J. (1991) 'Crime prevention: the British experience', in Stenson, K. and Cowell, D. (eds) *The Politics of Crime Control*, London, Sage.

Brinkley, I. (1997) 'Underworked and underpaid', *Soundings*, no. 6, pp. 161–71.

Brown, B. (1986) 'Women and crime: the dark figures of criminology', *Economy and Society*, vol. 15, no. 3, pp. 355–402.

Brown, D. and Hogg, R. (1992) 'Law and order politics – left realism and radical criminology: a view from down under', in Matthews, R. and Young, J. (eds) *Issues in Realist Criminology*, London, Sage.

Brown, I. and Hullin, R. (1992) 'A study of sentencing in the Leeds Magistrates' Courts. The treatment of ethnic minority and white offenders', *British Journal of Criminology*, vol. 32, no. 1, pp. 41–53.

Brown, S. (1998) *Understanding Youth and Crime: Listening to Youth?*, Buckingham, Open University Press.

Brown, S. (2003) *Crime and Law in Media Culture*, Buckingham, Open University Press.

Bull, R. and Green, J. (1980) 'The relationship between physical appearance and criminality', *Medicine, Science and the Law*, vol. 20, no. 2, pp. 79–83.

Bullock, K. and Tilley, N. (2002) *Shootings, Gangs and Violent Incidents in Manchester*, Crime Reduction Series Paper 13, London, Home Office.

Burbach, R., Nunez, O. and Kagarlistsky, B. (1997) *Globalization and its Discontents*, London, Pluto.

Burchell, G., Gordon, C. and Miller, P. (eds) (1991) *The Foucault Effect: Studies in Governmentality*, Hemel Hempstead, Harvester.

Burchill, J. and Parsons, T. (1978) *The Boy Looked at Johnny*, London, Pluto.

Burgess, P.K. (1972) 'Eysenck's theory of criminality: a new approach', *British Journal of Criminology*, vol. 12, no. 1, pp. 74–82.

Burke, T. (1996) *Policing and the Public: Findings from the 1994 British Crime Survey*, Research Findings, no. 28, London, Home Office.

Burney, E. (1985) *Sentencing Young People*, Aldershot, Gower.

Burney, E. (2002) 'Talking tough, acting coy: what happened to the Anti-Social Behaviour Order?', *Howard Journal*, vol. 41, no. 5, pp. 469–84.

Burt, C. (1925) *The Young Delinquent*, London, University of London Press.

Cain, M. (1985) 'Beyond informal justice', *Contemporary Crises*, vol. 9, pp. 335–73.

Cain, M. (ed.) (1989) *Growing Up Good*, London, Sage.

Cain, M. (1990) 'Towards transgression: new directions in feminist criminology', *International Journal of the Sociology of Law*, vol. 18, no. 1, pp. 1–18.

Callaghan, G. (1992) 'Locality and localism: the spatial orientation of young adults in Sunderland', *Youth and Policy*, no. 39, pp. 23–33.

Campbell, A. (1981) *Girl Delinquents*, Oxford, Blackwell.

Campbell, A. (1984) *The Girls in the Gang*, Oxford, Blackwell.

Campbell, A. and Muncer, S. (1989) 'Them and us: a comparison of the cultural context of American gangs and British subcultures', *Deviant Behaviour*, vol. 10, pp. 271–88.

Campbell, B. (1993) *Goliath: Britain's Dangerous Places*, London, Methuen.

Campbell, S. (2002) *A Review of Anti-social Behaviour Orders*, Home Office Research Study no. 236, London, Home Office.

Carlen, P. (1992) 'Criminal women and criminal justice: the limits to and potential of feminist and left realist perspectives', in Matthews, R. and Young, J. (eds) *Issues in Realist Criminology*, London, Sage.

Carlen, P. (1996) *Jigsaw: A Political Criminology of Youth Homelessness*, Buckingham, Open University Press.

Carpenter, M. (1853) *Juvenile Delinquents, Their Condition and Treatment*, London, Cash.

Carrington, B. and Wilson, B. (2002) 'Global club cultures: cultural flows and late modern dance music culture', in Cieslik, M. and Pollock, G. (eds) *Young People in Risk Society*, Aldershot, Ashgate.

Carrington, K. and Hogg, R. (eds) (2002) *Critical Criminology: Issues, Debates, Challenges*, Cullompton, Willan.

Casburn, M. (1979) *Girls Will be Girls*, London, WRRCP.

Cashmore, E. (1979) *Rastaman: The Rastafarian Movement in England*, London, Allen & Unwin.

Cashmore, E. (1997) *The Black Culture Industry*, London, Routledge.

Cashmore, E. and Troyna, B. (eds) (1982) *Black Youth in Crisis*, London, Allen & Unwin.

Caspi, A., McClay, J., Moffit, T., Mill, J., Martin, J., Craig, I., Taylor, A. and Poulton, R. (2002) 'Role of genotype in the cycle of violence in maltreated children', *Science*, vol. 297, no. 5582, pp. 851–4.

Cavadino, P. (1997) 'The Crime (Sentences) Bill and young offenders', *Youth Justice Newsletter*, no. 4, Peterborough, Vision Quest, pp. 1–6.

Cawson, P. and Martell, M. (1979) *Children Referred to Closed Units*, DHSS Research Report, no. 5, London, DHSS.

CCCS (Centre for Contemporary Cultural Studies) (1980) *Fads and Fashions*, London, Social Science Research Council/Sports Council.

Chambliss, W. (1975) 'Towards a political economy of crime', *Theory and Society*, vol. 2, pp. 149–70.

Chesney-Lind, M., Skelden, R. and Joe, K. (1996) 'Girls, delinquency and gang membership' in Huff, C.R. (ed.) *Gangs in America*, 2nd edn, London, Sage.

Chibnall, S. (1977) *Law and Order News*, London, Tavistock.

Children's Legal Centre (CLC) (1982) *Locked Up in Care*, London, CLC.

Children's Rights Alliance (2002) *Rethinking Child Imprisonment*, London, Children's Rights Alliance.

Children's Society (1989) *Penal Custody for Juveniles – the Line of Least Resistance*, London, Children's Society.

Children's Society (1993) *A False Sense of Security*, London, Children's Society.

Christiansen, K.O. (1977) 'A review of studies of criminality among twins', in Mednick, S. and Christiansen, K.O. (eds) *Biosocial Bases of Criminal Behaviour*, New York, Gardner.

Christie, N. (1977) 'Conflicts as property', *British Journal of Criminology*, vol. 17, no. 1 pp. 1–15.

Christie, N. (2000) *Crime Control as Industry*, 3rd edn, London, Routledge.

Chunn, D. and Gavigan, S. (1988) 'Social control: analytical tool or analytical quagmire', *Contemporary Crises*, vol. 12, no. 2, pp. 107–24.

Ciba Foundation Symposium (1996) *Genetics of Criminal and Antisocial Behaviour*, Chichester, Wiley.

Clarke, G. (1990) 'Defending ski jumpers: a critique of theories of youth subcultures', in Frith, S. and Goodwin, A. (eds) (1990) *On Record*, London, Routledge.

Clarke, J. (1975) *The Three R's – Repression, Rescue and Rehabilitation*, Birmingham, Centre for Contemporary Cultural Studies, University of Birmingham.

Clarke, J. (1976) 'Style', in Hall, S. and Jefferson, T. (eds) *Resistance through Rituals*, London, Hutchinson.

Clarke, J. (1984) 'Young, gifted and highly dangerous: media images of youth'. Unpublished paper, Milton Keynes, Faculty of Social Sciences, The Open University.

Clarke, J. (1985a) 'Managing the delinquent: the Children's Branch of the Home Office 1913–30', in Langan, M. and Schwarz, B. (eds) *Crises in the British State 1880–1930*, London, Hutchinson.

Clarke, J. (1985b) 'Whose justice? The politics of juvenile control', *International Journal of the Sociology of Law*, vol. 13, no. 4, pp. 405–21.

Clarke, J. (2000) 'A world of difference? Globalisation and the study of social policy', in Lewis, G., Gewirtz, S. and Clarke, J. (eds) *Rethinking Social Policy*, London, Sage.

Clarke, J. and Cochrane, A. (1998) 'The social construction of social problems', in Saraga, E. (ed.) *Embodying the Social: Constructions of Difference*, London, Routledge/Open University.

Clarke, J. and Jefferson, T. (1973) *The Politics of Popular Culture*, Birmingham, Centre for Contemporary Cultural Studies Occasional Paper, University of Birmingham.

Clarke, J. and Newman, J. (1997) *The Managerial State*, London, Sage.

Clarke, J., Hall, S., Jefferson, T. and Roberts, B. (1976) 'Subcultures, cultures and class: a theoretical overview', in Hall, S. and Jefferson, T. (eds) *Resistance through Rituals*, London, Hutchinson.

Clarke, J., Cochrane, A. and McLaughlin, E. (eds) (1994) *Managing Social Policy*, London, Sage.

Clarke, R. (ed.) (1992) *Situational Crime Prevention: Successful Case Studies*, Albany, NY, Harrow and Heston.

Clarke, R. and Sinclair, I. (1974) 'Toward more effective treatment evaluation,' *Collected Studies in Criminological Research*, vol. 12, pp. 55–82, Strasbourg, Council of Europe.

Cloonan, M. (1995) 'I fought the law: popular music and British obscenity law', *Popular Music*, vol. 14, no. 3, pp. 349–63.

Cloward, R. and Ohlin, L. (1961) *Delinquency and Opportunity: A Theory of Delinquent Gangs*, London, Routledge & Kegan Paul.

Cockburn, C. (1987) *Two-Track Training: Sex Inequalities and the YTS*, London, Macmillan.

Coffield, F. and Gofton, L. (1994) *Drugs and Young People*, London, Institute for Public Policy Research.

Coffield, F., Borrill, C. and Marshall, S. (1986) *Growing up at the Margins*, Milton Keynes, Open University Press.

Cohen, A. (1955) *Delinquent Boys: The Culture of the Gang*, Chicago, Chicago Free Press.

Cohen, N. (2003) '661 new crimes – and counting', *New Statesman*, 7 July.

Cohen, P. (1972) *Subcultural Conflict and Working Class Community*, Working Papers in Cultural Studies, no. 2, Birmingham, Centre for Contemporary Cultural Studies, University of Birmingham..

Cohen, P. (1979) 'Policing the working class city', in NDC/CSE, *Capitalism and the Rule of Law*, London, Hutchinson.

Cohen, P. (1982) 'School for dole', *New Socialist*, no. 3, pp. 43–7.

Cohen, P. (1986) *Rethinking the Youth Question*, Post-16 Education Centre, Working Paper no. 3, London, Institute of Education.

Cohen, P. (1997a) 'The same old generation game?', *Criminal Justice Matters*, no. 28, pp. 8–9.

Cohen, P. (1997b) *Rethinking the Youth Question*, London, Macmillan.

Cohen, P. (2000) 'In the country of the blind: youth studies and cultural studies in Britain', in Pickford, J. (ed.) *Youth Justice: Theory and Practice*, London, Cavendish.

Cohen, S. (1968) 'The politics of vandalism', *New Society*, 12 December, pp. 872–4.

Cohen, S. (1973a) *Folk Devils and Moral Panics: The Creation of Mods and Rockers*, London, Paladin.

Cohen, S. (1973b) 'The failures of criminology', *The Listener*, 8 November, pp. 622–5.

Cohen, S. (1973c) 'Property destruction: motives and meanings', in Ward, C. (ed.) *Vandalism*, London, Architectural Press.

Cohen, S. (1979) 'The punitive city: notes on the dispersal of social control', *Contemporary Crises*, vol. 3, no. 4, pp. 341–63.

Cohen, S. (1980) 'Symbols of trouble', Introduction to *Folk Devils and Moral Panics*, 2nd edn, Oxford, Martin Robertson.

Cohen, S. (1985) *Visions of Social Control*, Cambridge, Polity.

Cohen, S. (1987) 'Taking decentralization seriously: values, visions and policies', in Lowman, J., Menzies, R.J. and Palys, T.S. (eds) *Transcarceration: Essays in the Sociology of Social Control*, Aldershot, Gower.

Cohen, S. (1988) *Against Criminology*, New Brunswick, NJ, Transaction Publishers.

Cohen, S. (1989) 'The critical discourse on "social control": notes on the concept as a hammer', *International Journal of the Sociology of Law*, vol. 17, pp. 347–57.

Cohen, S. (1993) 'Human rights and crimes of the state: the culture of denial', *Australian and New Zealand Journal of Criminology*, vol. 26, no. 2, pp. 97–115.

Cohen, S. (1994) 'Social control and the politics of reconstruction', in Nelken, D. (ed.) *The Futures of Criminology*, London, Sage.

Cohen, S. (1998) 'Intellectual scepticism and political commitment: the case of radical criminology', in Walton, P. and Young, J. (eds) *The New Criminology Revisited*, Basingstoke, Macmillan.

Cohen, S. and Scull, A. (eds) (1983) *Social Control and the State: Historical and Comparative Essays*, Oxford, Martin Robertson.

Coleman, C. and Moynihan, J. (1996) *Understanding Crime Data*, Buckingham, Open University Press.

Coleman, J.C. (1980) *The Nature of Adolescence*, London, Methuen.

Coles, B. (1995) *Youth and Social Policy*, London, UCL Press.

Collin, M. (1997) *Altered State*, London, Serpent's Tail.

Commission for Racial Equality (2003) *Racial Equality in Prisons*, London, CRE.

Connell, R.W. (1987) *Gender and Power*, Cambridge, Polity.

Connell, R.W. (1995) *Masculinities*, Cambridge, Polity.

Corby, B. (1997) 'The mistreatment of young people', in Roche, R. and Tucker, S. (eds) *Youth in Society*, London, Sage/Open University.

Cornish, D. and Clarke, R. (eds) (1986) *The Reasoning Criminal*, New York, Springer-Verlag.

Corrigan, P. (1976) 'Doing nothing', in Hall, S. and Jefferson, T. (eds) *Resistance through Rituals*, London, Hutchinson.

Corrigan, P. (1979) *Schooling the Smash Street Kids*, London, Macmillan.

Council of Europe (1998) *Penological Information Bulletin*, no. 21.

Council of Europe (2000) *European Sourcebook of Crime and Criminal Justice Statistics*, Strasbourg, Council of Europe.

Coward, R. (1994) 'Whipping boys', *Guardian*, Weekend, 3 September, pp. 32–5.

Cowie, J., Cowie, V. and Slater, E. (1968) *Delinquency in Girls*, London, Heinemann.

Cox, P. and Shore, H. (eds) (2002) *Becoming Delinquent: British and European Youth 1650–1950*, Aldershot, Ashgate.

Craine, S. and Coles, B. (1995) 'Alternative careers: youth transitions and young people's involvement in crime', *Youth and Policy*, no. 48, pp. 6–27.

Crawford, A. (1997) *The Local Governance of Crime: Appeals to Community and Partnership*, Oxford, Clarendon Press.

Crawford, A. (2001) 'The growth of crime prevention in France as contrasted with the English experience', in Hughes, G., McLaughlin, E. and Muncie, J. (eds) *Crime Prevention and Community Safety: New Directions*, London, Sage.

Crawford, A. (2002) 'The governance of crime and insecurity in an anxious age: The trans-European and the local', in Crawford, A. (ed.) *Crime and Insecurity: The Governance of Safety in Europe*, Cullompton, Willan.

Crawford, A. and Jones, M. (1996) 'Kirkholt revisited: some reflections on the transferability of crime prevention initiatives', *Howard Journal*, vol. 35, no. 1, pp. 21–39.

Crawford, A. and Newburn, T. (2003) *Youth Offending and Restorative Justice*, Cullompton, Willan.

Crawford, A., Jones, T., Woodhouse, T. and Young, J. (1990) *Second Islington Crime Survey*, London, Middlesex Polytechnic.

CRE (Commission for Racial Equality) (1992) *Juvenile Cautioning – Ethnic Monitoring in Practice*, London, CRE.

Crookes, T. (1979) 'Sociability and behaviour disturbance', *British Journal of Criminology*, vol. 19, no. 1, pp. 60–6.

Cross, N., Evans, P. and Minkes, J. (2003) 'Still children first? Developments in youth justice in Wales', *Youth Justice*, vol. 2, no. 3, pp. 151–62.

Crowley, A. (1998) *A Criminal Waste: A Study of Child Offenders Eligible for Secure Training Centres*, London, Children's Society.

Cullen, F. and Gilbert, K. (1982) *Reaffirming Rehabilitation*, Cincinnati, Anderson.

Cunneen, C. (2003) 'Thinking critically about restorative justice', in McLaughlin, E. et al. (eds) *Restorative Justice: Critical Issues*, London, Sage/OU.

Cunneen, C. and White, R. (2002) *Juvenile Justice: Youth and Crime in Australia*, Melbourne, Oxford University Press.

Cunningham, H. (1995) *Children and Childhood in Western Society since 1500*, Harlow, Longman.

Currie, E. (1985) *Confronting Crime: An American Challenge*, New York, Pantheon.

Currie, E. (1993) *Reckoning: Drugs, the Cities and the American Future*, New York, Hill & Wang.

Daly, K. (2002) 'Restorative justice: the real story', *Punishment and Society*, vol. 4, no. 1, pp. 55–79.

Damer, S. (1977) 'Wine Alley: the sociology of the dreadful enclosure', in Carson, W. and Wiles, P. (eds) *The Sociology of Crime and Delinquency in Britain*, vol. 2, Oxford, Martin Robertson.

Davies, B. (1982) 'Juvenile justice in confusion', *Youth and Policy*, vol. 1, no. 2, pp. 33–6.

Davies, S. (1987) 'Towards the re-moralisation of society', in Loney, M. (ed.) *The State or the Market*, London, Sage.

Davis, J. (1990) *Youth and the Condition of Britain*, London, Athlone.

Davis, M. (1990) *City of Quartz*, London, Verso.

Davis, M. and Bourhill, M. (1997) '"Crisis": the demonisation of children and young people', in Scraton, P. (ed.) *'Childhood' in 'Crisis'?*, London, UCL Press.

Davis, N.Z. (1971) 'The reasons of misrule: youth groups and charivaris in sixteenth century France', *Past and Present*, no. 50, pp. 41–75.

Dean, M. (1999) *Governmentality: Power and Rule in Modern Society*, London, Sage.

De Haan, W. (1990) *The Politics of Redress*, London, Unwin Hyman.

De Haan, W. (1991) 'Abolitionism and crime control: a contradiction in terms', in Stenson, K. and Cowell, D. (eds) *The Politics of Crime Control*, London, Sage.

Dennis, N. (1993) *Rising Crime and the Dismembered Family*, London, Institute of Economic Affairs.

Dennis, N. (ed.) (1997) *Zero Tolerance: Policing a Free Society*, London, Institute of Economic Affairs.

Dennis, N. and Erdos, G. (1992) *Families without Fatherhood*, London, Institute of Economic Affairs.

Department of Education and Science (1983) *Young People in the 80s: A Survey*, London, HMSO.

DHSS (Department of Health and Social Security) (1981) *Offending by Young People: A Survey of Recent Trends*, London, DHSS.

Dickie, D. (1979) 'The social work role in Scottish juvenile justice', in Parker, M. (ed.) *Social Work and the Courts*, London, Edward Arnold.

Dickinson, D. (1995) 'Crime and unemployment', *New Economy*, vol. 2, no. 2, pp. 115–20.

Dignan, J. (1999) 'The Crime and Disorder Act and the prospects for restorative justice, *Criminal Law Review*, January, pp. 48–60.

Dingwall, R., Eekelaar, J.M. and Murray, T. (1984) 'Childhood as a social problem', *Journal of Law and Society*, vol. 11, no. 2, pp. 207–32.

Dinham, P. (1999) 'A conflict in the law?', *Youth Justice Matters*, December, pp. 12–14.

Ditchfield, J. (1976) *Police Cautioning in England and Wales*, Home Office Research Study, no. 37, London, HMSO.

Ditton, J. (1979) *Contrology: Beyond the New Criminology*, London, Macmillan.

Ditton, J. and Duffy, J. (1983) 'Bias in the newspaper reporting of crime news', *British Journal of Criminology*, vol. 23, no. 2, pp. 159–65.

Dolowitz, D. (ed.) (2000) *Policy Transfer and British Social Policy: Learning from the USA?*, Buckingham, Open University Press.

Dolowitz, D. and Marsh, D. (2000) 'Learning from abroad: The role of policy transfer in contemporary policy making', *Governance*, vol. 13, no. 1, pp. 5–24.

Donzelot, J. (1979) *The Policing of Families*, London, Hutchinson.

Dorn, N. and South, N. (1982) *Of Males and Markets*, Research Paper no. 1, Middlesex Polytechnic.

Downes, D. (1966) *The Delinquent Solution*, London, Routledge & Kegan Paul.

Downes, D. (1988) *Contrasts in Tolerance*, Oxford, Oxford University Press.

Downes, D. and Rock, P. (1995) *Understanding Deviance*, revised 2nd edn, Oxford, Clarendon.

Dugdale, R. (1910) *The Jukes*, New York, Putnam.

Dunkel, F. (1991) 'Legal differences in juvenile criminology in Europe', in Booth, T. (ed.) *Juvenile Justice in the New Europe*, Social Services Monographs, University of Sheffield.

Dunning, E., Murphy, P. and Williams, J. (1988) *The Roots of Football Hooliganism*, London, Routledge.

Durkheim, E. (1895/1964) *The Rules of Sociological Method*, reprinted 1964, New York, Free Press.

Durkheim, E. (1897/1952) *Suicide*, reprinted 1952, London, Routledge.

Dyhouse, C. (1981) *Girls Growing Up in Late Victorian and Edwardian England*, London, Routledge.

Einstadter, W. and Henry, S. (1995) *Criminological Theory*, Fort Worth, TX, Harcourt Brace.

Empey, L. (1982) *American Delinquency, Its Meaning and Construction*, Chicago, Dorsey.

Emsley, C. (1996) 'The origins and development of the police', in McLaughlin, E. and Muncie, J. (eds) *Controlling Crime*, London, Sage/Open University.

Ericson, R.V. (1991) 'Mass media, crime, law and justice', *British Journal of Criminology*, vol. 31, no. 3, pp. 219–49.

Ericson, R.V. and Haggerty, K.D. (1991) 'Governing the young', in Smandych, R. (ed.) *Governable Places*, Ashgate, Aldershot.

Erikson, E. (1968) *Identity, Youth and Crises*, London, Faber & Faber.

Esbensen, F.A. and Huizinga, D. (1991) 'Juvenile victimisation and delinquency', *Youth and Society*, vol. 23, no. 2, pp. 202–28.

Etzioni, A. (1995) *The Spirit of Community*, London, Fontana.

Eysenck, H. (1970) *Crime and Personality*, London, Paladin. First published 1964.

Farrington, D. (1989) 'The origins of crime: the Cambridge study of delinquent development', Home Office Research and Planning Unit, *Research Bulletin*, no. 27, London, HMSO, pp. 29–33.

Farrington, D. (1994) 'Human development and criminal careers', in Maguire, M., Morgan, R. and Reiner, R. (eds) *The Oxford Handbook of Criminology*, Oxford, Clarendon.

Farrington, D. (1996) *Understanding and Preventing Youth Crime*, Social Policy Research Findings, no. 93, York, Joseph Rowntree Foundation.

Farrington, D. (2000) 'Explaining and preventing crime: The globalisation of knowledge', *Criminology*, vol. 38, no. 1, pp. 1–24.

Farrington, D. (2002) 'Developmental and risk-focused prevention' in Maguire, M., Morgan, R., and Reiner, R. (eds) *The Oxford Handbook of Criminology*, 3rd edn, Oxford, Oxford University Press.

Farrington, D. (2003) 'Key results from the first 40 years of the Cambridge Study in delinquent development', in Thornberry, T. and Krohn, M. (eds) *Taking Stock of Delinquency*, New York, Kluwer.

Farrington, D. and Dowds, E. (1985) 'Disentangling criminal behaviour and police reaction', in Farrington, D. and Gunn, J. (eds) *Reactions to Crime*, Chichester, Wiley.

Farrington, D. and West, D. (1990) 'The Cambridge study in delinquent development', in Kerner, H.J. and Kaiser, G. (eds) *Criminality: Personality, Behaviour and Life History*, Berlin, Springer-Verlag.

Farrington, D., Barnes, G. and Lambert, S. (1996) 'The concentration of offending in families', *Legal and Criminological Psychology*, vol. 1, pp. 47–63.

Fass, P.S. (1977) *The Damned and the Beautiful*, New York, Oxford University Press.

Feeley, M. and Simon, J. (1992) 'The new penology', *Criminology*, vol. 30, no. 4, pp. 449–74.

Feest, J. (1991) 'Reducing the prison population: lessons from the West German experience', in Muncie, J. and Sparks, R. (eds) *Imprisonment: European Perspectives*, Hemel Hempstead, Harvester.

Felson, M. (1998) *Crime and Everyday Life*, 2nd edn, Thousand Oaks, CA, Pine Forge Press.

Fergusson, R. (2002) 'Rethinking youth transitions: policy transfer and new exclusions in New Labour's New Deal', *Policy Studies*, vol. 23, no. 3/4, pp. 173–90.

Fergusson, R., Pye, D., Esland, G., McLaughlin, E. and Muncie, J. (2000) 'Normalised dislocation and new subjectivities in post-16 markets for education and work', *Critical Social Policy*, vol. 20, no. 3, pp. 283–306.

Ferrell, J. (1996) *Crimes of Style: Urban Graffiti and the Politics of Criminality*, Boston, Northeastern University Press.

Ferrell, J. (1997) 'Youth, crime and cultural space', *Social Justice*, vol. 24, no. 4, pp. 21–38.

Ferrell, J. (1998) 'Criminological Verstehen: Inside the immediacy of crime', in Ferrell, J. and Hamm, M. (eds) *Ethnography at the Edge*, Boston, Northeastern University Press.

Ferrell, J. (1999) 'Cultural criminology', *Annual Review of Sociology*, vol. 25, pp. 395–418.

Ferrell, J. (2001) *Tearing Down the Streets: Adventures in Urban Anarchy*, Basingstoke, Palgrave.

Ferrell, J. and Sanders, C.R. (eds) (1995) *Cultural Criminology*, Boston, Northeastern University Press.

Ferri, E. (1901) *Criminal Sociology*, Boston, Little, Brown.

Field, S. (1990) *Trends in Crime and their Interpretation*, Home Office Research Study no. 119, London, HMSO.

Findlay, J., Bright, J. and Gill, K. (1990) *Youth Crime Prevention: A Handbook of Good Practice*, Swindon, Crime Concern.

Finn, D. (1983) 'The youth training schemes: a new deal?', *Youth and Policy*, vol. 1, no. 4, pp. 16–24.

Finn, D. (1987) *Training without Jobs*, London, Macmillan.

Fionda, J. (1998) 'The age of innocence? – The concept of childhood in the punishment of young offenders', *Child and Family Law Quarterly*, vol. 10, no. 1 pp. 77–87.

Fitzgerald, M. (1993) *Ethnic Minorities and the Criminal Justice System*, Royal Commission on Criminal Justice, Research Study no. 20, London, HMSO.

Fitzgerald, M. and Hale, C. (1996) *Ethnic Minorities, Victimisation and Racial Harassment*, Home Office Research Study no. 154, London, Home Office.

Flood-Page, C., Campbell, S., Harrington, V. and Miller, J. (2000) *Youth Crime: Findings from the 1998/99 Youth Lifestyles Survey*, Home Office research study, no. 209, London, Home Office.

Forester, T. (1981) 'Young and out of work: a political timebomb', *New Society*, 16 July, pp. 95–8.

Forrester, D., Chatterton, M. and Pease, K. (1988) *The Kirkholt Burglary Prevention Project*, Crime Prevention Unit, paper no. 13, London, HMSO.

Foster, J. (1990) *Villains*, London, Routledge.

Foucault, M. (1977) *Discipline and Punish*, London, Allen Lane.

Foucault, M. (1991) 'Governmentality', in Burchell, G., Gordon, C. and Miller, P. (eds) *The Foucault Effect: Studies in Governmentality*, Hemel Hempstead, Harvester.

Franklin, B. and Petley, J. (1996) 'Killing the age of innocence: newspaper reporting of the death of James Bulger', in Pilcher, J. and Wagg, S. (eds) *Thatcher's Children*, London, Falmer.

Freeman, D. (1983) *Margaret Mead and Samoa*, Cambridge, MA, Harvard University Press.

Freeman, M. (2002) 'Children's rights ten years after ratification', in Franklin, B. (ed.) *The New Handbook of Children's Rights*, London, Routledge.

Freud, A. (1952) 'Adolescence', *Psychoanalytical Study of the Child*, vol. 13, pp. 255–78.

Frith, S. (1978) 'The punk bohemians', *New Society*, 9 March, pp. 353–36.

Frith, S. (1983) *Sound Effects: Youth, Leisure and the Politics of Rock*, London, Constable.

Frith, S. (1984) *The Sociology of Youth*, Ormskirk, Causeway.

Frith, S. and McRobbie, A. (1978) 'Rock and sexuality', *Screen Education*, vol. 29, pp. 3–19.

Frost, N. and Stein, M. (1989) *The Politics of Child Welfare*, Hemel Hempstead, Harvester Wheatsheaf.

Furlong, A. and Cartmel, F. (1997) *Young People and Social Change*, Buckingham, Open University Press.

Fyvel, T.R. (1961) *The Insecure Offenders: Rebellious Youth in the Welfare State*, London, Chatto & Windus.

Garland, D. (1985) *Punishment and Welfare: A History of Penal Strategies*, Aldershot, Gower.

Garland, D. (1990) *Punishment and Modern Society*, Oxford, Oxford University Press.

Garland, D. (1996) 'The limits of the sovereign state: strategies of crime control in contemporary society', *British Journal of Criminology*, vol. 36, no. 4, pp. 445–71.

Garland, D. (2001) *The Culture of Control*, Oxford, Oxford University Press.

Garland, D. and Young, P. (eds) (1983) *The Power to Punish: Contemporary Penality and Social Analysis*, Aldershot, Gower.

Garrett, P.M. (2002) '"Encounters in the new welfare domains of the Third Way": social work, the connexions agency and personal advisers', *Critical Social Policy*, vol. 22, no. 4, pp. 596–618.

Gartside, P. (1997) 'By-passing politics? The contradictions of "DIY culture"', *Soundings*, no. 6, pp. 198–208.

Gatrell, V. (1990) 'Crime, authority and the policeman-state', in Thompson, F.M.L. (ed.) *Cambridge Social History of Britain 1750–1950*, vol. 3, Cambridge, Cambridge University Press.

Gelder, K. and Thornton, S. (eds) (1997) *The Subcultures Reader*, London, Routledge.

Gelsthorpe, L. (1984) 'Girls and juvenile justice', *Youth and Policy*, no. 11, pp. 1–5.

Gelsthorpe, L. and Morris, A. (1994) 'Juvenile justice 1945–1992', in Maguire, M., Morgan, R. and Reiner, R. (eds) *The Oxford Handbook of Criminology*, Oxford, Clarendon.

Gelsthorpe, L. and Morris, A. (2002) 'Restorative justice: the last vestiges of welfare?', in Muncie, J., Hughes, G. and McLaughlin, E. (eds) *Youth Justice: Critical Readings*, London, Sage.

Gibson, B., Cavadino, P., Rutherford, A., Ashworth, A. and Harding, J. (1994) *The Youth Court: One Year Onwards*, Winchester, Waterside.

Giddens, A. (1991) *Modernity and Self Identity*, Cambridge, Polity.

Gill, K. (1985) 'The Scottish hearings system', *Ajjust*, no. 5, pp. 18–21.

Gill, O. (1977) *Luke Street: Housing Policy, Conflict and the Creation of the Delinquency Area*, London, Macmillan.

Gillespie, M. and McLaughlin, E. (2003) *Media and the shaping of public knowledge and attitudes towards crime and punishment*, Rethinking Crime and Punishment Research Briefing, London, Esmée Fairbairn Foundation.

Gillis, J.R. (1974) *Youth and History*, London, Academic Press.

Gillis, J.R. (1975) 'The evolution of juvenile delinquency in England 1890–1914', *Past and Present*, no. 67, pp. 96–126.

Gilroy, P. (1987a) 'The myth of black criminality', in Scraton, P. (ed.) *Law, Order and the Authoritarian State*, Milton Keynes, Open University Press.

Gilroy, P. (1987b) *'There Ain't No Black in the Union Jack'*, London, Hutchinson.

Gilroy, P. (1993) *The Black Atlantic*, London, Verso.

Gilroy, P. and Lawrence, P. (1988) 'Two tone Britain: white and black youth and the politics of anti-racism', in Cohen, P. and Bains, H.S. (eds) *Multi-Racist Britain*, London, Macmillan.

Ginsberg, N. (1985) 'Striking back for the empire', *Critical Social Policy*, vol. 12, pp. 127–30.

Glueck, S. and Glueck, E. (1950) *Unravelling Juvenile Delinquency*, New York, Harper & Row.

Goddard, H. (1927) *The Kallikak Family: A Study in the Heredity of Feeble-mindedness*, London, Macmillan.

Goldblatt, P. and Lewis, C. (eds) (1998) *Reducing Offending*, Home Office Research Study, no. 187, London, HMSO.

Goldson, B. (1997a) 'Children, crime, policy and practice: neither welfare nor justice', *Children and Society*, vol. 11, no. 2, pp. 77–88.

Goldson, B. (1997b) 'Children in trouble: state responses to juvenile crime', in Scraton, P. (ed.) *'Childhood' in 'Crisis'?*, London, UCL Press.

Goldson, B. (1999) 'Youth (In)justice: contemporary developments in policy and practice' in Goldson, B. (ed.) *Youth Justice: Contemporary Policy and Practice*, Aldershot, Ashgate.

Goldson, B. (ed.) (2000a) *The New Youth Justice*, Lyme Regis, Russell House.

Goldson, B. (2000b) 'Children in need or young offenders?', *Child and Family Social Work*, vol. 5, pp. 255–265.

Goldson, B. (2001) 'A rational youth justice?', *Probation Journal*, vol. 48, no. 2, pp. 76–85.

Goldson, B. (2002a) 'New Labour, social justice and children: political calculation and the deserving-undeserving schism', *British Journal of Social Work*, vol. 32, pp. 683–95.

Goldson, B. (2002b) 'New punitiveness: the politics of child incarceration', in Muncie, J., Hughes, G. and McLaughlin, E. (eds) *Youth Justice: Critical Readings*, London, Sage.

Goldson, B. (2002c) *Vulnerable Inside: Children in Secure and Penal Settings*, London, The Children's Society.

Goldson, B. and Chigwada-Bailey, R. (1999) '(What) justice for black children and young people?', in Goldson, B. (ed.) *Youth Justice: Contemporary Policy and Practice*, Aldershot, Ashgate.

Goldson, B. and Jamieson, J. (2002) 'Youth crime, the parenting deficit and state intervention: a contextual critique', *Youth Justice*, vol. 2, no. 2, pp. 82–99.

Goldson, B. and Peters, E. (2000) *Tough Justice*, London, The Children's Society.

Goldson, B., Lavalette, M. and McKechnie, J. (eds) (2002) *Children, Welfare and the State*, London, Sage.

Goode, E. and Ben-Yehuda, N. (1994) *Moral Panics: The Social Construction of Deviance*, Oxford, Blackwell.

Goodey, J. (2001) 'The criminalization of British Asian youth', *Journal of Youth Studies*, vol. 4, no. 4, pp. 429–50.

Goring, C. (1913) *The English Convict*, London, HMSO.

Gottfredson, M.R. and Hirschi, T. (1990) *A General Theory of Crime*, Stanford, CA, Stanford University Press.

Graham, J. (1998) 'What works in preventing criminality', in Goldblatt, P. and Lewis, C. (eds) *Reducing Offending*, Home Office Research Study, no. 187, London, HMSO.

Graham, J. (ed.) (1990) *Crime Prevention Strategies in Europe and America*, Helsinki, Institute for Crime Prevention and Control.

Graham, J. and Bowling, B. (1995) *Young People and Crime*, Home Office Research Study, no. 145, London, HMSO.

Gramsci, A. (1971) *Selection from Prison Notebooks*, London, Lawrence & Wishart.

Gray, P. (2003) *An Evaluation of the Plymouth Restorative Justice Programme*, University of Plymouth, Department of Social Policy and Social Work.

Green, D. and Parton, A. (1990) 'Slums and slum life in Victorian England', in Gaskell, S.M. (ed.) *Slums*, Leicester, Leicester University Press.

Greenberg, D. (1977) 'Delinquency and the age structure of society', *Contemporary Crises*, vol. 1, no. 2, pp. 189–224.

Griffin, C. (1985) *Typical Girls?* London, Routledge.

Griffin, C. (1993) *Representations of Youth*, Cambridge, Polity.

Griffith, P. (2002) 'Juvenile delinquency in time', in Cox, P. and Shore, H. (eds) *Becoming Delinquent*, Aldershot, Ashgate.

Grisso, T. and Schwartz, R.G. (eds) (2000) *Youth on Trial*, Chicago, University of Chicago Press.

HAC (Home Affairs Committee) (1993) *Juvenile Offenders*, Sixth Report, London, HMSO.

Hagan, J. and McCarthy, B. (1998) *Mean Streets: Youth Crime and Homelessness*, Cambridge, Cambridge University Press.

Hagell, A. and Newburn, T. (1994) *Persistent Young Offenders*, London, Policy Studies Institute.

Hagell, A., Hazel, N. and Shaw, C. (2000) *Evaluation of Medway Secure Training Centre*, London, Home Office.

Haines, K. and Drakeford, M. (1998) *Young People and Youth Justice*, Basingstoke, Macmillan.

Hall, G.S. (1905) *Adolescence: Its Psychology and Its Relations to Physiology, Anthropology, Sociology, Sex, Crime, Religion and Education*, New York, Appleton.

Hall, S. (1969) 'The hippies: an American moment', in Nagel, J. (ed.) *Student Power*, London, Merlin.

Hall, S. (1978) 'The treatment of football hooliganism in the press', in Ingham, R. (ed.) *Football Hooliganism*, London, Inter-Action.

Hall, S. (1980) *Drifting into a Law and Order Society*, London, Cobden Trust.

Hall, S. (1988) 'New ethnicities', in Donald, J. and Rattansi, A. (eds) *'Race', Culture and Difference*, Milton Keynes, Sage/Open University.

Hall, S. (1992) 'The question of cultural identity', in Hall, S., Held, D. and McGrew, T. (eds) *Modernity and Its Futures*, Cambridge, Polity/Open University.

Hall, S. (1997) 'The terms of change', *New Ethnicities*, no. 2, University of East London. pp. 7–8.

Hall, S. and Jefferson, T. (eds) (1976) *Resistance through Rituals: Youth Subcultures in Post-war Britain*, London, Hutchinson.

Hall, S. and Scraton, P. (1981) 'Law, class and control', in Fitzgerald, M., McLennan, G. and Pawson, J. (eds) *Crime and Society*, London, Routledge/Open University.

Hall, S., Clarke, J., Critcher, C., Jefferson, T. and Roberts, B. (1975) *Newsmaking and Crime*, Occasional Paper, Birmingham Centre for Contemporary Cultural Studies, University of Birmingham.

Hall, S., Critcher, C., Jefferson, T., Clarke, J. and Roberts, B. (1978) *Policing the Crisis: Mugging, the State and Law and Order*, London, Macmillan.

Hammersley, R., Khan, F. and Ditton, J. (2002) *Ecstasy and the Rise of the Chemical Generation*, London, Routledge.

Hancock, L. (2001) *Community, Crime and Disorder*, Basingstoke, Palgrave.

Hargreaves, D.H. (1967) *Social Relations in a Secondary Modern School*, London, Routledge & Kegan Paul.

Harman, C. (2000) 'Anti-capitalism: theory and practice', *International Socialism*, no. 88.

Harris, R. (1982) 'Institutionalised ambivalence: social work and the Children and Young Persons Act 1969', *British Journal of Social Work*, vol. 12, no. 3, pp. 247–63.

Harris, R. and Timms, N. (1993) *Secure Accommodation in Child Care*, London, Routledge.

Harris, R. and Webb, P. (1987) *Welfare, Power and Juvenile Justice*, London, Tavistock.

Hartless, J., Ditton, J., Nair, G. and Phillips, S. (1995) 'More sinned against than sinning: a study of young teenagers' experience of crime', *British Journal of Criminology*, vol. 35, no. 1, pp. 114–33.

Hay, C. (1995) 'Mobilisation through interpellation: James Bulger, juvenile crime and the construction of a moral panic', *Social and Legal Studies*, vol. 4, no. 2, pp. 197–223.

Haydon, D. and Scraton, P. (2000) '"Condemn a little more, understand a little less": the political context and rights implications of the domestic and European rulings in the Venables – Thompson case', *Journal of Law and Society*, vol. 27, no. 3, pp. 416–48.

Hayek, F.A. (1983) *Knowledge, Evolution and Society*, London, Adam Smith Institute.

Hayward, K. (2002) 'The vilification and pleasures of youthful transgression', in Muncie, J., Hughes, G., and McLaughlin, E. (eds) *Youth Justice: Critical Readings*, London, Sage.

Healy, W. and Bronner, A. (1936) *New Light on Delinquency and its Treatment*, New Haven, CT, and London, Yale University Press.

Hebdige, D. (1976a) 'The meaning of mod', in Hall, S. and Jefferson, T. (eds) *Resistance through Rituals*, London, Hutchinson.

Hebdige, D. (1976b) 'Reggae, Rastas and Rudies', in Hall, S. and Jefferson, T. (eds) *Resistance through Rituals*, London, Hutchinson.

Hebdige, D. (1979) *Subculture: The Meaning of Style*, London, Methuen.

Hebdige, D. (1981) 'Skinheads and the search for white working class identity', *New Socialist*, vol. 1, September/October, pp. 38–41.

Hebdige, D. (1988) *Hiding in the Light*, London, Comedia.

Heidensohn, F. (1985) *Women and Crime*, London, Macmillan.

Hendrick, H. (1990) *Images of Youth: Age, Class and the Male Youth Problem 1880–1920*, Oxford, Clarendon.

Hendrick, H. (1997) 'Constructions and reconstructions of British childhood: an interpretative survey, 1800 to the present', in James, A. and Proat, A. (eds) *Constructing and Reconstructing Childhood*, 2nd edn, Basingstoke, Falmer.

Henry, S. and Milovanovic, D. (1994) 'The constitution of constitutive criminology: a postmodern approach to criminological theory', in Nelken, D. (ed.) *The Futures of Criminology*, London, Sage.

Henry, S. and Milovanovic, D. (1996) *Constitutive Criminology*, London, Sage.

Herrnstein, R.J. and Murray, C. (1994) *The Bell Curve*, New York, Basic Books.

Hester, S. and Eglin, P. (1992) *A Sociology of Crime*, London, Routledge.

Hetherington, K. (1998) 'Vanloads of uproarious humanity: New age travellers and the utopics of the countryside', in Skelton, T. and Valentine, G. (eds) *Cool Places: Geographies of Youth Cultures*, London, Routledge.

Hill, J. and Wright, G. (2003) 'Youth, community safety and the paradox of inclusion', *The Howard Journal*, vol. 42, no. 3, pp. 282–97.

Hobbs, D. (1997) 'Criminal collaboration: youth gangs, subcultures, professional criminals and organized crime', in Maguire, M., Morgan, R. and Reiner, R. (eds) *The Oxford Handbook of Criminology*, 2nd edn, Oxford, Clarendon.

Hoffman, A. (1968) *Revolution for the Hell of It*, Chicago, Dial Press.

Holdaway, S. et al., (2001) *New Strategies to Address Youth Offending: The National Evaluation of the Pilot Offending Teams*, Research Directorate Occasional paper, no. 69, London, Home Office.

Hollands, R. (1990) *The Long Transition: Class, Culture and Youth Training*, Basingstoke, Macmillan.

Hollands, R. (1995) *Friday Night, Saturday Night: Youth Cultural Identification in the Post-Industrial City*, Newcastle, University of Newcastle Press.

Hollands, R. (2002) 'Divisions in the dark; youth cultures, transitions and segmented consumption spaces in the night time economy', *Journal of Youth Studies*, vol. 5, no. 2 pp. 153–71.

Hollin, C. (1989) *Psychology and Crime*, London, Routledge.

Home Office (1927) *Report of the Departmental Committee on the Treatment of Young Offenders*, (The Molony Committee) Cmnd 2831, London, HMSO.

Home Office (1968) *Children in Trouble*, Cmnd 3601, London, HMSO.

Home Office (1990) *Crime, Justice and Protecting the Public*, Cmnd 965, London, HMSO.

Home Office (1991) *Safer Communities: The Local Delivery of Crime Prevention through the Partnership Approach* (The Morgan Report), London, HMSO.

Home Office (1995) *Strengthening Punishment in the Community*, London, HMSO.

Home Office (1997a) *Tackling Delays in the Youth Justice System*, London, Home Office.

Home Office (1997b) *Preventing Children Offending*, Cmnd 3566, London, HMSO.

Home Office (1997c) *Tackling Youth Crime: A Consultation Paper*, London, HMSO.

Home Office (1997d) *Prison Statistics, England and Wales 1996*, Cmnd 3732, London, HMSO.

Home Office (1997e) *No More Excuses: A New Approach to Tackling Youth Crime in England and Wales*, Cmnd 3809, London, HMSO.

Home Office (2002) *Criminal Statistics England and Wales 2001*, London, HMSO.

Home Office (2003a) *Respect and Responsibility: Taking a Stand against Anti-Social Behaviour*, Cmnd 5778, London, HMSO.

Home Office (2003b) *Youth Justice – the Next Steps*, London, Home Office.

Home Office (2003c) *Prison Statistics for England and Wales 2002*, Cmnd 5996, London, HMSO.

Home Office (2003d) *Prison Population Brief, May 2003*, London, HMSO.

Home Office, DES, DE, DHSS and Welsh Office (1984) *Crime Prevention* (Circular 8/1984) London, HMSO.

Hood, R. (1992) *Race and Sentencing: A Study in the Crown Court*, Oxford, Clarendon.

hooks, bell (1994) *Outlaw Culture: Resisting Representations*, New York and London, Routledge.

Hooton, E. (1939) *Crime and the Man*, Cambridge, MA, Harvard University Press.

Hopkins Burke, R. (2001) *An Introduction to Criminological Theory*, Cullompton, Willan.

Hough, M. (1996) *Drugs Misuse and the Criminal Justice System: A Review of the Literature*, Home Office Drugs Prevention Initiative Paper, no. 15, London, HMSO.

Hough, M. and Mayhew, P. (1983) *The British Crime Survey: First Report*, Home Office Research Study, no. 16, London, HMSO.

Hough, M. and Roberts, J. (1998) *Attitudes to Punishment*, Home Office Research Study, no. 179, London, HMSO.

Hough, M., Jacobson, J. and Millie, A. (2003) *The Decision to Imprison*, London, Prison Reform Trust.

Howard League (1995) *Banged Up, Beaten Up, Cutting Up*, London, The Howard League for Penal Reform.

Howard League (1999) *Protecting the Rights of Children*, London, The Howard League for Penal Reform.

Howard League (2003) *Howard League/Campaigns/Girls in Prison/htm*.

Hudson, A. (1988) 'Boys will be boys: masculinism and the juvenile justice system', *Criticial Social Policy*, no. 21, pp. 30–48.

Hudson, B. (1984) 'Femininity and adolescence', in McRobbie, A. and Nava, M. (eds) *Gender and Generation*, London, Macmillan.

Hudson, B. (1987) *Justice through Punishment*, London, Macmillan.

Hudson, B. (1989) 'Discrimination and disparity: the influence of race on sentencing', *New Community*, vol. 16, no. 1, pp. 23–34.

Hudson, J., Morris, A., Maxwell, G. and Galaway, B. (1996) *Family Group Conferences*, Annandale, Australia, Federation Press.

Huff, R. (1996) *Gangs in America*, 2nd edn, London, Sage.

Hughes, G. (1991) 'Taking crime seriously: a critical analysis of new left realism', *Sociology Review*, vol. 1, no. 2, pp. 18–23.

Hughes, G. (1996) 'Communitarianism and law and order', *Critical Social Policy*, vol. 16, no. 4, pp. 17–41.

Hughes, G. (1998) *Understanding Crime Prevention: Social Control, Risk and Late Modernity*, Buckingham, Open University Press.

Hughes, G. (2002) 'Crime and disorder partnerships: the future of community safety?', in Hughes, G., McLaughlin, E. and Muncie, J. (eds) *Crime Prevention and Community Safety: New Directions*, London, Sage.

Hughes, G., Leisten, R. and Pilkington, A. (1998) 'Diversion in a culture of severity', *Howard Journal*, vol. 37, no. 1, pp. 16–33.

Hughes, G., McLaughlin, J. and Muncie, J. (2002) 'Teetering on the edge: the futures of crime control and community safety', in Hughes, G., McLaughlin, E. and Muncie, J. (eds) *Crime Prevention and Community Safety: New Directions*, London, Sage.

Hulsman, L. (1986) 'Critical criminology and the concept of crime', *Contemporary Crises*, vol. 10, no. 1, pp. 63–80.

Human Rights Watch (1997) *Racist Violence in the United Kingdom*, New York, Human Rights Watch.

Humphries, S. (1981) *Hooligans or Rebels?* Oxford, Blackwell.

Humphries, S. (1994) 'Yesterday's yobs, today's grandfathers', *Independent*, 31 October, p. 21.

Hunt, A. (1991) 'Postmodernism and critical criminology', in McClean, B. and Milovanovic, D. (eds) *New Directions in Critical Criminology*, Vancouver, University of Vancouver Press.

Hutson, S. and Liddiard, M. (1994) *Youth Homelessness: The Construction of a Social Issue*, London, Macmillan.

Hyland, T. and Musson, D. (2001) 'Unpacking the New Deal for young people: promise and problems', *Educational Studies*, vol. 27, no. 1, pp. 55–67.

Hylton, J. (1981) ' Community corrections and social control: the case of Sastkatchewan, Canada', *Contemporary Crises*, vol. 5, no. 2, pp. 193–215.

Iadicola, P. (1986) 'Community crime control strategies', *Crime and Social Justice*, no. 25, pp. 140–65.

ISDD (Institute for the Study of Drug Dependence) (1996) *Drug Misuse in Britain 1995*, London, ISDD.

Jacques, M. (1973) 'Trends in youth culture: some aspects', *Marxism Today*, vol. 17, no. 9, pp. 268–80.

James, A. and James, A. (2001) 'Tightening the net: children, community and control', *British Journal of Sociology*, vol. 52, no. 2, pp. 211–28.

James, A. and Jenks, C. (1996) 'Public perceptions of childhood criminality', *British Journal of Sociology*, vol. 47, no. 2, pp. 315–31.

Jankowski, M. (1991) *Islands in the Street: Gangs and American Urban Society*, Berkeley, CA, University of California Press.

Jefferson, T. (1976) 'Cultural responses of the Teds', in Hall, S. and Jefferson, T. (eds) *Resistance through Rituals*, London, Hutchinson.

Jefferson, T. (1997) 'Masculinities and crime', in Maguire, M., Morgan, R. and Reiner, R. (eds) *The Oxford Handbook of Criminology*, 2nd edn, Oxford, Clarendon.

Jefferson, T. (2002) 'For a psychosocial criminology' in Carrington, K. and Hogg, R. (eds) *Critical Criminology*, Cullompton, Willan.

Jefferson, T., Sim, J. and Walklate, S. (1992) 'Europe, the Left and criminology in the 90s', in Farrington, D. and Walklate, S. (eds) *Offenders and Victims: Theory and Policy*, London, British Society of Criminology/ISTD.

Jeffery, C.R. (1978) 'Criminology as an interdisciplinary behavioural science', *Criminology*, vol. 16, no. 2, pp. 149–69.

Jeffs, T. and Smith, M. (1994) 'Young people, youth work and a new authoritarianism', *Youth and Policy*, no. 46, pp. 17–32.

Jeffs, T. and Smith, M. (1996) 'Getting the dirtbags off the streets – curfews and other solutions to juvenile crime', *Youth and Policy*, no. 53, pp. 1–14.

Jeffs, T. and Spence, J. (2000) 'New Deal for young people', *Youth and Policy*, no. 66, pp. 34–61.

Jenkins, R. (1983) *Lads, Citizens and Ordinary Kids*, London, Routledge.

Jenkins, S. (1987) 'Crime soars – or does it?', *Sunday Times*, 22 March, p. 25.

Jenks, C. (1996) *Childhood*, London, Routledge.

Johnstone, G. (2002) *Restorative Justice: Ideas, Values and Debates*, Cullompton, Willan.

Jones, D. (2001) 'Misjudged youth: a critique of the Audit Commissions reports on youth justice', *British Journal of Social Work*, vol. 31, no. 1, pp. 57–79.

Jones, J. and Newburn, T. (2002) 'Policy convergence and crime control in the USA and the UK', *Criminal Justice*, vol. 2, no. 2, pp. 173–203.

Jones, T., Maclean, B. and Young, J. (1986) *The Islington Crime Survey*, Aldershot, Gower.

Jordan, B. (1996) *Poverty: A Theory of Social Exclusion*, Cambridge, Polity.

Junger-Tas, J. (1987) 'Crime prevention in the Netherlands', *Research Bulletin*, no. 24, Home Office Research and Planning Unit, London, HMSO, pp. 33–6.

Junger-Tas, J. (2002) 'The juvenile justice system: Past and present trends in western society', in Weijers, I. and Duff, A. (eds) *Punishing Juveniles*, Oxford, Hart.

Jupp, V., Davies, P. and Francis, P. (1999) 'The features of invisible crimes', in Davies, P., Francis, P. and Jupp, V. (eds) *Invisible Crimes*, Basingstoke, Macmillan.

Justice (2000) *Restoring Youth Justice: New Directions in Domestic and International Law and Practice*, London, Justice.

Kalra, V., Fieldhouse, E. and Alam, S. (2001) 'Avoiding the New Deal', *Youth and Policy*, no. 72, pp. 63–79.

Karstedt, S. (2001) 'Comparing cultures, comparing crime: Challenges, prospects and problems for a global criminology', *Crime, Law and Social Change,* vol. 36, no. 3, pp. 285–308.

Katz, J. (1988) *Seductions of Crime: Moral and Sensual Attractions in Doing Evil*, New York, Basic Books.

Katz, J. (2000) 'The gang myth', in Karstedt, S. and Bussman, K.D. (eds) *Social Dynamics of Crime and Control*, Oxford, Hart.

Keane, J. (1997) 'Ecstasy in the unhappy society', *Soundings*, no. 6, pp. 127–39.

Keith, M. (1993) *Race, Riots and Policing*, London, UCL Press.

Kemp, A. and Rugg, J. (2001) 'Young people, housing benefit and the risk society', *Social Policy and Administration*, vol. 35, no. 6, pp. 688–700.

Kempf-Leonard, K. and Petersen, E. (2000) 'Expanding the realms of the new penology: the advent of actuarial justice for juveniles', *Punishment and Society*, vol. 2, no. 1, pp. 66–97.

Kerouac, J. (1957) *On the Road*, reprinted 1972, Harmondsworth, Penguin.

Kettle, M. (1982) 'The racial numbers game in our prisons', *New Society*, 30 September, pp. 535–7.

Killeen, D. (1992) 'Leaving home', in Coleman, J.C. and Warren Adamson, C. (eds) *Youth Policy in the 1990s*, London, Routledge.

King, M. (1988) *How to Make Social Crime Prevention Work: The French Experience*, London, NACRO.

King, M. (1989) 'Social crime prevention à la Thatcher', *Howard Journal*, vol. 28, no. 4, pp. 291–312.

King, M. (1995) 'The James Bulger murder trial: moral dilemmas and social solutions', *International Journal of Children's Rights*, vol. 3, no. 2, pp. 167–87.

King, P. (1998) 'The rise of juvenile delinquency in England 1780–1840: changing patterns of perception and prosecution', *Part and Present*, no. 160, pp. 116–66.

King, P. (2002) 'A brief history of panic', *Safer Society*, no. 13, pp. 8–10.

King, P. and Noel, J. (1993) 'The origins of the problem of juvenile delinquency: the growth of juvenile prosecutions in London in the late eighteenth and early nineteenth centuries', in *Criminal Justice History*, vol. 14, Westport, CT, Greenwood.

Klein, D. (1973) 'The etiology of female crime', *Issues in Criminology*, vol. 8, no. 2, pp. 3–30.

Klein, N. (2001) 'Farewell to the "end of history"', in Panitch, L. and Leys, C. (eds) *Socialist Register 2002*, London, Merlin.

Kobrin, S. and Klein, M. (1983) *Community Treatment of Juvenile Offenders: The DSO Experiments*, London, Sage.

Komen, M. (2002) 'Dangerous children: Juvenile delinquency and judicial intervention in the Netherlands, 1960–1995', *Crime, Law and Social Change*, vol. 37, pp. 379–401.

Krisberg, B. and Austin, J. (1993) *Reinventing Juvenile Justice*, London, Sage.

Kuure, T. (2002) 'Low custody in Finland', Paper delivered to the Children Law UK/NACRO Conference, 'Reducing Custodial sentencing for Young Offenders: The European Experience', London, 23 October.

Lacombe, D. (1996) 'Reforming Foucault: a critique of the social control thesis', *British Journal of Sociology*, vol. 47, no. 2, pp. 333–52.

Land, H. (1997) 'Families and the law', in Muncie, J., Wetherell, M., Langan, M., Dallos, R. and Cochrane, A. (eds) *Understanding the Family*, London, Sage/Open University.

Landau, S. and Nathan, G. (1983) 'Selecting delinquents for cautioning in the London metropolitan area', *British Journal of Criminology*, vol. 23, no. 2, pp. 128–49.

Lauritsen, J., Sampson, R. and Laub, J. (1991) 'The link between offending and victimisation among adolescents', *Criminology*, vol. 29, no. 2, pp. 265–92.

Lea, J. and Young, J. (1984) *What Is To Be Done about Law and Order?*, Harmondsworth, Penguin.

Lees, S. (1986) *Losing Out: Sexuality and Adolescent Girls*, London, Hutchinson.

Leffert, N. and Petersen, A. (1995) 'Patterns of development during adolescence', in Rutter, M. and Smith, D. (eds) *Psychosocial Disorders in Young People*, Chichester, Wiley.

Lemert, E. (1951) *Social Pathology*, New York, McGraw-Hill.

Lemert, E. (1967) *Human Deviance, Social Problems and Social Control*, Englewood Cliffs, NJ, Prentice-Hall.

Leonard, E. (1982) *Women, Crime and Society*, London, Longman.

Lerman, P. (1975) *Community Treatment and Social Control*, Chicago, Chicago University Press.

Lévi-Strauss, C. (1966) *The Savage Mind*, London, Weidenfeld & Nicolson.

Levitas, R. (1996) 'The concept of social exclusion and the new Durkheimian hegemony', *Critical Social Policy*, vol. 16, no. 1, pp. 5–20.

Levitas, R. (1998) *The Inclusive Society? Social Exclusion and New Labour*, London, Macmillan.

Liddle, M. and Solanki, A-R. (2002) *Persistent Young Offenders: Research on Individual Backgrounds and Life Experiences*, NACRO Research Briefing no. 1, London, NACRO.

Liebling, A. (1992) *Suicides in Prison*, London, Routledge.

Lilly, R., Cullen, F. and Ball, R. (1989) *Criminological Theory: Context and Consequences*, London, Sage.

Lipsey, M. (1995) 'What do we learn from 400 research studies on the effectiveness of treatment with juvenile delinquents?', in McGuire, J. (ed.) *What Works: Reducing Reoffending*, London, Wiley.

Lipsitz, G. (1994) 'We know what time it is: race, class and youth culture in the nineties', in Ross, A. and Rose, T. (eds) *Microphone Fiends: Youth Music and Youth Culture*, London and New York, Routledge.

Livingstone, S. (1996) 'On the continuing problem of media effects', in Curran, J. and Gurevitch, M. (eds) *Mass Media and Society*, 2nd edn, London, Arnold.

Lloyd, C., Mair, G. and Hough, M. (1994) *Explaining Reconviction Rates: A Critical Analysis*, Home Office Research Findings, no. 12, London, HMSO.

Loader, I. (1996) *Youth, Policing and Democracy*, London, Macmillan.

Lockyer, A. and Stone, F. (eds) (1998) *Juvenile Justice in Scotland: Twenty Five Years of the Welfare Approach*, Edinburgh, T. & T. Clark.

Lombroso, C. (1876) *L'Uomo Delinquente*, Milan, Hoepli.

Loney, M. (1981) 'Making myths', *Youth in Society*, June, pp. 10–11.

Lowman, J., Menzies, R.J. and Palys, T.S. (eds) (1987) *Transcarceration: Essays in the Sociology of Social Control*, Aldershot, Gower.

Lyng, S. (1990) 'Edgework: a social psychological analysis of voluntary risk taking', *American Journal of Sociology*, vol. 95, no. 4, pp. 851–86.

MacDonald, R. (ed.) (1997) *Youth, the 'Underclass' and Social Exclusion*, London, Routledge.

MacLean, B. (1991) 'In partial defense of socialist realism', *Crime, Law and Social Change*, vol. 15, pp. 213–54.

Magarey, S. (1978) 'The invention of juvenile delinquency in early nineteenth century England', *Labour History* (Sydney), vol. 34, pp. 11–25.

Malek, B. (1997) 'Not such tolerant times', *Soundings*, no. 6, pp. 140–51.

Mann, K. (1991) *The Making of an English 'Underclass'?*, Milton Keynes, Open University Press.

Marcuse, H. (1964) *One Dimensional Man*, London, Routledge.

Marcuse, H. (1972) *An Essay on Liberation*, Harmondsworth, Penguin.

Marsh, P. (1977) 'Dole queue rock', *New Society*, 20 January, pp. 112–14.

Martin, C. (1997) *The ISTD Handbook of Community Programmes for Young and Juvenile Offenders*, Winchester, Waterside.

Martinson, R. (1974) 'What works? – questions and answers about prison reform', *The Public Interest*, no. 35, pp. 22–54.

Marx, K. (1859) Preface to *A Contribution to the Critique of Political Economy*, reprinted in Marx and Engels (1968) *Selected Works*, London, Lawrence & Wishart.

Marx, K. (1865) *Theories of Surplus Value*, reprinted 1964, London, Lawrence & Wishart.

Marx, K. and Engels, F. (1848) *Manifesto of the Communist Party*, reprinted 1952, Moscow, Progress.

Mason, D. (2001) *Building Safer Communities for Children*, London, NSPCC.

Matthews, R. (1987a) 'Taking realist criminology seriously', *Contemporary Crises*, vol. 11, pp. 371–401.

Matthews, R. (1987b) 'Decarceration and social control: fantasies and realities', in Lowman, J., Menzies, R.J. and Palys, T.S. (eds) *Transcarceration: Essays in the Sociology of Social Control*, Aldershot, Gower.

Matthews, R. and Trickey, J. (1996) *Drugs and Crime: A Study amongst Young People in Leicester*, Leicester, Centre for the Study of Public Order.

Matza, D. (1964) *Delinquency and Drift*, New York, Wiley.

Mawby, R. (1979) 'The victimization of juveniles: a comparative study of three areas of publicly owned housing in Sheffield', *Journal of Crime and Delinquency*, vol. 16, no. 1, pp. 98–114.

Maxfield, M. and Baumer, T. (1990) 'Home detention with electronic monitoring', *Crime and Delinquency*, vol. 36, no. 4, pp. 521–36.

May, D. (1977) 'Delinquent girls before the courts', *Medical Science Law*, vol. 17, no. 2, pp. 203–10.

May, M. (1973) 'Innocence and experience: the evolution of the concept of juvenile delinquency in the mid-nineteenth century', *Victorian Studies*, vol. 17, no. 1. pp. 7–29.

Mayhew, H. (1861) *London Labour and London Poor*, vol. 1, London, Griffin, Bohn & Co.

Mayhew, P., Clarke, R., Sturman, A. and Hough, M. (1976) *Crime as Opportunity*, Home Office Research Study, no. 34, London, HMSO.

Mayhew, P., Mirrlees-Black, C. and Maung, N.A. (1994) *Trends in Crime: Findings from the 1994 British Crime Survey*, Home Office Research Findings, no. 14, London, HMSO.

McAra, L. and Young, P. (1997) 'Juvenile Justice in Scotland', *Criminal Justice*, vol. 15, no. 3, pp. 8–10.

McCaghy, C. (1976) *Deviant Behaviour*, London, Macmillan.

McGhee, J., Waterhouse, L. and Whyte, B. (1996) 'Children's hearings and children in trouble', in Asquith, S. (ed.) *Children and Young People in Conflict with the Law*, London, Jessica Langley.

McGuigan, J. (1992) *Cultural Populism*, London, Routledge.

McGuire, J. (ed.) (1995) *What Works: Reducing Reoffending*, London, Wiley.

McKay, G. (1996) *Senseless Acts of Beauty: Cultures of Resistance since the Sixties*, London, Verso.

McKay, G. (ed.) (1998) *DIY Culture: Party and Protest in Nineties Britain*, London, Verso.

McLaughlin, E. and Muncie, J. (1993) 'Juvenile delinquency', in Dallos, R. and McLaughlin, E. (eds) *Social Problems and the Family*, London, Sage/Open University.

McLaughlin, E. and Muncie, J. (1994) 'Managing the criminal justice system', in Clarke, J. Cochrane, A. and McLaughlin, E. (eds) *Managing Social Policy*, London, Sage.

McLaughlin, E. and Muncie, J. (1999) 'Walled cities: surveillance, regulation and segregation' in Pile, S., Brook, C. and Mooney, G. (eds) *Unruly Cities?*, London, Routledge.

McLaughlin, E., Muncie, J. and Hughes, G. (2001) 'The permanent revolution: New Labour, new public management and the modernization of criminal justice', *Criminal Justice*, vol. 1, no. 3, pp. 301–18.

McLaughlin, E., Muncie, J. and Hughes, G. (eds) (2003a) *Criminological Perspectives: Essential Readings*, 2nd edn, London, Sage.

McLaughlin, E. et al. (2003b) *Restorative Justice: Critical Issues*, London, Sage/Open University.

McMahon, M. (1990) 'Net-widening: vagaries in the use of a concept', *British Journal of Criminology*, vol. 30, no. 2, pp. 121–49.

McNeish, D. (1996) 'Young people, crime, justice and punishment', in Roberts, H. and Sachdev, D. (eds) *Young People's Attitudes*, Ilford, Dr Barnardo's.

McQuail, D. (1993) *Media Performance*, London, Sage.

McQueen, R. (1990) 'The prospects for left realist criminology in Australia', *The Critical Criminologist*, vol. 2, no. 2, pp. 9–10, 13–15.

McRobbie, A. (1978) 'Working class girls and the culture of femininity', in Centre for Contemporary Cultural Studies, *Women Take Issue*, London, Hutchinson.

McRobbie, A. (1980) 'Settling accounts with subcultures: a feminist critique', *Screen Education*. no. 34, pp. 37–49.

McRobbie, A. (1991) *Feminism and Youth Culture*, London, Macmillan.

McRobbie, A. (1994) *Postmodernism and Popular Culture*, London, Routledge.

McRobbie, A. and Garber, J. (1976) 'Girls and subcultures', in Hall, S. and Jefferson, T. (eds) *Resistance through Rituals*, London Hutchinson.

McRobbie, A. and Nava, M. (eds) (1984) *Gender and Generation*, London, Macmillan.

McRobbie, A. and Thornton, S. (1995) 'Rethinking moral panic for multi-mediated social worlds', *British Journal of Sociology*, vol. 46, no. 4, pp. 559–74.

Mead, M. (1928) *Coming of Age in Samoa*, New York, Morrow.

Mead, G.H. (1934) *Mind, Self and Society*, Chicago, Chicago University Press.

Measor, L. and Squires, P. (2000) *Young People and Community Safety*, Aldershot, Ashgate.

Measham, F., Newcombe, R. and Parker, H. (1994) 'The normalisation of recreational drug use amongst young people in the north-west of England', *British Journal of Sociology*, vol. 45, no. 2, pp. 287–311.

Mednick, S. and Volavka, J. (1980) 'Biology and crime', in Morris, N. and Tonry, M. (eds) *Crime and Justice*, vol. 2, Chicago, Chicago University Press.

Mednick, S.A., Gabrielli, W. and Hutchings, B. (1987) 'Genetic factors in the etiology of criminal behaviour', in Mednick, S., Moffit, T. and Stack, S. (eds) *The Causes of Crime: New Biological Approaches*, Cambridge, Cambridge University Press.

Melossi, D. (2000) 'Translating social control: Reflections on the comparison of Italian and North American cultures', in Karstedt, S. and Bussman, K-D. (eds) *Social Dynamics of Crime and Control*, Oxford, Hart.

Melly, G. (1972) *Revolt into Style*, Harmondsworth, Penguin.

Mérigeau, M. (1996) 'Legal frameworks and interventions', in McCarney, W. (ed.) *Juvenile Delinquents and Young People in Danger in an Open Environment*, Winchester, Waterside.

Merton, R. (1938) 'Social structure and anomie', *American Sociological Review*, vol. 3, pp. 672–82.

Merton, R. (1957) *Social Theory and Social Structure*, New York, Free Press.

Messerschmidt, J.W. (1993) *Masculinities and Crime*, Lanham, MD, Rowman & Littlefield.

Michael, J. and Adler, M. (1933) *Crime, Law and Social Science*, New York, Harcourt Brace Jovanovich.

Miles, S. (2000) *Youth Lifestyles in a Changing World*, Buckingham, Open University Press.

Miller, P. and Plant, M. (1996) 'Drinking, smoking and illicit drug use among 15 and 16 year olds in the United Kingdom', *British Medical Journal*, vol. 313, pp. 394–7.

Millett, K. (1970) *Sexual Politics*, New York, Doubleday.

Millham, S., Bullock, R. and Hosie, R. (1978) *Locking Up Children*, London, Saxon House.

Mirrlees-Black, C., Mayhew, P. and Percy, A. (1996) *The 1996 British Crime Survey*, Home Office Statistical Bulletin, issue 19/96, London, HMSO.

Mirrlees-Black, C., Budd, T., Partridge, S. and Mayhew, P. (1998) *The 1998 British Crime Survey: England and Wales*, Home Office Statistical Bulletin, issue 21/98, London, HMSO.

Mishra, R. (1999) *Globalisation and the Welfare State*, Cheltenham, Edward Elgar.

Mirza, H.S. (1992) *Young, Female and Black*, London, Routledge.

Mizen, P. (1995) *The State, Young People and Youth Training*, London, Mansell.

Mizen, P. (2003) 'Tomorrow's future or signs of a misspent youth?', *Youth and Policy*, no. 79, pp. 1–18.

Mizen, P. (2004) *The Changing State of Youth*, Basingstoke, Palgrave.

Mooney, J. (2003) 'It's the family, stupid', in Matthews, R. and Young, J. (eds) *The New Politics of Crime and Punishment*, Cullompton, Willan.

Monaghan, G., Hibbert, P. and Moore, S. (2003) *Children in Trouble: Time for Change*, London, Barnardo's.

Morgan, D. (1981) 'Youth call-up: social policy for the young', *Critical Social Policy*, vol. 1, no. 2, pp. 101–10.

Morgan, J. and Zedner, L. (1992) *Child Victims*, Oxford, Clarendon.

Morgan, P. (1978) *Delinquent Fantasies*, Aldershot, Temple Smith.

MORI (2002) *Youth Survey: Summary*, London, Youth Justice Board.

Morris, A. (1974) 'Scottish juvenile justice: a critique', in Hood, R. (ed.) *Crime, Criminology and Public Policy*, London, Heinemann.

Morris, A. and Giller, M. (1987) *Understanding Juvenile Justice*, London, Croom Helm.

Morris, A. and Maxwell, G. (eds) (2001) *Restorative Justice for Juveniles*, Oxford, Hart.

Morris, A. and McIsaac, M. (1978) *Juvenile Justice?*, London, Heinemann.

Morris, A., Giller, H., Geach, H. and Szwed, E. (1980) *Justice for Children*, London, Macmillan.

Morris, T. (1957) *The Criminal Area: A Study in Social Ecology*, London, Routledge.

Morrison, W. (1995) *Theoretical Criminology: From Modernity to Post-Modernism*, London, Cavendish.

Muncie, J. (1984) *The Trouble with Kids Today: Youth and Crime in Post-War Britain*, London, Hutchinson.

Muncie, J. (1987) 'Much ado about nothing? The sociology of moral panics', *Social Studies Review*, vol. 3, no. 2, pp. 42–7.

Muncie, J. (1990) 'Failure never matters: detention centres and the politics of deterrence', *Critical Social Policy*, no. 28, pp. 53–66.

Muncie, J. (1997a) 'Investing in our future', *Criminal Justice Matters*, no. 28, pp. 4–5.

Muncie, J. (1997b) 'Shifting sands: care, community and custody in youth justice discourse', in Roche, J. and Tucker, S. (eds) *Youth in Society*, London, Sage/Open University.

Muncie, J. (1998) 'Reassessing competing paradigms in criminological theory', in Walton, P. and Young, J. (eds) *The New Criminology Revisited*, Basingstoke, Macmillan.

Muncie, J. (1999a) 'Institutionalized intolerance: youth justice and the 1998 Crime and Disorder Act', *Critical Social Policy*, vol. 19, no. 2, pp. 147–75.

Muncie, J. (1999b) *Youth and Crime: A Critical Introduction*, London, Sage.

Muncie, J. (2000a) 'Decriminalizing criminology', in Lewis, G., Gewirtz, S. and Clarke, J. (eds) *Rethinking Social Policy*, London, Sage.

Muncie, J. (2000b) 'Pragmatic Realism? Searching for criminology in the New Youth Justice' in Goldson, B (ed.) *The New Youth Justice*, Lynne Regis, Russell House.

Muncie, J. (2001) 'The construction and deconstruction of crime', in Muncie, J. and McLaughlin, E. (eds) *The Problem of Crime*, 2nd edn, London, Sage.

Muncie, J. (2002) 'A new deal for youth?: Early intervention and correctionalism', in Hughes, G., McLaughlin, E. and Muncie, J. (eds) *Crime Prevention and Community Safety: New Directions*, London, Sage.

Muncie, J. (2003a) 'Juvenile justice in Europe: some conceptual, analytical and statistical comparisons', *Childright*, no. 202, pp. 14–17.

Muncie, J. (2003b) 'Youth, risk and victimisation', in Davies, P., Francis, P. and Jupp, V. (eds) *Victimisation: Theory, Research and Policy*, Basingstoke, Palgrave Macmillan.

Muncie, J. (2004) 'Youth justice: globalisation and multi-modal governance', in Newburn, T. and Sparks, R. (eds) *Criminal Justice and Political Cultures*, Cullompton, Willan.

Muncie, J. and Fitzgerald, M. (1981) 'Humanizing the deviant', in Fitzgerald, M., McLellan, G. and Pawson, J. (eds) *Crime and Society*, London, Routledge/Open University.

Muncie, J. and Hughes, G. (2002) 'Modes of youth governance: political rationalities, criminalisation and resistance', in Muncie, J., Hughes, G. and McLaughlin, E. (eds) *Youth Justice: Critical Readings*, London, Sage.

Muncie, J. and McLaughlin, E. (eds) (2001) *The Problem of Crime*, London, 2nd edn, Sage/Open University.

Muncie, J., Coventry, G. and Walters, R. (1995) 'The politics of youth crime prevention', in Noaks, L., Maguire, M. and Levi, M. (eds) *Contemporary Issues in Criminology*, Cardiff, University of Wales Press.

Muncie, J., McLaughlin, E. and Langan, M. (eds) (1996) *Criminological Perspectives: A Reader*, London, Sage/Open University.

Muncie, J., Hughes, G. and McLaughlin, E. (2002) *Youth Justice: Critical Readings*, London, Sage.

Mungham, G. and Pearson, G. (eds) (1976) *Working Class Youth Culture*, London, Routledge & Kegan Paul.

Murdock, G. and McCron, R. (1973) 'Scoobies, skins and contemporary pop', *New Society*, 29 March, pp. 690–2.

Murdock, G. and McCron, R. (1976) 'Youth and class: the career of a confusion', in Mungham, G. and Pearson, G. (eds) *Working Class Youth Culture*, London, Routledge & Kegan Paul.

Murdock, G. and Troyna, B. (1981) 'Recruiting racists', *Youth in Society*, November, pp. 9–10.

Murray, C. (1984) *Losing Ground*, New York, Basic Books.

Murray, C. (1990) *The Emerging Underclass*, London, Institute of Economic Affairs.

Murray, C. (1994) *Underclass: The Crisis Deepens*, London, Institute of Economic Affairs.

Murray, C. (2000) 'Baby beware', *Sunday Times*, February 13.

Musgrove, F. (1964) *Youth and the Social Order*, London, Routledge.

Myrdal, G. (1964) *Challenge to Affluence*, London, Victor Gollancz.

NACRO (National Association for the Care and Resettlement of Offenders) (1993) *Community Provision for Young People in the Youth Justice System*, London, NACRO.

NACRO (1995) *Family Group Conferencing*, NACRO Briefing Paper, September, London, NACRO.

NACRO (1997) *Facts about Young Offenders in 1995*, London, NACRO Youth Crime Section.

NACRO (1998) *Facts about Young Offenders in 1996*, London, NACRO Youth Crime Section.

NACRO (2001) *Girls in the Youth Justice System*, Youth Crime Briefing, London, NACRO.

NACRO (2003a) 'Some facts about young people who offend – 2001', *Youth Crime Briefing*, March.

NACRO (2003b) *A Failure of Justice: Reducing Child Imprisonment*, London, NACRO.

NACRO Young Offenders Committee (1992) 'Stopping youth crime', *Childright*, no. 83, pp. 9–10.

NAJC (New Approaches to Juvenile Crime) (1993) *Creating More Criminals*, Briefing Paper no. 1, June, London, NAJC.

Nathan, S. (1995) *Boot Camps: Return of the Short Sharp Shock*, London, Prison Reform Trust.

National Audit Office (NAO) (2002) *The New Deal for Young People*, 28 February, HC639, London, HMSO.

National Research Institute of Legal Policy (1998) *Regulating the Prison Population*, Research Communications no. 38 Helsinki, NRILP.

Nelken, D. (1989) 'Discipline and punish: some notes on the margin', *Howard Journal*, vol. 28, no. 4, pp. 245–54.

Nelken, D. (1994) 'Whom can you trust? The future of comparative criminology', in Nelken, D. (ed.) *The Futures of Criminology*, London, Sage.

Nellis, M. (1991) 'The electronic monitoring of offenders in England and Wales', *British Journal of Criminology*, vol. 31. no. 2, pp. 165–85.

Nellis, M. (2002) 'Community justice, time and the new National Probation Service', *The Howard Journal*, vol. 41, no. 1, pp. 59–86.

Neustatter, A. (1998) 'Kids – what the papers say', *Guardian*, 8 April, pp. 8–9.

Neville, R. (1971) *Playpower*, London, Paladin.

Newburn, T. (1996) 'Back to the future? Youth crime, youth justice and the rediscovery of "authoritarian populism"', in Pilcher, J. and Wagg, S. (eds) *Thatcher's Children*, London, Falmer.

Newburn, T. (2002) 'Young people, crime and youth justice', in Maguire, M., Morgan, R. and Reiner, R. (eds) *The Oxford Handbook of Criminology*, 3rd edn, Oxford, Oxford University Press.

Newburn, T. and Stanko, E. (eds) (1994) *Just Boys Doing Business?* London, Routledge.

Newman, J. (2001) *Modernising Governance*, London, Sage.

Norrie, K. (1997) *Children's Hearings in Scotland*, Edinburgh, Sweet and Maxwell.

Norris, C. and Armstrong, G. (1999) *The Maximum Surveillance Society: The Rise of CCTV*, Oxford, Berg.

NSPCC (2002) *Child Abuse in Britain*, London, NSPCC.

NSPCC (2003) *Child Killings in England and Wales*, London, NSPCC.

O'Mahony, D. and Deazley, R. (2000) *Juvenile Crime and Justice: Review of the Criminal Justice System in Northern Ireland*, Research Report no. 17, Belfast, Northern Ireland Office.

O'Malley, P. (1992) 'Risk, power and crime prevention', *Economy and Society*, vol. 21, no. 3, pp. 252–75.

O'Malley, P. (2002) 'Criminologies of catastrophe?: Understanding criminal justice on the edge of the New Millennium', *Australian and New Zealand Journal of Criminology*, vol. 33, no. 2, pp. 153–67.

O'Malley, P. and Mugford, S. (1994) 'Crime, excitement and modernity', in Barak, G. (ed) *Varieties of Criminology*, Westport, Praeger.

Oakley, A. (1972) *Sex, Gender and Society*, New York, Harper & Row.

Osborne, R. (1995) 'Crime and the media: from media studies to post-modernism', in Kidd-Hewitt, D. and Osborne, R. (eds) *Crime and the Media*, London, Pluto.

Osgerby, B. (1998) *Youth in Britain since 1945*, Oxford, Blackwell.

Pakes, F. (2000) 'League champions in mid table: On the major changes in Dutch prison policy', *Howard Journal*, vol. 39, no. 1 pp. 30–39.

Pakes, F. (2004) *Comparative Criminal Justice*, Cullompton, Willan.

Palmer, T. (1971) *The Trials of OZ*. London, Blond & Briggs.

Parent, D. G. (1995) 'Boot camps failing to achieve goals', in Tonry, M. and Hamilton, K. (eds) *Intermediate Sanctions in Over-Crowded Times*, Boston, MA, Northeastern University Press.

Park, R. and Burgess, E. (1925) *The City*, Chicago, Chicago University Press.

Parker, H. (1974) *View from the Boys*, Newton Abbot, David & Charles.

Parker, H. (1996) 'Alcohol, young adult offenders and criminological cul-de-sacs', *British Journal of Criminology*, vol. 36, no. 2, pp. 282–98.

Parker, H. and Measham, F. (1994) 'Pick 'n' mix: changing patterns of illicit drug use amongst 1990s adolescents', *Drugs: Education, Prevention and Policy*, vol. 1, no. 1, pp. 5–13.

Parker, H. and Newcombe, R. (1987) 'Heroin use and acquisitive crime in an English community', *British Journal of Sociology*, vol. 38, no. 3, pp. 331–48.

Parker, H., Casburn, M. and Turnbull, D. (1981) *Receiving Juvenile Justice*, Oxford, Blackwell.

Parker, H., Jarvis, G. and Sumner, M. (1987) 'Under new orders: the redefinition of social work with young offenders', *British Journal of Social Work*, vol. 17, no. 1, pp. 21–43.

Parker, H., Newcombe, R. and Bakx, K. (1988) *Living with Heroin*, Milton Keynes, Open University Press.

Parker, H., Measham, F. and Aldridge, J. (1995) *Drugs Futures: Changing Patterns of Drug Use amongst English Youth*, Research Monograph no. 7, London, ISDD.

Parker, H., Aldridge, J. and Measham, F. (1998) *Illegal Leisure: The Normalisation of Adolescent Recreational Drug Use*, London, Routledge.

Parker, H., Williams, L. and Aldridge, J. (2002) 'The normalisation of "sensible" recreational drug use', *Sociology*, vol. 36, no. 4, pp. 941–64.

Parkin, F. (1968) *Middle Class Radicalism*, Manchester, Manchester University Press.

Parsons, T. (1942) 'Age and sex in the social structure of the United States', *American Sociological Review*, vol. 7, pp. 604–16.

Patrick, J. (1973) *A Glasgow Gang Observed*, London, Methuen.

Pearce, F. and Tombs, S. (1992) 'Realism and corporate crime', in Matthews, R. and Young, J. (eds) *Issues in Realist Criminology*, London, Sage.

Pearson, G. (1975) 'Vandals in the park', *New Society*, 9 October, p. 69.

Pearson, G. (1976) 'Paki-bashing in a north east Lancashire cotton town', in Mungham, G. and Pearson, G. (eds) *Working Class Youth Culture*, London, Routledge & Kegan Paul.

Pearson, G. (1983) *Hooligan: A History of Respectable Fears*, London, Macmillan.

Pearson, G. (1985) 'Lawlessness, modernity and social change: a historical appraisal', *Theory, Culture and Society*, vol. 2, no. 3, pp. 15–35.

Pearson, G. (1987) *The New Heroin Users*, London, Batsford.

Pearson, G. (1991) 'Drug-control policies in Britain', in Tonry, M. (ed.) *Crime and Justice: A Review of Research*, vol. 14, Chicago, Chicago University Press.

Pearson, G. (1993–4) 'Youth crime and moral decline: permissiveness and tradition', *The Magistrate*, December/January, pp. 190–2.

Pearson, G. (1994) 'Youth, Crime and Society', in Maguire, M., Morgan, R. and Reiner, R. (eds) *The Oxford Handbook of Criminology*, Oxford, Clarendon.

Percy, A. (1998) *Ethnicity and Victimisation: Findings from the 1996 British Crime Survey*, Home Office Statistical Bulletin, issue 6/98, London, HMSO.

Percy-Smith, B. and Weil, S. (2002) 'New Deal or raw deal? Dilemmas and paradoxes of state interventions into the youth labour market', in Cieslik, M. and Pollock, G. (eds) *Young People in Risk Society*, Aldershot, Ashgate.

Percy-Smith, J. (ed.) (2000) *Policy Responses to Social Exclusion*, Buckingham, Open University Press.

Perri, 6., Jupp, B., Parry, H. and Lasky, K. (1997) *The Substance of Youth: The Place of Drugs in Young People's Lives*, York, Joseph Rowntree Trust.

Pinchbeck, I. and Hewitt, M. (1973) *Children in English Society*, vol. 2, London, Routledge.

Pitts, J. (1988) *The Politics of Juvenile Crime*, London, Sage.

Pitts, J. (1992) 'The end of an era', *Howard Journal*, vol. 31, no. 2, pp. 133–49.

Pitts, J. (1995) 'Public issues and private troubles: a tale of two cities', *Social Work in Europe*, vol. 2, no. 1, pp. 3–11.

Pitts, J. (1997) 'Youth crime, social change and crime control in Britain and France' in the 1980s and 1990s', in Jones, H. (ed.) *Towards a Classless Society*, London, Routledge.

Pitts, J. (1999/2000) 'New youth justice, new youth crime', *Criminal Justice Matters*, no. 38, pp. 24–5.

Pitts, J. (2001) *The New Politics of Youth Crime: Discipline or Solidarity?*, Basingstoke, Palgrave.

Platt, A. (1969) *The Child Savers*, Chicago, Chicago University Press.

Platt, A. and Takagi, P. (1977) 'Intellectuals for law and order: a critique of the new realists', *Crime and Social Justice*, no. 8, pp. 1–16.

Plummer, K. (1979) 'Misunderstanding labelling perspectives', in Downes, D. and Rock, P. (eds) *Deviant Interpretations*, Oxford, Martin Robertson.

Pollock, L. (1983) *Forgotten Children: Parent–Child Relations from 1500 to 1900*, Cambridge, Cambridge University Press.

Polsky, N. (1971) *Hustlers, Beats and Others*, Harmondsworth, Penguin.

Porteous, M.A. and Colston, N.J. (1980) 'How adolescents are reported in the British Press', *Journal of Adolescence*, vol. 3, pp. 197–207.

Porter, R. (1996) 'The history of the "drugs problem"', *Criminal Justice Matters*, no. 24, pp. 3–4.

Pratt, J. (1983) 'Reflections on the approach of 1984: recent developments in social control in the UK', *International Journal of the Sociology of Law*, vol. 11, pp. 339–60.

Pratt, J. (1989) 'Corporatism: the third model of juvenile justice', *British Journal of Criminology*, vol. 29, no. 3, pp. 236–54.

Pratt, J. (1999) 'Governmentality, neo-Liberalism and dangerousness', in Smandych, R. (ed.) *Governable Places: Readings on Governmentality and Crime Control*, Aldershot, Ashgate.

Presdee, M. (1994) 'Young people, culture and the construction of crime: doing wrong versus doing crime', in Barak, G. (ed.) *Varieties of Criminology*, Westport, CT, Praeger.

Presdee, M. (2000) *Cultural Criminology and the Carnival of Crime*, London, Routledge.

Puffer, J. (1912) *The Boy and His Gang*, Boston, Houghton Mifflin.

Quetelet, M.A. (1842) *A Treatise on Man*, Edinburgh, Chambers.

Quinney, R. (1970) *The Social Reality of Crime*, Boston, Little, Brown.

Qvortrup, J., Bardy, M., Sgritta, G. and Wintersberger, H. (eds) (1994) *Childhood Matters*, Aldershot, Avebury.

Radzinowicz, L. and Hood, A. (1990) *The Emergence of Penal Policy*, Oxford, Clarendon.

Ramsay, M. (1997) *Persistent Drug-Misusing Offenders*, Home Office Research Findings, no. 50, London, HMSO.

Ramsay, M. and Percy, A. (1996) *Drug Misuse Declared: Results of the 1994 British Crime Survey*, Home Office Research Findings, no. 33, London, HMSO.

Ramsay, M. and Spiller, J. (1997) *Drug Misuse Declared in 1996: Key Results from the British Crime Survey*, Home Office Research Findings, no. 56, London, HMSO.

Ramsay, M., Baker, P., Goulden, C., Sharp, C. and Sandi, A. (2001) *Drug Misuse Declared in 2000: Results from the British Crime Survey*, Home Office Research Study, no. 224, London, Home Office.

Redhead, S. (1990) *The End of the Century Party*, Manchester, Manchester University Press.

Redhead, S. (1993) *Rave Off: Politics and Deviance in Contemporary Youth Culture*, Aldershot, Avebury.

Reiner, R. (2002) 'Media made criminality', in Maguire, M., Morgan, R. and Reiner, R. (eds) *The Oxford Handbook of Criminology*, 3rd edn, Oxford, Oxford University Press.

Release (1997) *Drugs and Dance Survey: An Insight into the Culture*, London, Release.

Report of Committee into Juvenile Delinquency (1816) *Committee for Investigating the Alarming Increase of Juvenile Delinquency in the Metropolis*, London, Dove.

Rex, J. and Moore, R. (1967) *Race, Community and Conflict*, London, Oxford University Press for the Institute of Race Relations.

Rice, M. (1990) 'Challenging orthodoxies in feminist theory: a black feminist critique', in Gelsthorpe, L. and Morris, A. (eds) *Feminist Perspectives in Criminology*, Milton Keynes, Open University Press.

Riddell, P. (1989) *The Thatcher Effect*, Oxford, Blackwell.

Ritchie, J. (2000) 'New Deal for young people: participants perspectives', *Policy Studies*, vol. 21, no. 4, pp. 301–12.

Roberts, H. (1996) '"It wasn't like this in our day": young people, religion and right and wrong', in Roberts, H. and Sachdev, D. (eds) *Young People's Social Attitudes*, Ilford, Dr. Barnado's.

Roberts, H. and Sachdev, D. (eds) (1996) *Young People's Social Attitudes*, Ilford, Dr. Barnado's.

Roberts, K. (1995) *Youth and Employment in Modern Britain*, Oxford, Oxford University Press.

Roberts, K. and Parsell, G. (1994) 'Youth cultures in Britain: the middle class take-over', *Leisure Studies*, vol. 13, no. 1, pp. 33–48.

Roche, S. (2002) 'Toward a new governance of crime and insecurity in France', in A. Crawford (ed.) *Crime and Insecurity: The Governance of Safety in Europe*, Cullompton, Willan.

Rock, P. and Cohen, S. (1970) 'The teddy boys', in Bogdanor, V. and Skidelsky, R. (eds) *The Age of Affluence*, London, Macmillan.

Rose, N. (1989) *Governing the Soul*, London, Routledge.

Rose, N. (1996a) 'Governing "advanced" Liberal democracies', in Barry, A., Osborne, T. and Rose, N. (eds) *Foucault and Political Reason*, London, UCL Press.

Rose, N. (1996b) 'The death of the social? Refiguring the territory of government', *Economy and Society*, vol. 25, no. 3, pp. 327–46.

Rose, N. (1999) *Powers of Freedom: Reframing Political Thought*, Cambridge, Cambridge University Press.

Rose, N. (2000) 'Government and control', *British Journal of Criminology*, vol. 40, pp. 321–39.

Rose, N. and Miller, P. (1992) 'Political power beyond the state: problematics of government', *British Journal of Sociology*, vol. 43, no. 2, pp. 173–205.

Rose, T. (1994) 'A style nobody can deal with: politics, style and the post-industrial city in hip hop', in Ross, A. and Rose, T. (eds) *Microphone Fiends*, New York and London, Routledge.

Rosenbaum, D. (1988) 'Community crime prevention: a review and synthesis of the literature', *Justice Quarterly*, vol. 5, no. 3. pp. 323–95.

Roshier, B. (1973) 'The selection of crime news by the press', in Cohen, S. and Young, J. (eds) *The Manufacture of News*, London, Constable.

Ross, R., Fabiano, E. and Ewles, C. (1988) 'Reasoning and rehabilitation', *International Journal of Offender Therapy and Comparative Criminology*, vol. 32, pp. 29–33.

Roszak, T. (1971) *The Making of a Counter-Culture*, London, Faber & Faber.

Rowbotham, J., Stevenson, K. and Pegg, S. (2003) 'Children of misfortune', *Howard Journal*, vol. 42, no. 2, pp. 107–22.

Rowbotham, S. (1973) *Women's Consciousness, Man's World*, Harmondsworth, Penguin.

Rubin, J. (1970) *Do It!*, New York, Simon & Schuster.

Runciman, W.G. (1966) *Relative Deprivation and Social Justice*, London, Routledge.

Rush, P. (1992) 'The government of a generation: the subject of juvenile delinquency', *Liverpool Law Review*, vol. 14, no. 1, pp. 3–41.

Russell, C. (1917) *The Problem of Juvenile Crime*, Oxford, Oxford University Press.

Rutherford, A. (1986) *Growing Out of Crime*, Harmondsworth, Penguin.

Rutherford, A. (1989) 'The mood and temper of penal policy: curious happenings in England during the 1980s', *Youth and Policy*, no. 27, pp. 27–31.

Rutherford, A. (1992) *Growing out of Crime: The New Era*, Winchester, Waterside.

Rutherford, A. (1993) *Criminal Justice and the Pursuit of Decency*, Oxford, Oxford University Press.

Rutherford, J. (1997) 'Young Britain', *Soundings*, no. 6, pp. 112–25.

Rutter, M. and Giller, H. (1983) *Juvenile Delinquency: Trends and Perspectives*, Harmondsworth, Penguin.

Rutter, M. and Smith, D. (eds) (1995) *Psychosocial Disorders in Young People*, Chichester, Wiley.

Rutter, M., Graham, P., Chadwick, O. and Yule, W. (1976) 'Adolescent turmoil: fact or fiction?', *Journal of Child Psychology and Psychiatry*, vol. 17, pp. 35–56.

Rutter, M., Giller, H. and Hagell, A. (1998) *Anti-social Behaviour by Young People*, Cambridge, Cambridge University Press.

Ruxton, S. (1996) *Children in Europe*, London, NCH Action for Children.

Said, E. (1991) *Orientalism*, Harmondsworth, Penguin.

Sanders, C.R. and Lyon, E. (1995) 'Repetitive retribution: media images and the cultural construction of criminal justice', in Ferrell, J. and Sanders, C. (eds) *Cultural Criminology*, Boston, MA, Northeastern University Press.

Saraga, E. (2001) 'Dangerous places: the family as a site of crime', in Muncie, J. and McLaughlin, E. (eds) *The Problem of Crime*, 2nd edn, London, Sage/Open University.

Saville, J. (1957) 'The welfare state: an historical approach', *New Reasoner*, vol. 3, pp. 5–24.

Schlesinger, P. and Tumber, H. (1994) *Reporting Crime: The Media Politics of Criminal Justice*, Oxford, Clarendon.

Schwartz, M. and Dekeseredy, W. (1991) 'Left realist criminology: strengths, weaknesses and the feminist critique', *Crime, Law and Social Change*, vol. 15, no. 1, pp. 51–72.

Scott, A. (1990) *Ideology and the New Social Movements*, London, Unwin Hyman.

Scottish Consortium on Crime and Criminal Justice (2000) *Rethinking Criminal Justice in Scotland*, Edinburgh, Scottish Consortium.

Scottish Executive (2003) *Youth Court Feasibility Project Group Report*, Edinburgh, Scottish Executive.

Scraton, P. (ed.) (1987) *Law, Order and the Authoritarian State*, Milton Keynes, Open University Press.

Scraton, P. (1997a) 'Whose "childhood"? What "crisis"?', in Scraton, P. (ed.) *'Childhood' in 'Crisis'?*, London, UCL Press.

Scraton, P. (ed.) (1997b) *'Childhood' in 'Crisis'?* London, UCL Press.

Scraton, P. and Chadwick, K. (1991) 'The theoretical and political priorities of critical criminology', in Stenson, K. and Cowell, D. (eds) *The Politics of Crime Control*, London, Sage.

Scraton, P. and Haydon, D. (2002) 'Challenging the criminalisation of children and young people: securing a rights based agenda', in Muncie, J., Hughes, G. and McLaughlin, E. (eds) *Youth Justice: Critical Readings*, London, Sage.

Scruton, R. (1980) *The Meaning of Conservatism*, Harmondsworth, Pelican.

Scull, A. (1977) *Decarceration*, Englewood Cliffs, NJ, Prentice-Hall.

Segal, L. (1990) *Slow Motion: Changing Masculinities, Changing Men*, London, Virago.

Sellin, T. (1938) *Culture, Conflict and Crime*, New York, Social Science Research Council.

Shacklady Smith, L. (1978) 'Sexist assumptions and female delinquency', in Smart, C. and Smart, B. (eds) *Women, Sexuality and Social Control*, London, Routledge.

Shallice, A. and Gordon, P. (1990) *Black People, White Justice? Race and the Criminal Justice System*, London, Runnymede.

Sharma, A. (1996) 'Sounds oriental: the (im)possibility of theorizing Asian musical cultures', in Sharma, S., Hutnyk, J. and Sharma, A. (eds) *Dis-orienting Rhythms*, London, Zed.

Sharma, S., Hutnyk, J. and Sharma, A. (eds) (1996) *Dis-orienting Rhythms: The Politics of the New Asian Dance Music*, London, Zed.

Shaw, C.R. (1929) *Delinquency Areas*, Chicago, Chicago University Press.

Shaw, C.R. and McKay, H.D. (1942) *Juvenile Delinquency and Urban Areas*, Chicago, Chicago University Press.

Sheldon, W. (1949) *Varieties of Delinquent Youth*, New York, Harper.

Sherman, L. et al. (1997) *Preventing Crime: What Works, What Doesn't, What's Promising*, Washington, US Department of Justice.

Shore, H. (1999) *Artful Dodgers: Youth and Crime in Early Nineteenth Century London*, London, Royal Historical Society.

Shore, H. (2002) 'Reforming the juvenile: gender, justice and the child criminal in nineteenth century England', in Muncie, J., Hughes, G. and McLaughlin, E. (eds) *Youth Justice: Critical Readings*, London, Sage.

Sibley, D. (1995) *Geographies of Exclusion*, London, Routledge.

Sim, J., Scraton, P. and Gordon, P. (1987) 'Crime, the state and critical analysis', in Scraton, P. (ed.) *Law, Order and the Authoritarian State*, Milton Keynes, Open University Press.

Simmons, C. and Wade, W. (1984) *I Like to Say What I Think*, London, Kogan Page.

Simmons, J. and Dodd, T. (2003) *Crime in England and Wales 2002/2003*, Home Office Statistical Bulletin, London, Home Office.

Simon, J. (1995) 'The boot camp and the limits of modern penality', *Social Justice*, vol. 22, no. 2, pp. 25–48.

Simon, J. (1997) 'Governing through crime', in Friedman, L. and Fisher, G. (eds) *The Crime Conundrum*, Boulder, CO, Westview.

Simon, J. (2001) 'Entitlement to cruelty: neo Liberalism and the punitive mentality in the United States', in Stenson, K. and Sullivan, R. (eds) *Crime, Risk and Justice*, Cullompton, Willan.

Singer, S. (1996) *Recriminalising Delinquency*, Cambridge, Cambridge University Press.

Sivanandan, A. (1976) 'Race, class and the state: in black experience in Britain', *Race and Class*, vol. 17, no. 4, pp. 347–68.

Skelton, T. and Valentine, G. (eds) (1998) *Cool Places: Geographies of Youth Cultures*, London, Routledge.

Smandych, R. (ed.) (1999) *Governable Places: Readings on Governmentality and Crime Control*, Aldershot, Ashgate.

Smandych, R. (ed.) (2001) *Youth Justice: History, Legislation and Reform*, Toronto, Harcourt.

Smart, C. (1976) *Women, Crime and Criminology*, London, Routledge.

Smart, C. (1989) *Feminism and the Power of Law*, London, Routledge.

Smart, C. (1990) 'Feminist approaches to criminology or postmodern woman meets atavistic man', in Morris, A. and Gelsthorpe, L. (eds) *Feminist Perspectives in Criminology*, Buckingham, Open University Press.

Smith, D. (1990) 'Juvenile delinquency in Britain in the First World War', in *Criminal Justice History*, vol. 11, Westport, CT, Meckler.

Smith, D. (2000) 'Learning from the Scottish Juvenile Justice System', *Probation Journal*, vol. 47, no 1, pp. 12–17.

Smith, D. and Gray, S. (1983) *Police and People in London*, London, Policy Studies Institute.

Smith, R. (2003) *Youth Justice: Ideas, Policy, Practice*, Collumpton, Willan.

Smith, S. (1973) 'The London apprentices as seventeenth-century adolescents', *Past and Present*, no. 61, pp. 149–61.

Smith, S.J. (1984) 'Crime in the news', *British Journal of Criminology*, vol. 24, no. 3, pp. 289–95.

Smithies, E. (1982) *Crime in Wartime: A Social History of Crime in World War II*, London, Allen & Unwin.

Social Exclusion Unit (SEU) (2001) *Preventing Social Exclusion*, London, HMSO.

Social Exclusion Unit (SEU) (2002) *Young Runaways*, London, HMSO.

Solomos, J. (1988) *Black Youth, Racism and the State*, Cambridge, Cambridge University Press.

Spergel, I. (1992) 'Youth gangs: an essay review', *Social Service Review*, vol. 66, pp. 121–40.

Spitzer, S. (1975) 'Toward a Marxian theory of deviance', *Social Problems*, vol. 22, no. 5, pp. 638–51.

Springhall, J. (1977) *Youth, Empire and Society*, London, Croom Helm.

Springhall, J. (1983–4) 'The origins of adolescence', *Youth and Policy*, vol. 2, no. 3, pp. 20–4.

Springhall, J. (1986) *Coming of Age: Adolescence in Britain 1860–1960*, London, Gill & Macmillan.

Stack, J.A. (1992) 'Children, urbanisation and the chances of imprisonment in mid-Victorian England', *Criminal Justice History*, vol. 13, Westport, CT, Greenwood.

Stafford, A. (1982) 'Learning not to labour', *Capital and Class*, no. 17, pp. 55–77.

Stanko, E.A. (1994) 'Challenging the problem of men's individual violence', in Newburn, T. and Stanko, B. (eds) *Just Boys Doing Business?*, London, Routledge.

Stanko, E.A. and Hobdell, K. (1993) 'Assault of men: masculinity and male victimisation', *British Journal of Criminology*, vol. 33, no. 3, pp. 400–15.

Stansill, P. and Mairowitz, D.Z. (1971) *BAMN: Outlaw Manifestos and Ephemera 1965–70*, Harmondsworth, Penguin.

Stedman-Jones, G. (1971) *Outcast London*, Oxford, Clarendon.

Stedman-Jones, G. (1977) 'Class expression versus social control? A critique of recent trends in the social history of "leisure"', *History Workshop Journal*, no. 4, pp. 162–70.

Stenson, K. (2000) 'Crime control, social policy and liberalism', in Lewis, G. et al. (eds) *Rethinking Social Policy*, London, Sage.

Stenson, K. and Factor, F. (1994) 'Youth work, risk and crime prevention', *Youth and Policy*, no. 45, pp. 1–15.

Stenson, K. and Sullivan, R. (eds) (2001) *Crime, Risk and Justice*, Cullompton, Willan.

Stevens, P. and Willis, C. (1979) *Race, Crime and Arrests*, Home Office Research Study, no. 58, London, HMSO.

Stewart, G. and Tutt, N. (1987) *Children in Custody*, Aldershot, Avebury.

Straus, M. (1994) *Beating the Devil out of them: Corporal Punishment in American Families*, New York, Lexington.

Straw, J. (1998) 'New approaches to crime and punishment', *Prison Service Journal*, no. 116, pp. 2–6.

Straw, J. and Michael, A. (1996) *Tackling the Causes of Crime: Labour's proposals to prevent crime and criminality*, London, Labour Party.

Sugarman, B. (1967) 'Involvement in youth culture, academic achievement and conformity', *British Journal of Sociology*, vol. 18, pp. 151–64.

Sumner, C. (ed.) (1990) *Censure, Politics and Criminal Justice*, Buckingham, Open University Press.

Sumner, C. (1994) *The Sociology of Deviance: An Obituary*, Buckingham, Open University Press.

Surette, R. (1998) *Media, Crime and Criminal Justice*, Belmont, CA, Wadsworth.

Sutherland, E. (1939) *Principles of Criminology*, Philadelphia, Lippincott.

Sutherland, E. and Cressey, D. (1970) *Criminology*, 8th edn, Philadelphia, Lippincott.

Sykes, G.M. and Matza, D. (1957) 'Techniques of neutralisation: a theory of delinquency', *American Sociological Review*, vol. 22, pp. 664–70.

Tame, C. (1991) 'Freedom, responsibility and justice: the criminology of the New Right', in Stenson, K. and Cowell, D. (eds) *The Politics of Crime Control*, London, Sage.

Tannenbaum, F. (1938) *Crime and the Community*, New York, Columbia University Press.

Tarling, R. (1982) *Unemployment and Crime*, Home Office Research Bulletin, no. 14, London, HMSO.

Tarling, R. (1993) *Analysing Offending: Data, Models and Interpretations*, London, HMSO.

Taylor, H. (1998) 'The politics of the rising crime statistics of England and Wales 1914–1960', *Crime, History and Societies*, vol. 2, no. 1, pp. 5–28.

Taylor, I. (1971) 'Soccer consciousness and soccer hooliganism', in Cohen, S. (ed.) *Images of Deviance*, Harmondsworth, Pengiun.

Taylor, I. (1981a) 'Crime waves in post-war Britain', *Contemporary Crises*, no. 5, pp. 43–62.

Taylor, I. (1981b) *Law and Order: Arguments for Socialism*, London, Macmillan.

Taylor, I. (1992) 'Left Realist criminology and the free market experiment in Britain', in Young, J. and Matthews, R. (eds) *Rethinking Criminology: The Realist Debate*, London, Sage.

Taylor, I. (1999) *Crime in Context: A Critical Criminology of Market Societies*, Cambridge, Polity.

Taylor, I. and Wall, D. (1976) 'Beyond the skinheads: comments on the emergence and significance of the glam rock cult', in Mungham, G. and Pearson, G. (eds) *Working Class Youth Culture*, London, Routledge & Kegan Paul.

Taylor, I., Walton, P. and Young, J. (1973) *The New Criminology*, London, Routledge.

Taylor, I., Walton, P. and Young, J. (eds) (1975) *Critical Criminology*, London, Routledge.

Taylor, I., Evans, K. and Fraser, P. (1996) *A Tale of Two Cities*, London, Routledge.

Taylor, L. (1971) *Deviance and Society*, London, Michael Joseph.

Taylor, L., Lacey, R. and Bracken, D. (1979) *In Whose Best Interests?*, London, Cobden Trust/Mind.

Tham, H. (2002) 'Law and order as a leftist project?: The case of Sweden', *Punishment and Society*, vol. 3, no. 3, pp. 409–26.

Thane, P. (1981) 'Childhood in history', in King, M. (ed.) *Childhood, Welfare and Justice*, London, Batsford.

Thompson, E. P. (1963) *The Making of the English Working Class*, Harmondsworth, Penguin.

Thornton, D., Curran, C., Grayson, D. and Holloway, V. (1984) *Tougher Regimes in Detention Centres*, London, HMSO.

Thornton, S. (1995) *Club Cultures: Music, Media and Subcultural Capital*, Cambridge, Polity.

Thorpe, D.H., Smith, D., Green, C.J. and Paley, J.H. (1980) *Out of Care: The Community Support of Juvenile Offenders*, London, Allen & Unwin.

Thrasher, F. (1927) *The Gang*, Chicago, Chicago University Press.

Tierney, J. (1980) 'Political deviance: a critical commentary on a case study', *Sociological Review*, vol. 28, no. 4, pp. 829–50.

Tierney, J. (1996) *Criminology: Theory and Context*, Hemel Hempstead, Prentice-Hall/Harvester Wheatsheaf.

Tilley, N. (2003) 'The rediscovery of learning: crime prevention and scientific realism', in Hughes, G. and Edwards, A. (eds) *Crime Control and Community*, Cullompton, Willan.

Tonge, J. (1999) 'New packaging, old deal? New Labour and employment policy innovation', *Critical Social Policy*, vol. 19, no. 2, pp. 217–32.

Toomey, C. (2002) 'School of hard locks', *Sunday Times Magazine*, 4 August.

UK Government (1999) *Convention on the Rights of the Child: Second Report to the UN Committee on the Rights of the Child by the United Kingdom*, London, HMSO.

United Nations (1989) *The United Nations Convention on the Rights of the Child*, New York, United Nations.

Urwick, E.J. (ed.) (1904) *Studies of Boy Life in Our Cities*, London, Dent.

Utting, D. (1996) *Reducing Criminality among Young People: A Sample of Relevant Programmes in the UK*, Home Office Research Study, no. 161, London, HMSO.

Vague, T. (1997) *Anarchy in the UK: The Angry Brigade*, Edinburgh, AK Press.

Valier, C. (2002) *Theories of Crime and Punishment*, Harlow, Longman/Pearson Education.

Van den Haag, E. (1975) *Punishing Criminals*, New York, Basic Books.

Vaneigem, R. (2001) *The Revolution of Everyday Life*, London, Rebel Press.

Vaughan, B. (2000) 'The government of youth: disorder and dependence', *Social and Legal Studies*, vol. 9, no. 3, pp. 347–66.

Vigil, J. (1988) *Barrio Gangs: Street Life and Identity in Southern California*, Austin, University of Texas Press.

Vold, G. and Bernard, T. (1986) *Theoretical Criminology*, 3rd edn, Oxford, Oxford University Press.

Von Hirsch, A. (1976) *Doing Justice: The Choice of Punishments*, New York, Hill & Wang.

Wacquant, L. (1999) 'How penal commonsense comes to Europeans', *European Societies*, vol. 1, no. 3, pp. 319–52.

Waddington, P.A.J. (1986) 'Mugging as a moral panic: a question of proportion', *British Journal of Sociology*, vol. 32, no. 2, pp. 245–59.

Waiton, S. (2001) *Scared of the Kids! Curfews, crime and the regulation of young people*, Sheffield, Sheffield Hallam Press.

Waldo, G. and Dinitz, S. (1967) 'Personality attributes of the criminal', *Journal of Research in Crime and Delinquency*, vol. 4, no. 2, pp. 185–201.

Walgrave, L. (1995) 'Restorative justice for juveniles: just a technique or a fully fledged alternative?', *Howard Journal*, vol. 34, no. 3, pp. 228–49.

Walgrave, L. and Mehlbye, J. (eds) (1998) *Confronting Youth in Europe – Juvenile Crime and Juvenile Justice*, Copenhagen, Denmark, Institute of Local Government Studies.

Walker, M. (1983) 'Some problems in interpreting statistics relating to crime', *Journal of the Royal Statistical Society Series A*, no. 146, part 3, pp. 282–93.

Walker, M. (1988) 'The court disposal of young males, by race, in London in 1983', *British Journal of Criminology*, vol. 28, no. 4, pp. 441–60.

Walker, M., Jefferson, T. and Seneviratne, M. (1990) *Ethnic Minorities, Young People and the Criminal Justice System*, ESRC Project no. E06250023, Centre for Criminological and Socio-Legal Studies, University of Sheffield.

Walklate, S. (1995) *Gender and Crime: An Introduction*, Hemel Hempstead, Prentice-Hall/Harvester.

Walklate, S. (1998) *Understanding Criminology: Current Theoretical Debates*, Buckingham, Open

University Press.

Walklate, S. (2001) *Gender, Crime and Criminal Justice*, Cullompton, Willan.

Wallace, C. (1987) *For Richer, for Poorer: Growing up in and out of Work*, London, Tavistock.

Walsh, C. (2002) 'Curfews: No more hanging around', *Youth Justice*, vol. 2, no. 2, pp. 70–81.

Walton, P. and Young, J. (eds) (1998) *The New Criminology Revisited*, Basingstoke, Macmillan.

Waterhouse, L., McGhee, J., Whyte, B., Loucks, N., Kay, H. and Stewart, R. (2000) *The Evaluation of Children's Hearings in Scotland*, vol. 3, *Children in Focus*, Edinburgh, Scottish Executive.

Webb, S. (2001) 'Some considerations on the validity of evidence based practice in social work', *British Journal of Social Work* vol. 31, no. 1, pp. 57–79.

Webster, C. (1997) 'The construction of British "Asian" criminality', *International Journal of the Sociology of Law*, vol. 25, pp. 65–86.

Weinberger, B. (1993) 'Policing juveniles: delinquency in late nineteenth and early twentieth century Manchester', *Criminal Justice History*, vol. 14, Westport, CT, Greenwood.

Weiner, M.J. (1990) *Reconstructing the Criminal: Culture, Law and Policy in England, 1830–1914*, Cambridge, Cambridge University Press.

Weiss, R.P. (1987) 'The community and prevention', in Johnson, E.H. (ed.) *Handbook on Crime and Delinquency Prevention*, New York, Greenwood Press.

Weitekamp, E. (2001) 'Mediation in Europe: paradoxes, problems and promises', in Morris, A. and Maxwell, G. (eds) *Restorative Justice for Juveniles*, Oxford, Hart.

West, D. (1967) *The Young Offender*, Harmondsworth, Penguin.

West, D. and Farrington, D. (1973) *Who Becomes Delinquent?*, London, Heinemann.

West, D. and Farrington, D. (1977) *The Delinquent Way of Life*, London, Heinemann.

Westergaard, J. (1965) 'The withering away of class: a contemporary myth', in Anderson, P. and Blackburn, R. (eds) *Towards Socialism*, London, Fontana.

White, R. (1990) *No Space of Their Own: Young People and Social Control in Australia*, Cambridge, Cambridge University Press.

White, R. (2001) 'Social justice, community building and restorative strategies', *Contemporary Justice Review*, vol. 3, no. 1, pp. 55–72.

White, R. (2003) 'Communities, conferences and restorative social justice', *Criminal Justice*, vol. 3, no. 2, pp. 139–60.

White, R. and Haines, F. (2000) *Crime and Criminology*, 2nd edn, Oxford, Oxford University Press.

Whitfield, D. (1997) *Tackling the Tag*, Winchester, Waterside.

Whyte, B. (2000) 'Youth justice in Scotland', in Pickford, J. (ed.) *Youth Justice: Theory and Practice*, London, Cavendish.

Whyte, W.F. (1943) *Street Corner Society*, Chicago, Chicago University Press.

Widdicombe, S. and Wooffitt, R. (1995) *The Language of Youth Subcultures*, Hemel Hempstead, Harvester.

Wilcox, A. (2003) 'Evidence based youth justice?', *Youth Justice*, vol. 3, no. 1, pp. 19–33.

Wilkins, L. (1964) *Social Deviance*, London, Tavistock.

Wilkinson, C. (1995) *The Drop-Out Society: Young People on the Margin*, Leicester, Youth Work Press.

Williams, K.S. (1994) *Textbook on Criminology*, 2nd edn, London, Blackstone.

Williams, P. and Dickinson, J. (1993) 'Fear of crime: read all about it?', *British Journal of Criminology*, vol. 33, no. 1, pp. 33–56.

Williamson, H. (1993) 'Youth policy in the United Kingdom and the marginalization of young people', *Youth and Policy*, no. 40, pp. 33–48.

Williamson, H. (1997) 'Status zero youth and the underclass', in MacDonald, R. (ed.) *Youth, the 'Underclass' and Social Exclusion*, London, Routledge.

Willis, P. (1977) *Learning to Labour*, London, Saxon House.

Willis, P. (1978) *Profane Culture*, London, Chatto & Windus.

Willis, P. (1990) *Common Culture*, Buckingham, Open University Press.

Willmott, P. (1966) *Adolescent Boys of East London*, London, Routledge.

Wilson, D. and Moore, S. (2003) *Playing the game: the experiences of young black men in custody*, London, Children's Society/Community Fund.

Wilson, J.Q. (1975) *Thinking about Crime*, New York, Vintage.

Wilson, J.Q. and Herrnstein, R.J. (1985) *Crime and Human Nature*, New York, Simon & Schuster.

Wilson, J.Q. and Kelling, G. (1982) 'Broken windows', *Atlantic Monthly*, March, pp. 29–38.

Wincup, E., Buckland, G. and Bayliss, R. (2003) *Youth Homelessness and Substance Use*, Home Office Research Study, no. 258, London, HMSO.

Winterdyk, J. (ed.) (2002) *Juvenile Justice Systems: International Perspectives*, 2nd edn, Toronto, Canadians Scholars Press.

Wolfe, T. (1969) *The Electric Kool-Aid Acid Test*, New York, Bantam.

Worrall, A. (1997) *Punishment in the Community*, Harlow, Longman.

Worrall, A. (1999) 'Troubled or troublesome? Justice for girls and young women', in Goldson, B. (ed.) *Youth Justice: Contemporary Policy and Practice*, Aldershot, Ashgate.

Worrall, A. (2001) 'Girls at risk? Reflections on changing attitudes to young women's offending', *Probation Journal*, vol. 48, no. 2, pp. 86–92.

Wyn, J. and White, R. (1997) *Rethinking Youth*, London, Sage.

Yablonsky, L. (1968) *The Hippie Trip*, New York, Pegasus.

Yeates, N. (2001) *Globalisation and Social Policy*, London, Sage.

Yeates, N. (2002) 'Globalisation and social policy: from global neo-liberal hegemony to global political pluralism', *Global Social Policy*, vol. 2, no. 1, pp. 66–91.

Yinger, J.M. (1960) 'Contraculture and subculture', *American Sociological Review*, vol. 55, pp. 625–35.

Young, A. (1996) *Imagining Crime*, London, Sage.

Young, J. (1971) *The Drugtakers*, London, Paladin.

Young, J. (1974) 'Mass media, drugs and deviance', in Rock, P. and McKintosh, M. (eds) *Deviance and Social Control*, London, Tavistock.

Young, J. (1975) 'Working class criminology', in Taylor, I., Walton, P. and Young, J. (eds) *Critical Criminology*, London, Routledge.

Young, J. (1979) 'Left idealism, reformism and beyond', in Fine, B., Kinsey, R., Lea, J., Picciotto, S. and Young, J. (eds) *Capitalism and the Rule of Law*, London, Hutchinson.

Young, J. (1986) 'The failure of criminology: the need for a radical realism', in Young, J. and Matthews, R. (eds) *Confronting Crime*, London, Sage.

Young, J. (1990) 'Asking questions of Left Realism', *Critical Criminologist*, vol. 2, no. 2, pp. 1–2; 10.

Young, J. (1992) 'Ten points of realism', in Young, J. and Matthews, R. (eds) *Rethinking Criminology: The Realist Debate*, London, Sage.

Young, J. (1999) *The Exclusive Society*, London, Sage.

Young, J. (2002) 'Critical criminology in the 21st century: critique, irony and the always unfinished', in Carrington, K. and Hogg, R. (eds) *Critical Criminology*, Cullompton, Willan.

Young, J. (2003) 'Winning the fight against crime? New Labour, populism and lost opportunities', in Matthews, R. and Young, J. (eds) *The New Politics and Crime and Punishment*, Cullompton, Willan.

Young, J. and Matthews, R. (2003) 'New Labour, crime control and social exclusion', in Matthews, R. and Young, J. (eds) *The New Politics of Crime and Punishment*, Cullompton, Willan.

Young, R. and Hoyle, C. (2002) *An Evaluation of the Implementation and Effectiveness of an Initiative in Restorative Cautioning*, Findings no. 542, York, Joseph Rowntree Foundation.

Youth Justice Board (2000) *National Standards for Youth Justice*, London, Youth Justice Board.

Youth Justice Board (2001) *Risk and Protective Factors Associated with Youth Crime and Effective Interventions to Prevent It*, YJB research note, no. 5, London, Youth Justice Board.

Zedner, L. (1991) *Women, Crime and Custody in Victorian England*, Oxford, Clarendon.

Zedner, L. (1994) 'Child Victims', in Jones, I.G. and Williams, G. (eds) *Social Policy, Crime and Punishment*, Cardiff, University of Wales Press.

Zehr, H. and Mika, H. (1998) 'Fundamental concepts of restorative justice', *Contemporary Justice Review*, vol. 1, pp. 47–55.

Index

An asterisk* after a word refers to an entry in the glossary.